Toshiaki Iwashiro

The novelization of Psyren has been published!

Between that and various other factors, my workload has increased dramatically over the past couple of months!

But it was all worth it. I hope you'll read the novel as well!

Toshiaki Iwashiro was born December 11, 1977, in Tokyo and has the blood type of A. His debut manga was the popular *Mieru Hito*, which ran from 2005 to 2007 in Japan in *Weekly Shonen Jump*, where *Psyren* was also serialized.

PSYREN VOL. 13
SHONEN JUMP Manga Edition

STORY AND ART BY TOSHIAKI IWASHIRO

Translation/Camellia Nieh
Lettering/Annaliese Christman
Design/Matt Hinrichs
Editor/Joel Enos

PSYREN © 2007 by Toshiaki Iwashiro
All rights reserved.
First published in Japan in 2007 by SHUEISHA Inc., Tokyo.
English translation rights arranged by SHUEISHA Inc.

The stories, characters and incidents mentioned in this publication are
entirely fictional.

Printed in the U.S.A.

Published by VIZ Media, LLC
P.O. Box 77010
San Francisco, CA 94107

10 9 8 7 6 5 4 3 2 1
First printing, November 2013

www.viz.com

THE WORLD'S
MOST POPULAR MANGA

SHONEN JUMP

www.shonenjump.com

SHONEN JUMP MANGA EDITION

PSYREN

13

INFILTRATION

Story and Art by
Toshiaki Iwashiro

AGEHA YOSHINA

SAKURAKO AMAMIYA

KABUTO KIRISAKI

Welcome to PSYREN

Characters

JUNAS

KYLE

MIROKU AMAGI

SHAO

Story

THIS IS THE STORY OF A GROUP OF TEENAGERS CAUGHT IN THE LIFE-OR-DEATH GAME OF PSYREN. SENT HURTLING BACK AND FORTH THROUGH TIME, THEY MUST PARTICIPATE IN A DESPERATE BATTLE TO PROTECT THE FUTURE OF THEIR WORLD.

HAVING SURVIVED THEIR FOURTH TRIP TO PSYREN, AGEHA AND HIS FRIENDS SET OUT TO LEARN MORE ABOUT MIROKU AMAGI IN ORDER TO COMBAT HIS EVIL PLOT. A RESEARCHER FROM MIROKU'S PAST REVEALS A WAY TO STOP THE MADMAN, CONTAINED DEEP WITHIN A HIGH-SECURITY RESEARCH LAB. AGEHA AND MATSURI INFILTRATE THE LAB, NARROWLY ESCAPING A TWISTED TRAP SET BY ONE OF MIROKU'S FOLLOWERS, BUT IN THE PROCESS THE KEY TO STOPPING MIROKU IS LOST FOREVER.

VOL. 13
INFILTRATION
CONTENTS

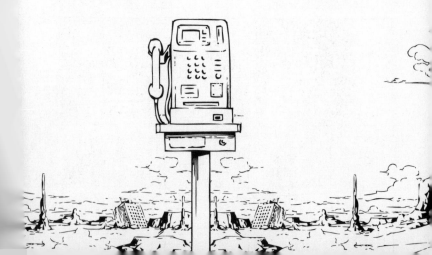

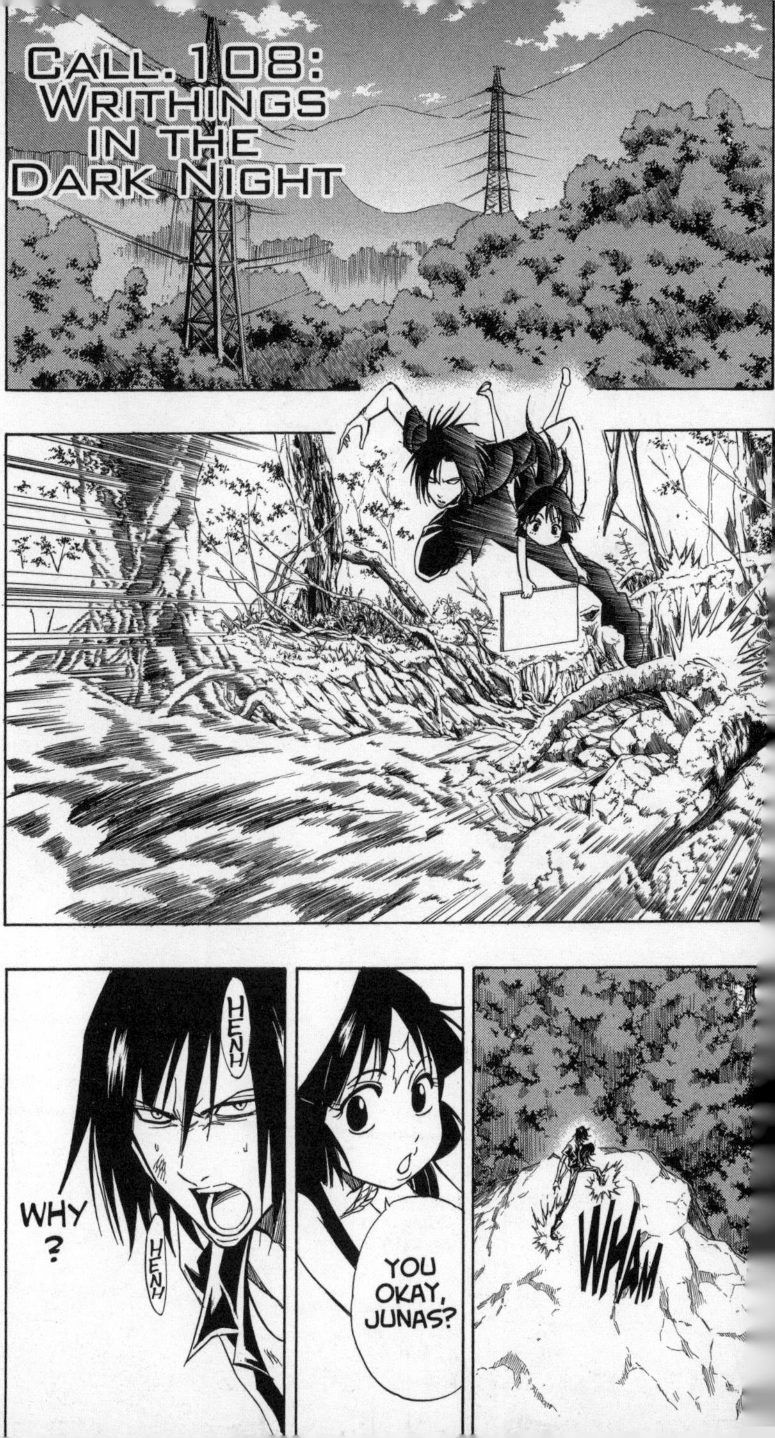
CALL. 108: WRITHINGS IN THE DARK NIGHT
WHAM
YOU OKAY, JUNAS?
HENH
HENH
WHY?

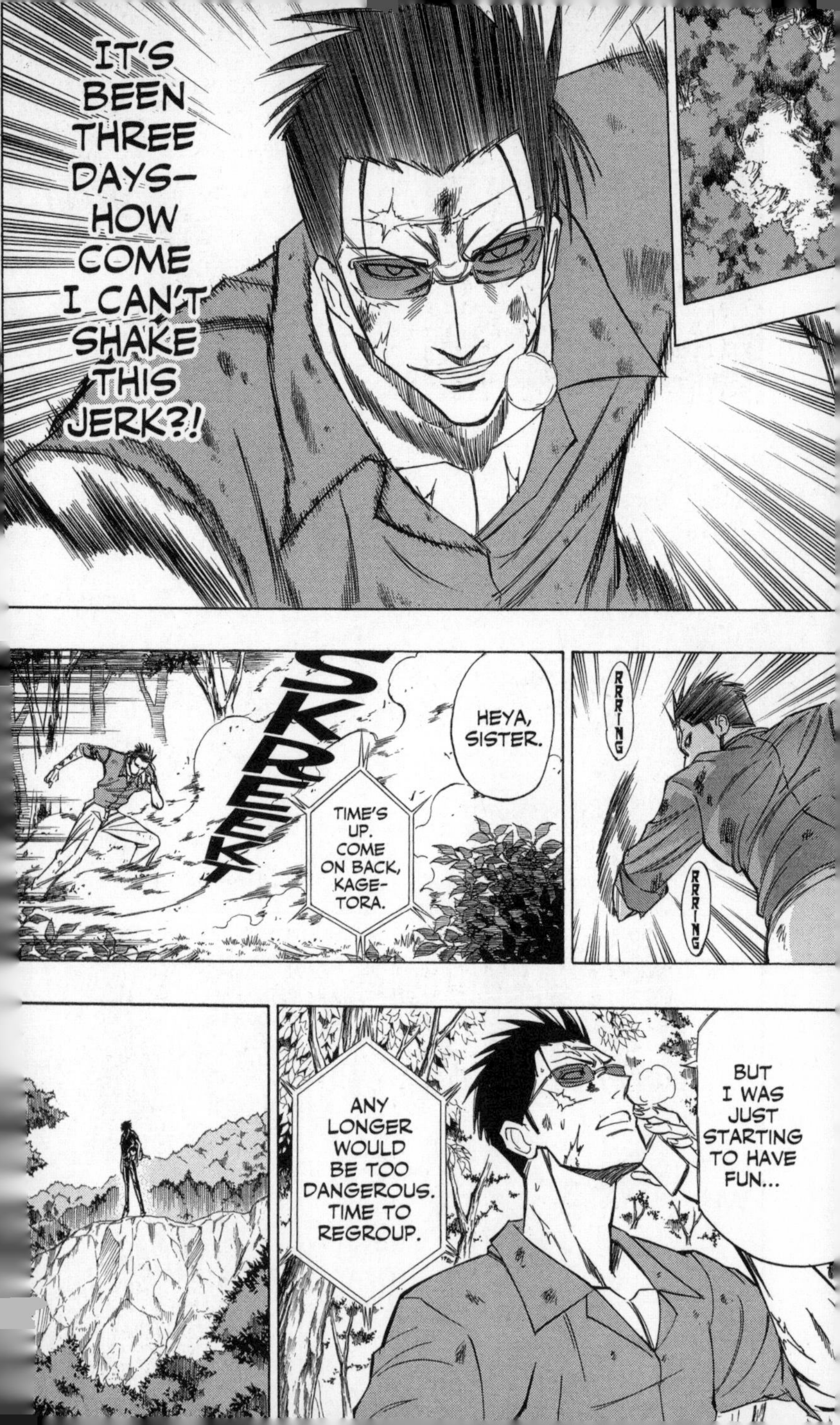
IT'S BEEN THREE DAYS—HOW COME I CAN'T SHAKE THIS JERK?!
RRRING
RRRING
SKREEK
HEYA, SISTER.
TIME'S UP. COME ON BACK, KAGE-TORA.
BUT I WAS JUST STARTING TO HAVE FUN...
ANY LONGER WOULD BE TOO DANGEROUS. TIME TO REGROUP.

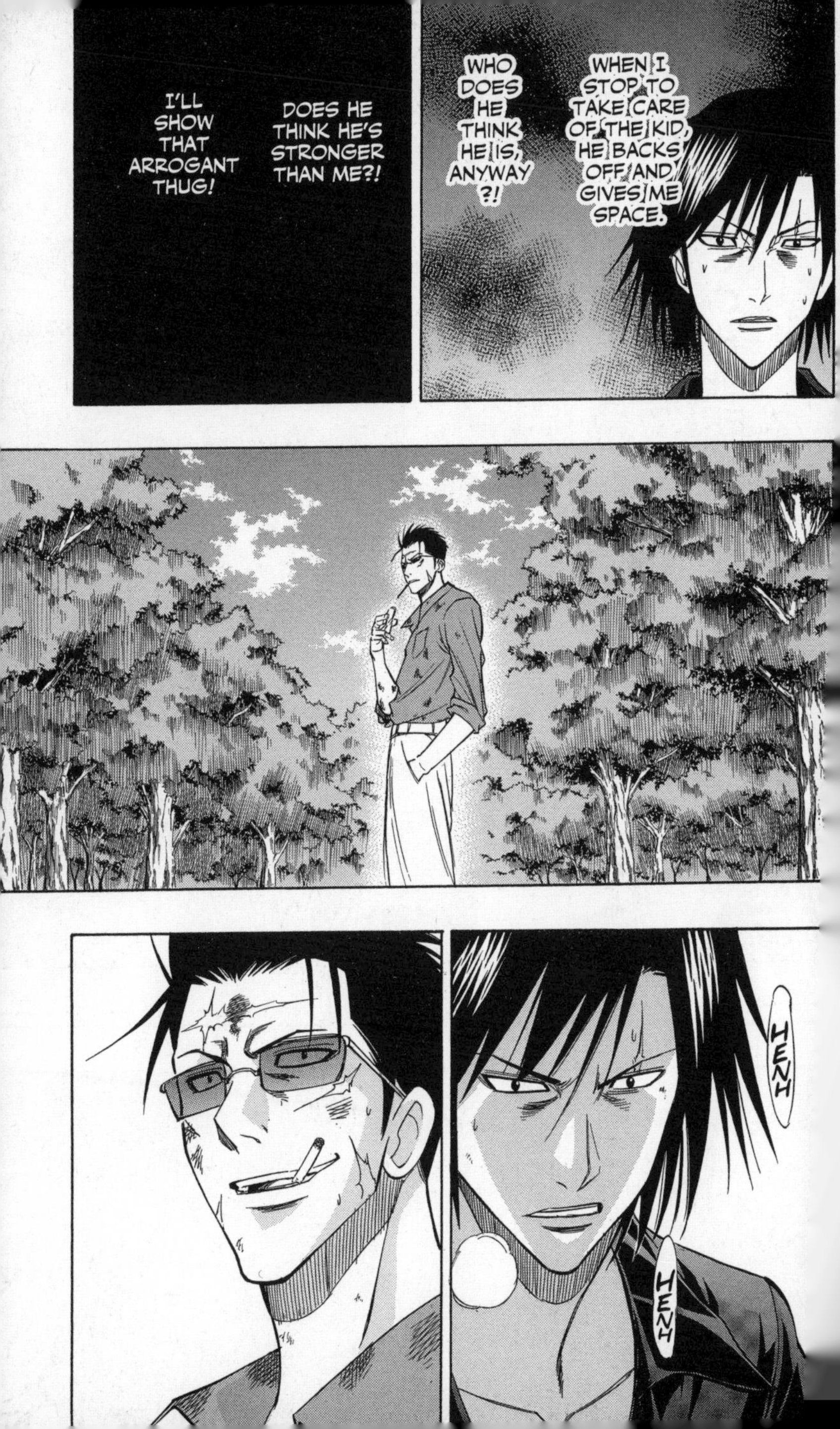
WHEN I STOP TO TAKE CARE OF THE KID, HE BACKS OFF AND GIVES ME SPACE.
WHO DOES HE THINK HE IS, ANYWAY?!
DOES HE THINK HE'S STRONGER THAN ME?!
I'LL SHOW THAT ARROGANT THUG!
HENH
HENH

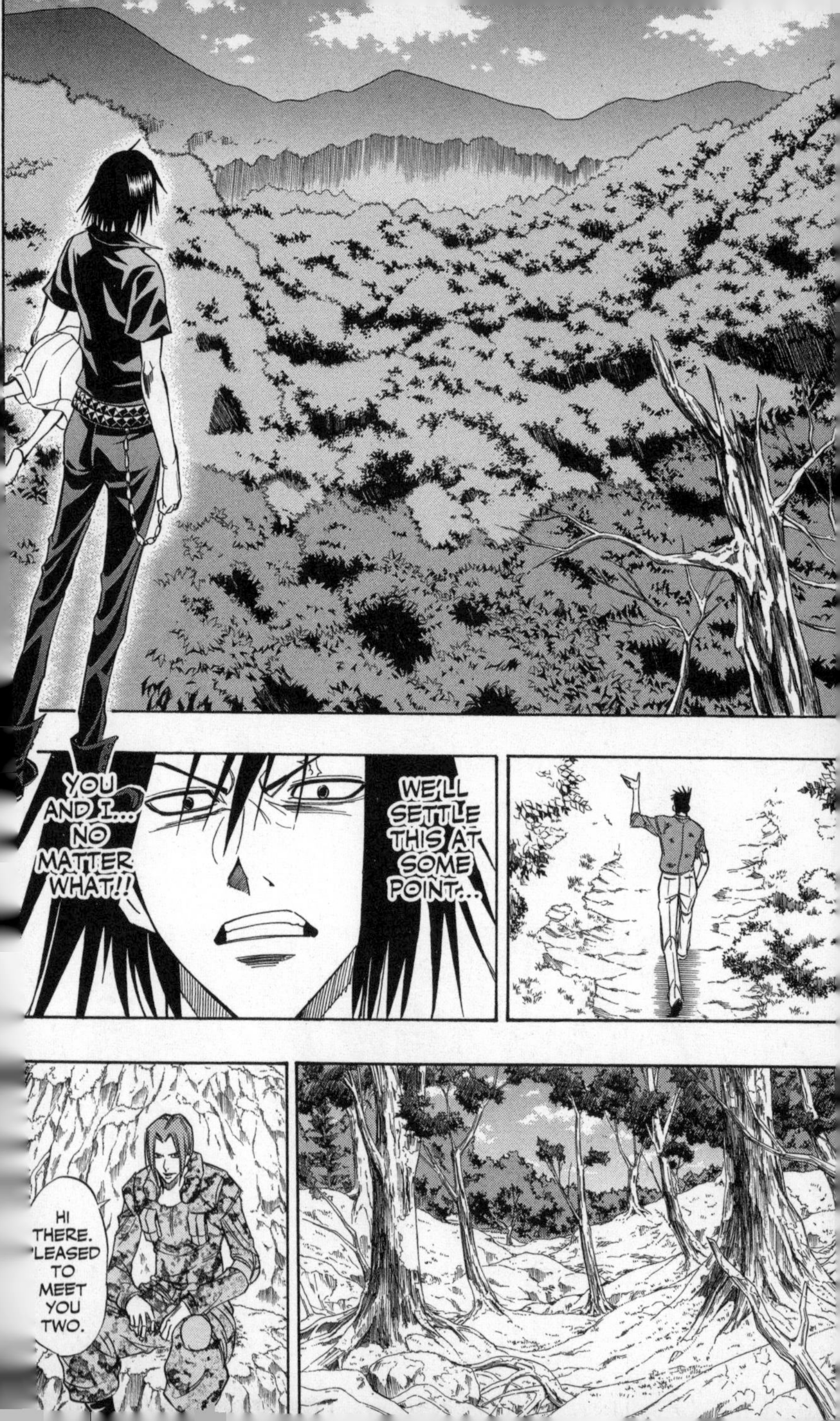
WE'LL SETTLE THIS AT SOME POINT...
YOU AND I... NO MATTER WHAT!!
HI THERE. LEASED TO MEET YOU TWO.

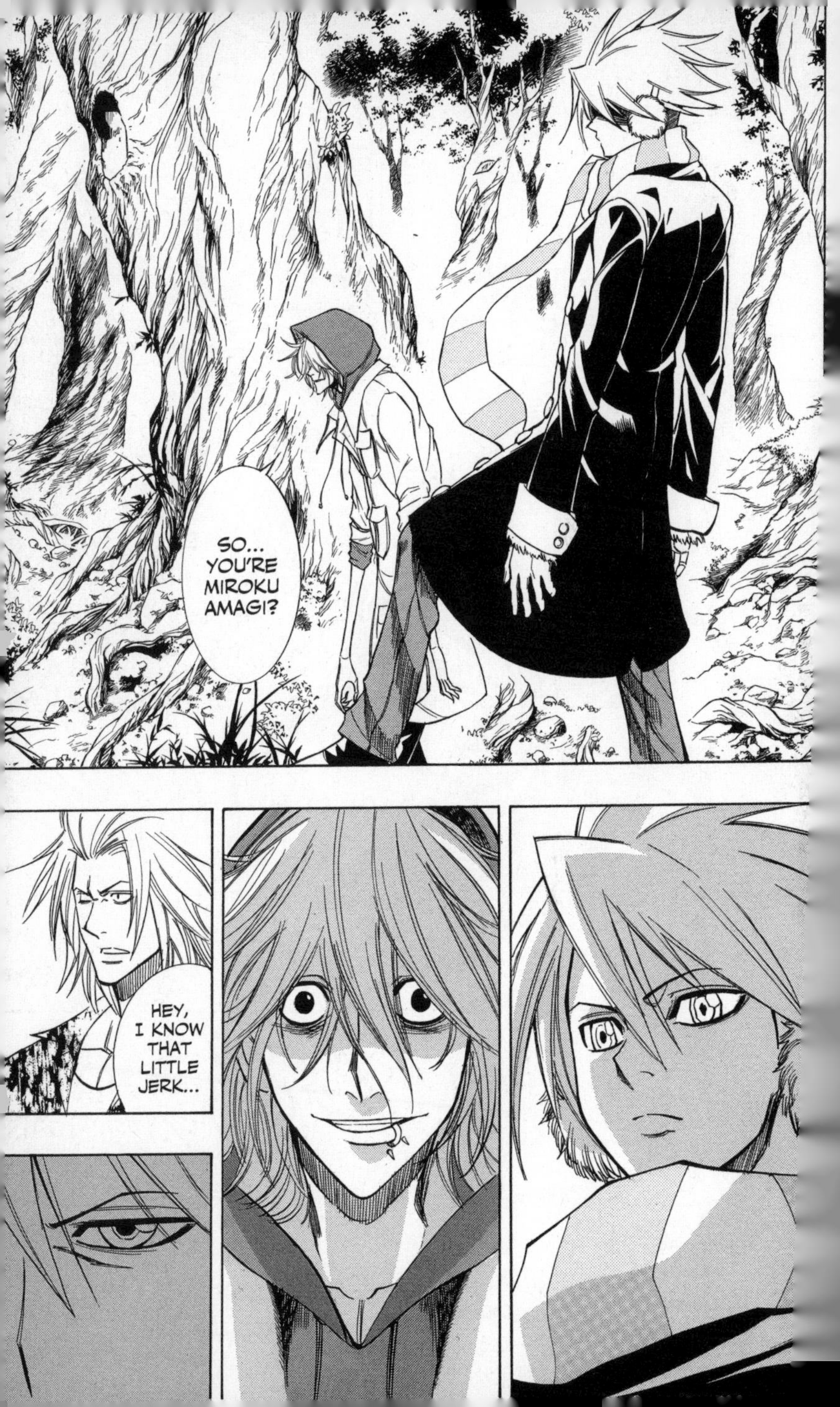
SO... YOU'RE MIROKU AMAGI?
HEY, I KNOW THAT LITTLE JERK...

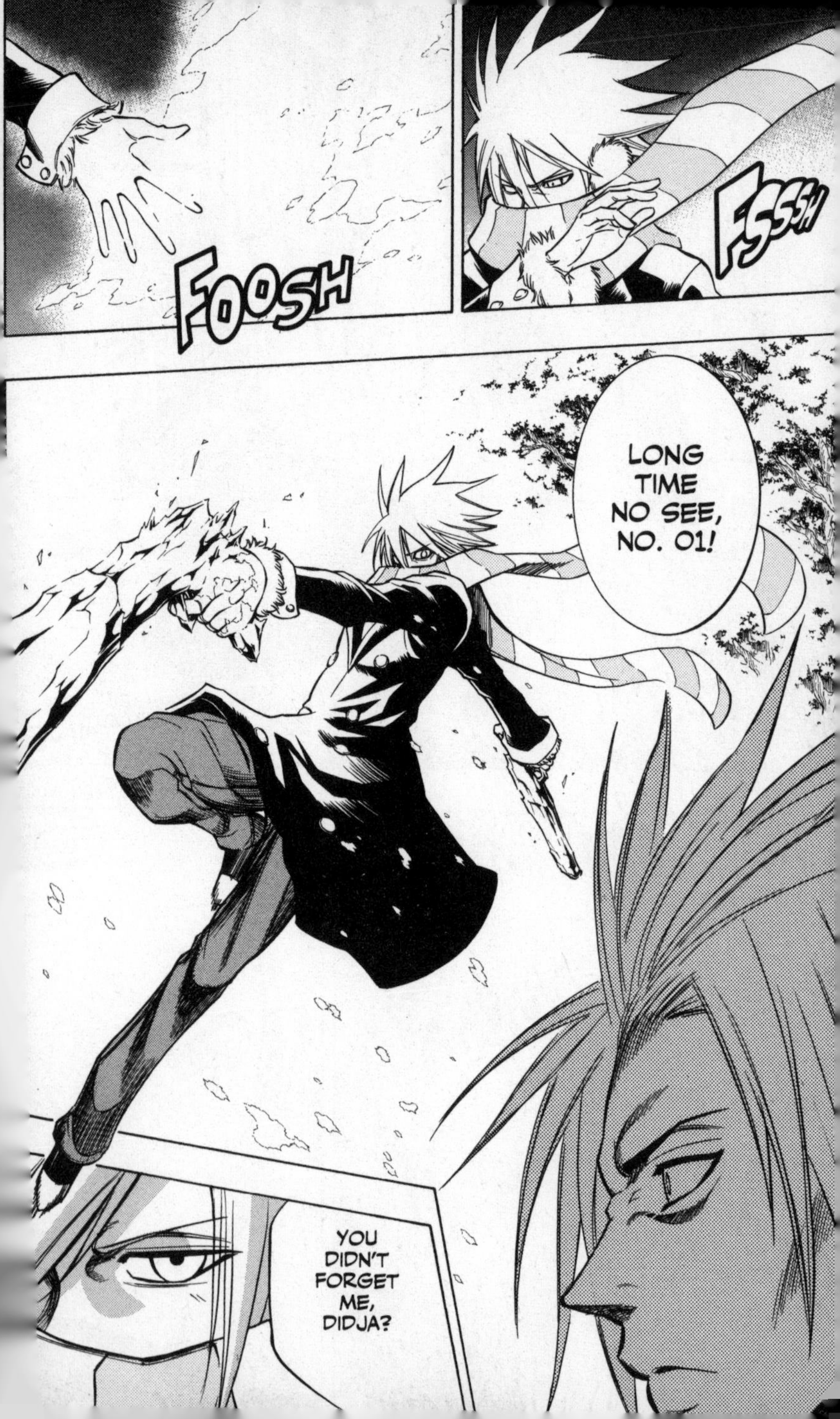
FSSSH
FOOSH
LONG TIME NO SEE, NO. 01!
YOU DIDN'T FORGET ME, DIDJA?

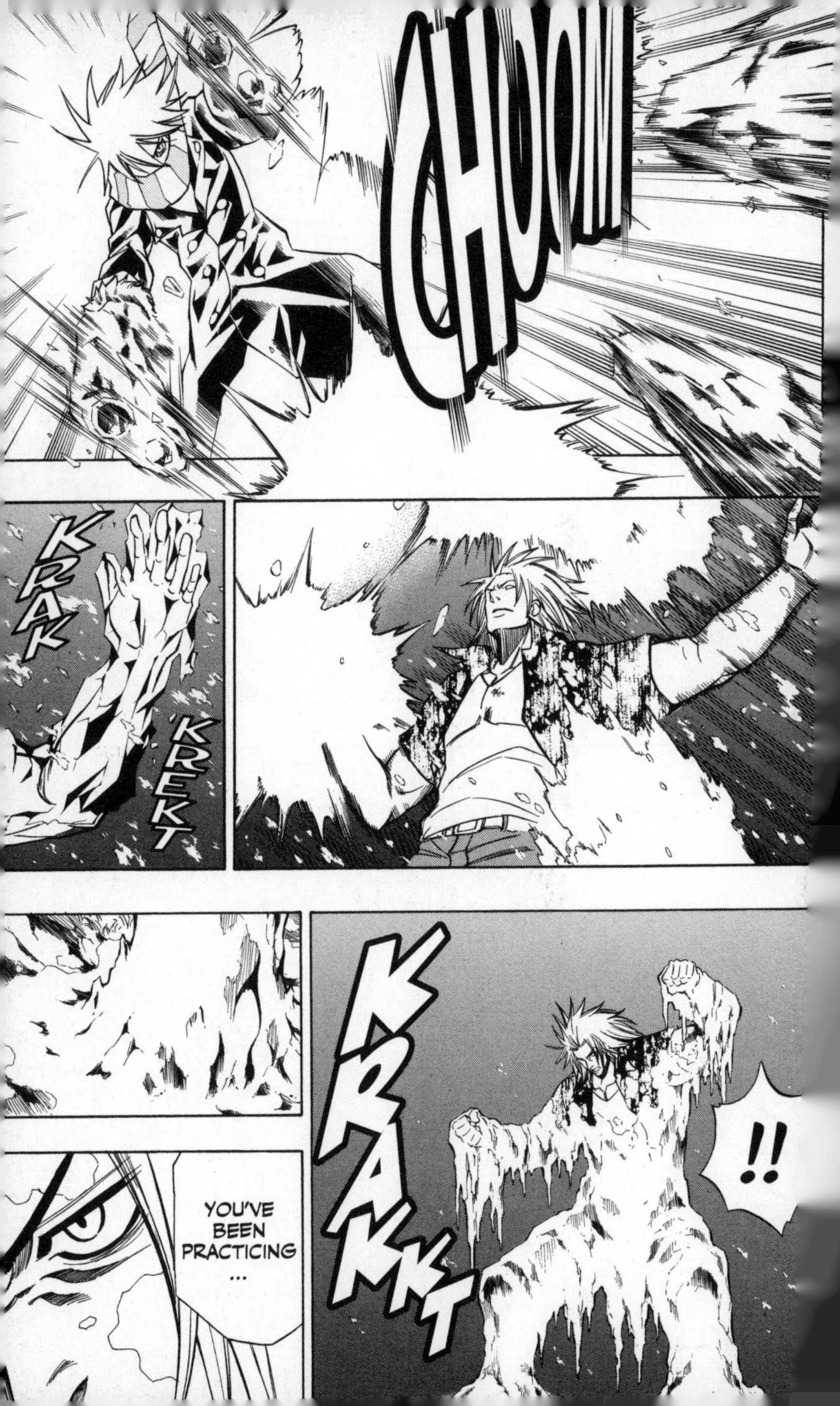
CHOOM!
KRAK
KREKT
KRAKKT
!!
YOU'VE BEEN PRACTICING ...

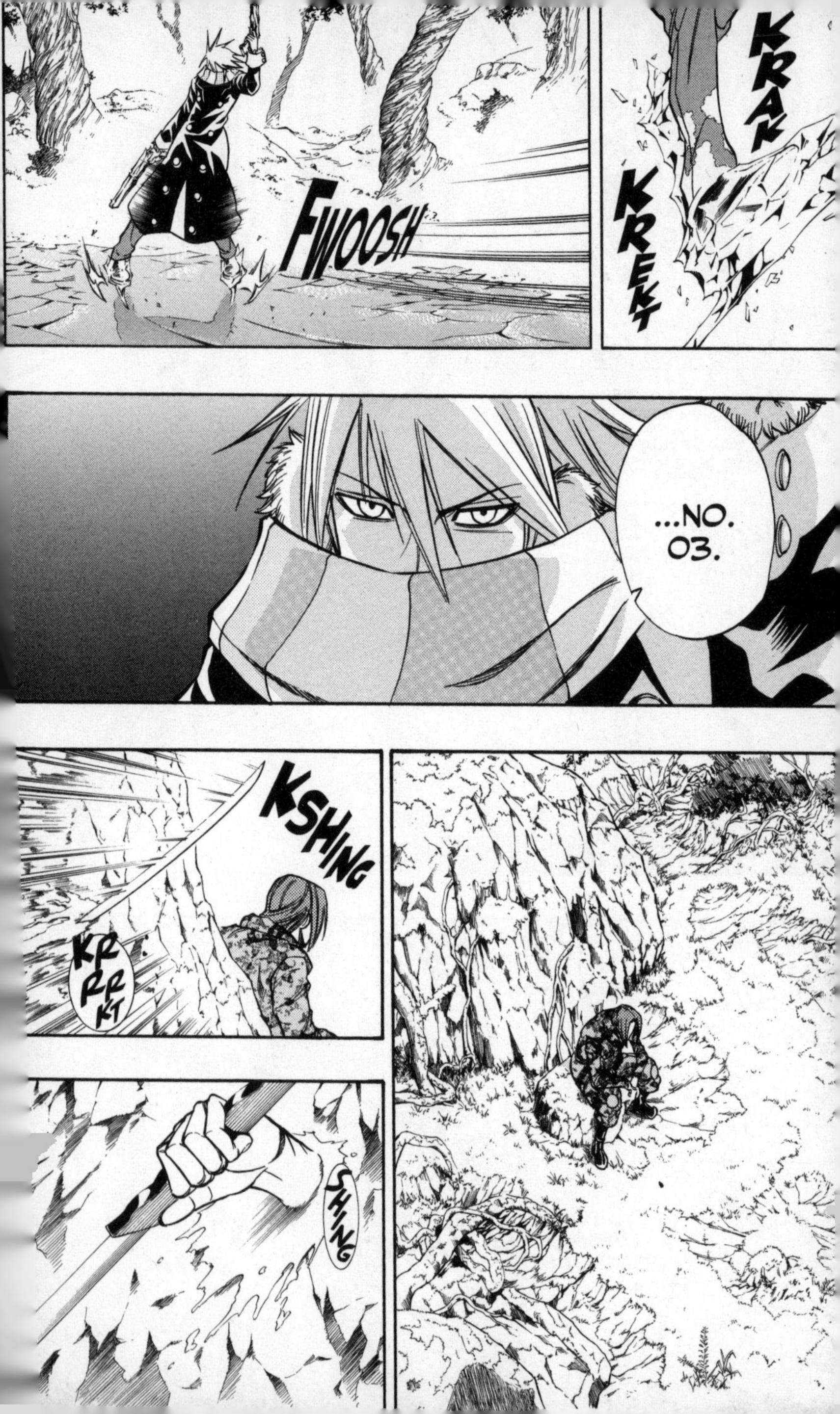
KRAK
KREKT
FWOOSH
...NO. 03.
KSHING
KRRRKT
SHING

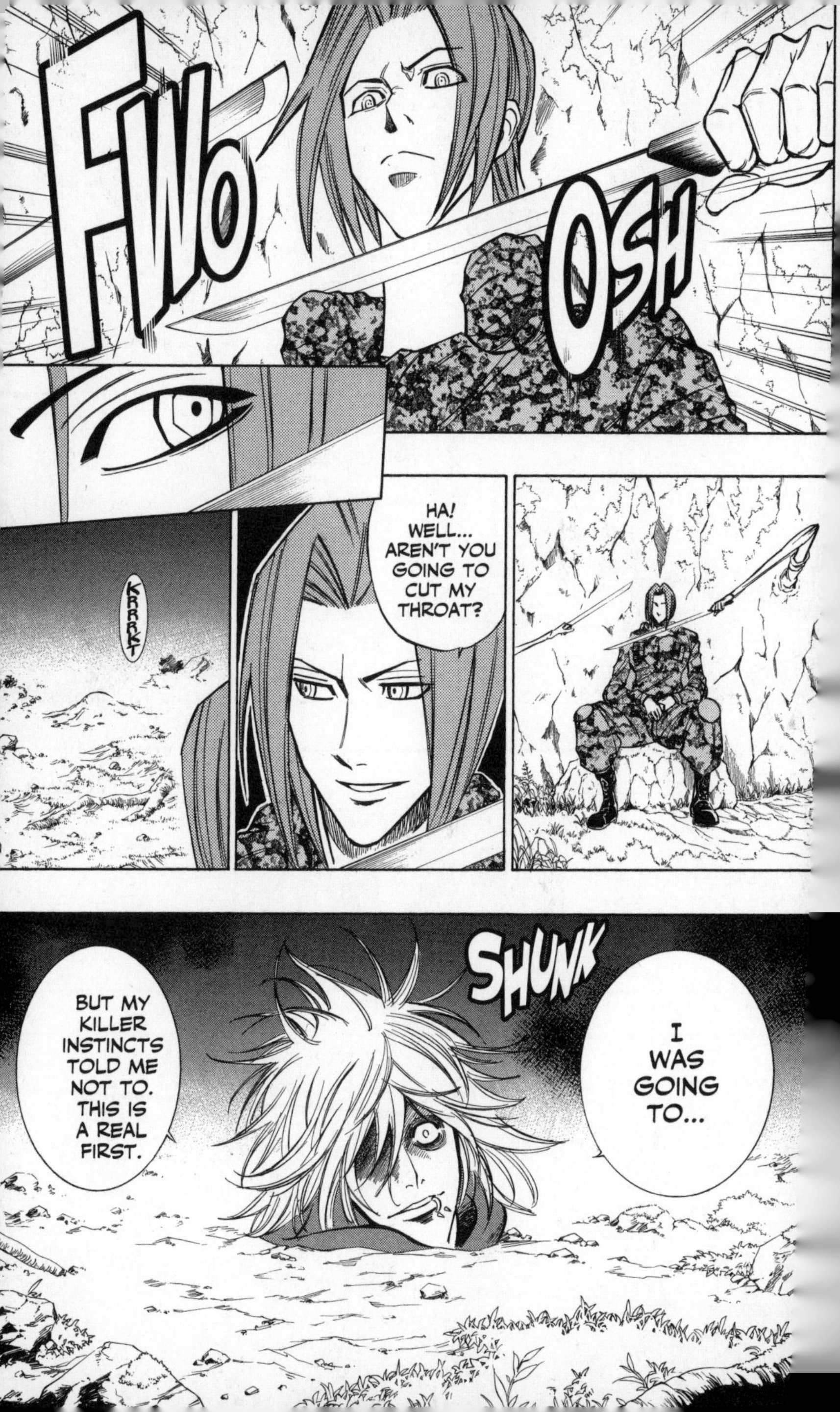
FWOOSH
HA! WELL... AREN'T YOU GOING TO CUT MY THROAT?
KRRRKT
SHUNK
I WAS GOING TO...
BUT MY KILLER INSTINCTS TOLD ME NOT TO. THIS IS A REAL FIRST.

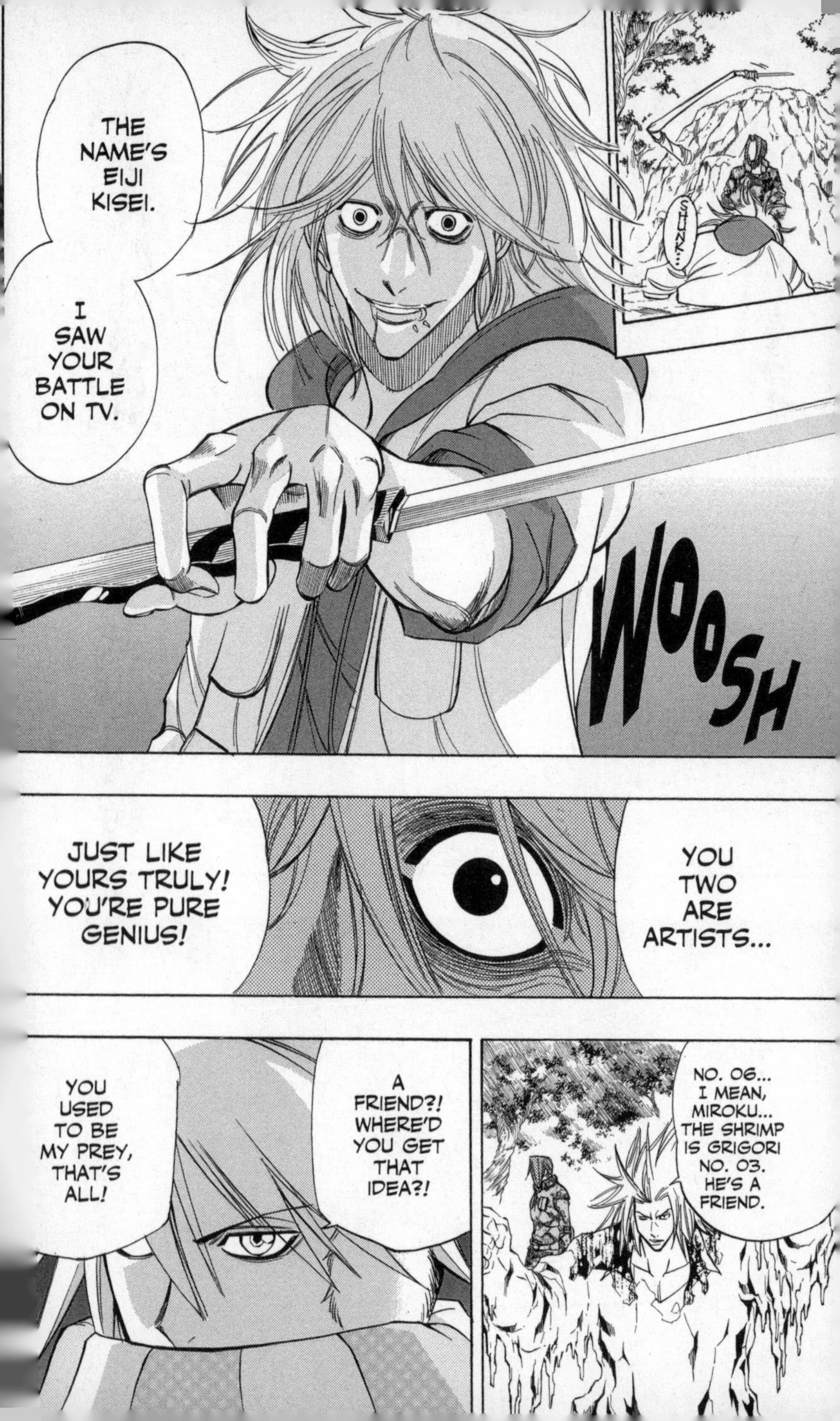
SHUNK...
THE NAME'S EIJI KISEI.
I SAW YOUR BATTLE ON TV.
WOOSH
YOU TWO ARE ARTISTS...
JUST LIKE YOURS TRULY! YOU'RE PURE GENIUS!
NO. 06... I MEAN, MIROKU... THE SHRIMP IS GRIGORI NO. 03. HE'S A FRIEND.
A FRIEND?! WHERE'D YOU GET THAT IDEA?!
YOU USED TO BE MY PREY, THAT'S ALL!

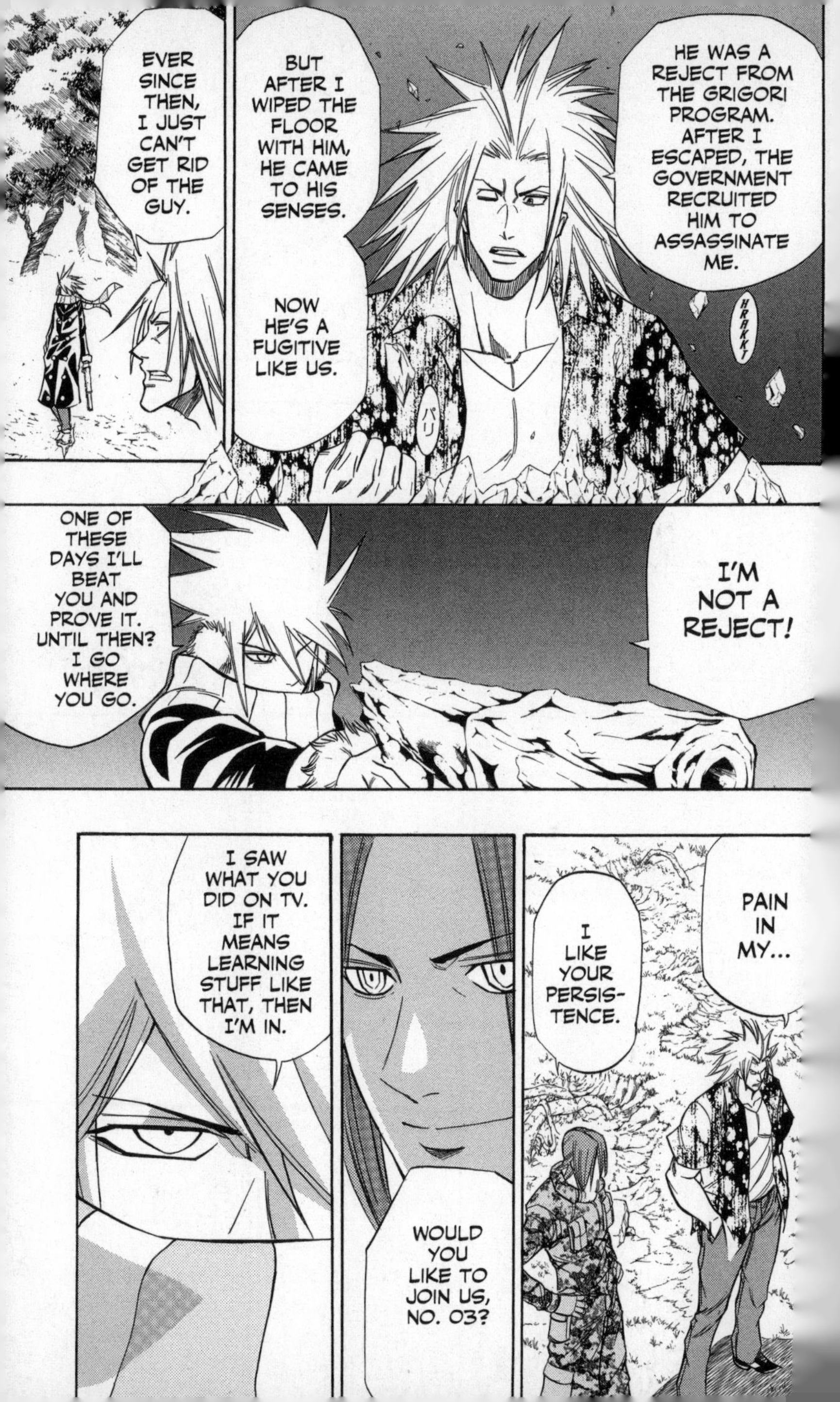
HE WAS A REJECT FROM THE GRIGORI PROGRAM. AFTER I ESCAPED, THE GOVERNMENT RECRUITED HIM TO ASSASSINATE ME.
HRAKKT
BUT AFTER I WIPED THE FLOOR WITH HIM, HE CAME TO HIS SENSES.
NOW HE'S A FUGITIVE LIKE US.
パリ
EVER SINCE THEN, I JUST CAN'T GET RID OF THE GUY.
I'M NOT A REJECT!
ONE OF THESE DAYS I'LL BEAT YOU AND PROVE IT. UNTIL THEN? I GO WHERE YOU GO.
PAIN IN MY...
I LIKE YOUR PERSIS-TENCE.
WOULD YOU LIKE TO JOIN US, NO. 03?
I SAW WHAT YOU DID ON TV. IF IT MEANS LEARNING STUFF LIKE THAT, THEN I'M IN.

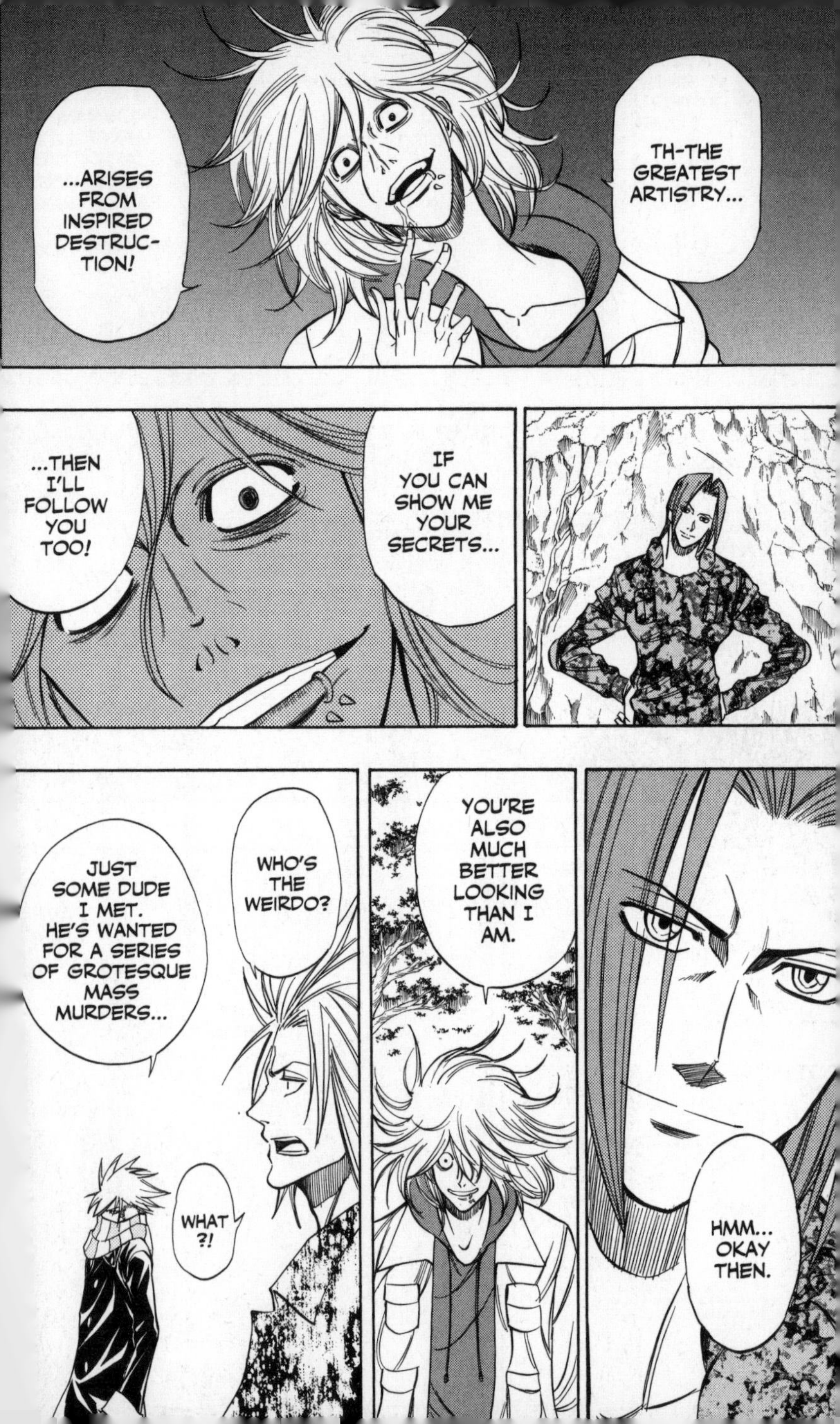
TH-THE GREATEST ARTISTRY...
...ARISES FROM INSPIRED DESTRUC-TION!
IF YOU CAN SHOW ME YOUR SECRETS...
...THEN I'LL FOLLOW YOU TOO!
HMM... OKAY THEN.
YOU'RE ALSO MUCH BETTER LOOKING THAN I AM.
WHO'S THE WEIRDO?
JUST SOME DUDE I MET. HE'S WANTED FOR A SERIES OF GROTESQUE MASS MURDERS...
WHAT?!

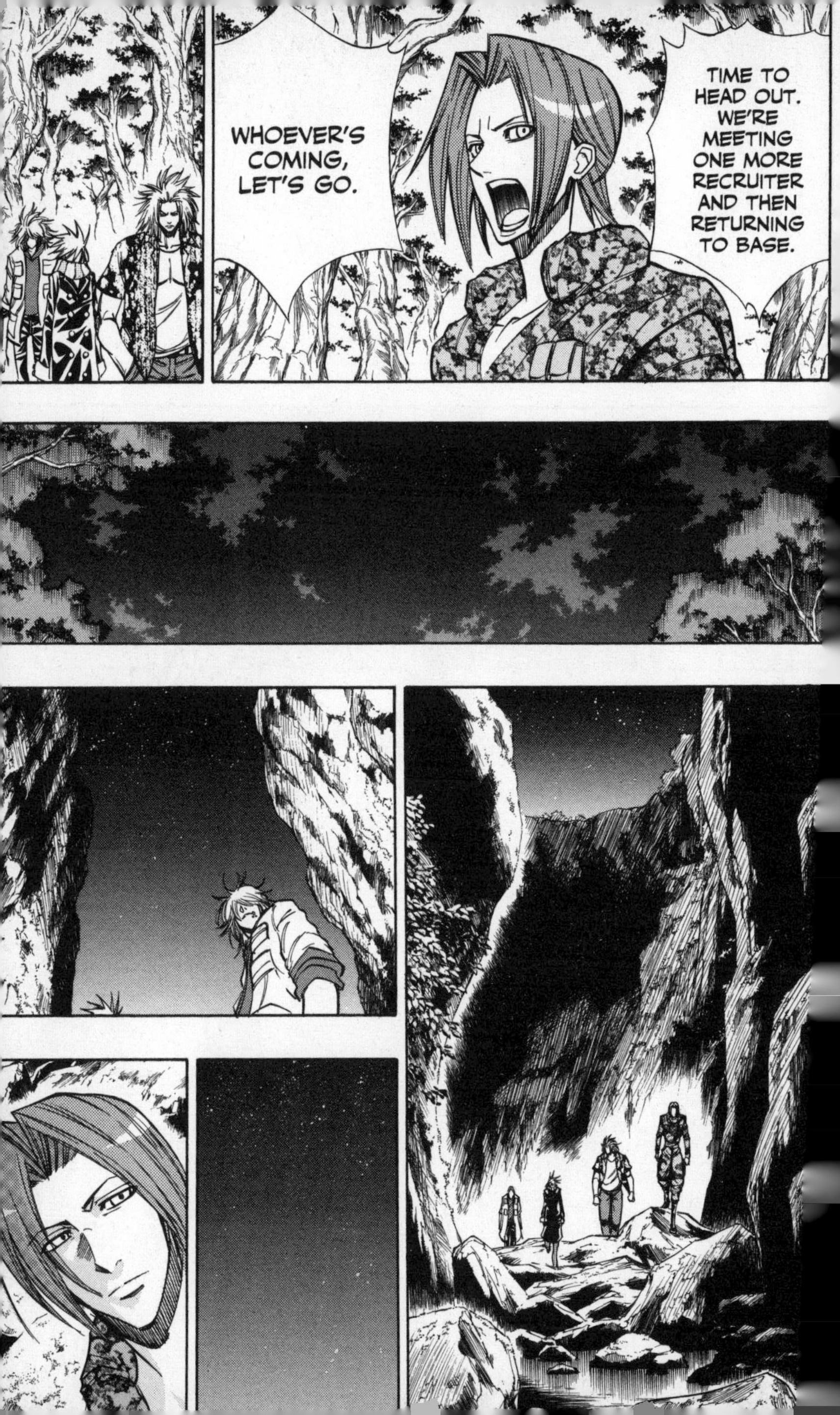
TIME TO HEAD OUT. WE'RE MEETING ONE MORE RECRUITER AND THEN RETURNING TO BASE.
WHOEVER'S COMING, LET'S GO.

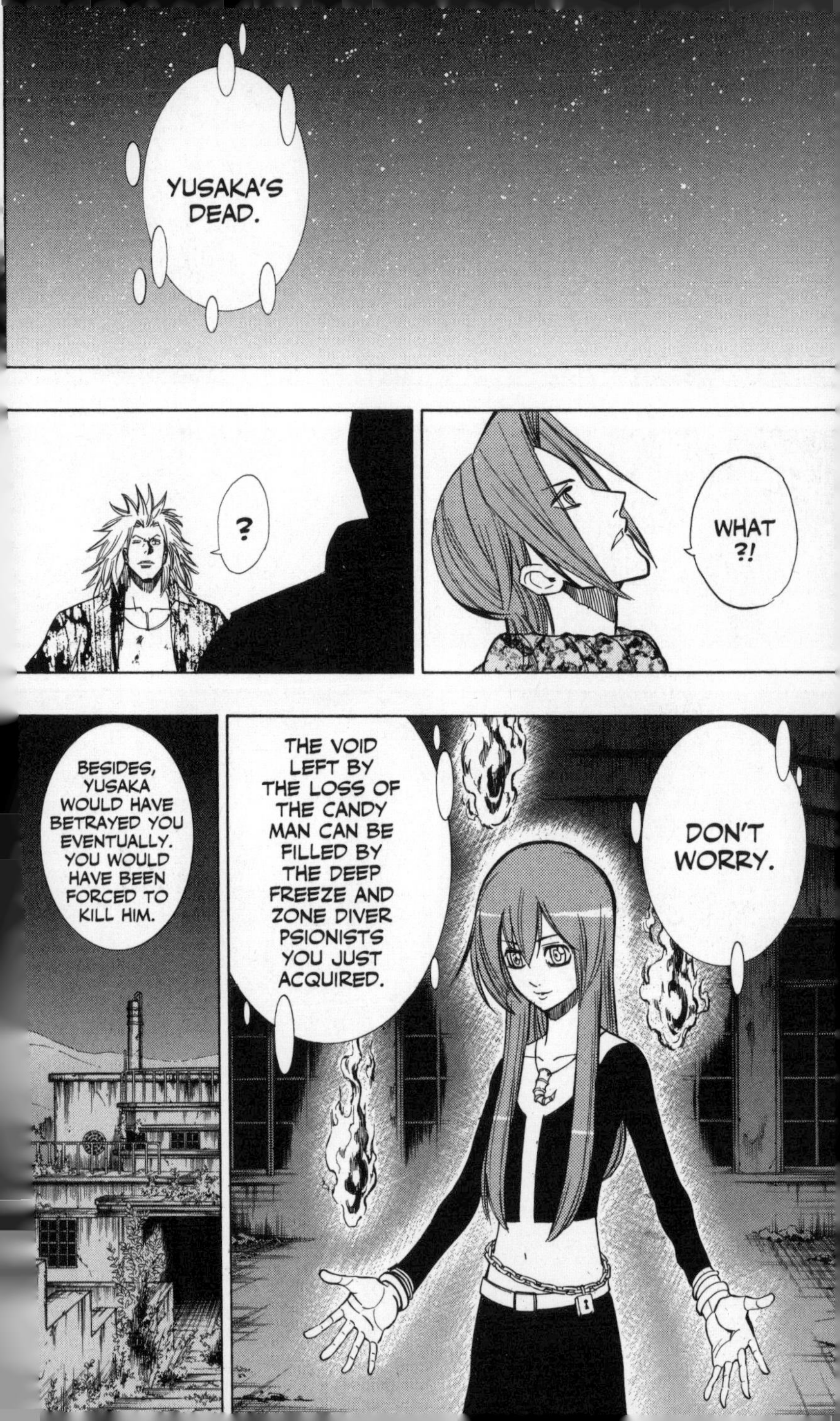
YUSAKA'S DEAD.
WHAT?!
?
DON'T WORRY.
THE VOID LEFT BY THE LOSS OF THE CANDY MAN CAN BE FILLED BY THE DEEP FREEZE AND ZONE DIVER PSIONISTS YOU JUST ACQUIRED.
BESIDES, YUSAKA WOULD HAVE BETRAYED YOU EVENTUALLY. YOU WOULD HAVE BEEN FORCED TO KILL HIM.

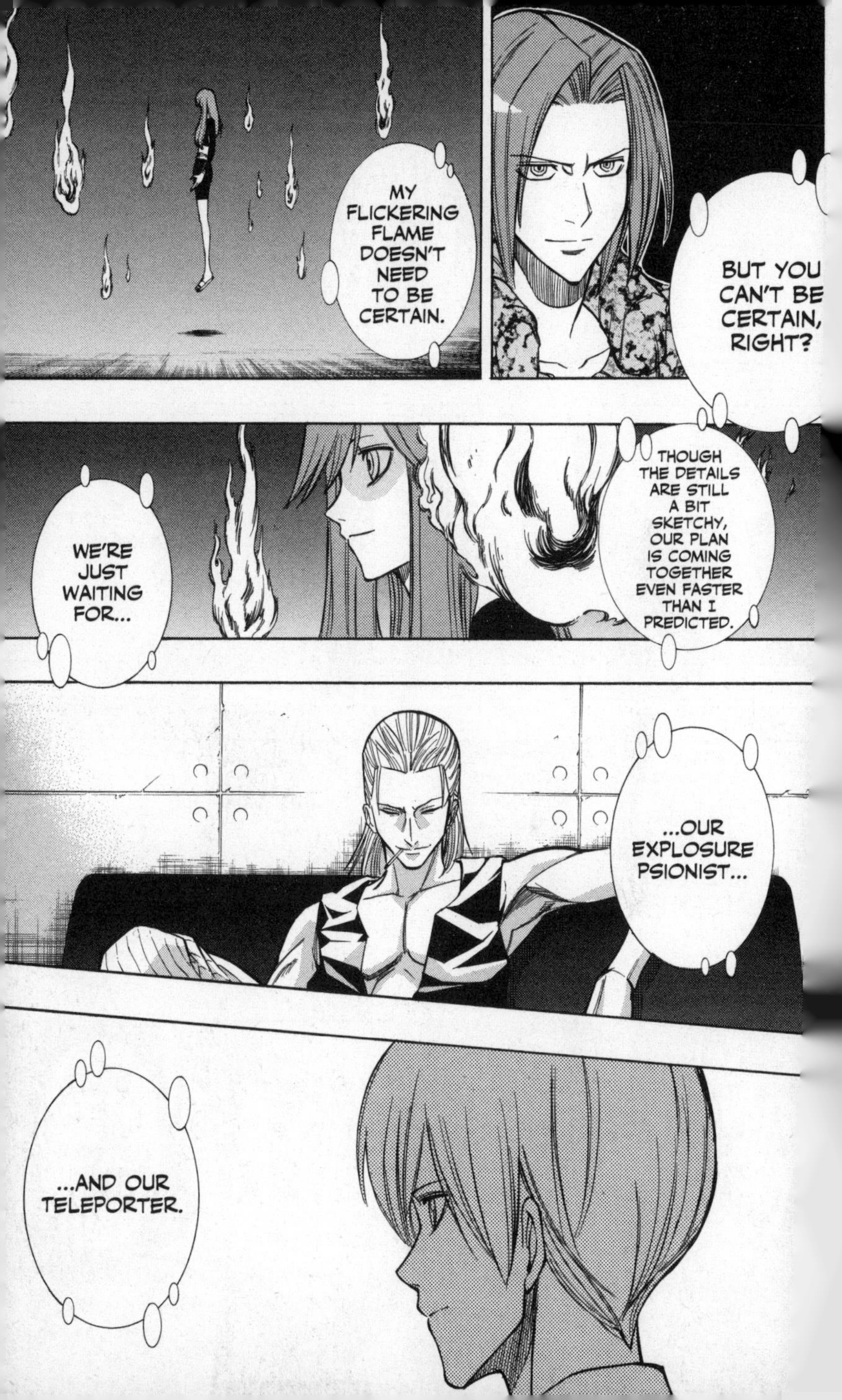
BUT YOU CAN'T BE CERTAIN, RIGHT?
MY FLICKERING FLAME DOESN'T NEED TO BE CERTAIN.
THOUGH THE DETAILS ARE STILL A BIT SKETCHY, OUR PLAN IS COMING TOGETHER EVEN FASTER THAN I PREDICTED.
WE'RE JUST WAITING FOR...
...OUR EXPLOSURE PSIONIST...
...AND OUR TELEPORTER.

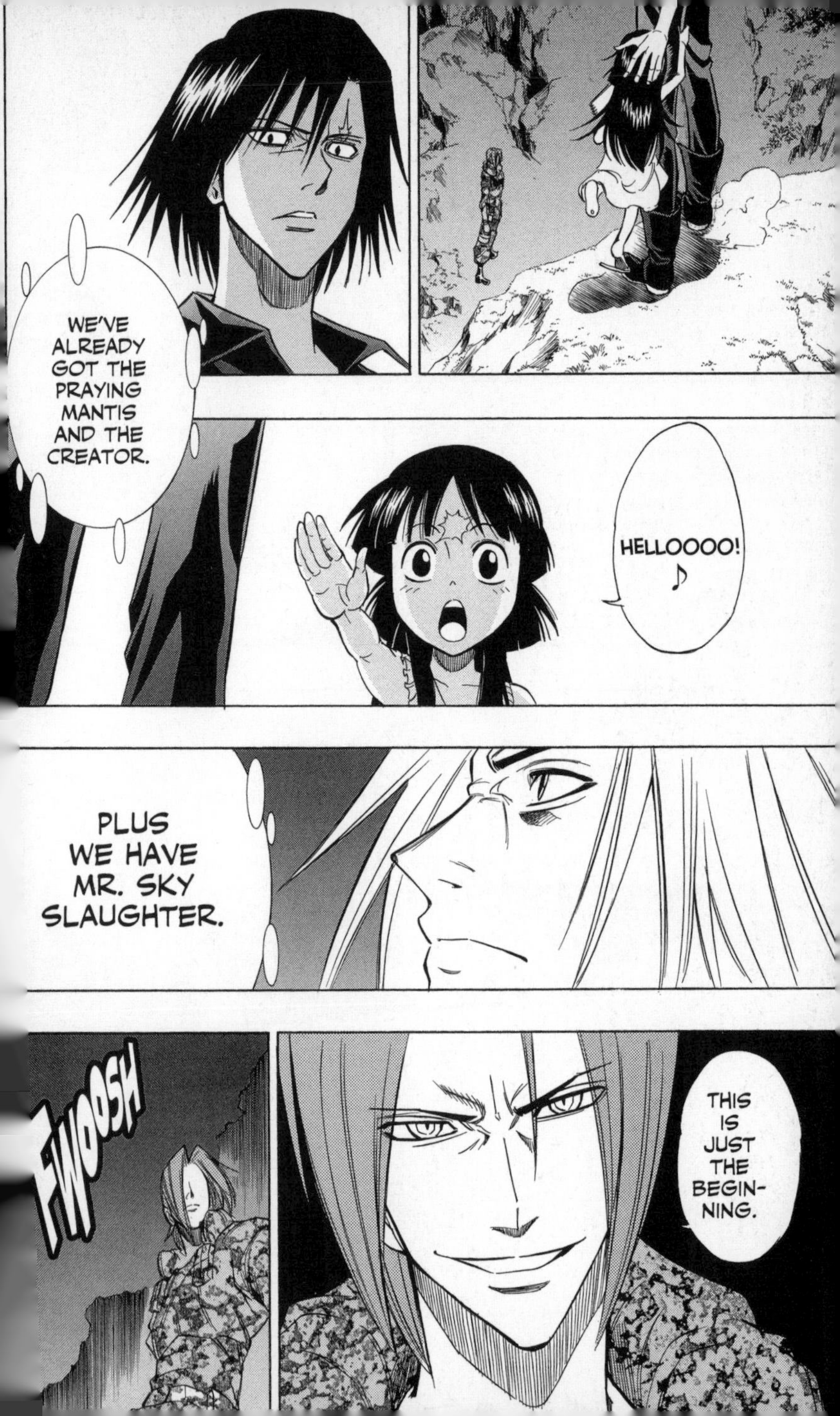
WE'VE ALREADY GOT THE PRAYING MANTIS AND THE CREATOR.
HELLOOOO! ♪
PLUS WE HAVE MR. SKY SLAUGHTER.
THIS IS JUST THE BEGIN- NING.
FWOOSH

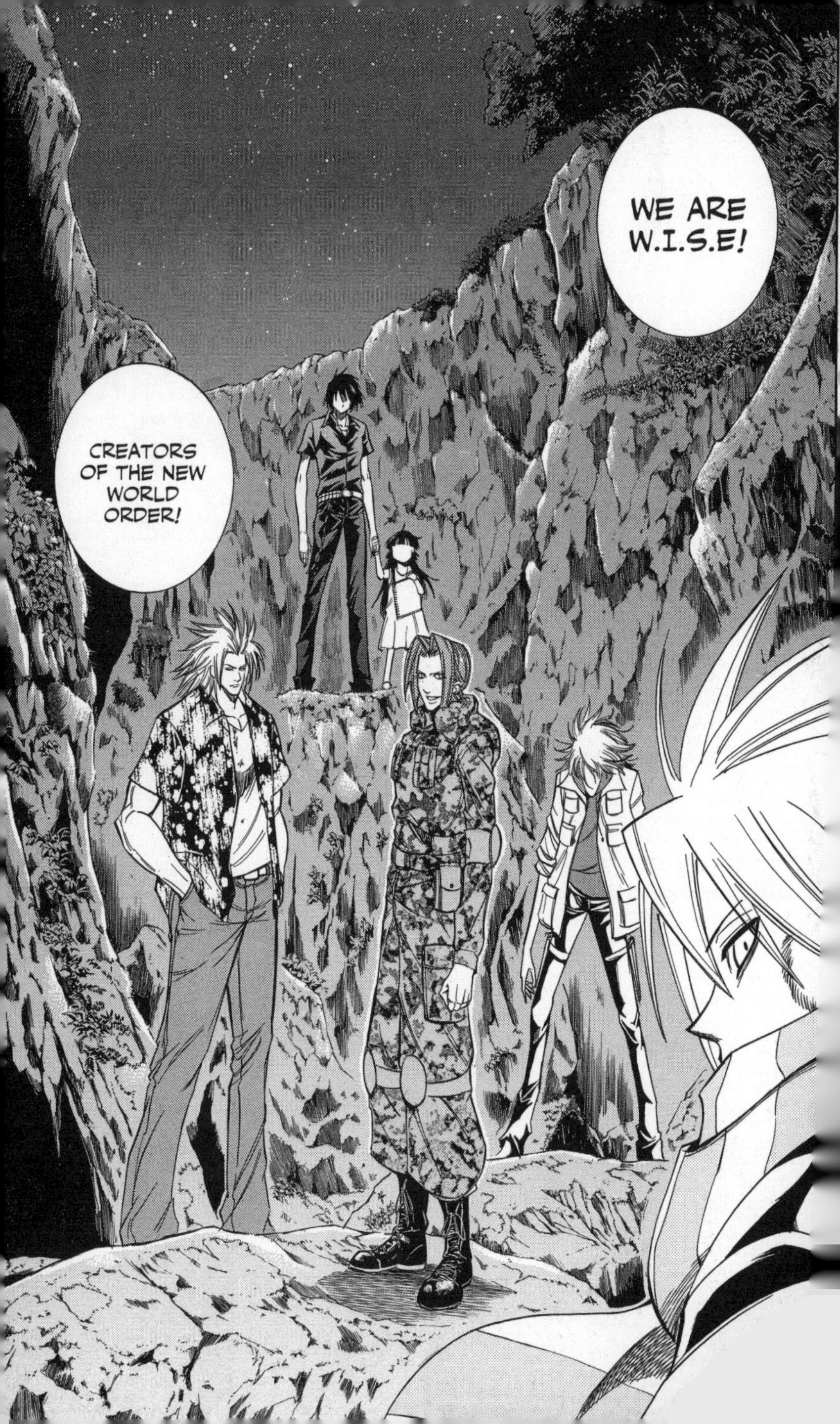
WE ARE W.I.S.E!
CREATORS OF THE NEW WORLD ORDER!

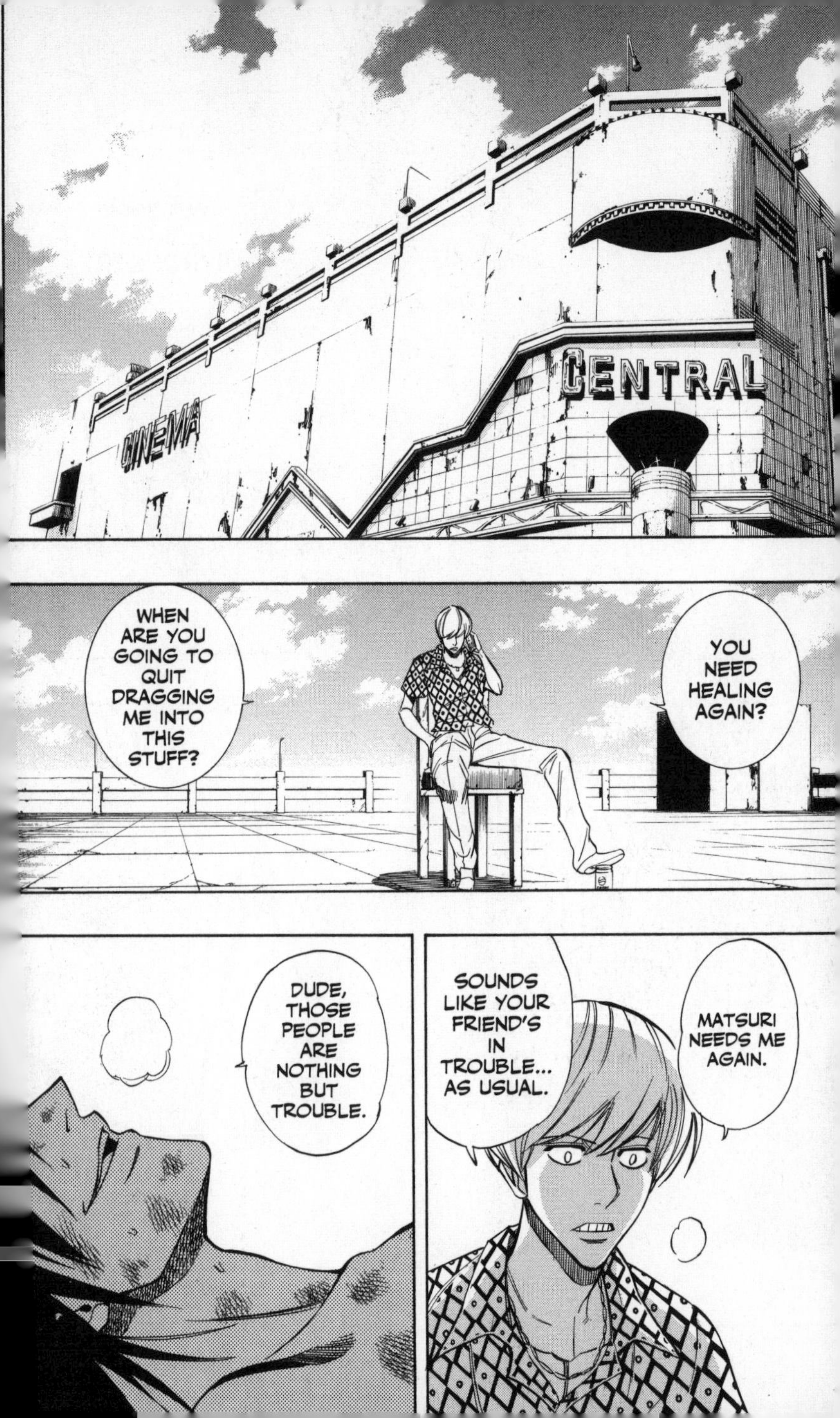
CENTRAL
CINEMA
YOU NEED HEALING AGAIN?
WHEN ARE YOU GOING TO QUIT DRAGGING ME INTO THIS STUFF?
MATSURI NEEDS ME AGAIN.
SOUNDS LIKE YOUR FRIEND'S IN TROUBLE... AS USUAL.
DUDE, THOSE PEOPLE ARE NOTHING BUT TROUBLE.

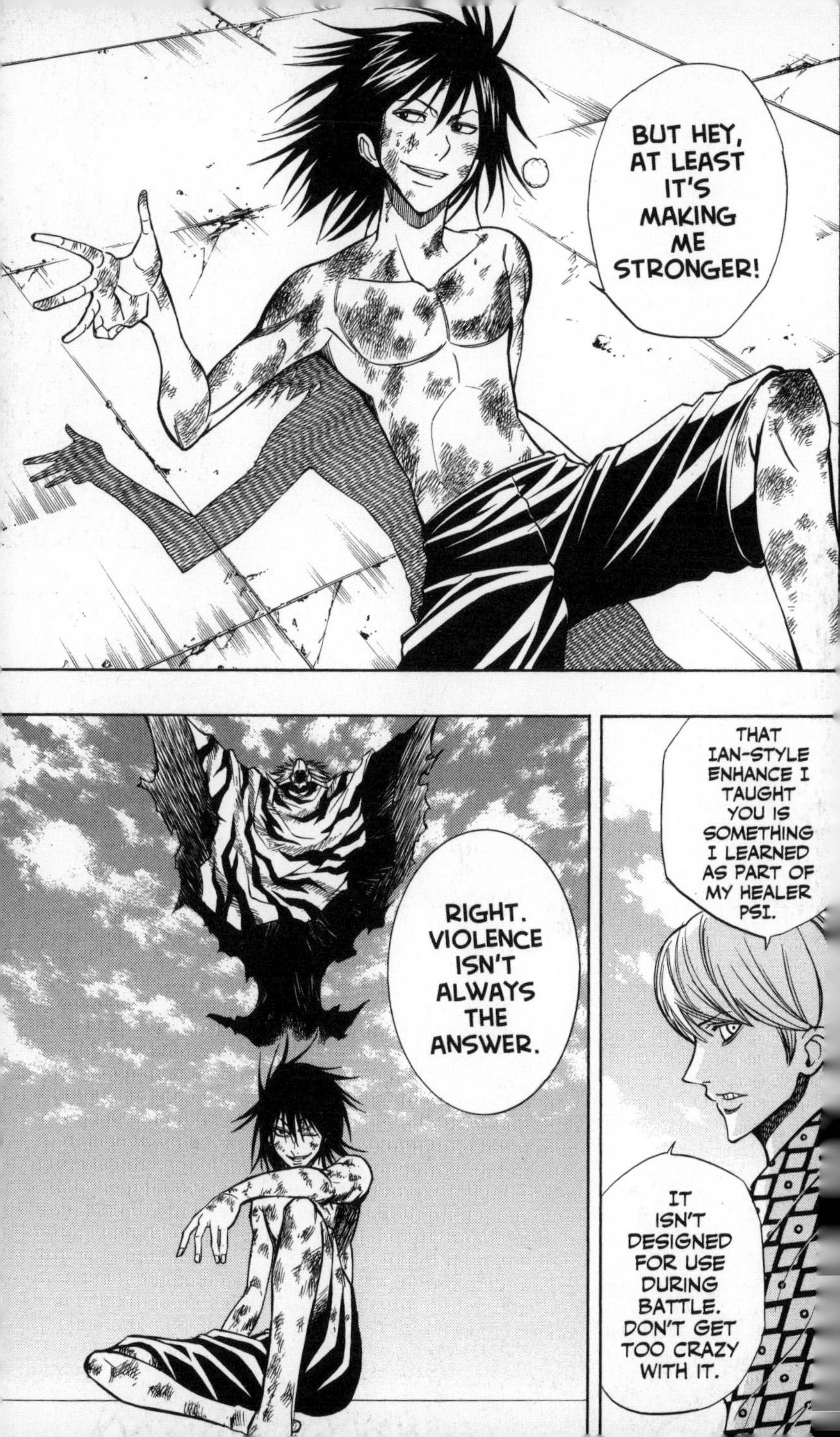
BUT HEY, AT LEAST IT'S MAKING ME STRONGER!
THAT IAN-STYLE ENHANCE I TAUGHT YOU IS SOMETHING I LEARNED AS PART OF MY HEALER PSI.
IT ISN'T DESIGNED FOR USE DURING BATTLE. DON'T GET TOO CRAZY WITH IT.
RIGHT. VIOLENCE ISN'T ALWAYS THE ANSWER.

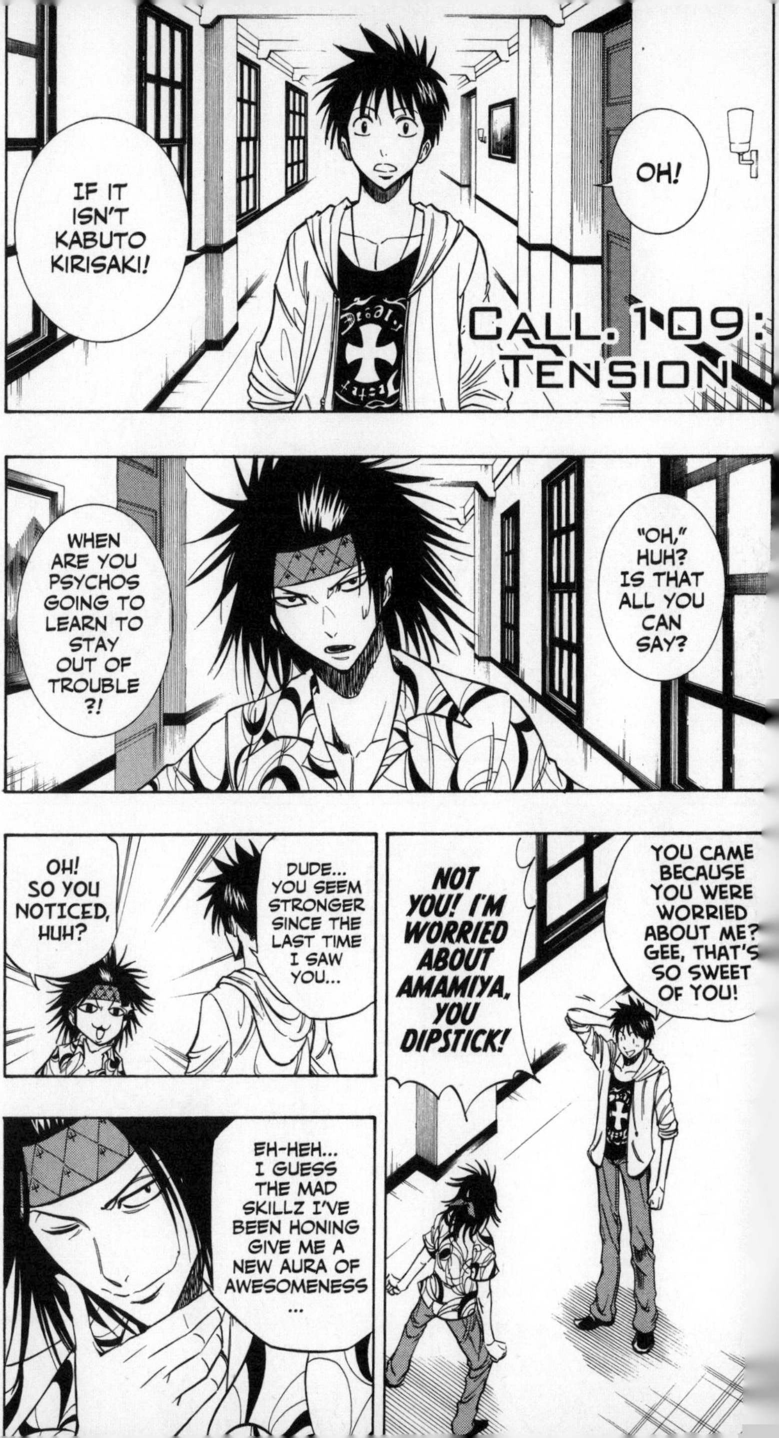
OH!
IF IT ISN'T KABUTO KIRISAKI!
CALL. 109: TENSION
"OH," HUH? IS THAT ALL YOU CAN SAY?
WHEN ARE YOU PSYCHOS GOING TO LEARN TO STAY OUT OF TROUBLE ?!
YOU CAME BECAUSE YOU WERE WORRIED ABOUT ME? GEE, THAT'S SO SWEET OF YOU!
NOT YOU! I'M WORRIED ABOUT AMAMIYA, YOU DIPSTICK!
DUDE... YOU SEEM STRONGER SINCE THE LAST TIME I SAW YOU...
OH! SO YOU NOTICED, HUH?
EH-HEH... I GUESS THE MAD SKILLZ I'VE BEEN HONING GIVE ME A NEW AURA OF AWESOMENESS ...

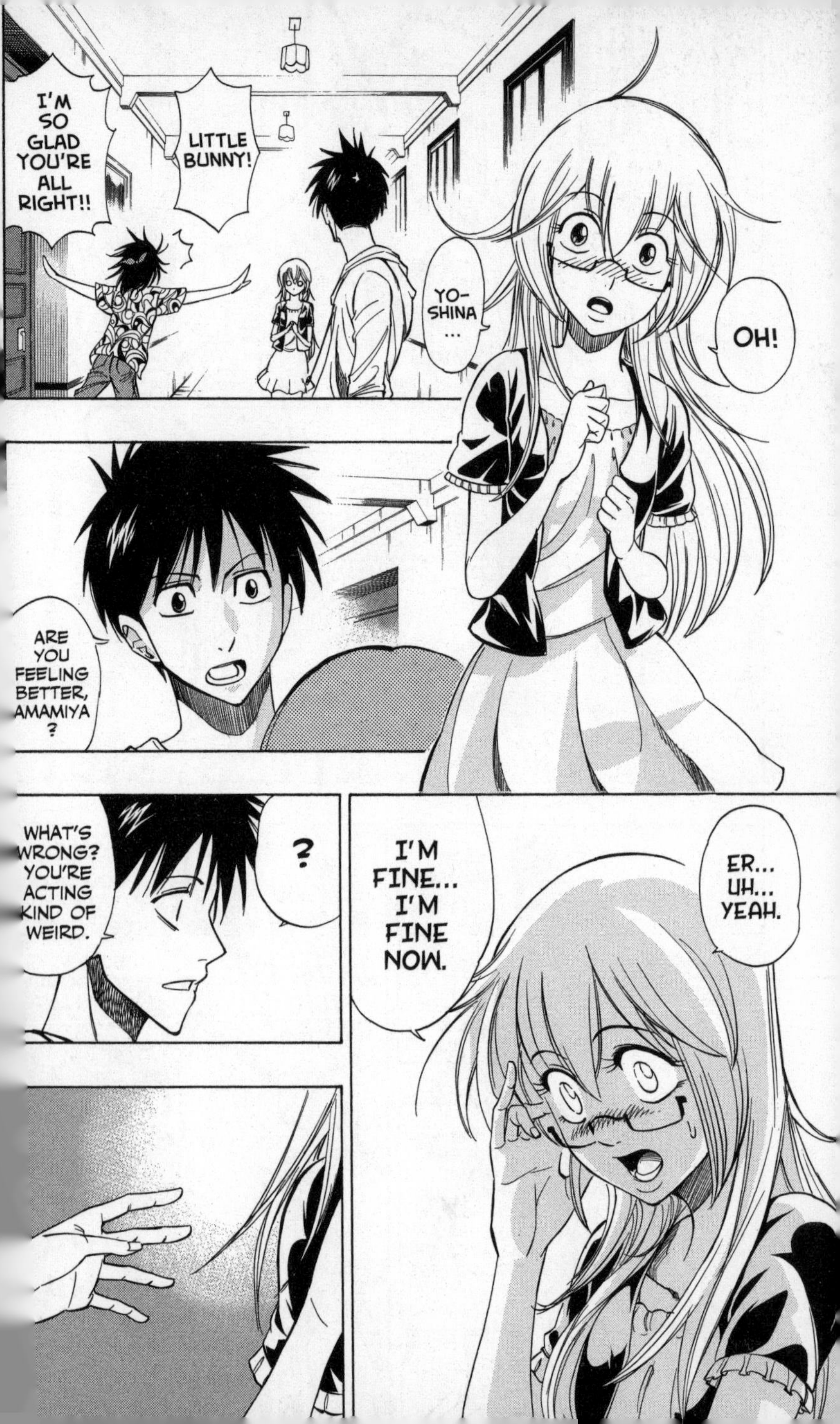
OH!
YO-SHINA...
LITTLE BUNNY!
I'M SO GLAD YOU'RE ALL RIGHT!!
ARE YOU FEELING BETTER, AMAMIYA?
ER... UH... YEAH.
I'M FINE... I'M FINE NOW.
?
WHAT'S WRONG? YOU'RE ACTING KIND OF WEIRD.

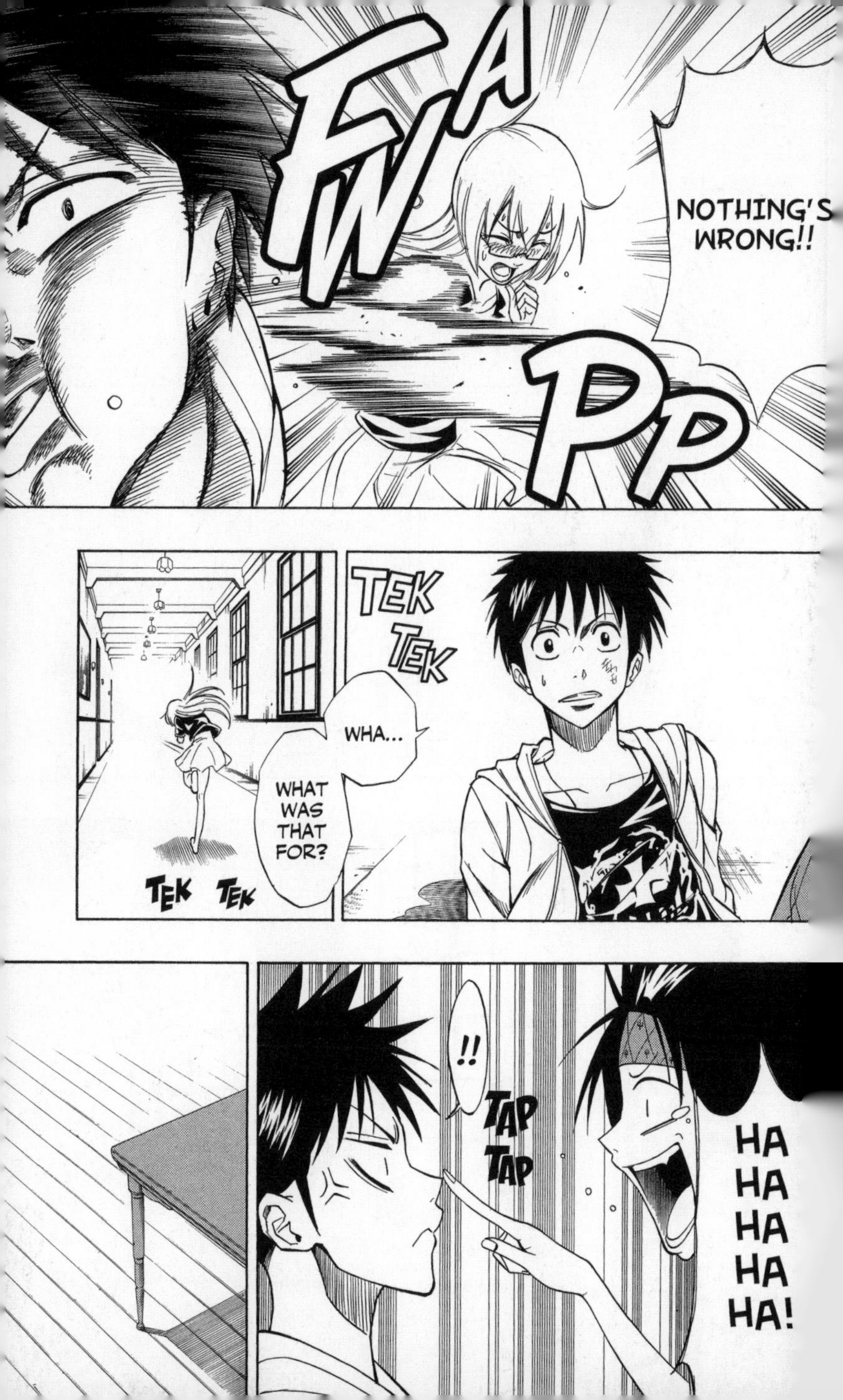
NOTHING'S WRONG!!
FWAPP
TEK TEK
WHA...
WHAT WAS THAT FOR?
TEK TEK
HA HA HA HA HA HA!
!!
TAP TAP

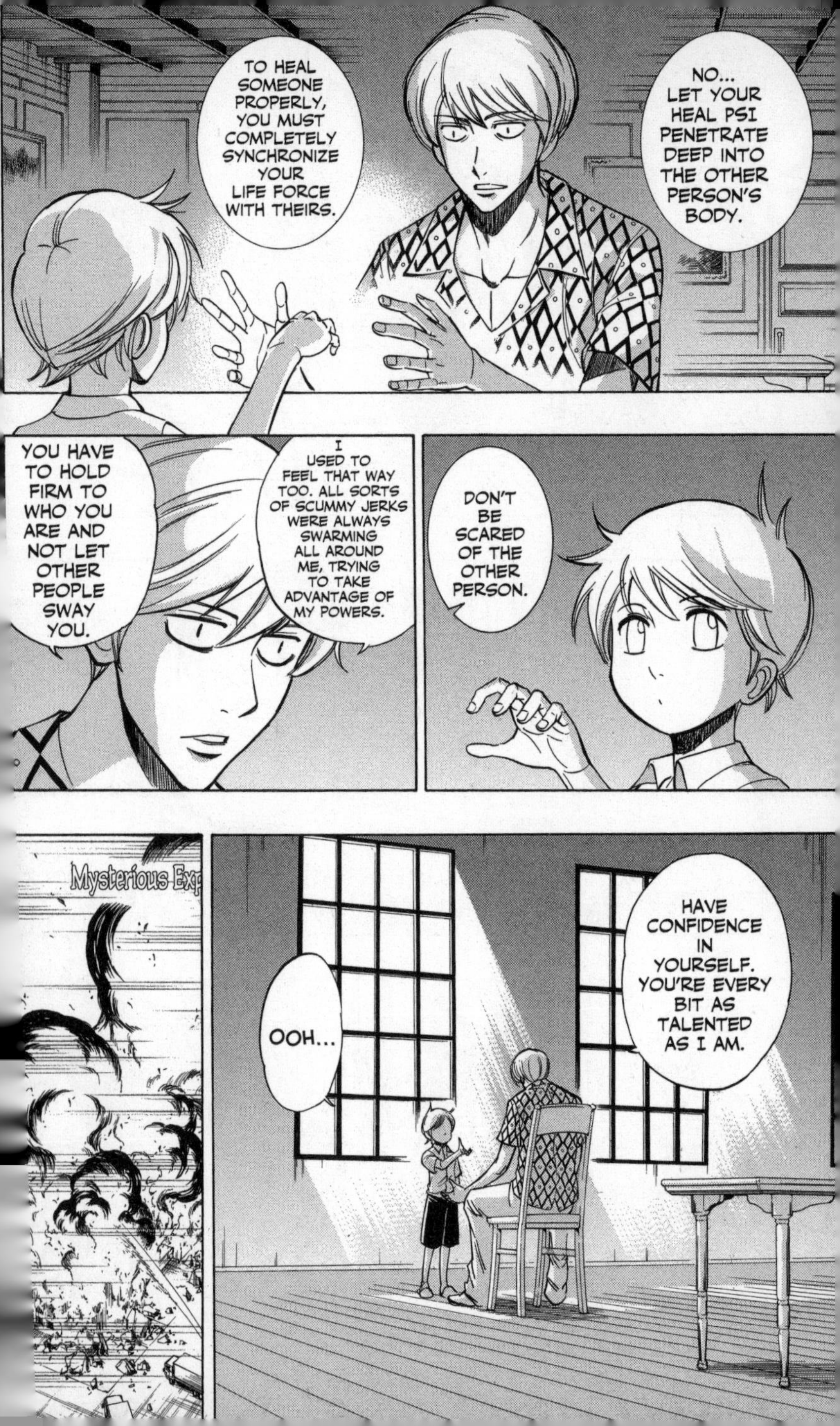
NO... LET YOUR HEAL PSI PENETRATE DEEP INTO THE OTHER PERSON'S BODY.
TO HEAL SOMEONE PROPERLY, YOU MUST COMPLETELY SYNCHRONIZE YOUR LIFE FORCE WITH THEIRS.
DON'T BE SCARED OF THE OTHER PERSON.
I USED TO FEEL THAT WAY TOO. ALL SORTS OF SCUMMY JERKS WERE ALWAYS SWARMING ALL AROUND ME, TRYING TO TAKE ADVANTAGE OF MY POWERS.
YOU HAVE TO HOLD FIRM TO WHO YOU ARE AND NOT LET OTHER PEOPLE SWAY YOU.
HAVE CONFIDENCE IN YOURSELF. YOU'RE EVERY BIT AS TALENTED AS I AM.
OOH...

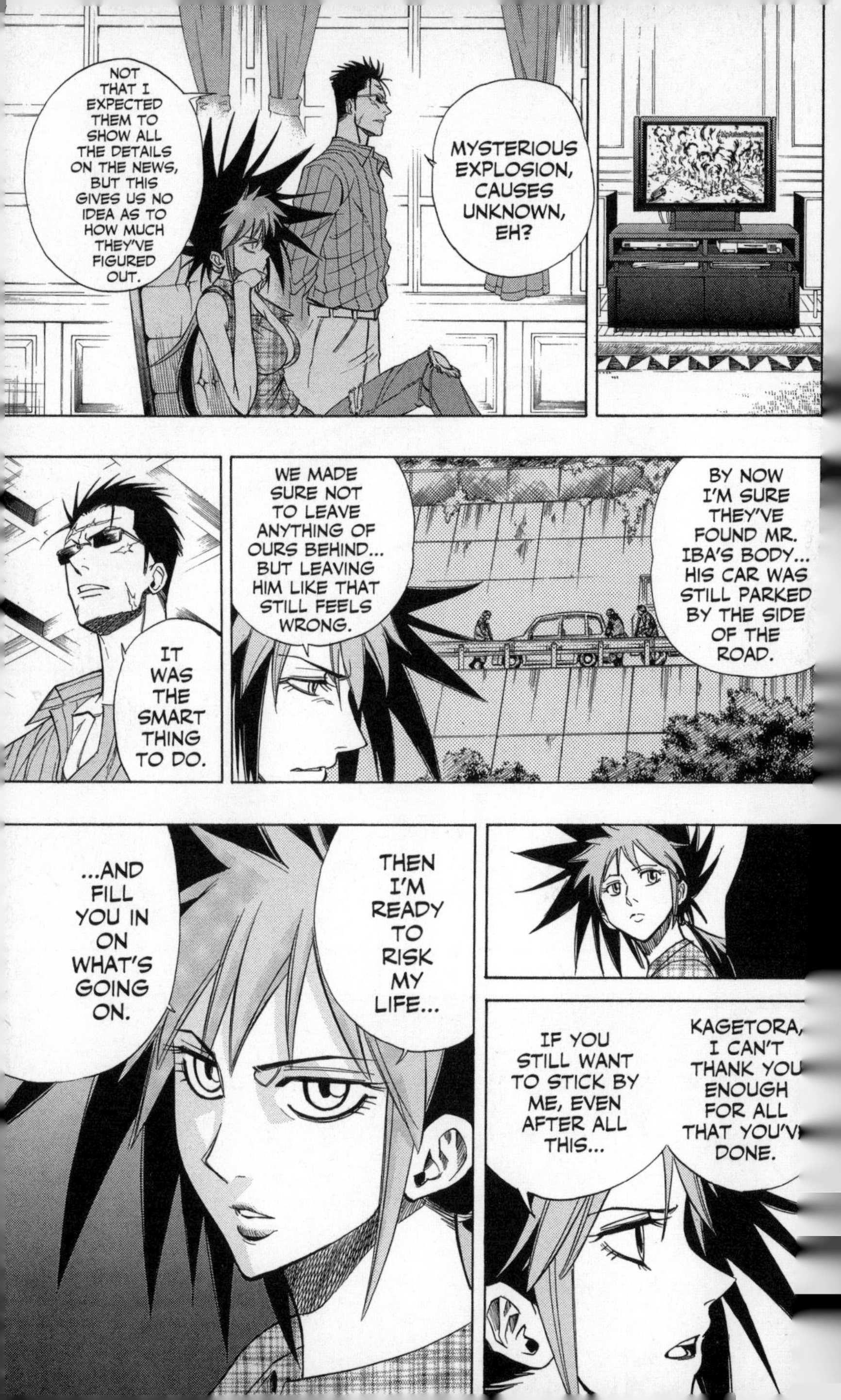
MYSTERIOUS EXPLOSION, CAUSES UNKNOWN, EH?
NOT THAT I EXPECTED THEM TO SHOW ALL THE DETAILS ON THE NEWS, BUT THIS GIVES US NO IDEA AS TO HOW MUCH THEY'VE FIGURED OUT.
BY NOW I'M SURE THEY'VE FOUND MR. IBA'S BODY... HIS CAR WAS STILL PARKED BY THE SIDE OF THE ROAD.
WE MADE SURE NOT TO LEAVE ANYTHING OF OURS BEHIND... BUT LEAVING HIM LIKE THAT STILL FEELS WRONG.
IT WAS THE SMART THING TO DO.
KAGETORA, I CAN'T THANK YOU ENOUGH FOR ALL THAT YOU'VE DONE.
IF YOU STILL WANT TO STICK BY ME, EVEN AFTER ALL THIS...
THEN I'M READY TO RISK MY LIFE...
...AND FILL YOU IN ON WHAT'S GOING ON.

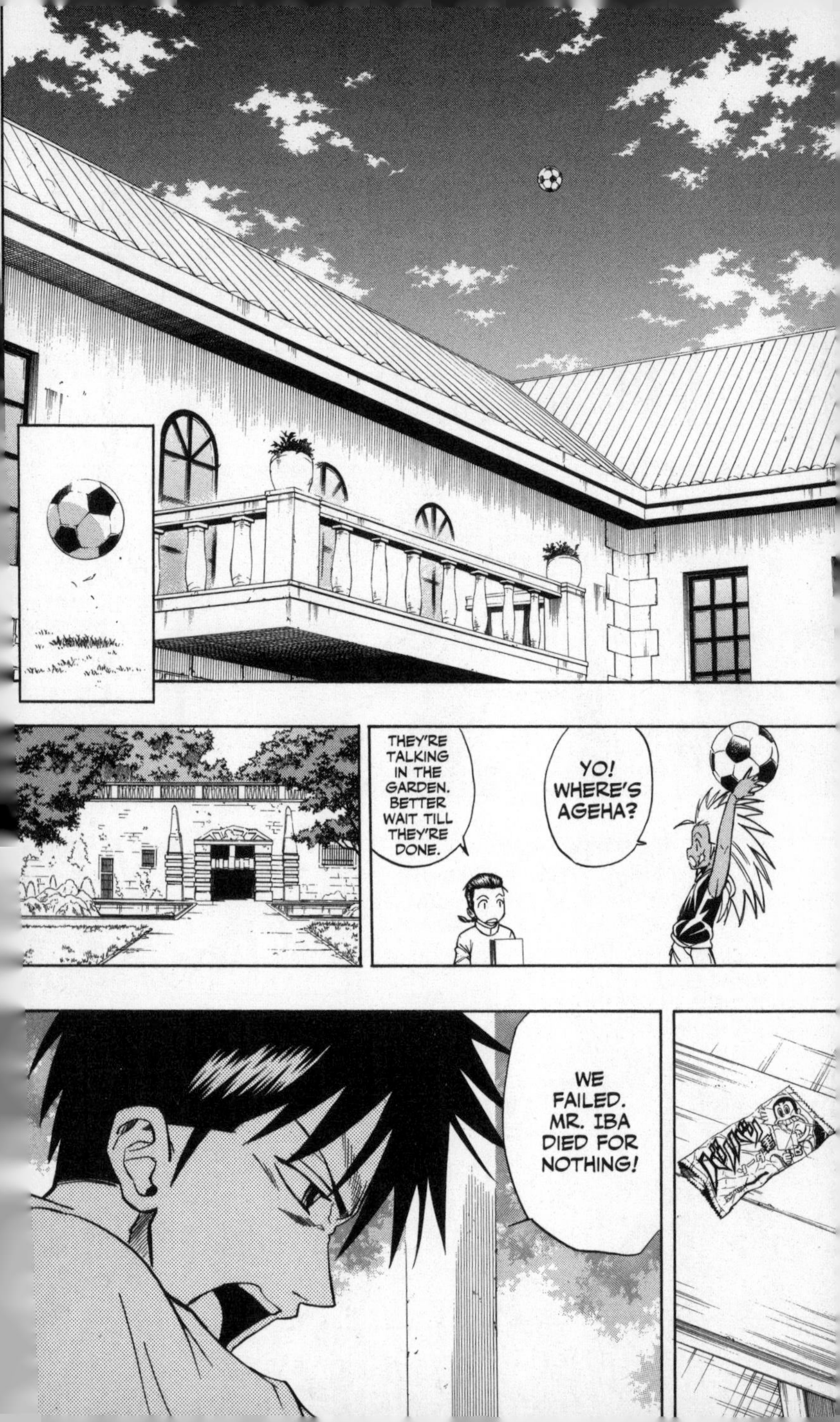
YO! WHERE'S AGEHA?
THEY'RE TALKING IN THE GARDEN. BETTER WAIT TILL THEY'RE DONE.
WE FAILED. MR. IBA DIED FOR NOTHING!

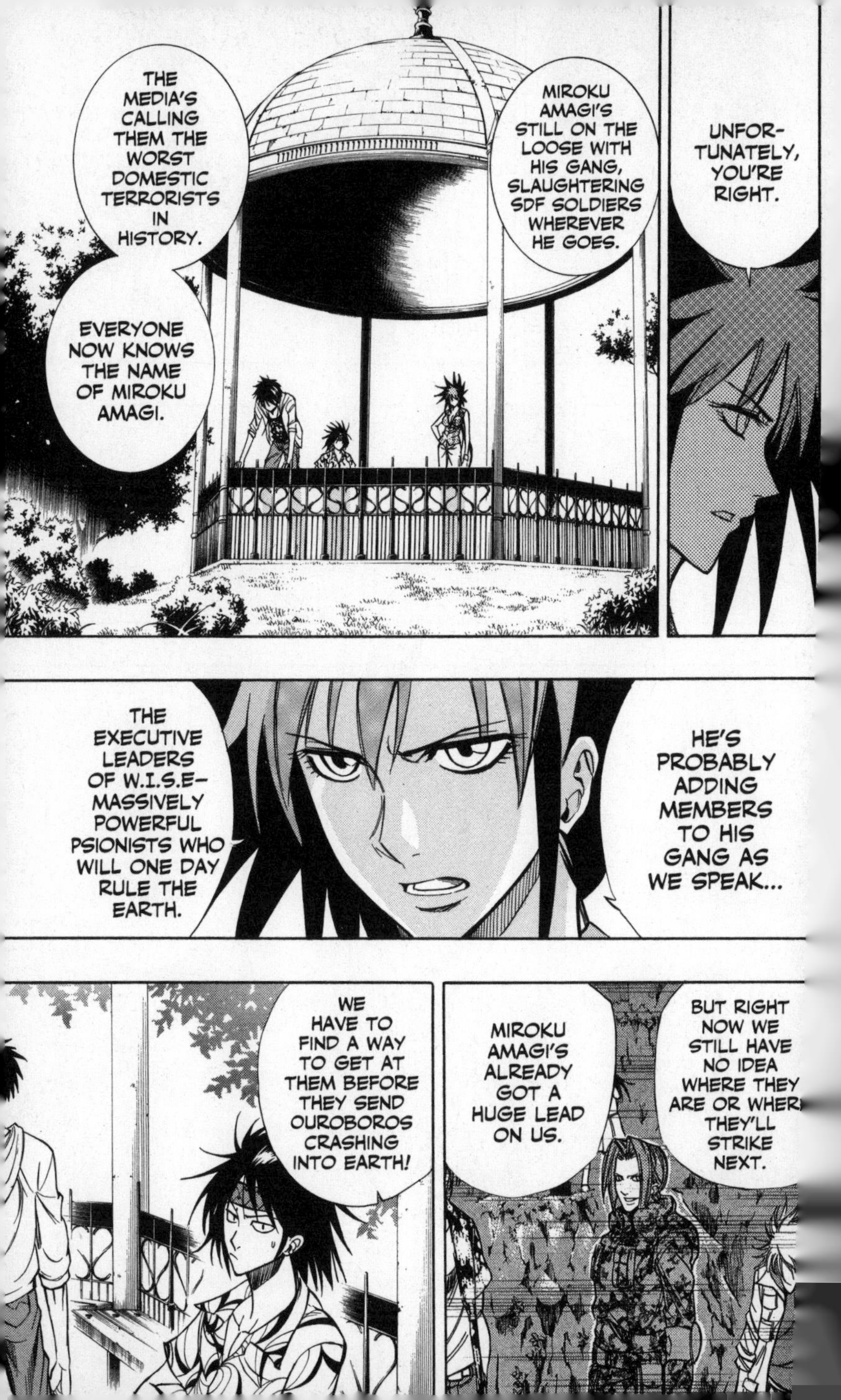

UNFORTUNATELY, YOU'RE RIGHT.
MIROKU AMAGI'S STILL ON THE LOOSE WITH HIS GANG, SLAUGHTERING SDF SOLDIERS WHEREVER HE GOES.
THE MEDIA'S CALLING THEM THE WORST DOMESTIC TERRORISTS IN HISTORY.
EVERYONE NOW KNOWS THE NAME OF MIROKU AMAGI.
HE'S PROBABLY ADDING MEMBERS TO HIS GANG AS WE SPEAK...
THE EXECUTIVE LEADERS OF W.I.S.E–MASSIVELY POWERFUL PSIONISTS WHO WILL ONE DAY RULE THE EARTH.
BUT RIGHT NOW WE STILL HAVE NO IDEA WHERE THEY ARE OR WHER THEY'LL STRIKE NEXT.
MIROKU AMAGI'S ALREADY GOT A HUGE LEAD ON US.
WE HAVE TO FIND A WAY TO GET AT THEM BEFORE THEY SEND OUROBOROS CRASHING INTO EARTH!

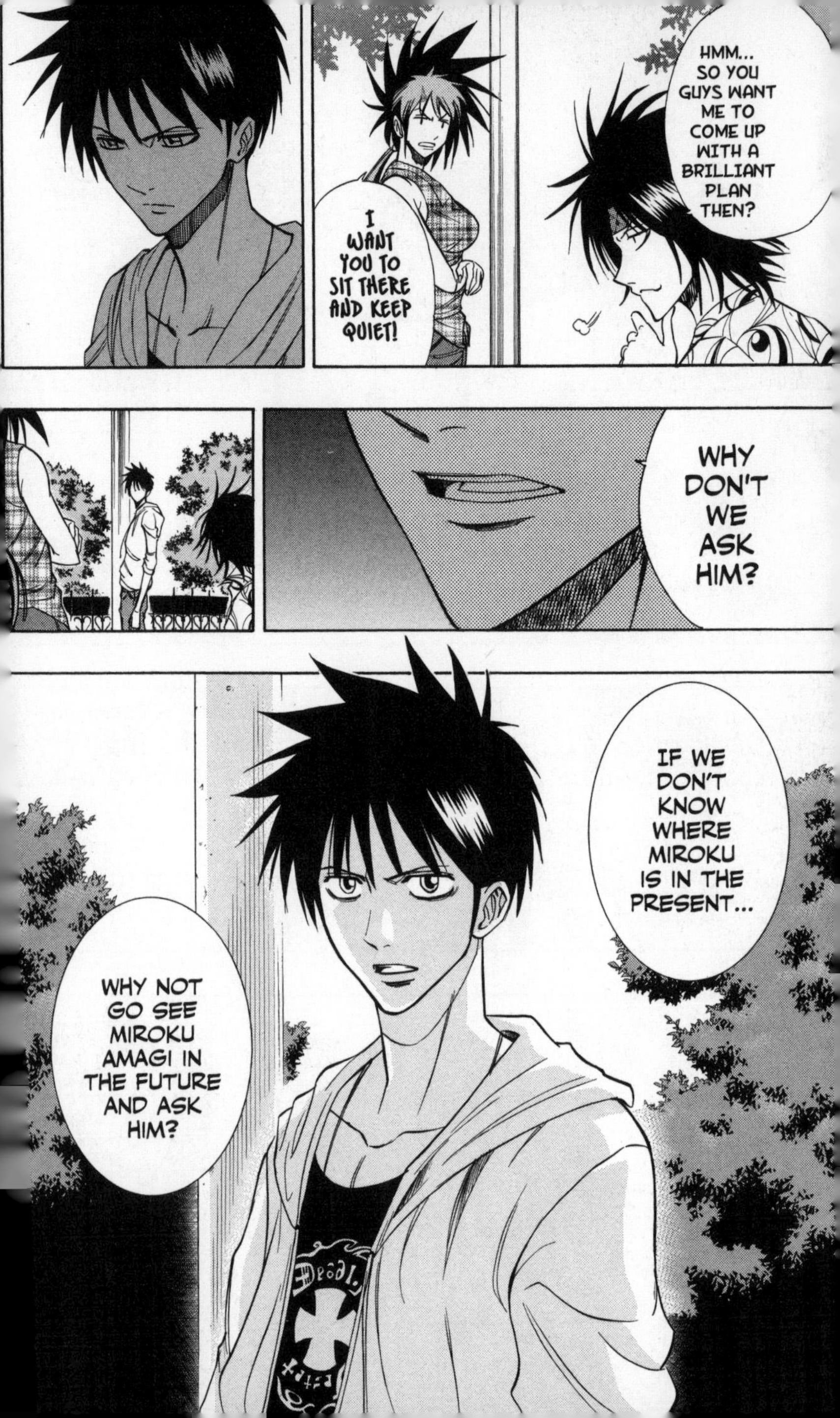
HMM... SO YOU GUYS WANT ME TO COME UP WITH A BRILLIANT PLAN THEN?
I WANT YOU TO SIT THERE AND KEEP QUIET!
WHY DON'T WE ASK HIM?
IF WE DON'T KNOW WHERE MIROKU IS IN THE PRESENT...
WHY NOT GO SEE MIROKU AMAGI IN THE FUTURE AND ASK HIM?

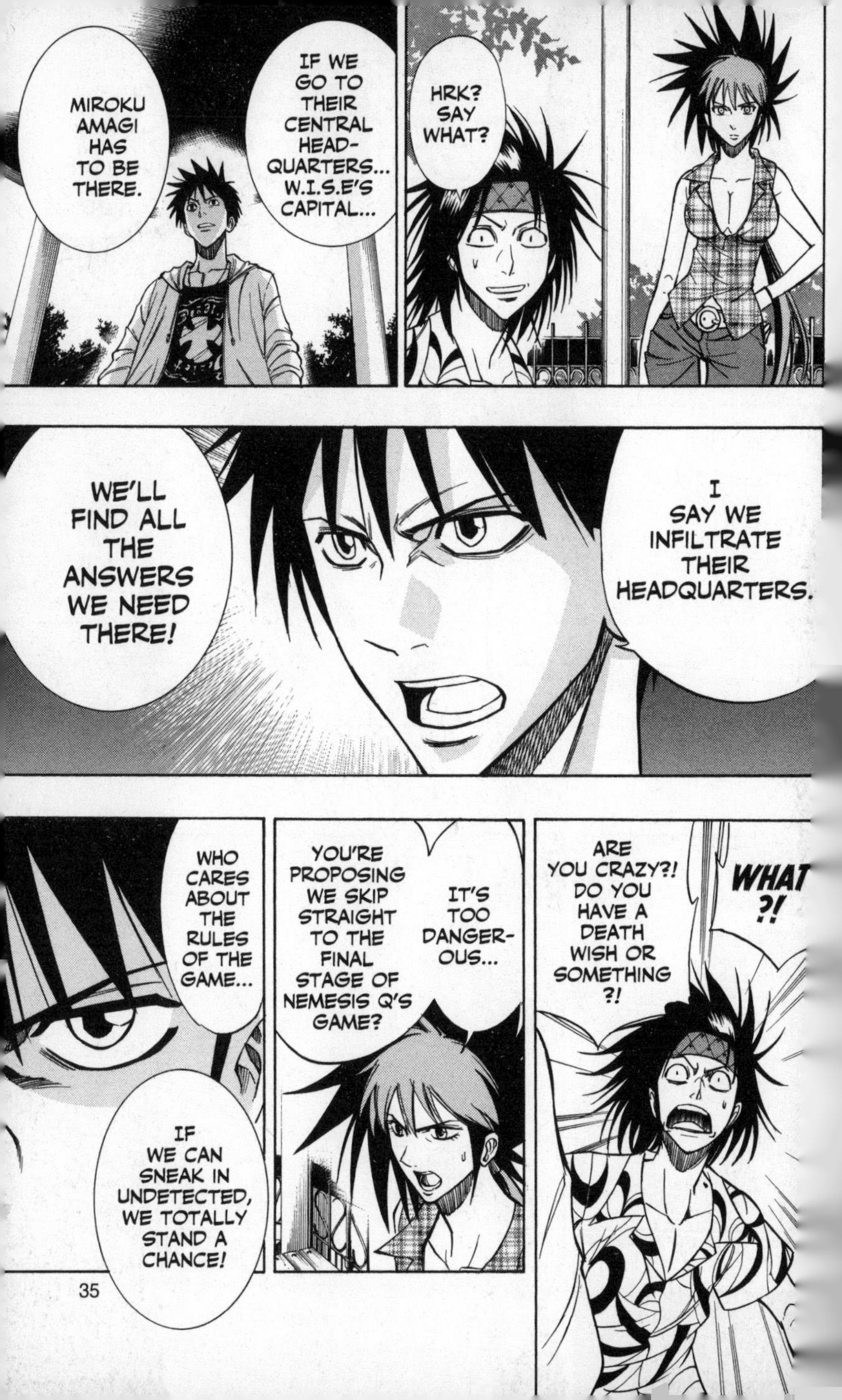

HRK? SAY WHAT?
IF WE GO TO THEIR CENTRAL HEAD-QUARTERS... W.I.S.E'S CAPITAL...
MIROKU AMAGI HAS TO BE THERE.
I SAY WE INFILTRATE THEIR HEADQUARTERS.
WE'LL FIND ALL THE ANSWERS WE NEED THERE!
WHAT?!
ARE YOU CRAZY?! DO YOU HAVE A DEATH WISH OR SOMETHING?!
IT'S TOO DANGER-OUS...
YOU'RE PROPOSING WE SKIP STRAIGHT TO THE FINAL STAGE OF NEMESIS Q'S GAME?
WHO CARES ABOUT THE RULES OF THE GAME...
IF WE CAN SNEAK IN UNDETECTED, WE TOTALLY STAND A CHANCE!

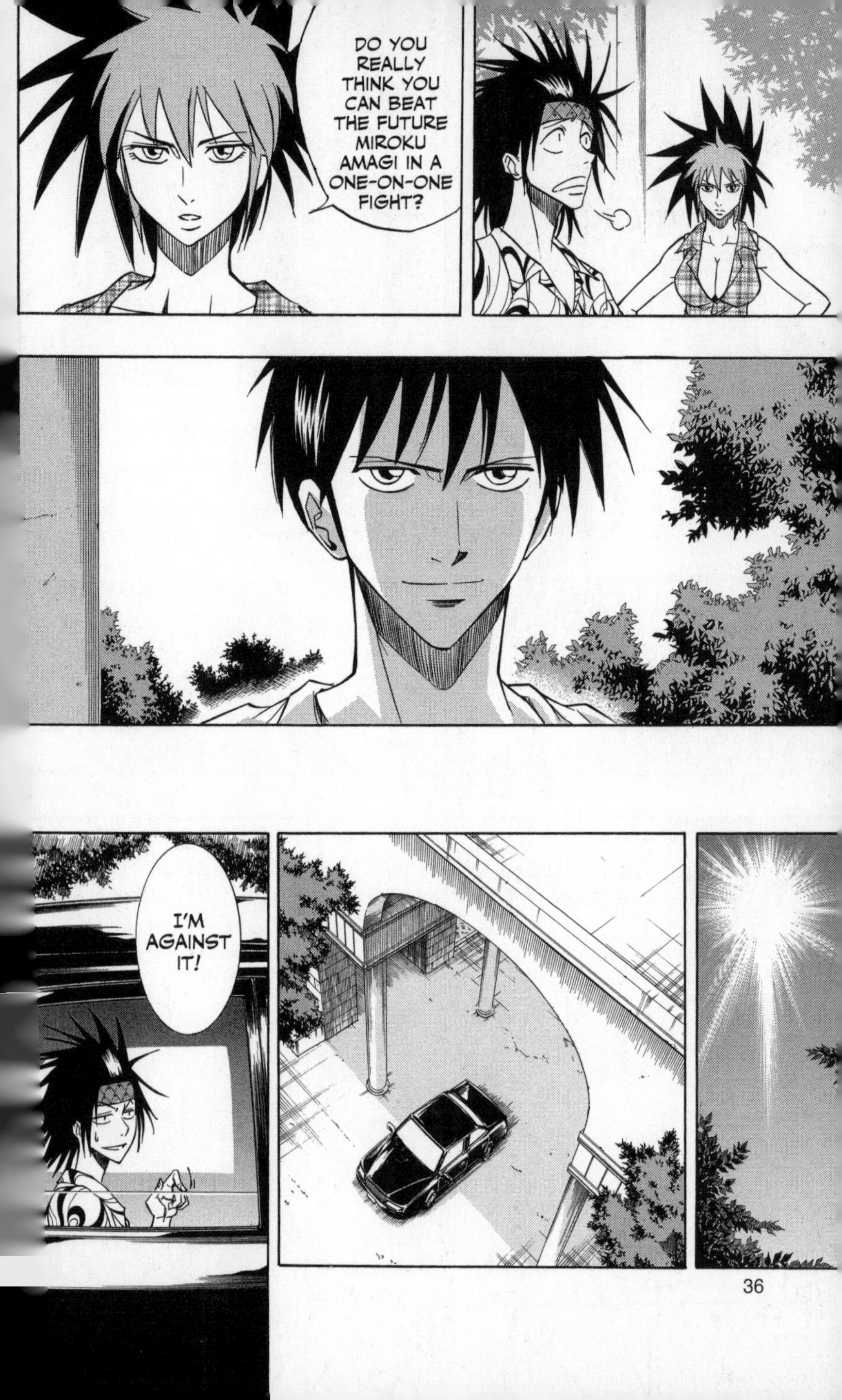
DO YOU REALLY THINK YOU CAN BEAT THE FUTURE MIROKU AMAGI IN A ONE-ON-ONE FIGHT?
I'M AGAINST IT!

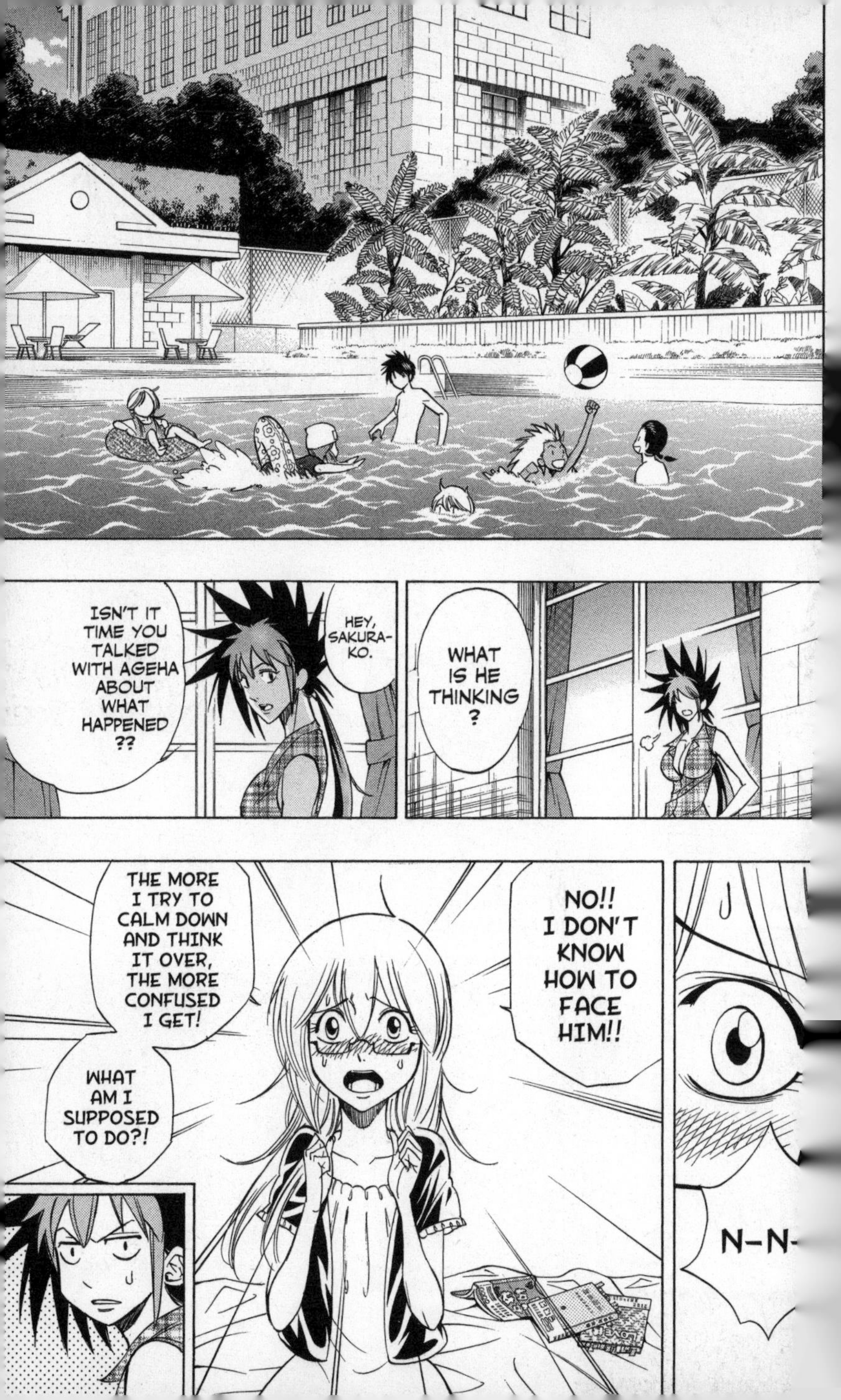
WHAT IS HE THINKING?
HEY, SAKURA-KO.
ISN'T IT TIME YOU TALKED WITH AGEHA ABOUT WHAT HAPPENED??
N-N-
NO!! I DON'T KNOW HOW TO FACE HIM!!
THE MORE I TRY TO CALM DOWN AND THINK IT OVER, THE MORE CONFUSED I GET!
WHAT AM I SUPPOSED TO DO?!

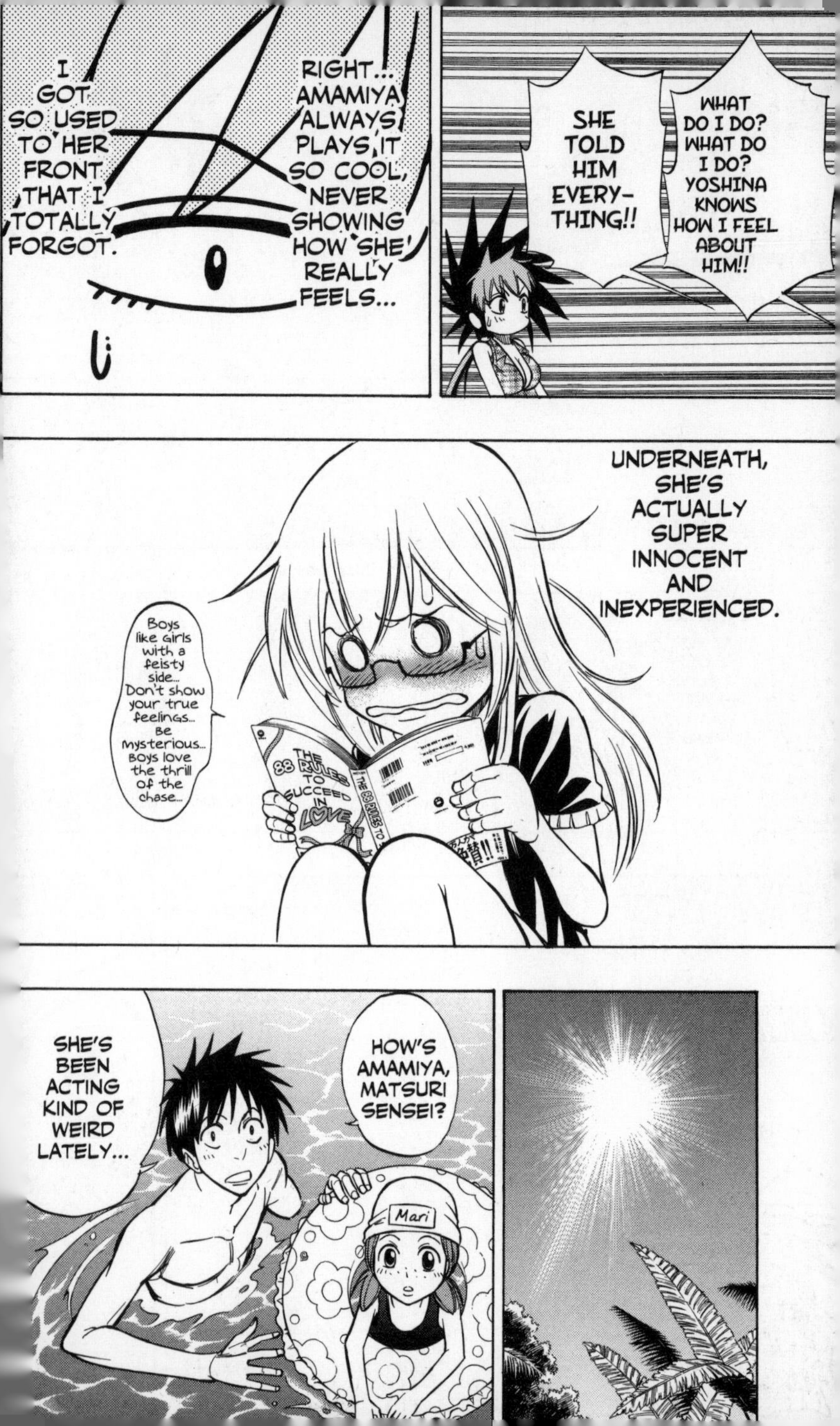
WHAT DO I DO? WHAT DO I DO? YOSHINA KNOWS HOW I FEEL ABOUT HIM!!
SHE TOLD HIM EVERYTHING!!
RIGHT... AMAMIYA ALWAYS PLAYS IT SO COOL, NEVER SHOWING HOW SHE REALLY FEELS...
I GOT SO USED TO HER FRONT THAT I TOTALLY FORGOT.
UNDERNEATH, SHE'S ACTUALLY SUPER INNOCENT AND INEXPERIENCED.
Boys like girls with a feisty side... Don't show your true feelings... Be mysterious... Boys love the thrill of the chase...
THE 88 RULES TO SUCCEED IN LOVE
HOW'S AMAMIYA, MATSURI SENSEI?
SHE'S BEEN ACTING KIND OF WEIRD LATELY...
Mari

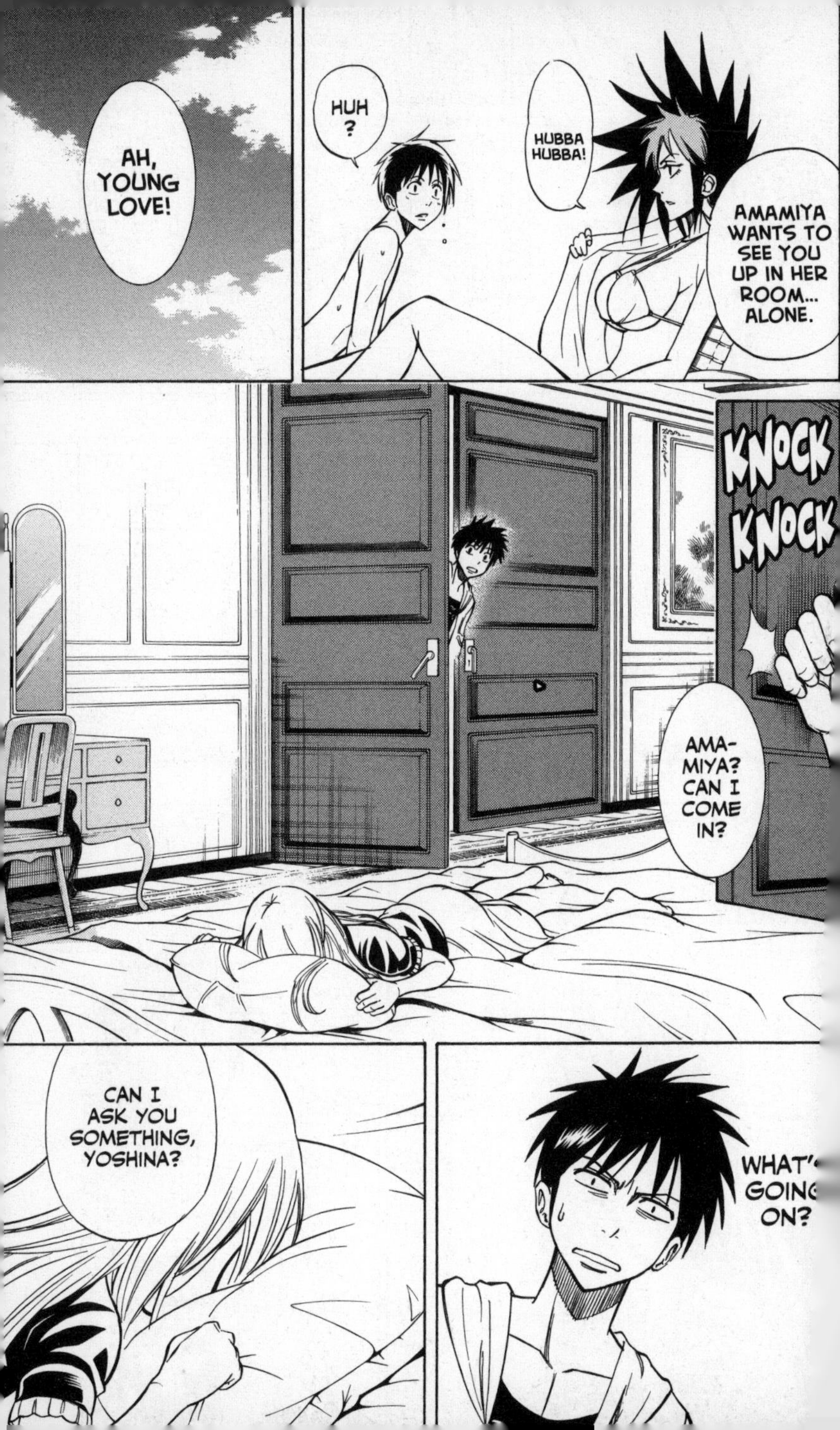
AMAMIYA WANTS TO SEE YOU UP IN HER ROOM... ALONE.
HUBBA HUBBA!
HUH?
AH, YOUNG LOVE!
KNOCK KNOCK
AMA-MIYA? CAN I COME IN?
WHAT'S GOING ON?
CAN I ASK YOU SOMETHING, YOSHINA?

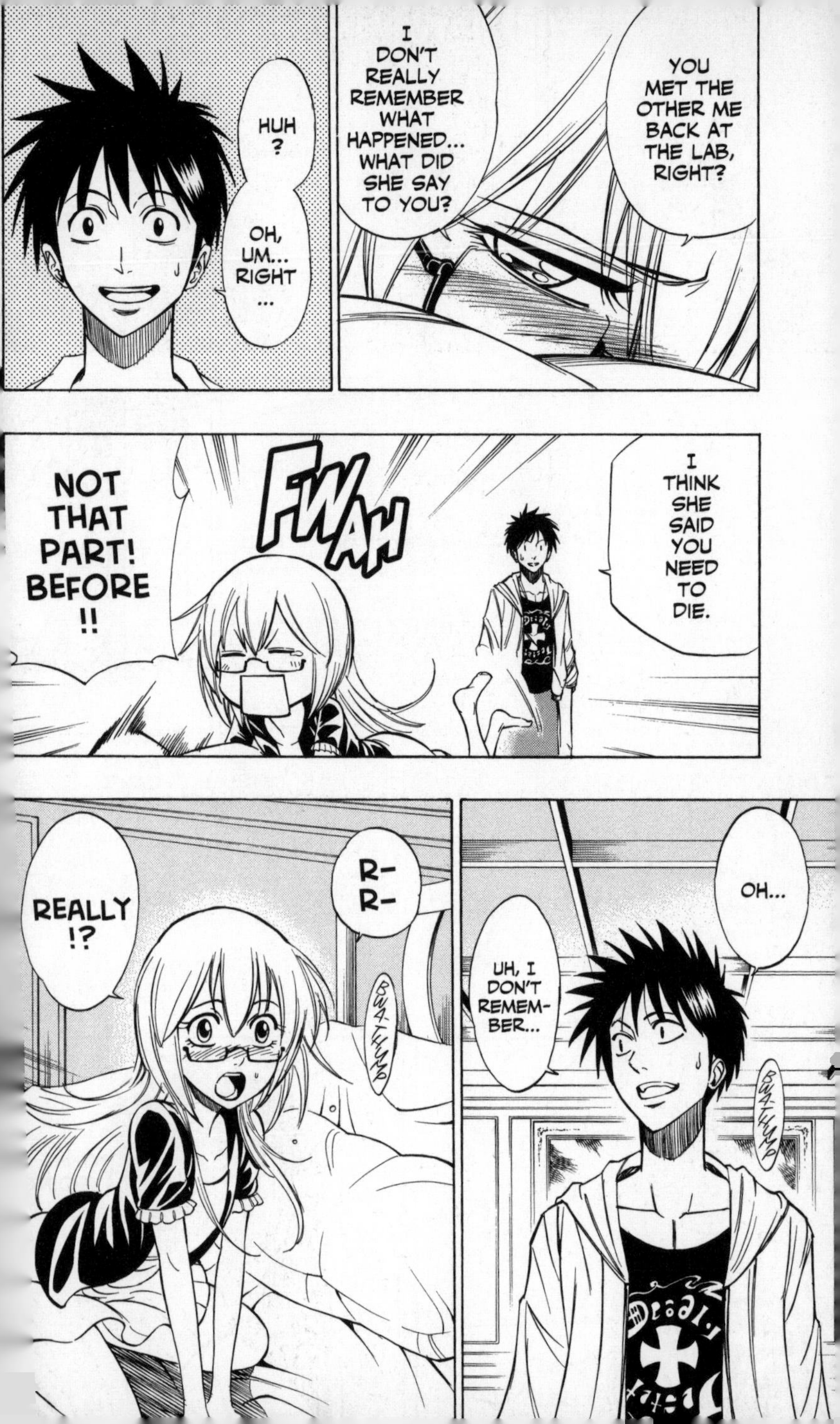
YOU MET THE OTHER ME BACK AT THE LAB, RIGHT?
I DON'T REALLY REMEMBER WHAT HAPPENED... WHAT DID SHE SAY TO YOU?
HUH?
OH, UM... RIGHT...
I THINK SHE SAID YOU NEED TO DIE.
FWAH
NOT THAT PART! BEFORE!!
OH...
UH, I DON'T REMEMBER...
BWA-THUMP
R-R-
REALLY!?
BWA-THUMP

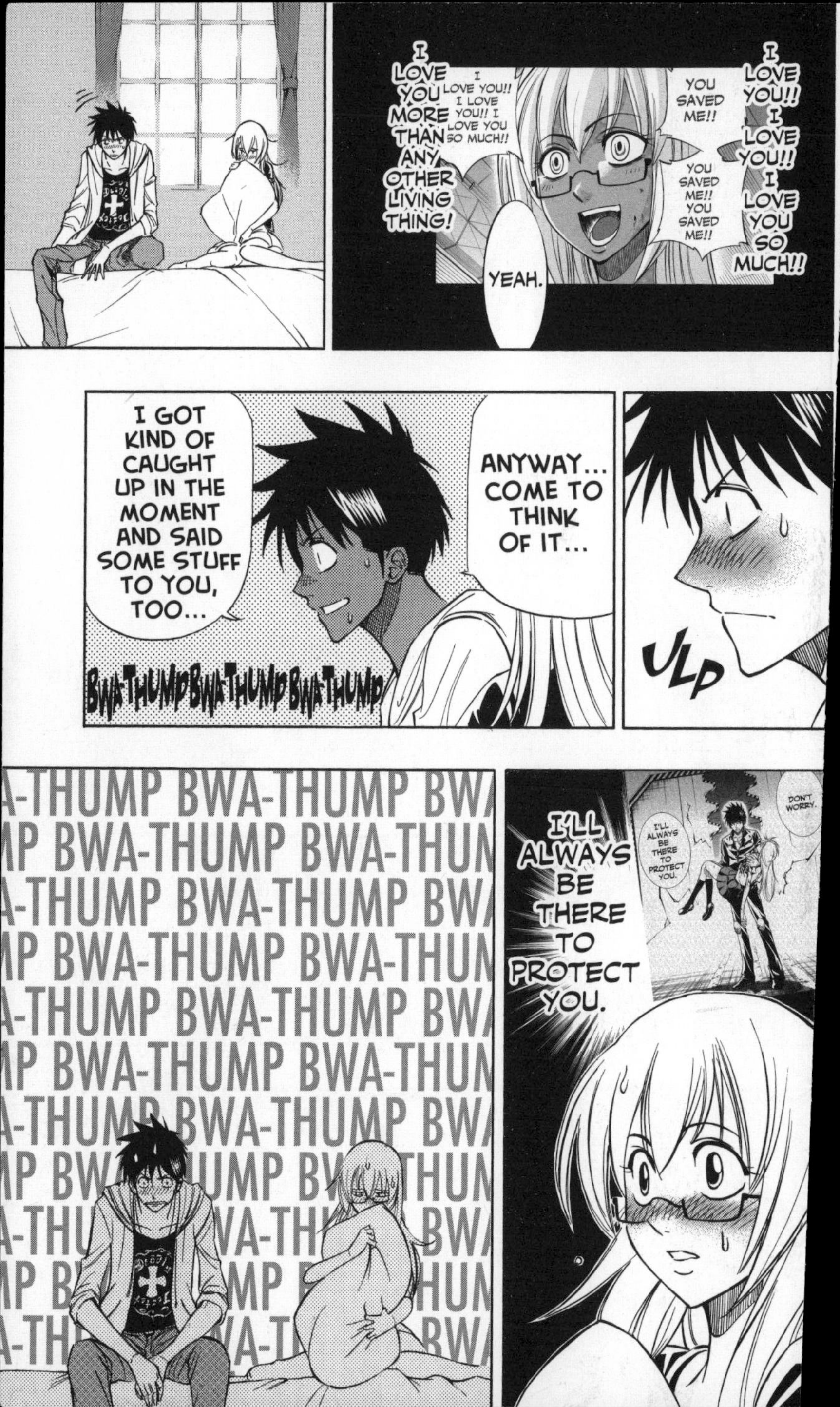
I LOVE YOU!! I LOVE YOU!! I LOVE YOU SO MUCH!!
YOU SAVED ME!!
YOU SAVED ME!! YOU SAVED ME!!
I LOVE YOU!! I LOVE YOU!! I LOVE YOU SO MUCH!!
I LOVE YOU MORE THAN ANY OTHER LIVING THING!
YEAH.
ULP
ANYWAY... COME TO THINK OF IT...
I GOT KIND OF CAUGHT UP IN THE MOMENT AND SAID SOME STUFF TO YOU, TOO...
BWA-THUMP BWA-THUMP BWA-THUMP
DON'T WORRY.
I'LL ALWAYS BE THERE TO PROTECT YOU.
I'LL ALWAYS BE THERE TO PROTECT YOU.
BWA-THUMP BWA-THUMP BWA-THUMP BWA-THUMP BWA-THUMP BWA-THUMP BWA-THUMP BWA-THUMP BWA-THUMP BWA-THUMP

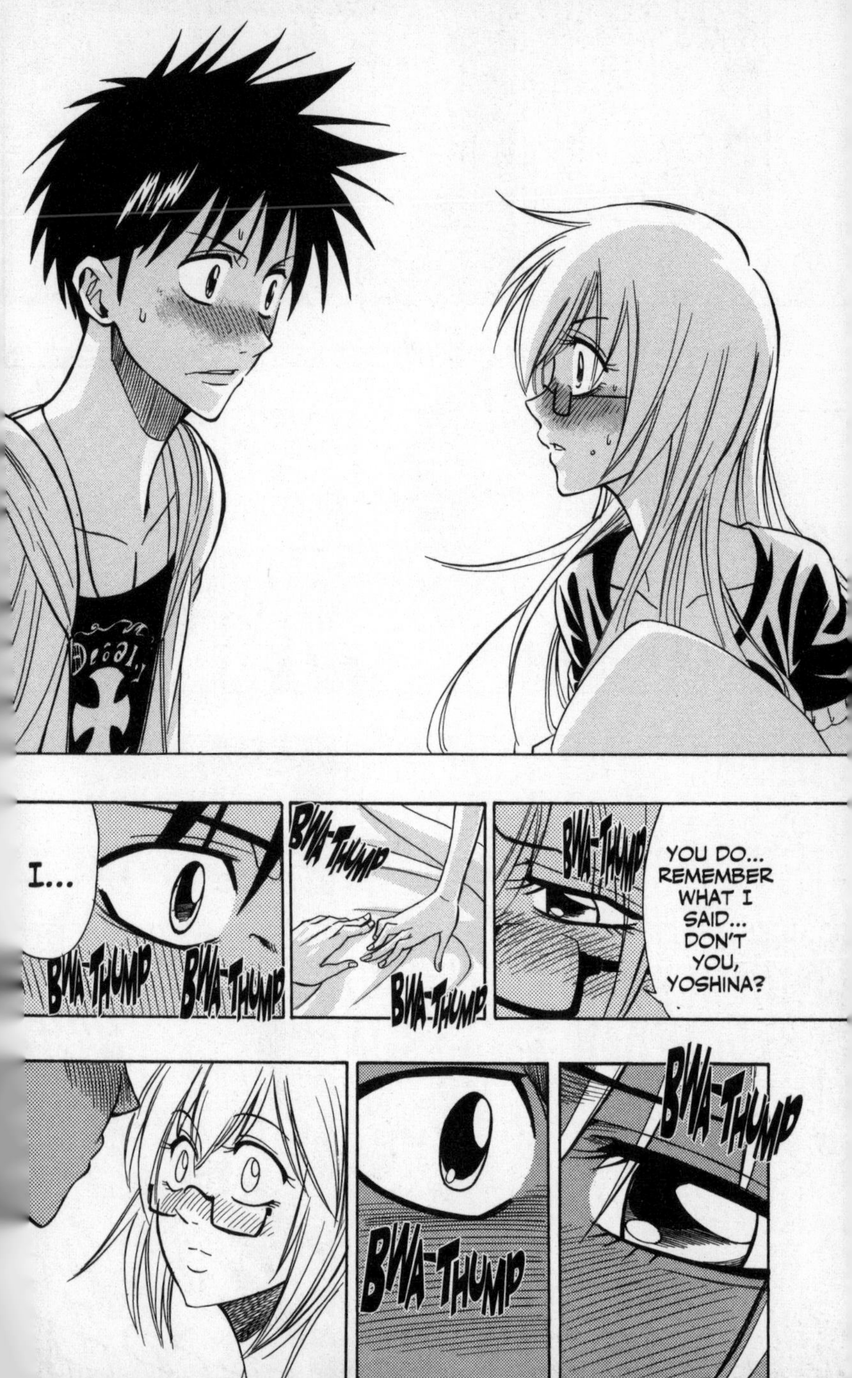
BWA-THUMP
YOU DO... REMEMBER WHAT I SAID... DON'T YOU, YOSHINA?
BWA-THUMP
BWA-THUMP
I...
BWA-THUMP
BWA-THUMP
BWA-THUMP
BWA-THUMP

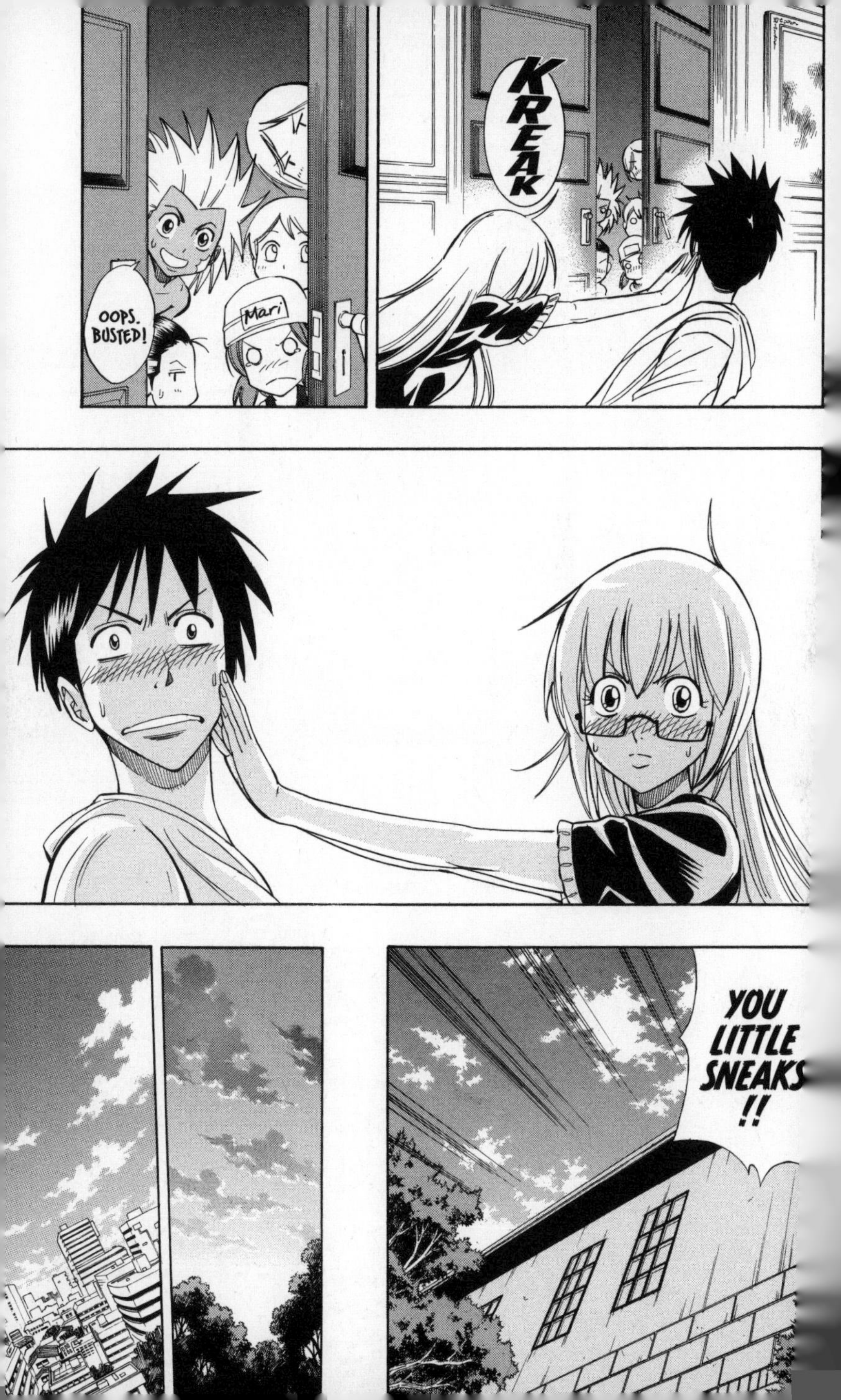
KREAK
OOPS. BUSTED!
Mari
YOU LITTLE SNEAKS!!

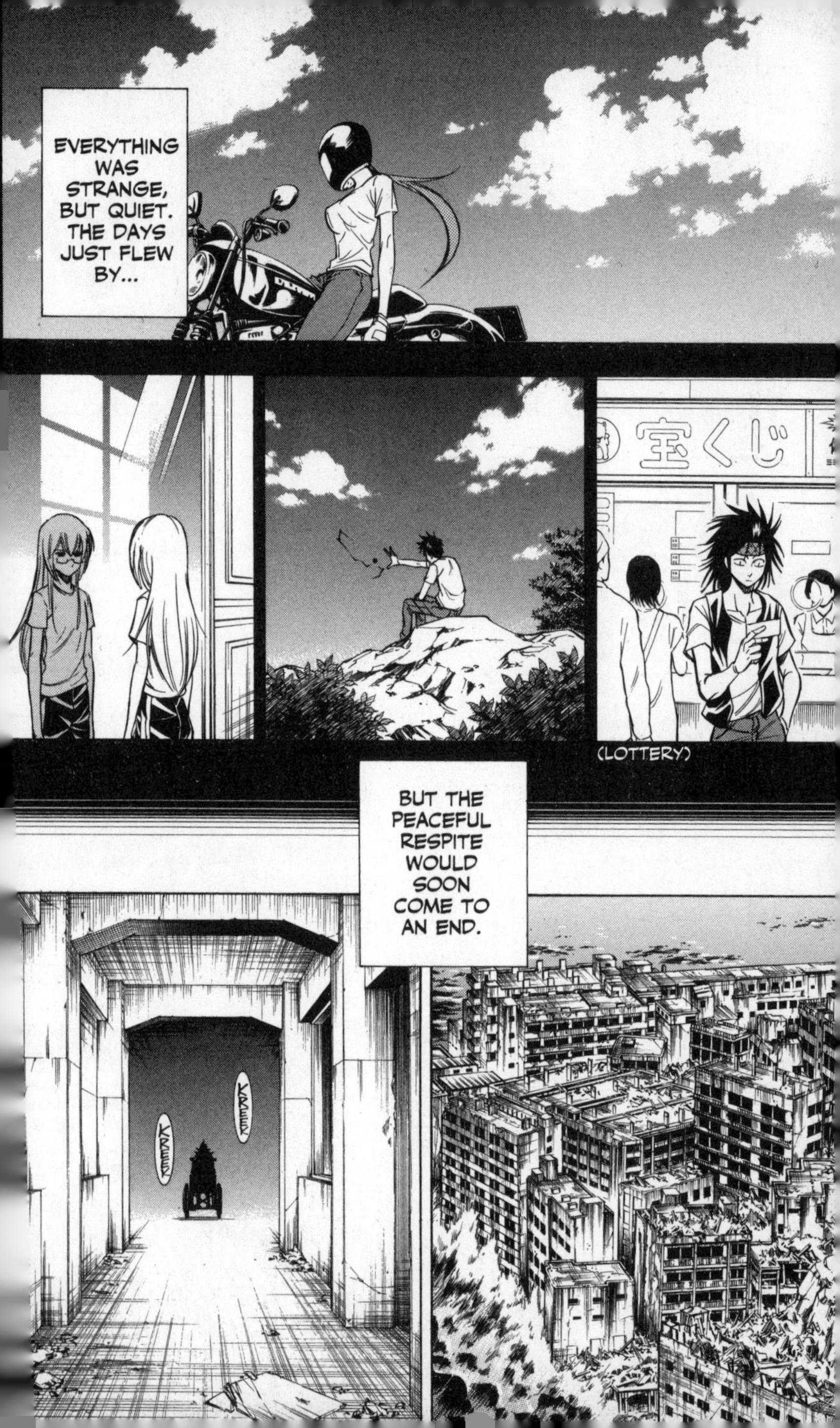
EVERYTHING WAS STRANGE, BUT QUIET. THE DAYS JUST FLEW BY...
宝くじ
(LOTTERY)
BUT THE PEACEFUL RESPITE WOULD SOON COME TO AN END.
KREEK
KREEK

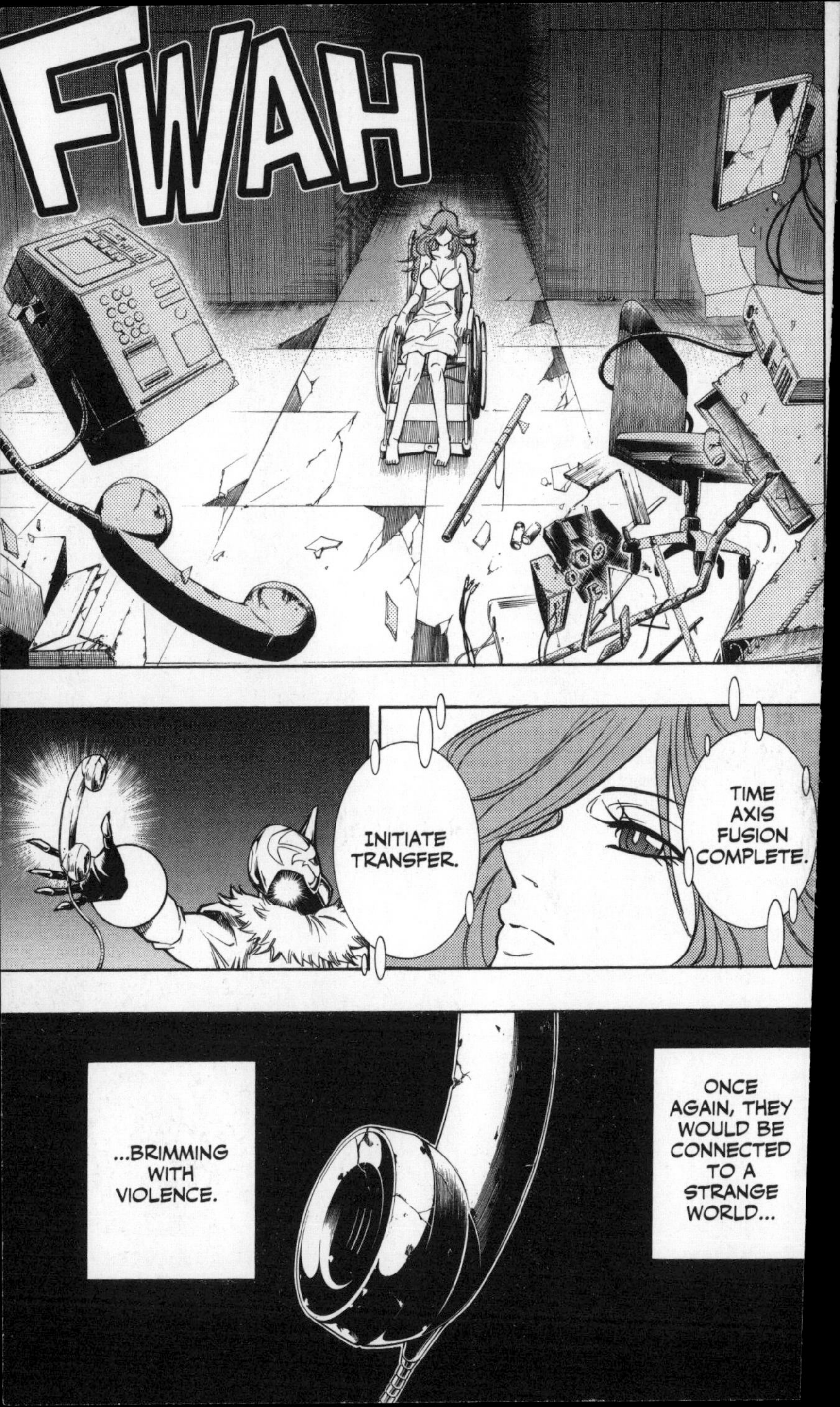
FWAH
TIME AXIS FUSION COMPLETE.
INITIATE TRANSFER.
ONCE AGAIN, THEY WOULD BE CONNECTED TO A STRANGE WORLD...
...BRIMMING WITH VIOLENCE.

YOUR FAVORITE PSYREN PSIONIC POWERS! VOTING RESULTS!

TOTAL RESULTS 6,836 votes!!

Which move is more powerful than all the rest?

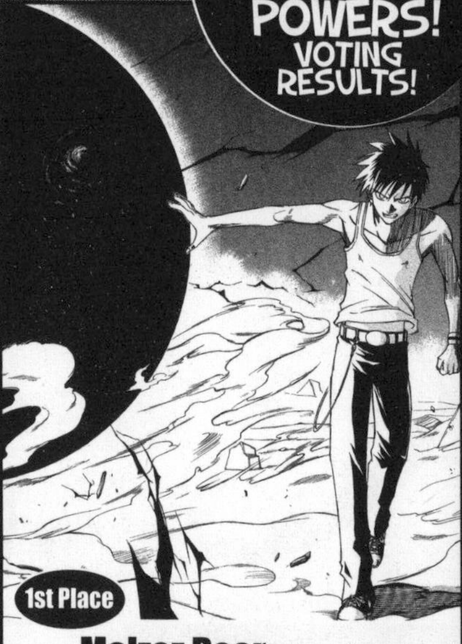

1st Place

Melzez Door Ageha 735 votes

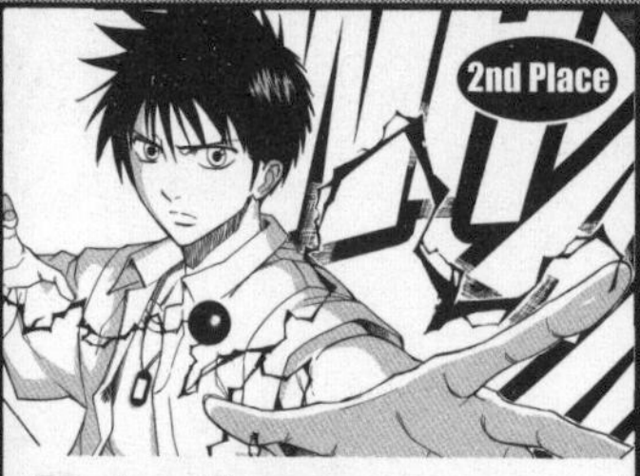

2nd Place

Melzez Lance Ageha 706 votes

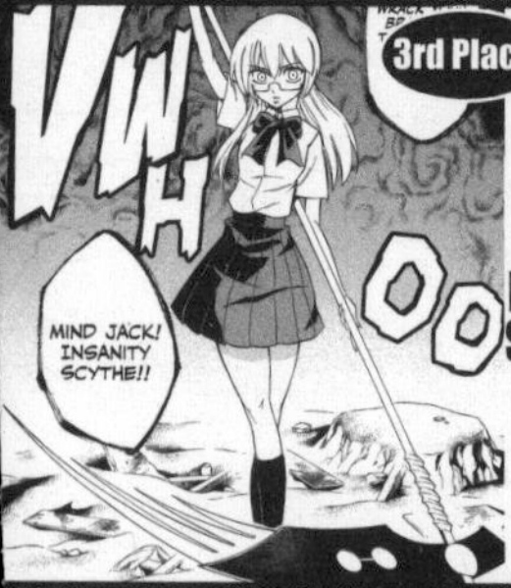
MIND JACK! INSANITY SCYTHE!!

3rd Place

Mind Jack! Insanity Scythe!! Amamiya 566 votes

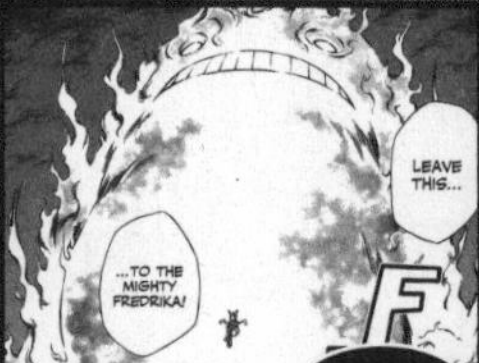
LEAVE THIS...
...TO THE MIGHTY FREDRIKA!

4th Place

Pyro Queen! Salamandra!! Fredrika (of the future) 400 votes

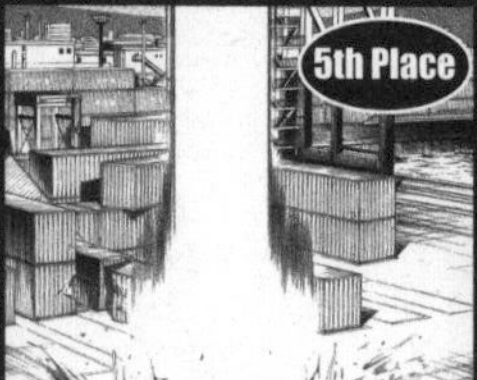

5th Place

Dying Sun Granar 385 votes

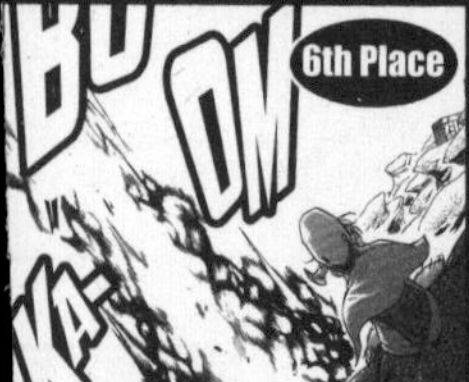

6th Place

Explosure Dolkey 363 votes

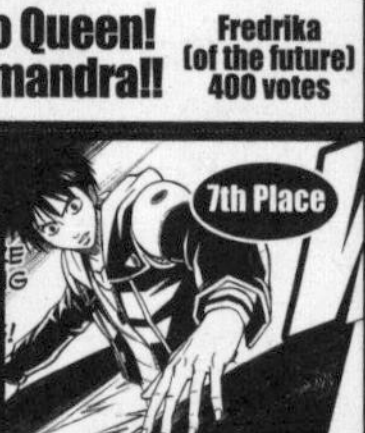

7th Place

Melzez Disk Version Ageha 294 votes

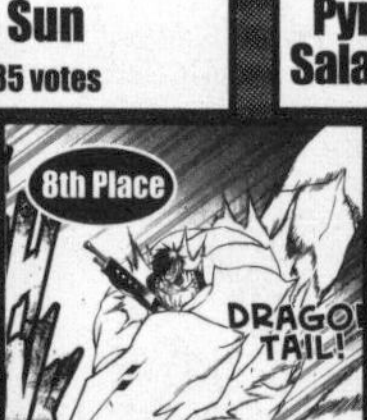

8th Place

Dragon Tail! Asaga 258 votes

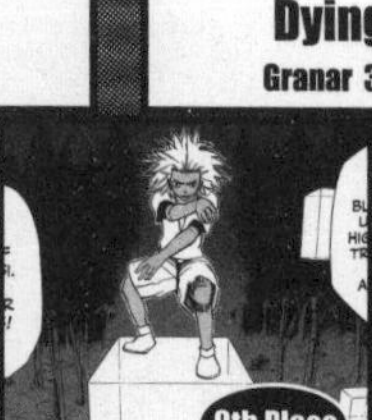

9th Place

Air Blocks Kyle 227 votes

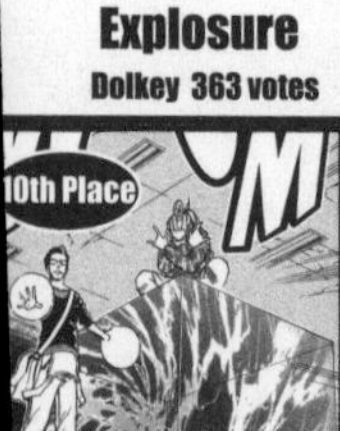

10th Place

Trick Room Ran 198 votes

CONTINUED ON PAGE 66!

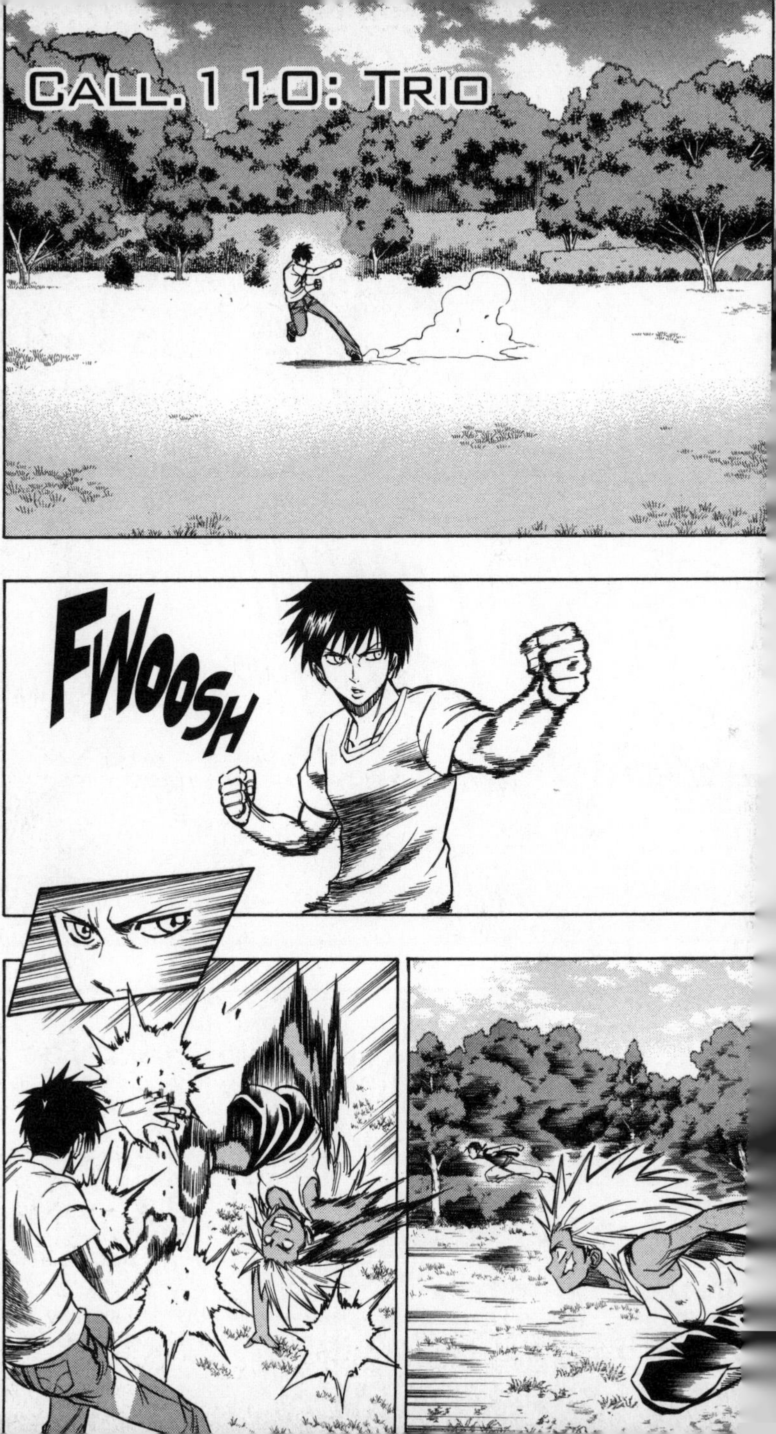
CALL. 110: TRIO
FWOOSH

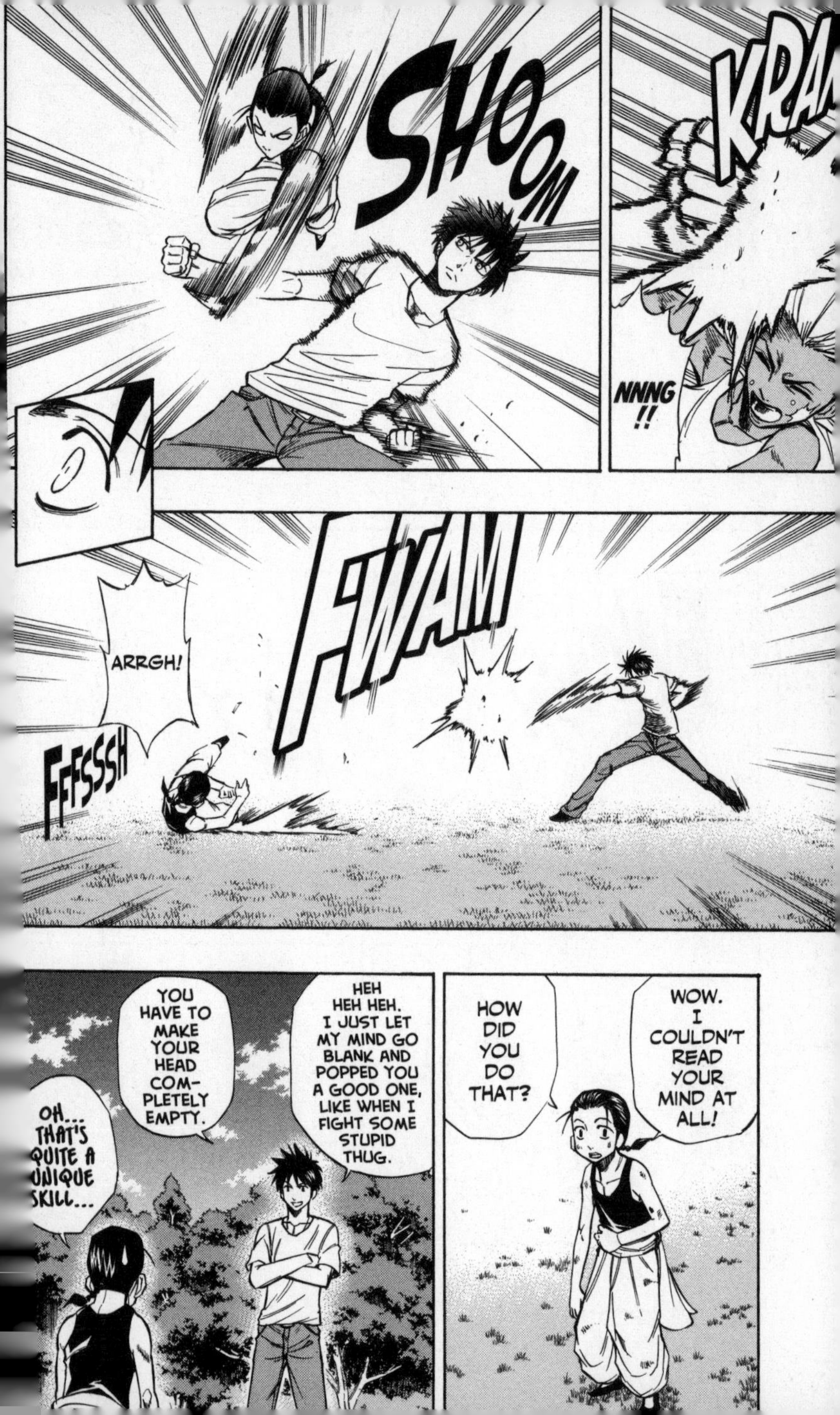
KRA
NNNG!!
SHOOM
FWAM
ARRGH!
FFFSSSH
WOW. I COULDN'T READ YOUR MIND AT ALL!
HOW DID YOU DO THAT?
HEH HEH HEH. I JUST LET MY MIND GO BLANK AND POPPED YOU A GOOD ONE, LIKE WHEN I FIGHT SOME STUPID THUG.
YOU HAVE TO MAKE YOUR HEAD COM-PLETELY EMPTY.
OH... THAT'S QUITE A UNIQUE SKILL...

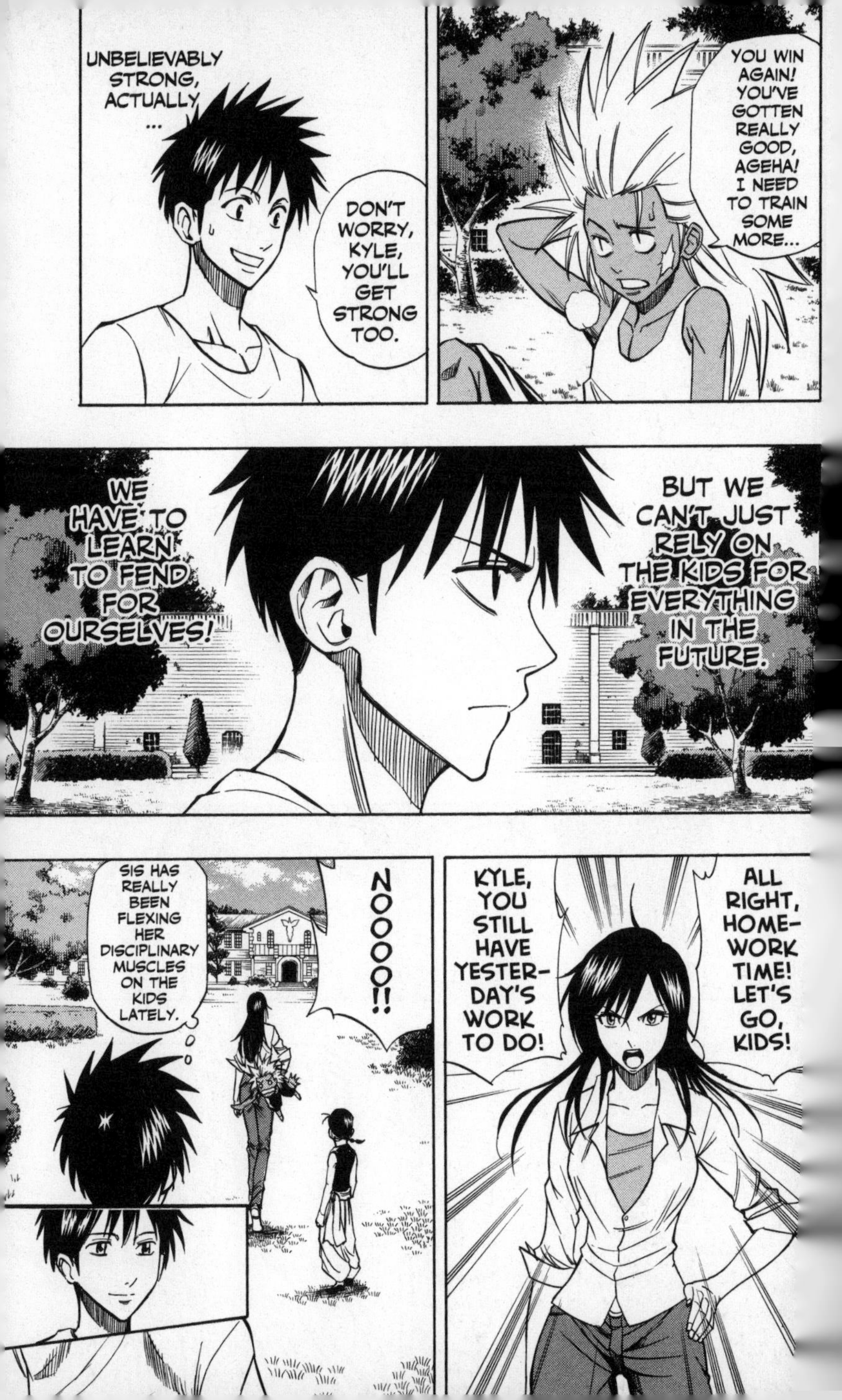
YOU WIN AGAIN! YOU'VE GOTTEN REALLY GOOD, AGEHA! I NEED TO TRAIN SOME MORE...
DON'T WORRY, KYLE, YOU'LL GET STRONG TOO.
UNBELIEVABLY STRONG, ACTUALLY ...
BUT WE CAN'T JUST RELY ON THE KIDS FOR EVERYTHING IN THE FUTURE.
WE HAVE TO LEARN TO FEND FOR OURSELVES!
ALL RIGHT, HOME-WORK TIME! LET'S GO, KIDS!
KYLE, YOU STILL HAVE YESTER-DAY'S WORK TO DO!
NOOOOO!!
SIS HAS REALLY BEEN FLEXING HER DISCIPLINARY MUSCLES ON THE KIDS LATELY.

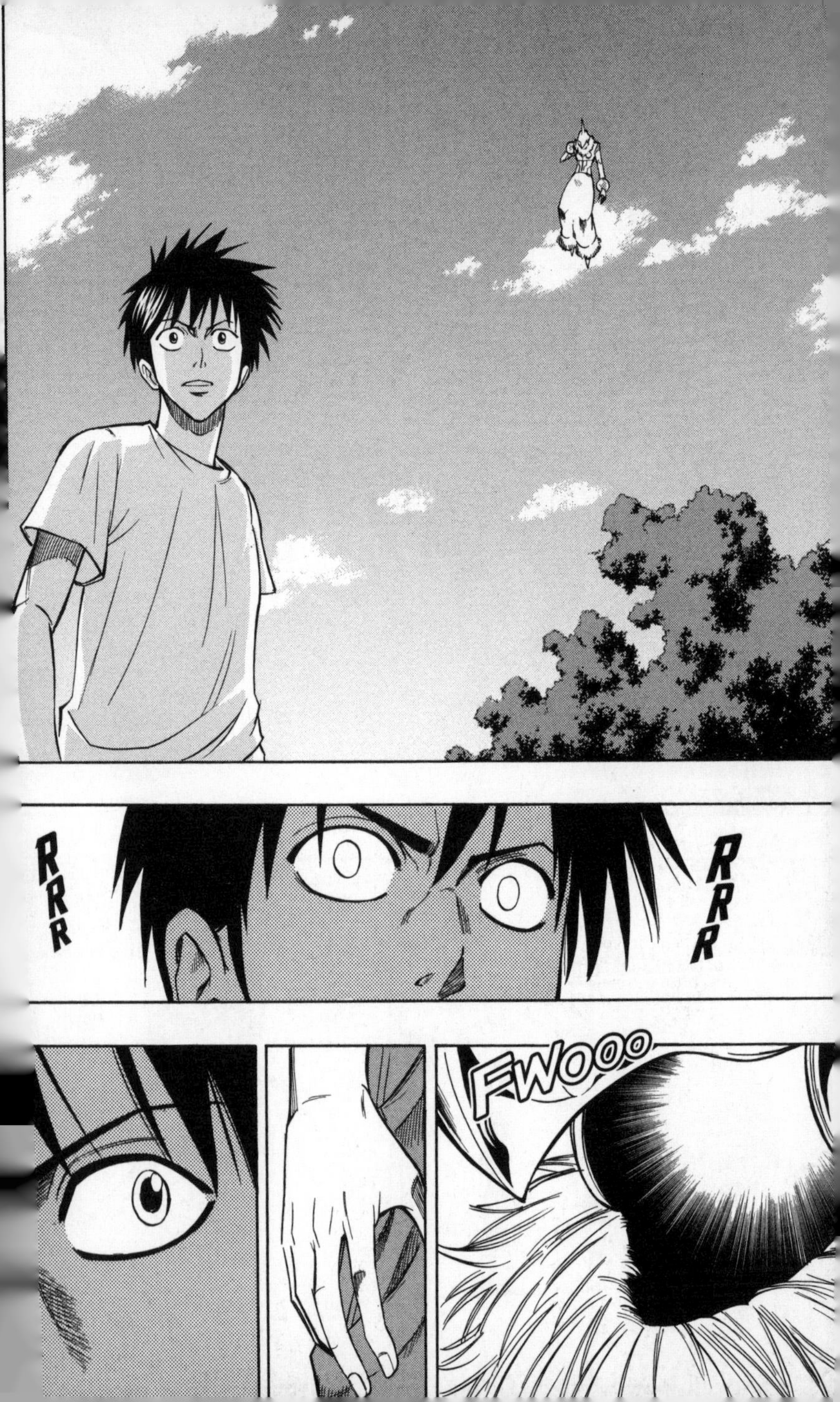
RRR
RRR
FWOOO

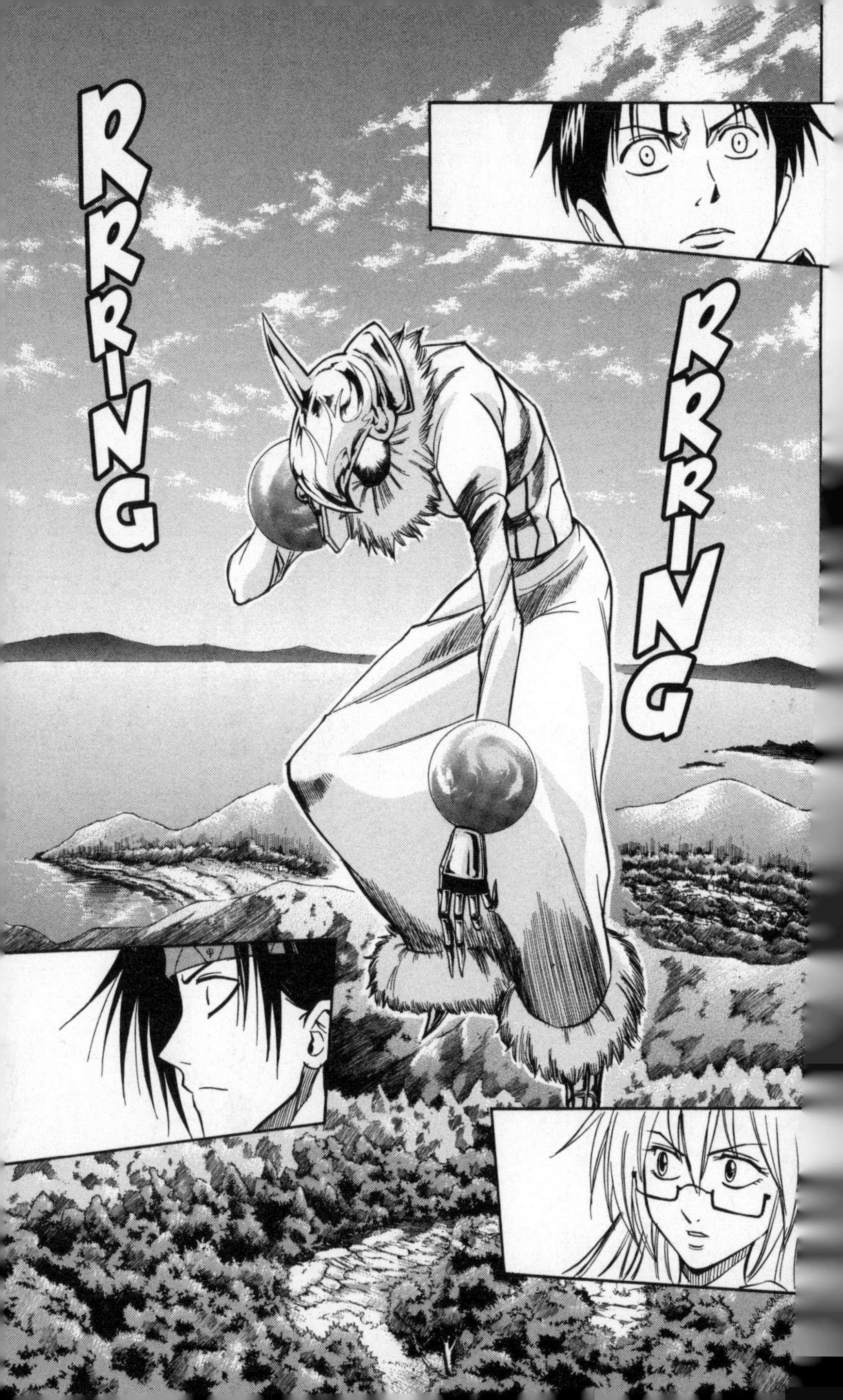
RRRING
RRRING

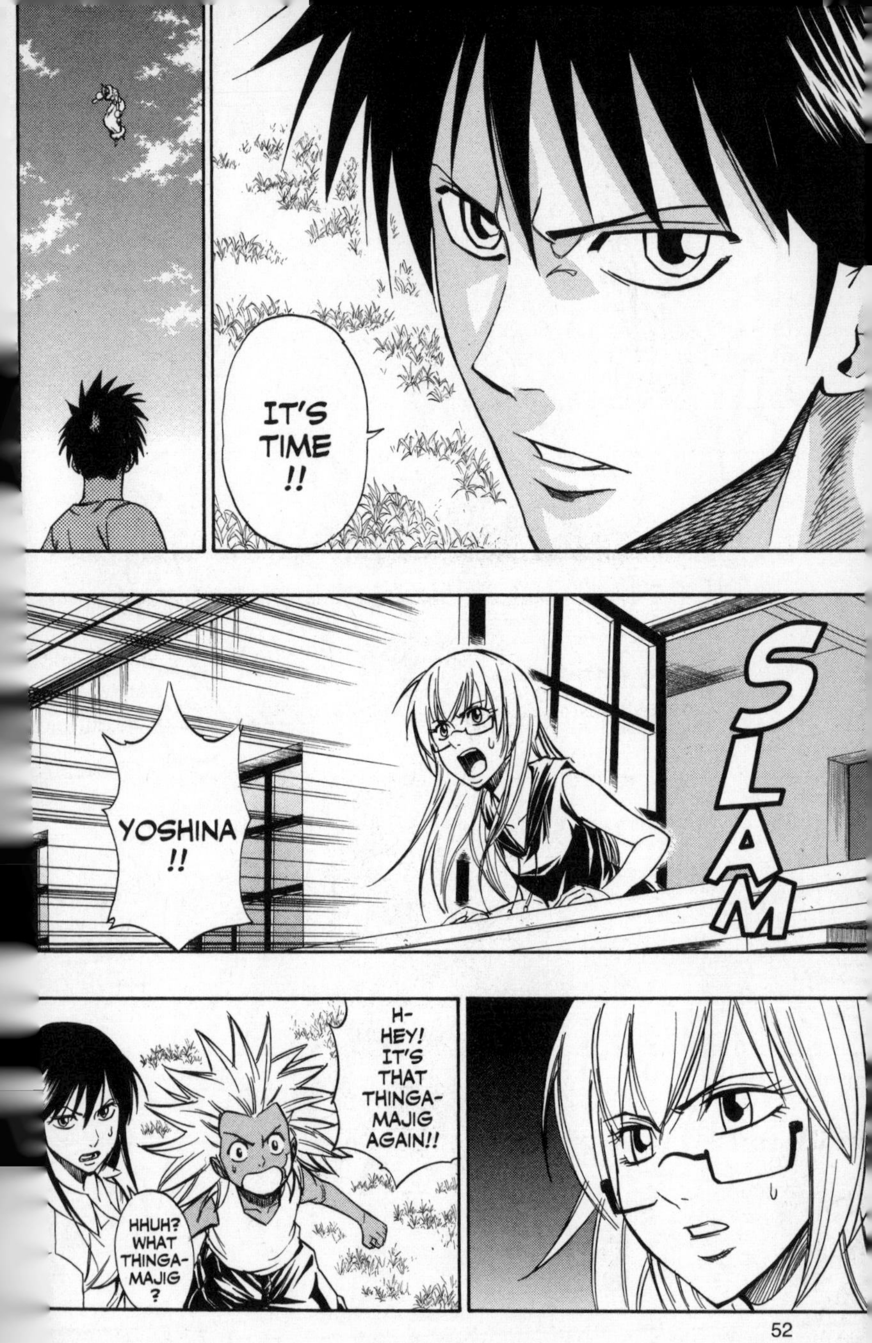
IT'S TIME!!
SLAM
YOSHINA!!
H-HEY! IT'S THAT THINGA-MAJIG AGAIN!!
HHUH? WHAT THINGA-MAJIG?

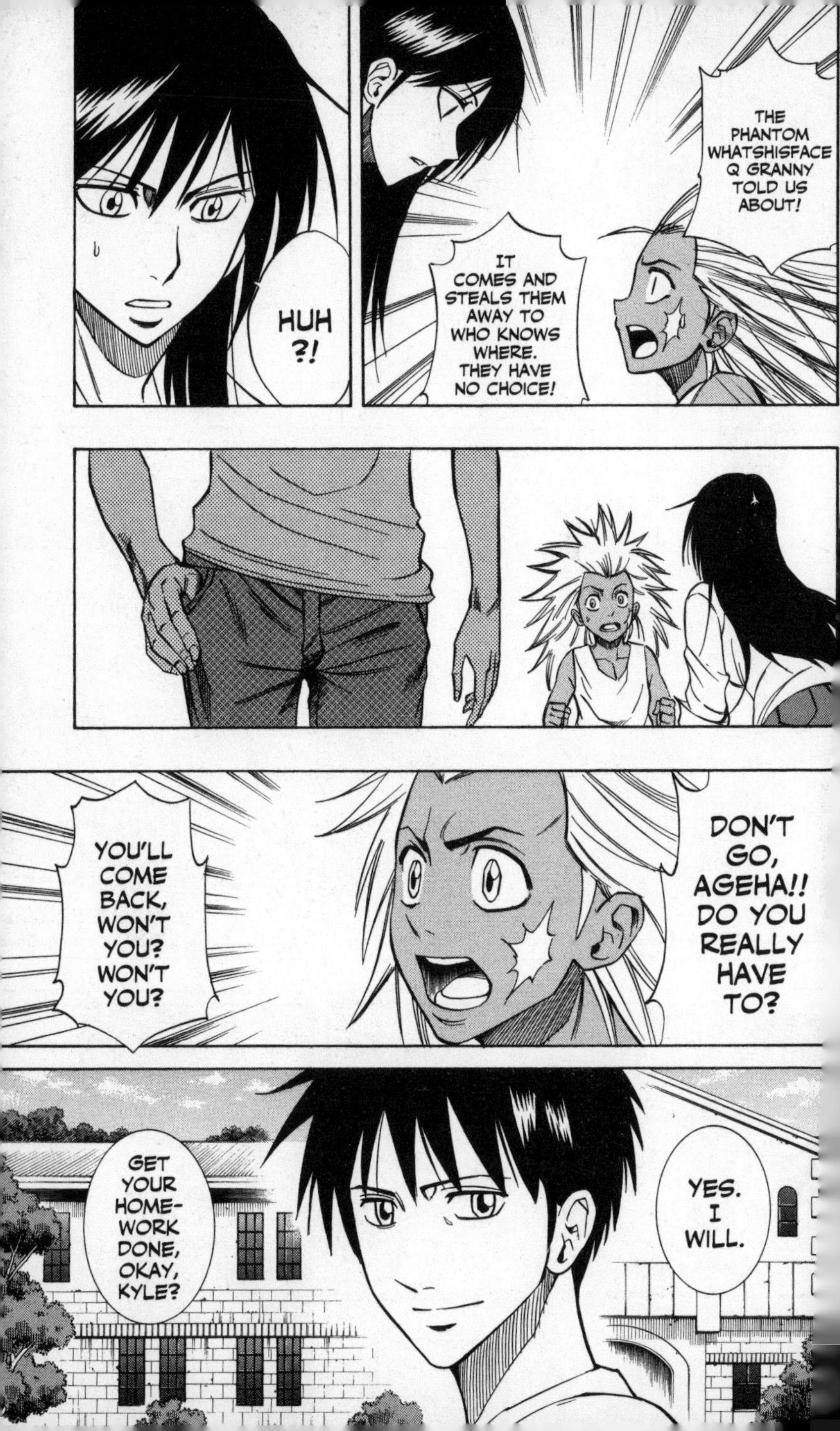
THE PHANTOM WHATSHISFACE Q GRANNY TOLD US ABOUT!
IT COMES AND STEALS THEM AWAY TO WHO KNOWS WHERE. THEY HAVE NO CHOICE!
HUH ?!
DON'T GO, AGEHA!! DO YOU REALLY HAVE TO?
YOU'LL COME BACK, WON'T YOU? WON'T YOU?
YES. I WILL.
GET YOUR HOME-WORK DONE, OKAY, KYLE?

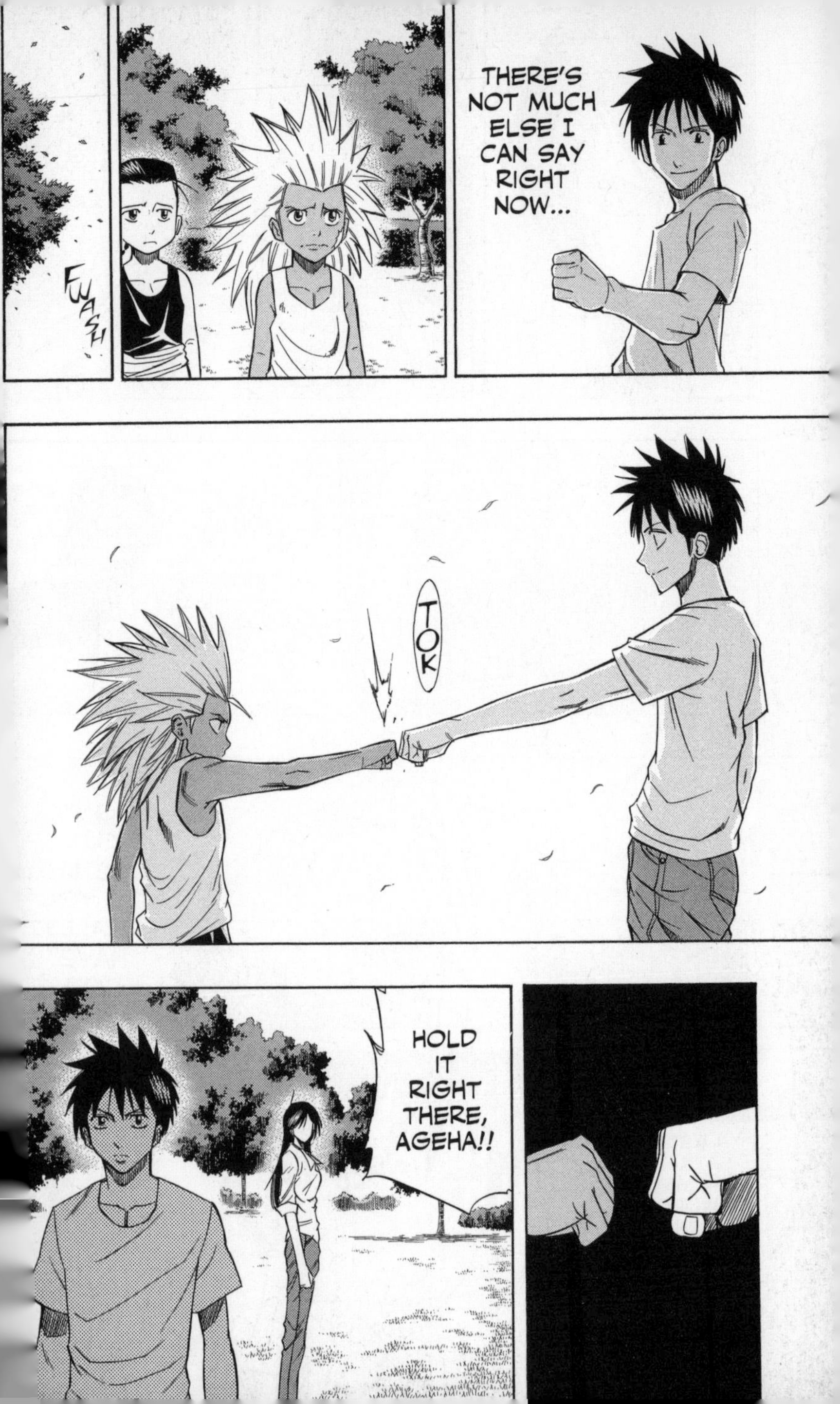
THERE'S NOT MUCH ELSE I CAN SAY RIGHT NOW...
FWASH
TOK
HOLD IT RIGHT THERE, AGEHA!!

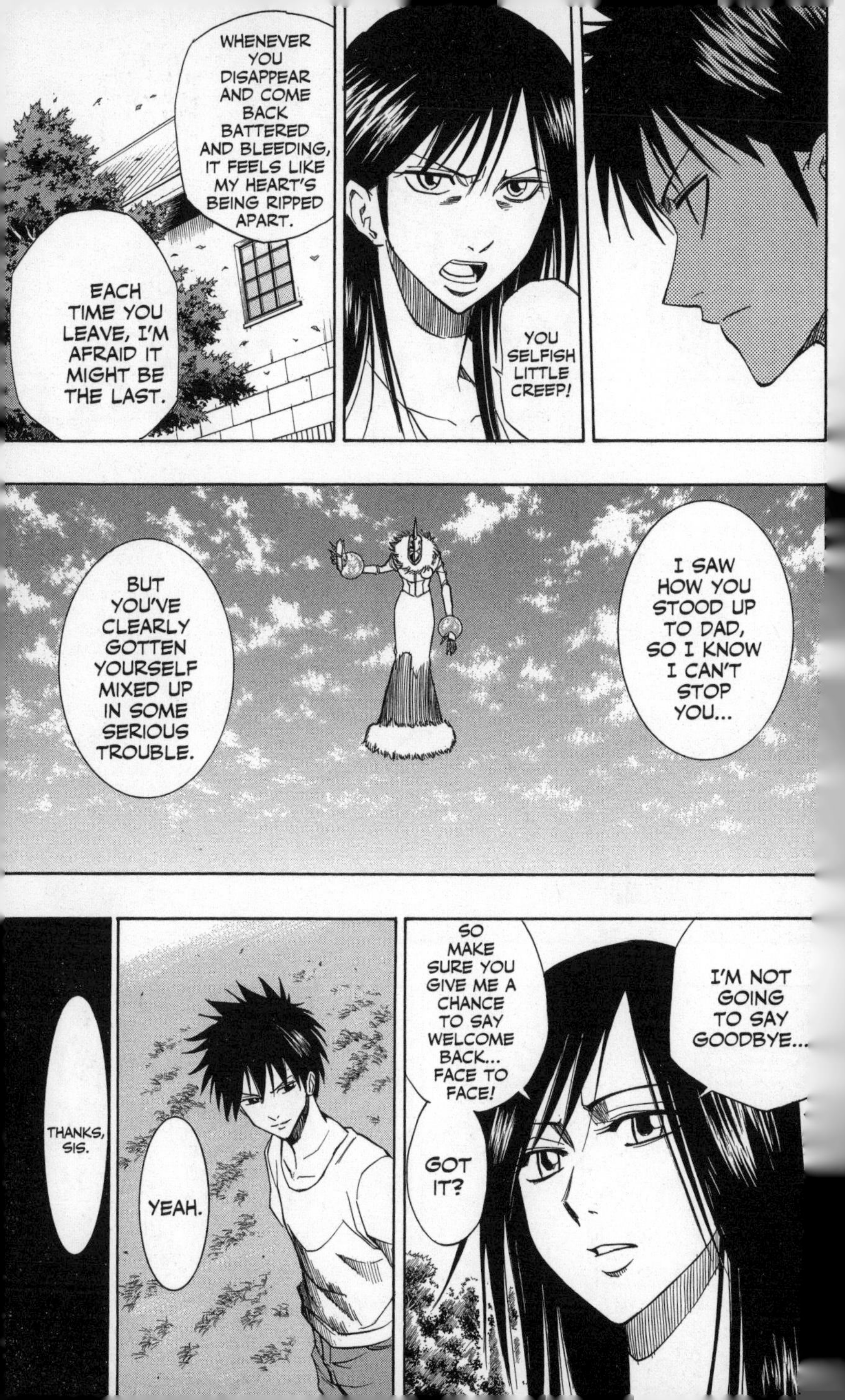
YOU SELFISH LITTLE CREEP!
WHENEVER YOU DISAPPEAR AND COME BACK BATTERED AND BLEEDING, IT FEELS LIKE MY HEART'S BEING RIPPED APART.
EACH TIME YOU LEAVE, I'M AFRAID IT MIGHT BE THE LAST.
I SAW HOW YOU STOOD UP TO DAD, SO I KNOW I CAN'T STOP YOU...
BUT YOU'VE CLEARLY GOTTEN YOURSELF MIXED UP IN SOME SERIOUS TROUBLE.
I'M NOT GOING TO SAY GOODBYE...
SO MAKE SURE YOU GIVE ME A CHANCE TO SAY WELCOME BACK... FACE TO FACE!
GOT IT?
YEAH.
THANKS, SIS.

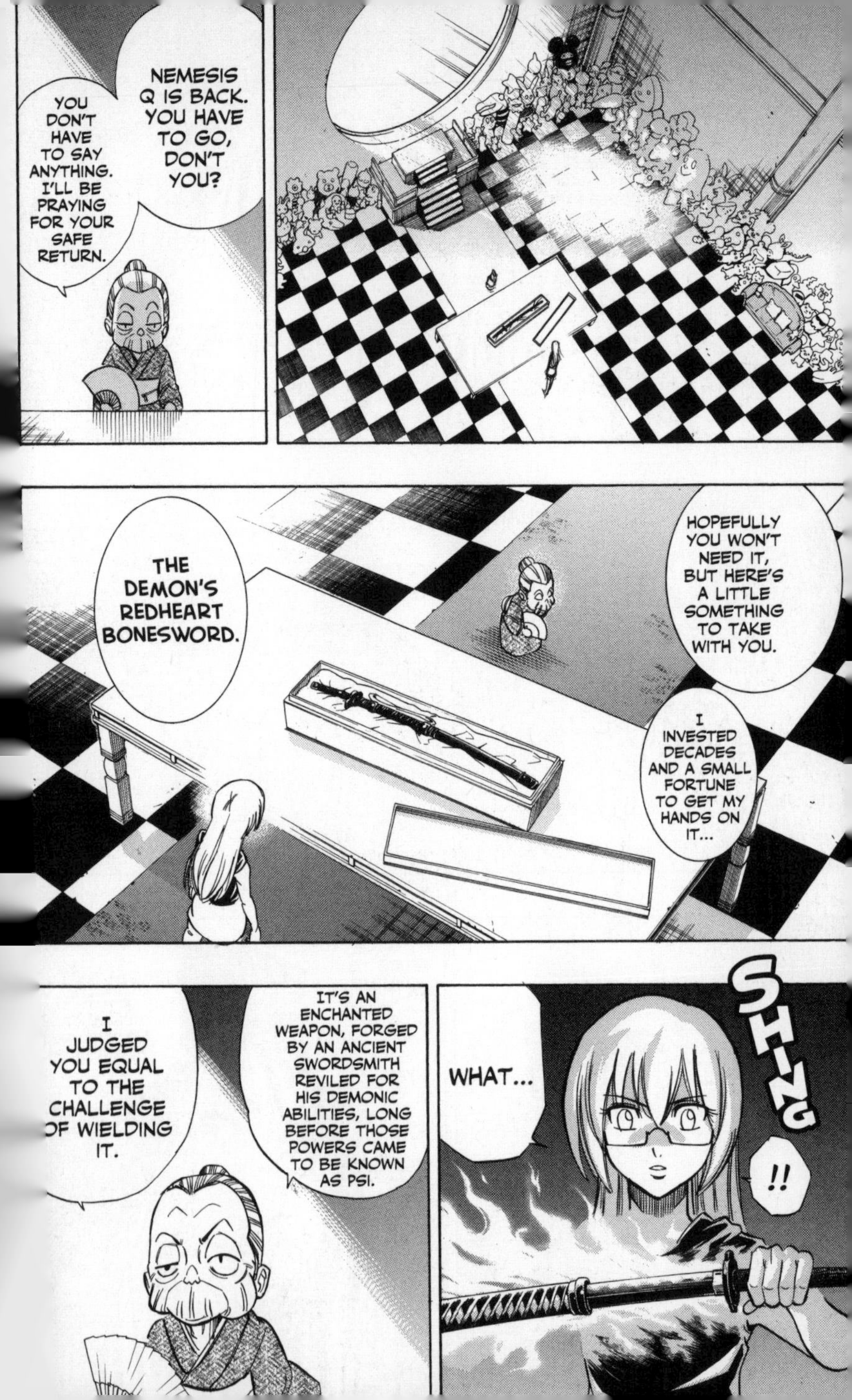
NEMESIS Q IS BACK. YOU HAVE TO GO, DON'T YOU?
YOU DON'T HAVE TO SAY ANYTHING. I'LL BE PRAYING FOR YOUR SAFE RETURN.
HOPEFULLY YOU WON'T NEED IT, BUT HERE'S A LITTLE SOMETHING TO TAKE WITH YOU.
I INVESTED DECADES AND A SMALL FORTUNE TO GET MY HANDS ON IT...
THE DEMON'S REDHEART BONESWORD.
SHING
WHAT...
!!
IT'S AN ENCHANTED WEAPON, FORGED BY AN ANCIENT SWORDSMITH REVILED FOR HIS DEMONIC ABILITIES, LONG BEFORE THOSE POWERS CAME TO BE KNOWN AS PSI.
I JUDGED YOU EQUAL TO THE CHALLENGE OF WIELDING IT.

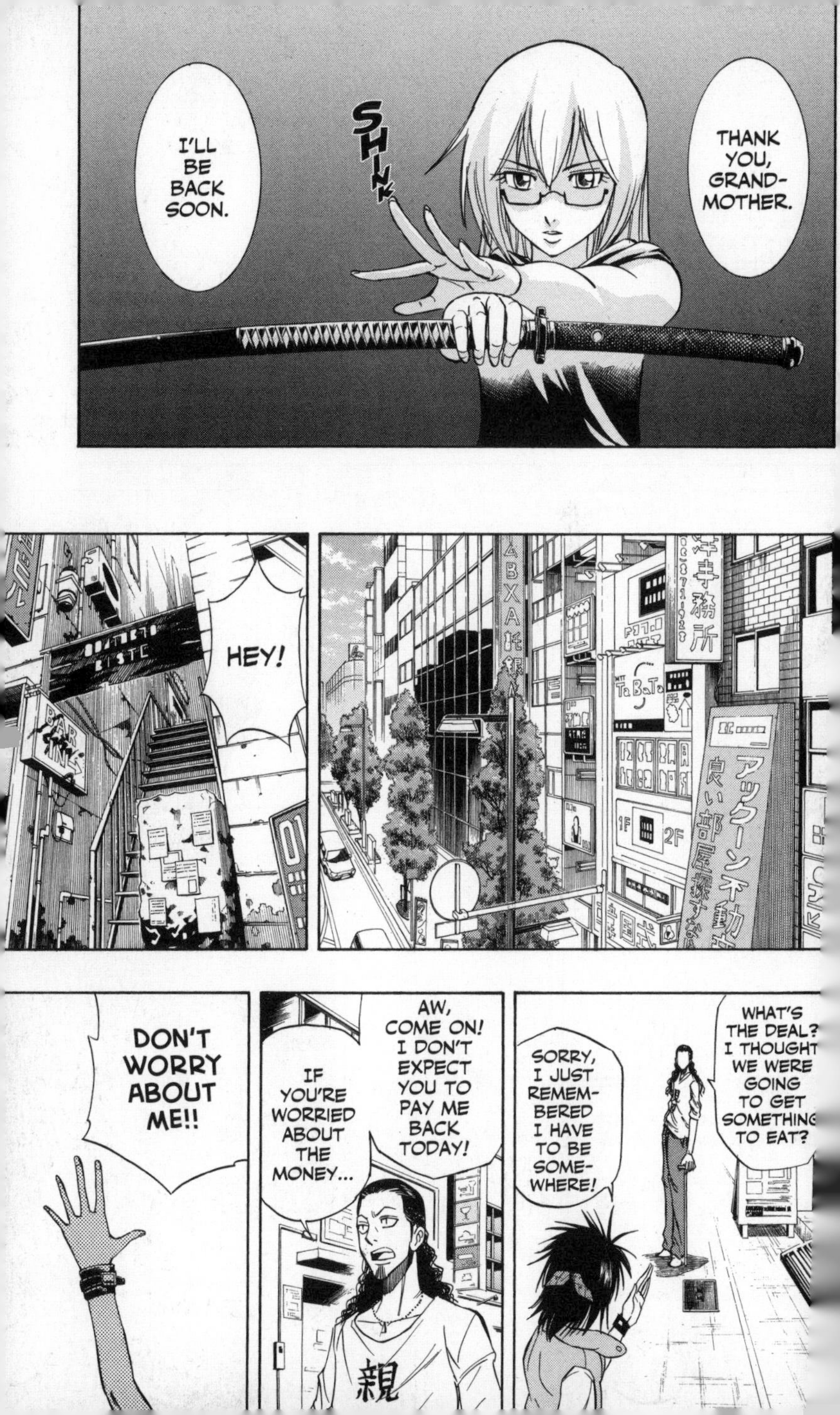
THANK YOU, GRAND-MOTHER.
SHINK
I'LL BE BACK SOON.
HEY!
WHAT'S THE DEAL? I THOUGHT WE WERE GOING TO GET SOMETHING TO EAT?
SORRY, I JUST REMEM-BERED I HAVE TO BE SOME-WHERE!
AW, COME ON! I DON'T EXPECT YOU TO PAY ME BACK TODAY!
IF YOU'RE WORRIED ABOUT THE MONEY...
DON'T WORRY ABOUT ME!!

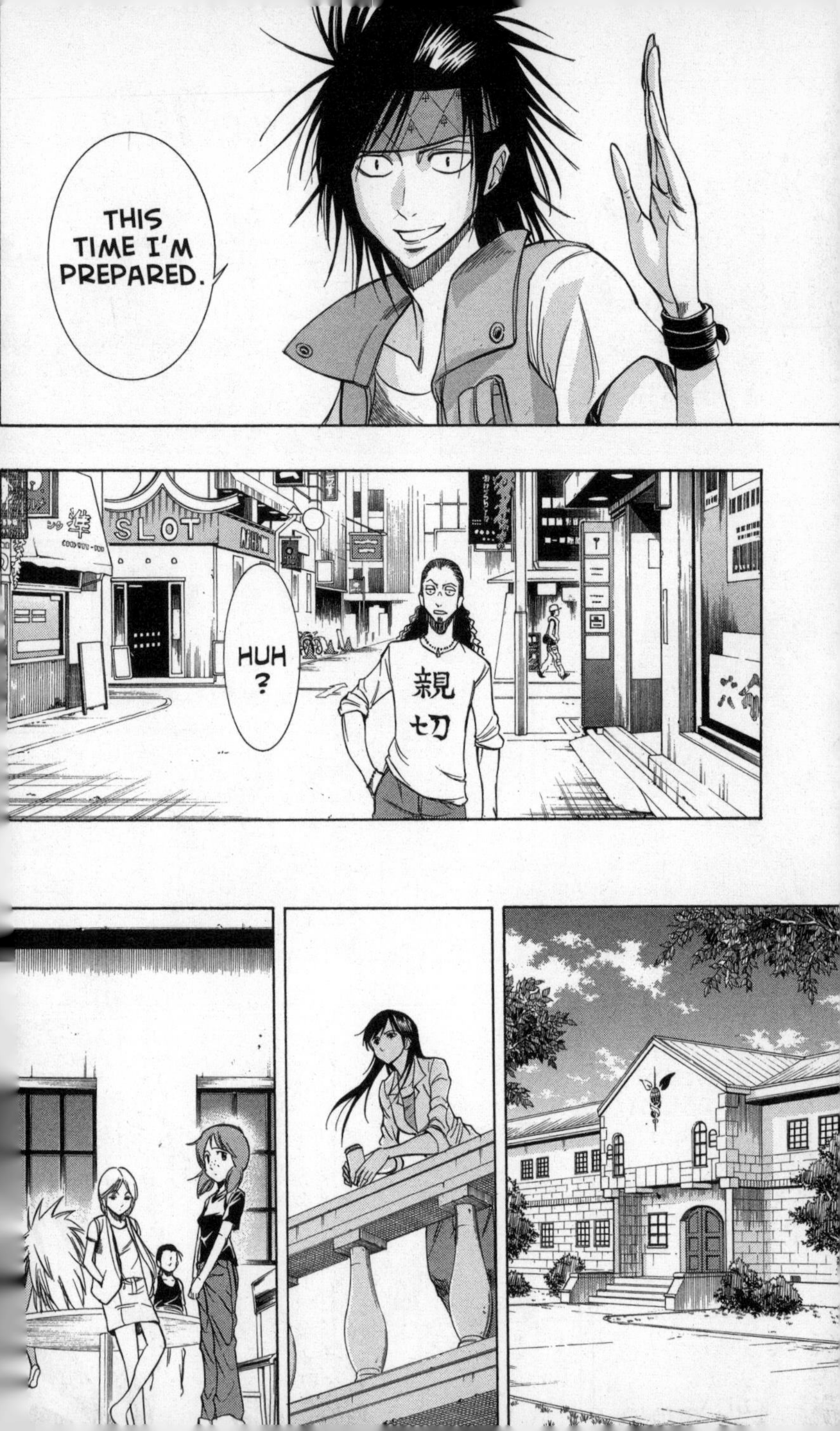
THIS TIME I'M PREPARED.
SLOT
HUH?
親切

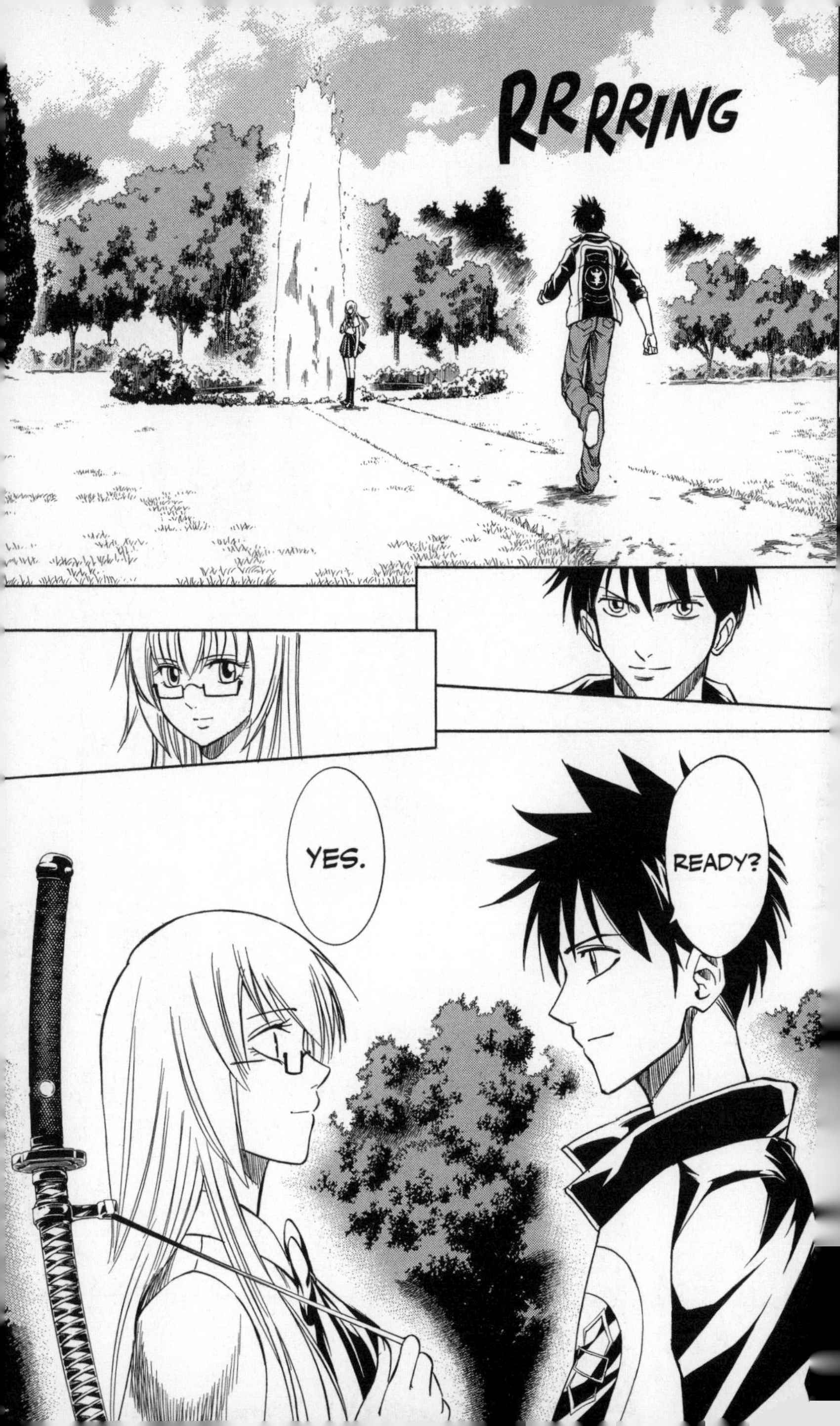
RRRRING
READY?
YES.

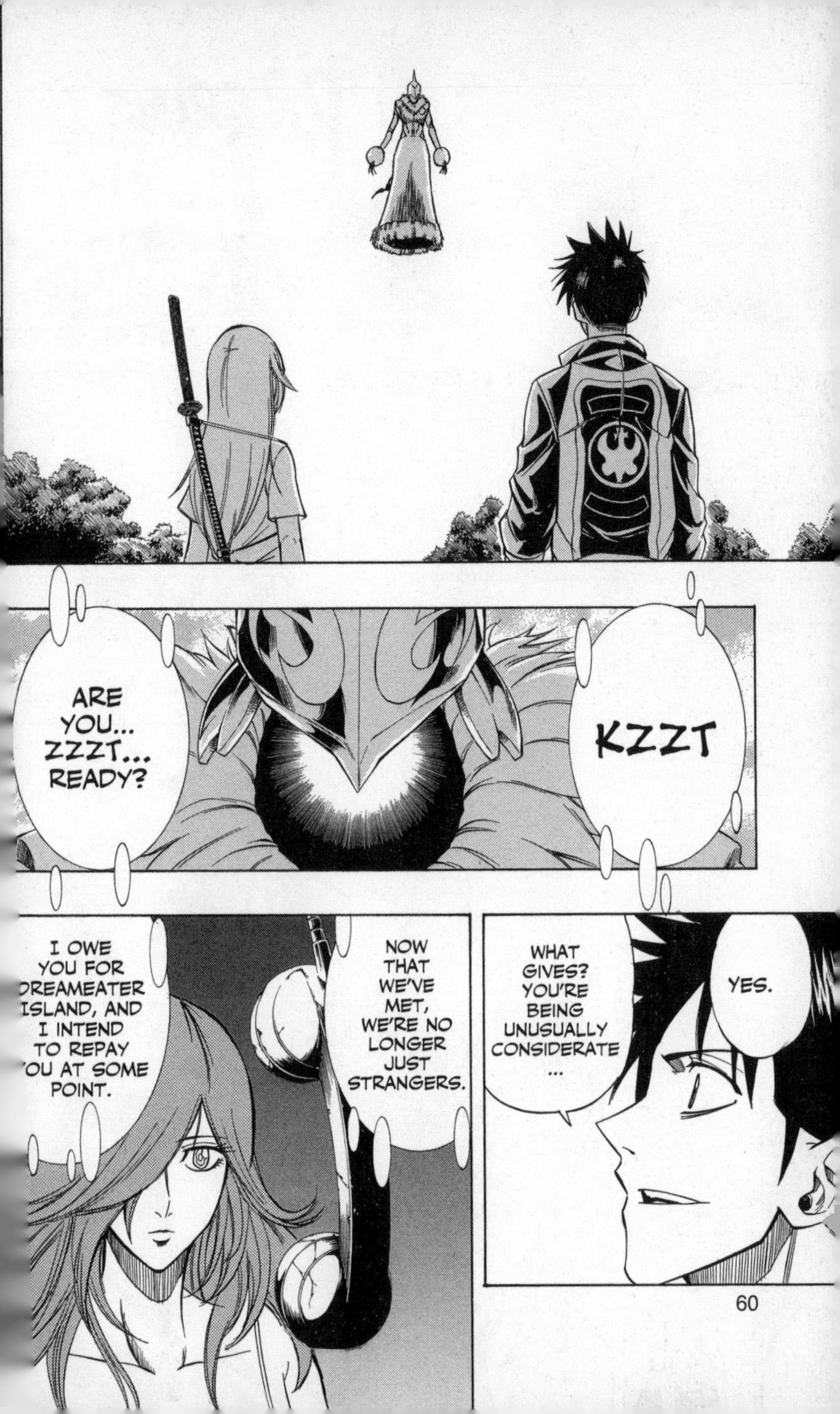
KZZT
ARE YOU... ZZZT... READY?
YES.
WHAT GIVES? YOU'RE BEING UNUSUALLY CONSIDERATE ...
NOW THAT WE'VE MET, WE'RE NO LONGER JUST STRANGERS.
I OWE YOU FOR DREAMEATER ISLAND, AND I INTEND TO REPAY YOU AT SOME POINT.

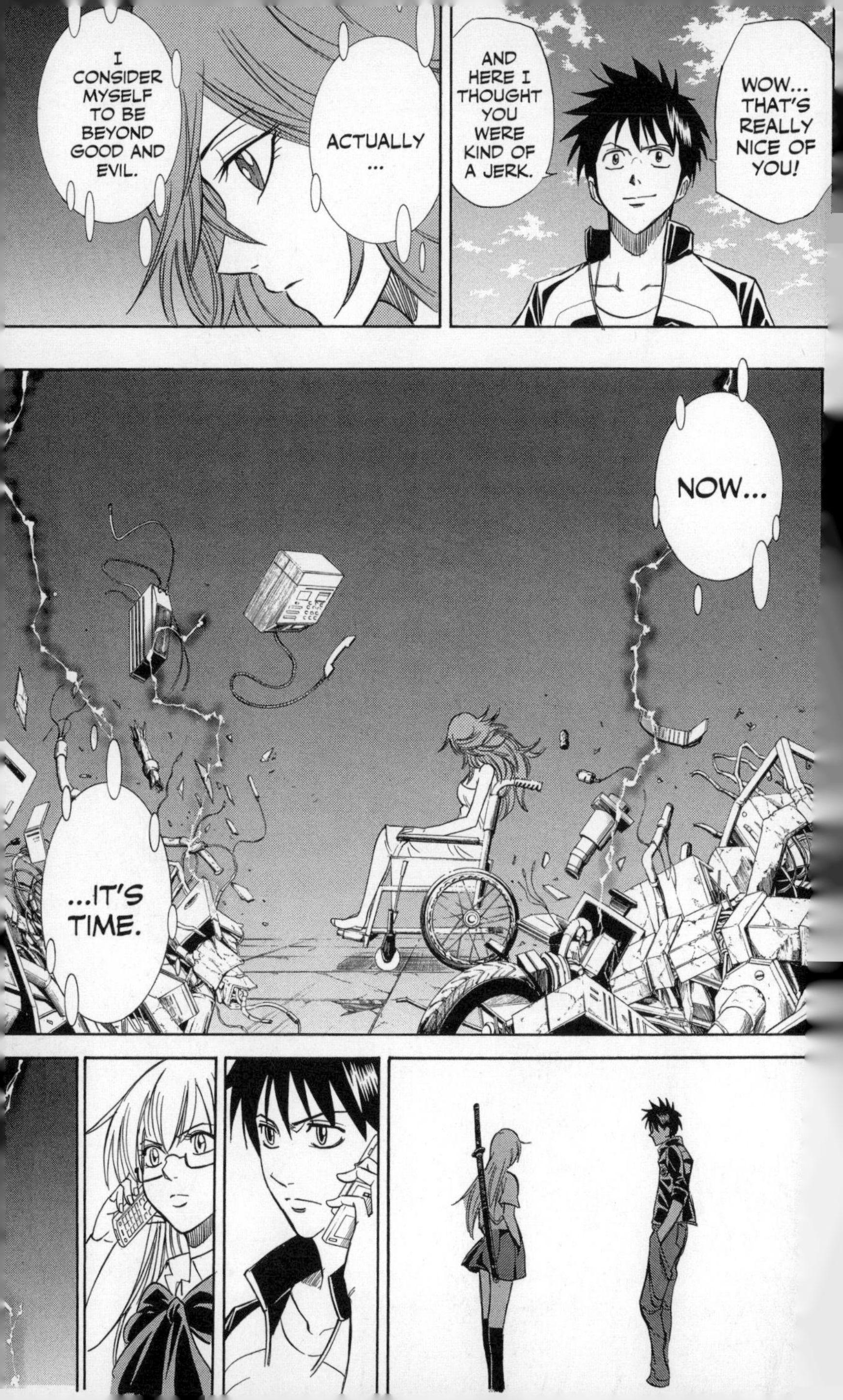
WOW... THAT'S REALLY NICE OF YOU!
AND HERE I THOUGHT YOU WERE KIND OF A JERK.
ACTUALLY ...
I CONSIDER MYSELF TO BE BEYOND GOOD AND EVIL.
NOW...
...IT'S TIME.

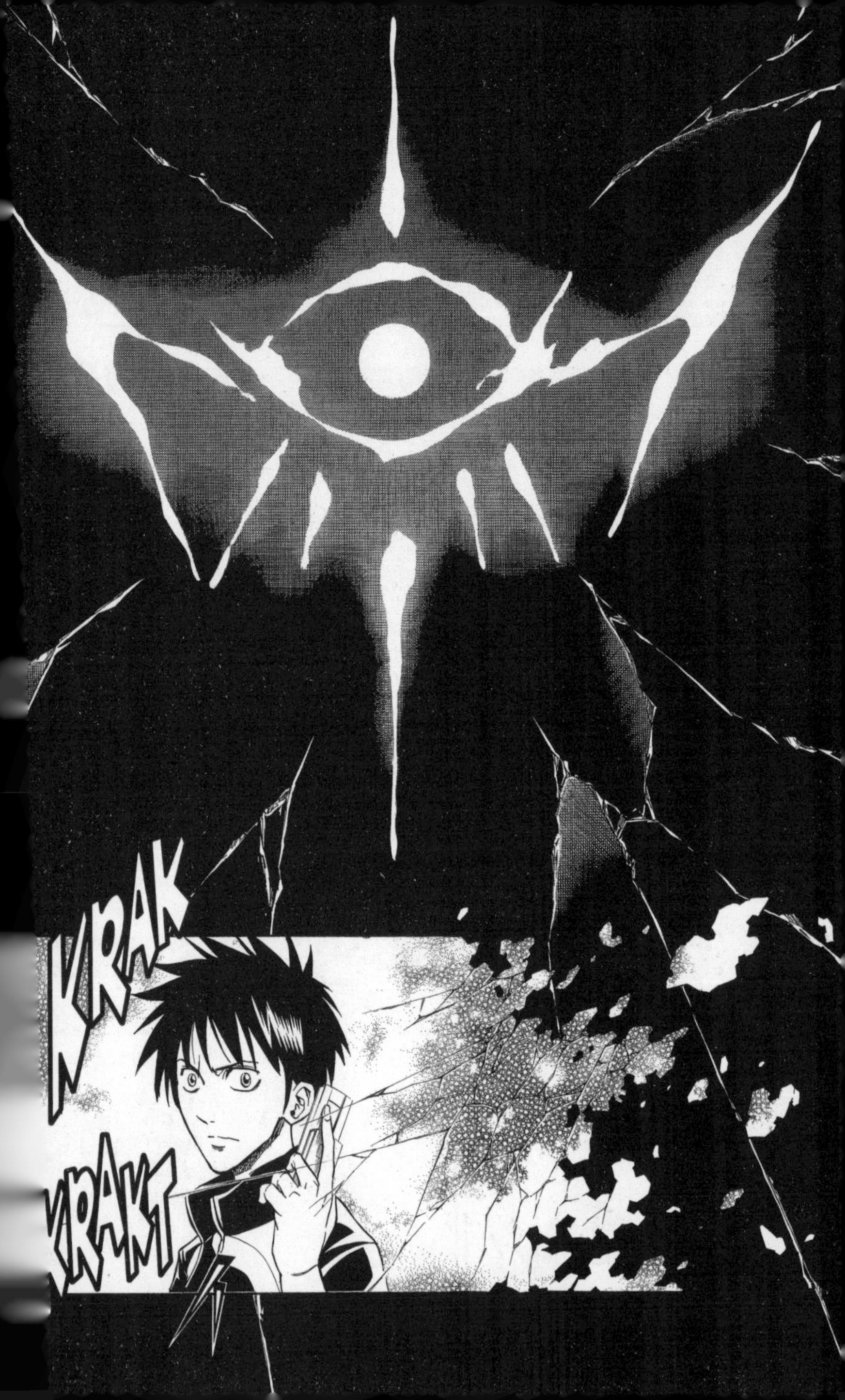
KRAK
KRAK

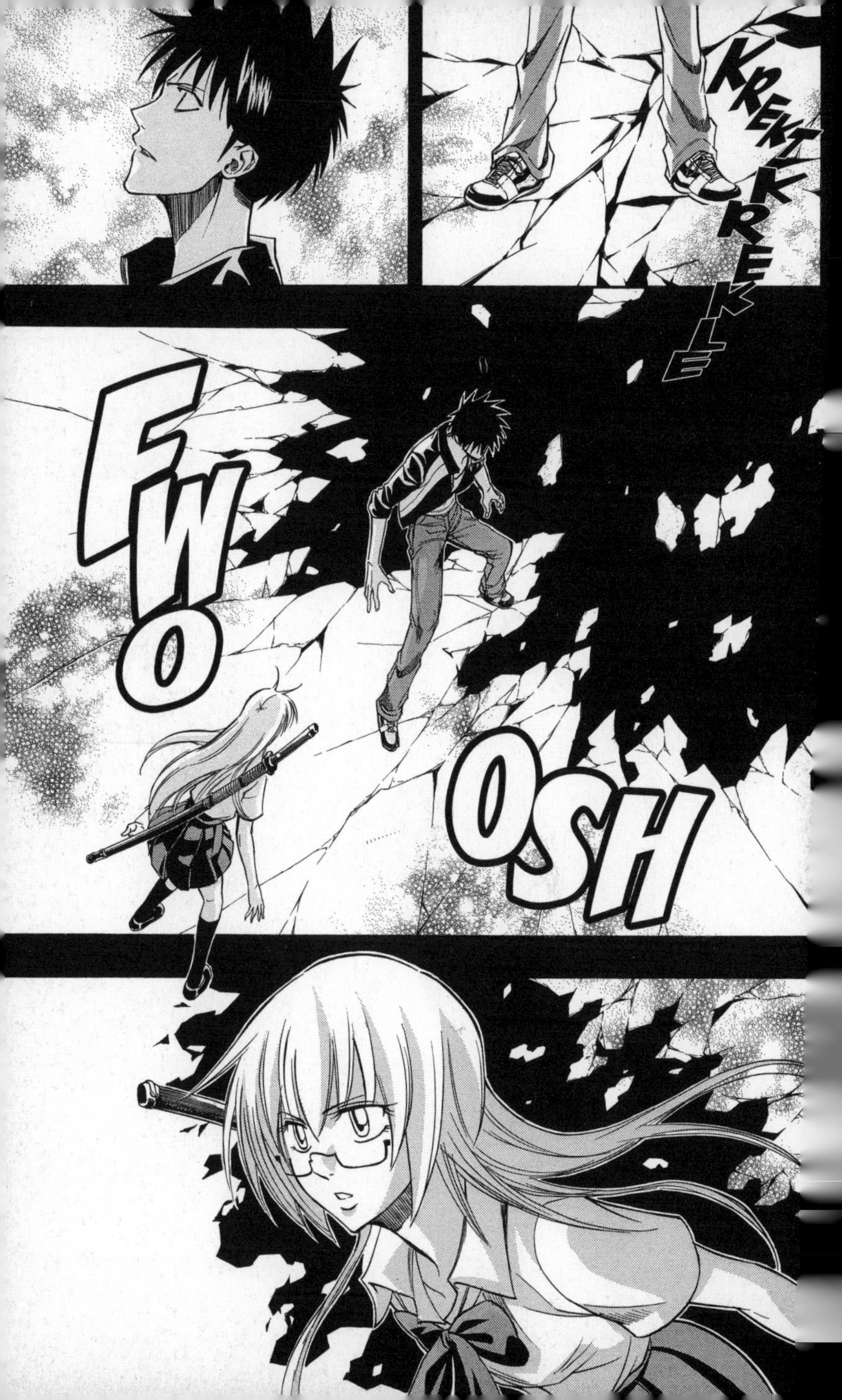
KREKT KREKKLE
FWOOSH

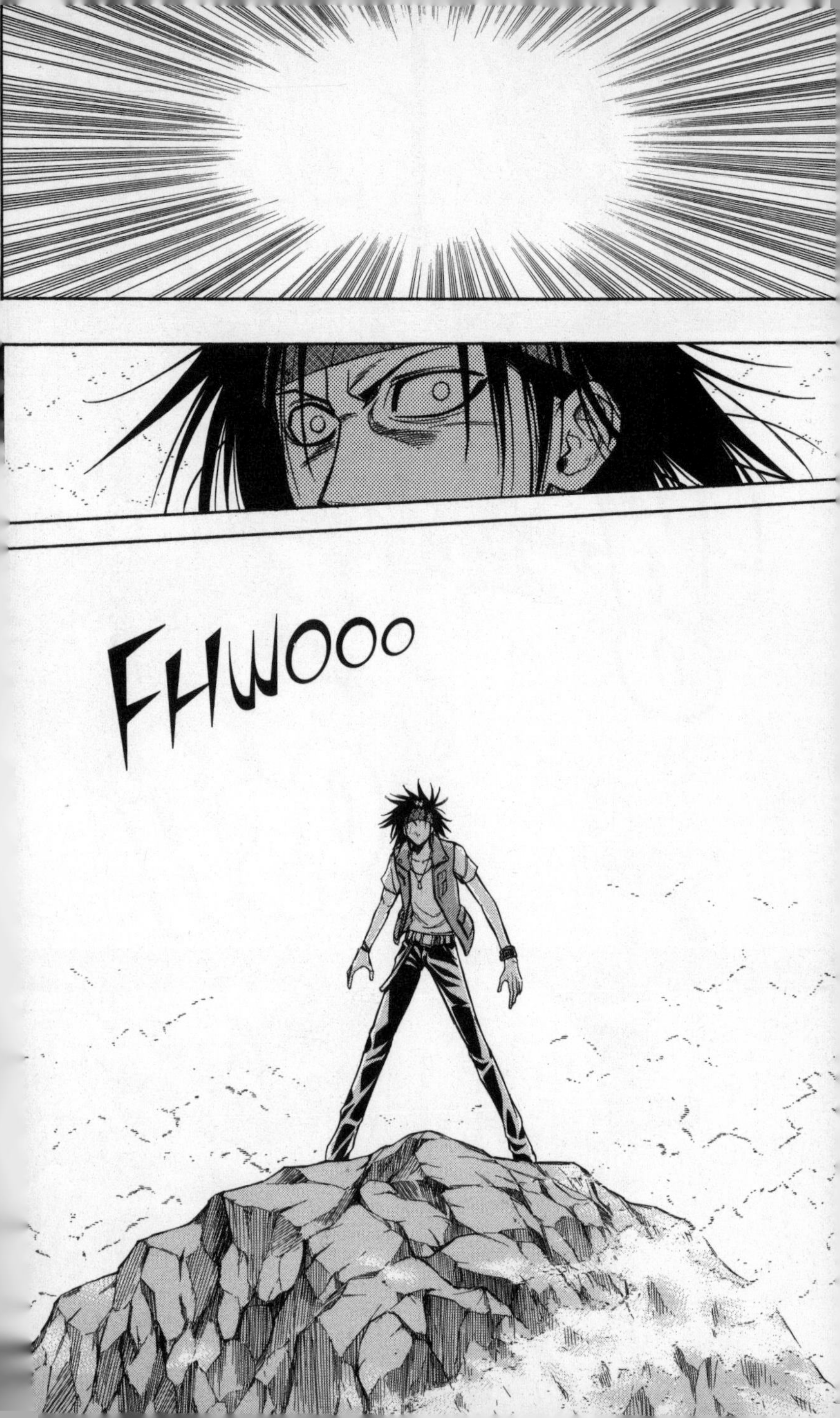
FHWOOO

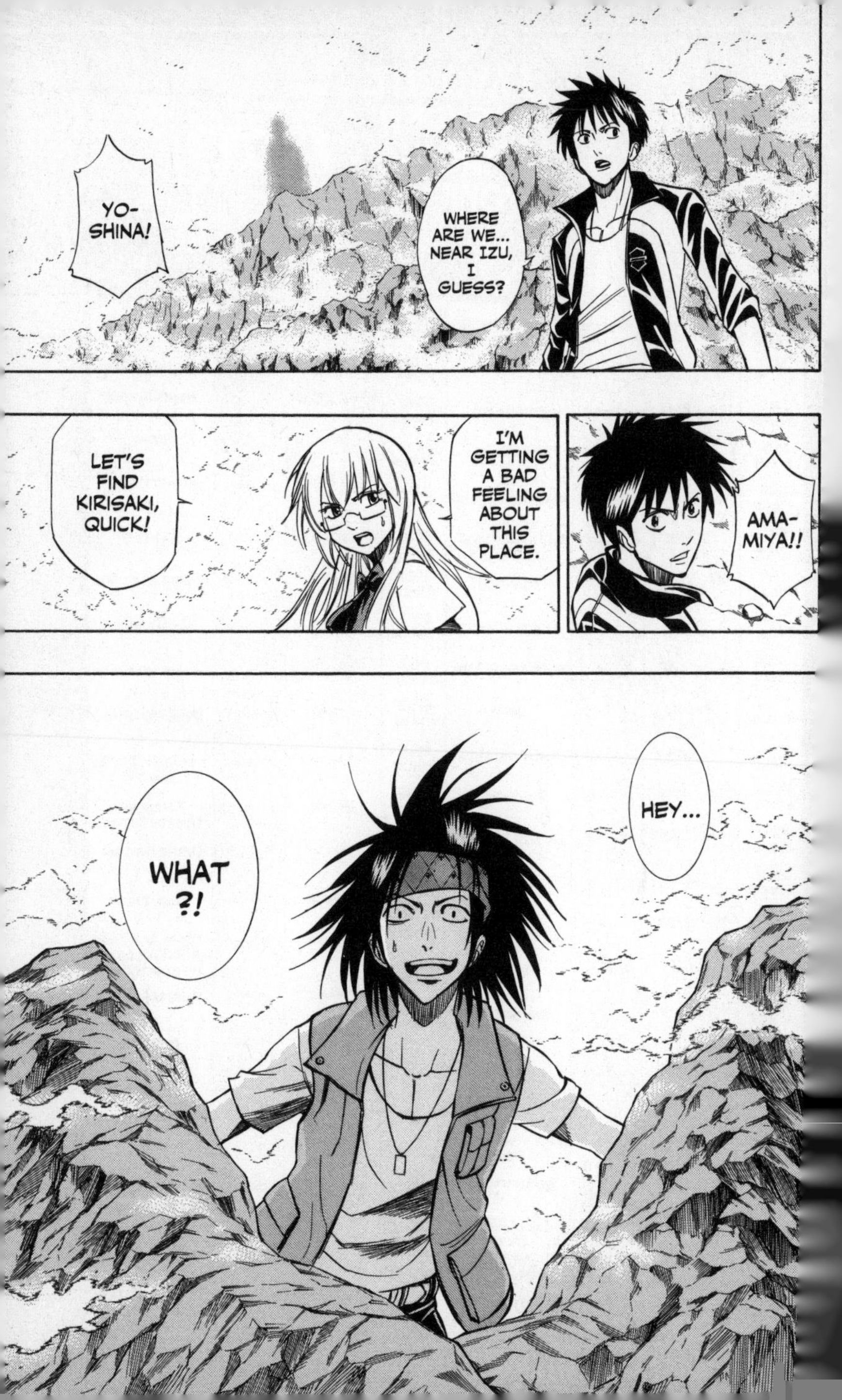
WHERE ARE WE... NEAR IZU, I GUESS?
YO-SHINA!
AMA-MIYA!!
I'M GETTING A BAD FEELING ABOUT THIS PLACE.
LET'S FIND KIRISAKI, QUICK!
HEY...
WHAT ?!

YOUR FAVORITE PSYREN PSIONIC POWERS! VOTING RESULTS!

Part 2

Whose tricks made it into the ranking?

11TH PLACE AND BEYOND!

11th Place	Miroku	190 votes	Tree of Sephiroth: Gevurah
12th Place	Amamiya (Avis)	161 votes	Blast
13th Place	Amamiya	159 votes	Telepathy
14th Place	Mari	158 votes	Telekinesis
15th Place	Kabuto	148 votes	Visions: Menace
16th Place	Yusaka	129 votes	Sulfur Mustard: Toxic Moth
17th Place	Kagetora	110 votes	Enhance
18th Place	Fredrika	105 votes	Pyro Queen
19th Place	Amamiya	101 votes	Wired Mind Jack
20th Place	Oboro	79 votes	Heal
21st Place	Tatsuo	77 votes	Blast Bazooka
22nd Place	Mistress (No. 07)	70 votes	Nemesis Q
23rd Place	Shao (future)	68 votes	Ying-Yang Shinra
24th Place	Shao	65 votes	Connect
25th Place	Haruhiko	62 votes	Shocker-N
26th Place	Taiga	55 votes	Chakram
27th Place	Matsuri	54 votes	Mega-Blast
28th Place	Ian	51 votes	Heal
29th Place	Junas	49 votes	Ashura Unlock
30th Place	Miroku	46 votes	Sephiroth Gate: Open
31st Place	Shiner	44 votes	Teleportation
32nd Place	Miroku	39 votes	Tree of Sephiroth: Tiferet

33rd Place	Okugo	38 votes	Orgous
34th Place	Junas	37 votes	Bishamon Mura
35th Place	Riko (Capriko)		Ogre Drawing
36th Place	Van	36 votes	Heal
37th Place	Ageha	32 votes	Melzez Vortex
38th Place	Mistress (No. 07)	31 votes	Klutzy Q
39th Place	Junas	30 votes	Bishamon Pellets
40th Place	Inui	29 votes	Angry Gory
41st Place	Oboro	28 votes	Skeletonization
42nd Place	Usui	24 votes	Deletion Spider
43rd Place	Miroku	22 votes	Tree of Sephiroth: Malchut
44th Place	Shiner	20 votes	Hexagonal Transfer System
45th Place	Shao	19 votes	White Dowser
46th Place	Yusaka	18 votes	Candy Man
47th Place	Elmore	16 votes	Thousand Year Kaleidoscope (Precognition)
48th Place	Amamiya	12 votes	Peeping Lover
49th Place	Miyake	11 votes	Octopus
	Ageha		Touching Amamiya!!!

THANKS SO MUCH FOR SUBMITTING SO MANY RESPONSES!

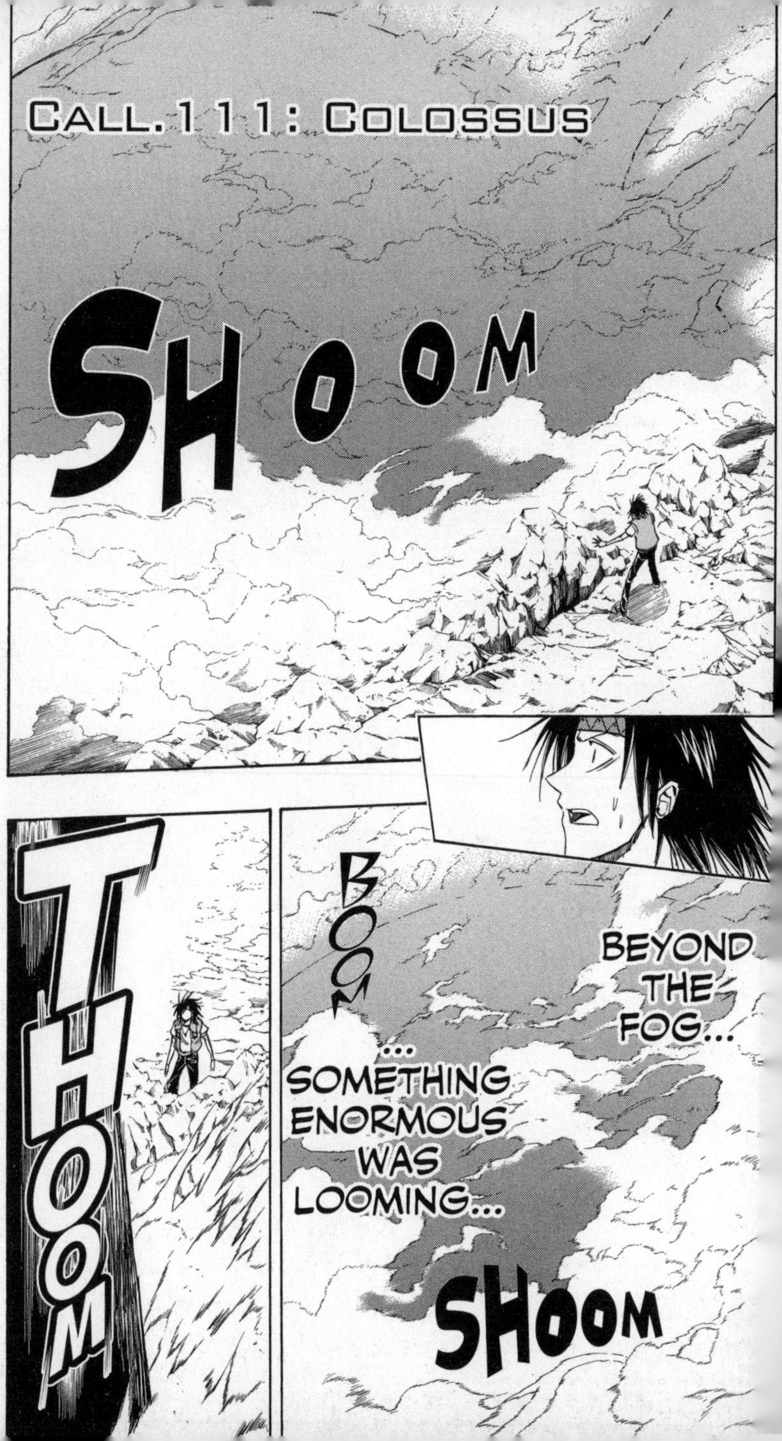
CALL. 111: COLOSSUS
SHOOM
BOOM
BEYOND THE FOG...
...SOMETHING ENORMOUS WAS LOOMING...
SHOOM
THOOM

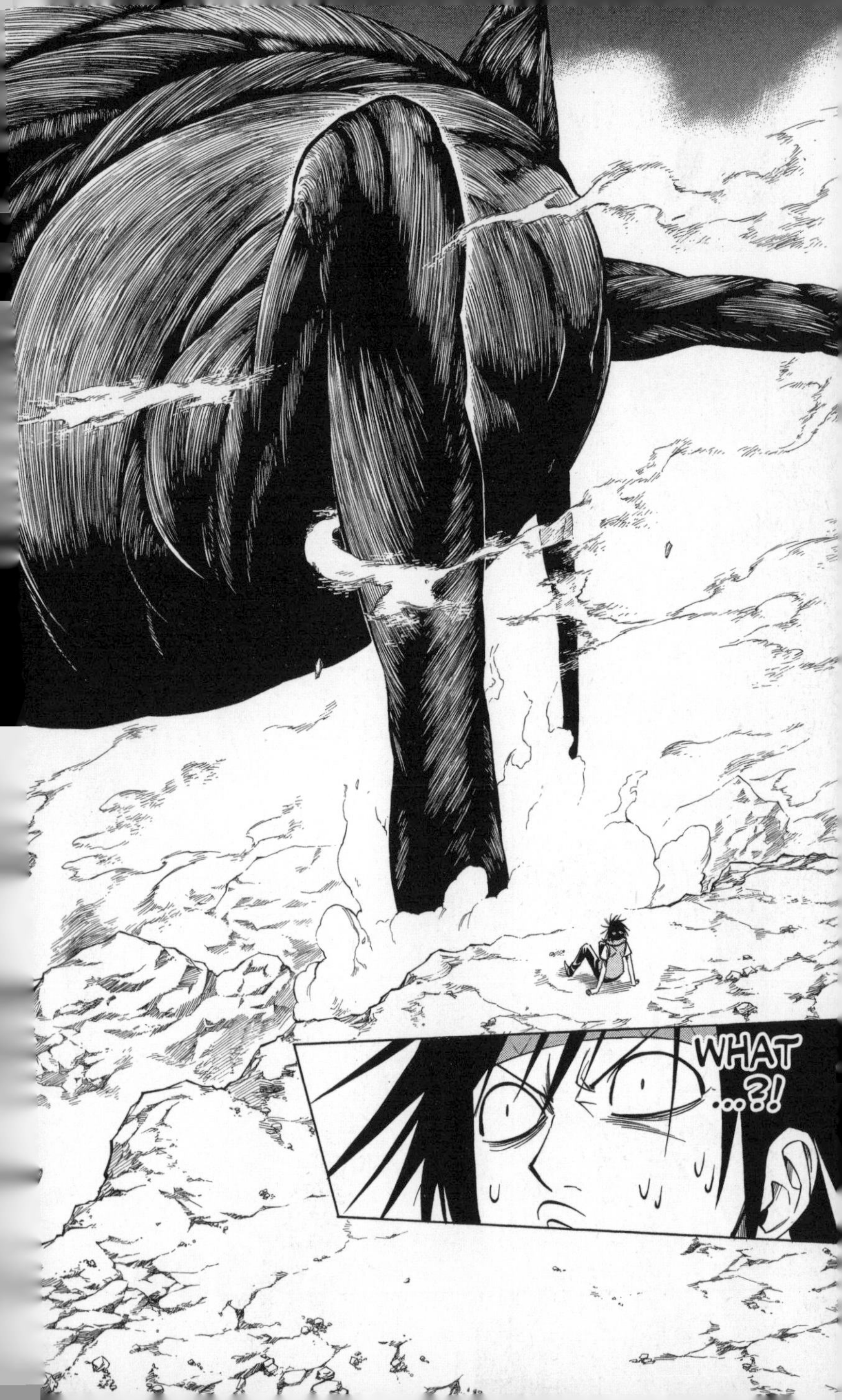
WHAT ...?!

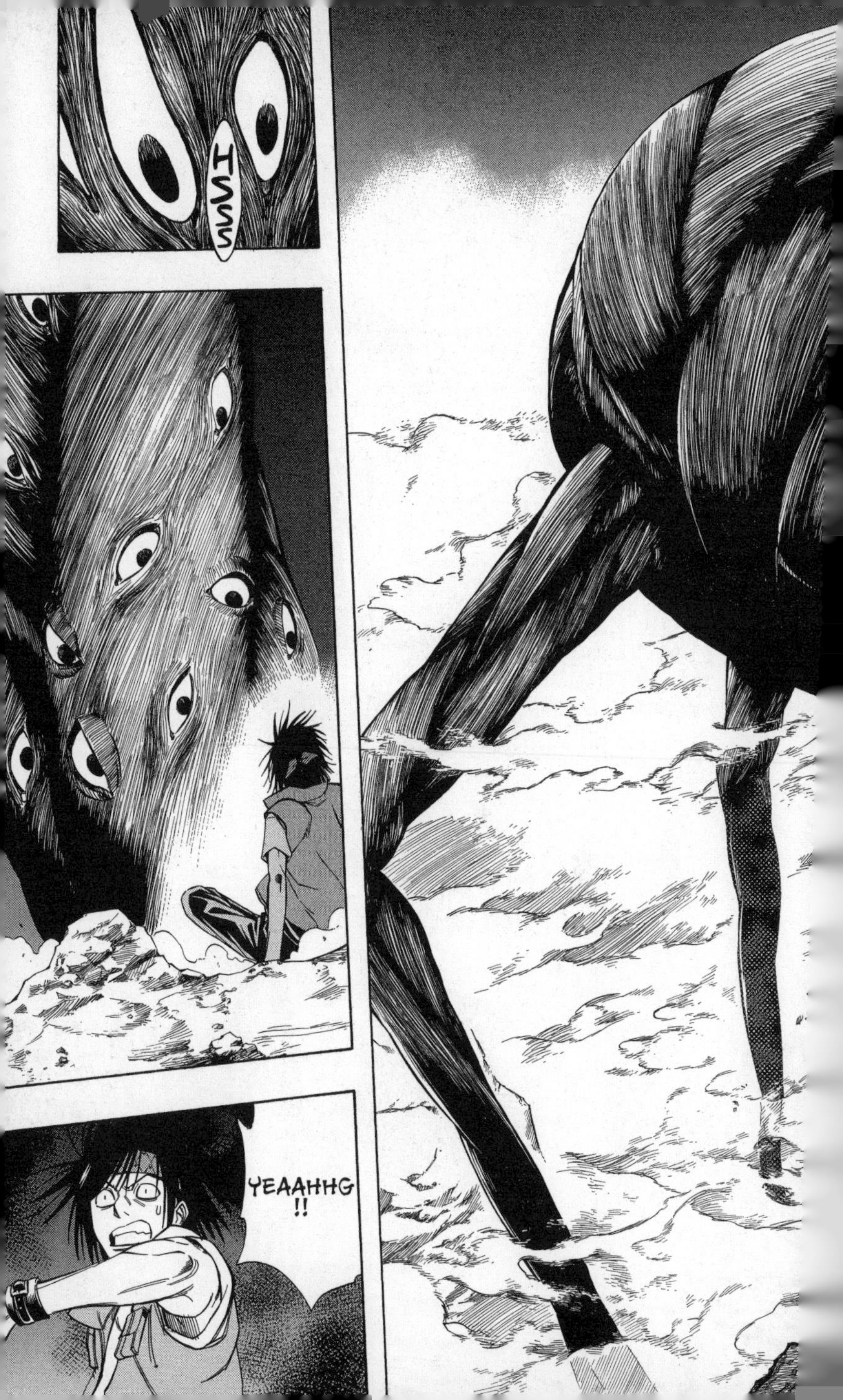
HSSSS
YEAAHHG !!

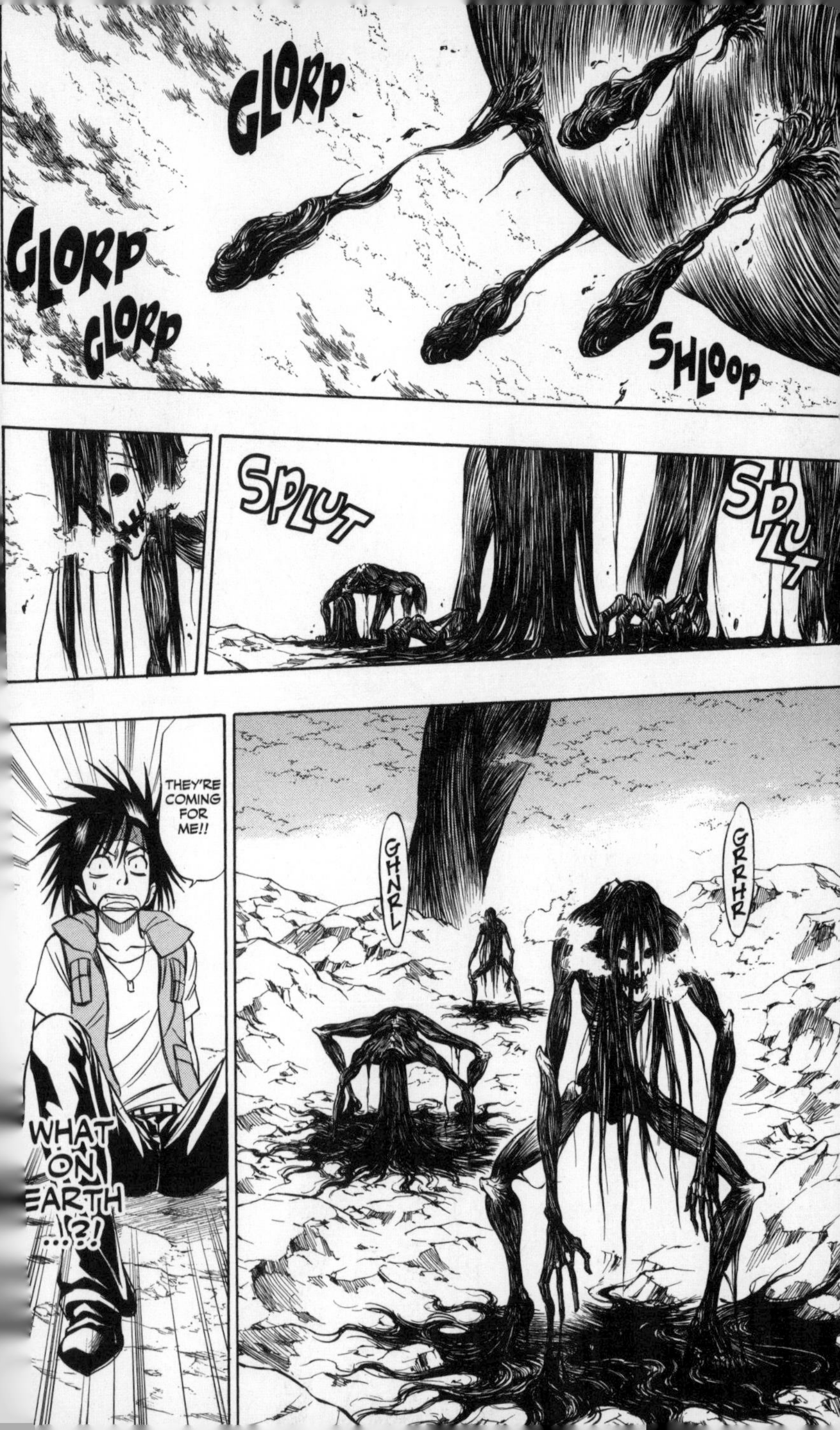
GLORP
SHLOOP
GLORP
GLORP
SPLUT
SPLUT
GRRHR
GHNRL
THEY'RE COMING FOR ME!!
WHAT ON EARTH ...!?!

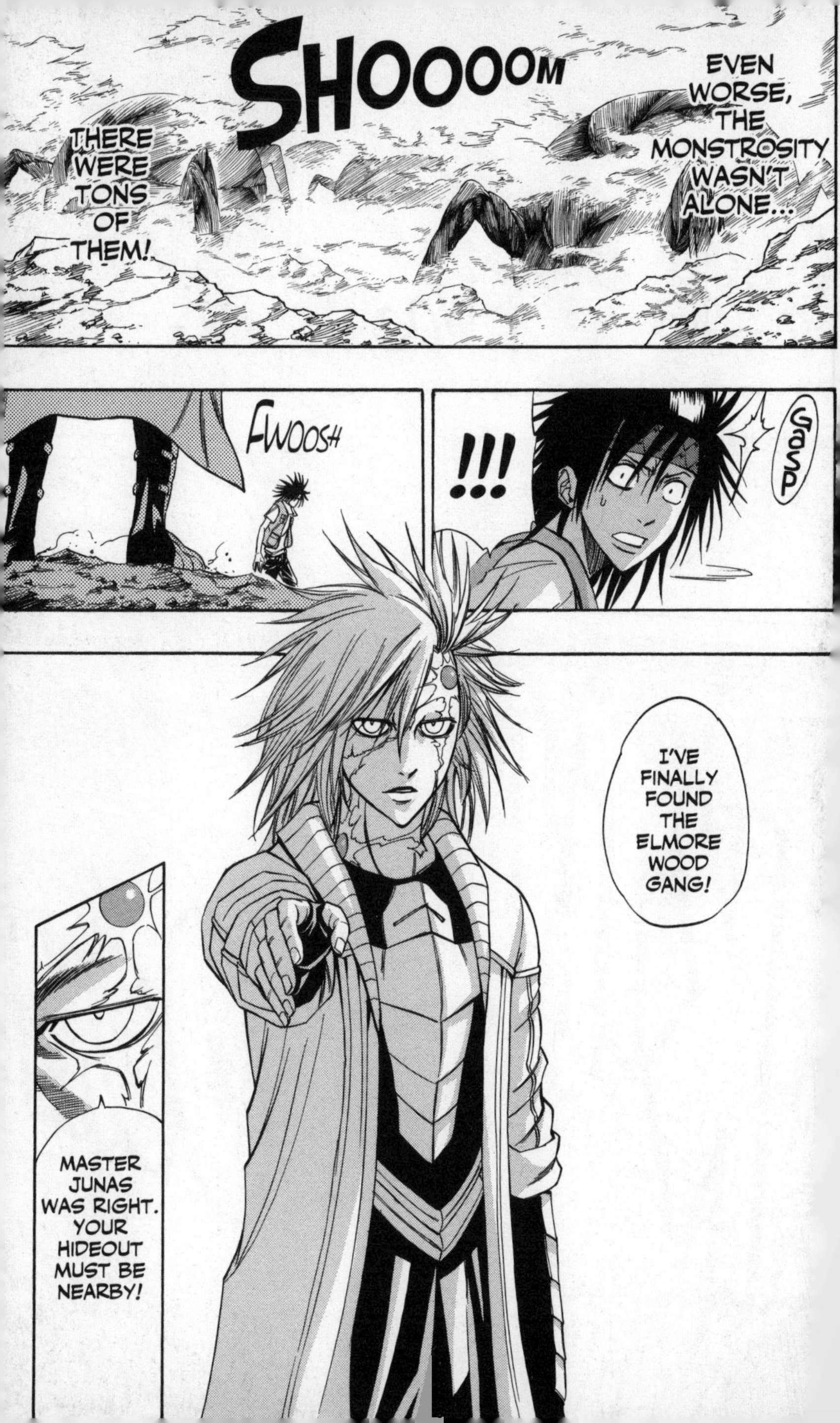
SHOOOOM
EVEN WORSE, THE MONSTROSITY WASN'T ALONE...
THERE WERE TONS OF THEM!
GASP
!!!
FWOOSH
I'VE FINALLY FOUND THE ELMORE WOOD GANG!
MASTER JUNAS WAS RIGHT. YOUR HIDEOUT MUST BE NEARBY!

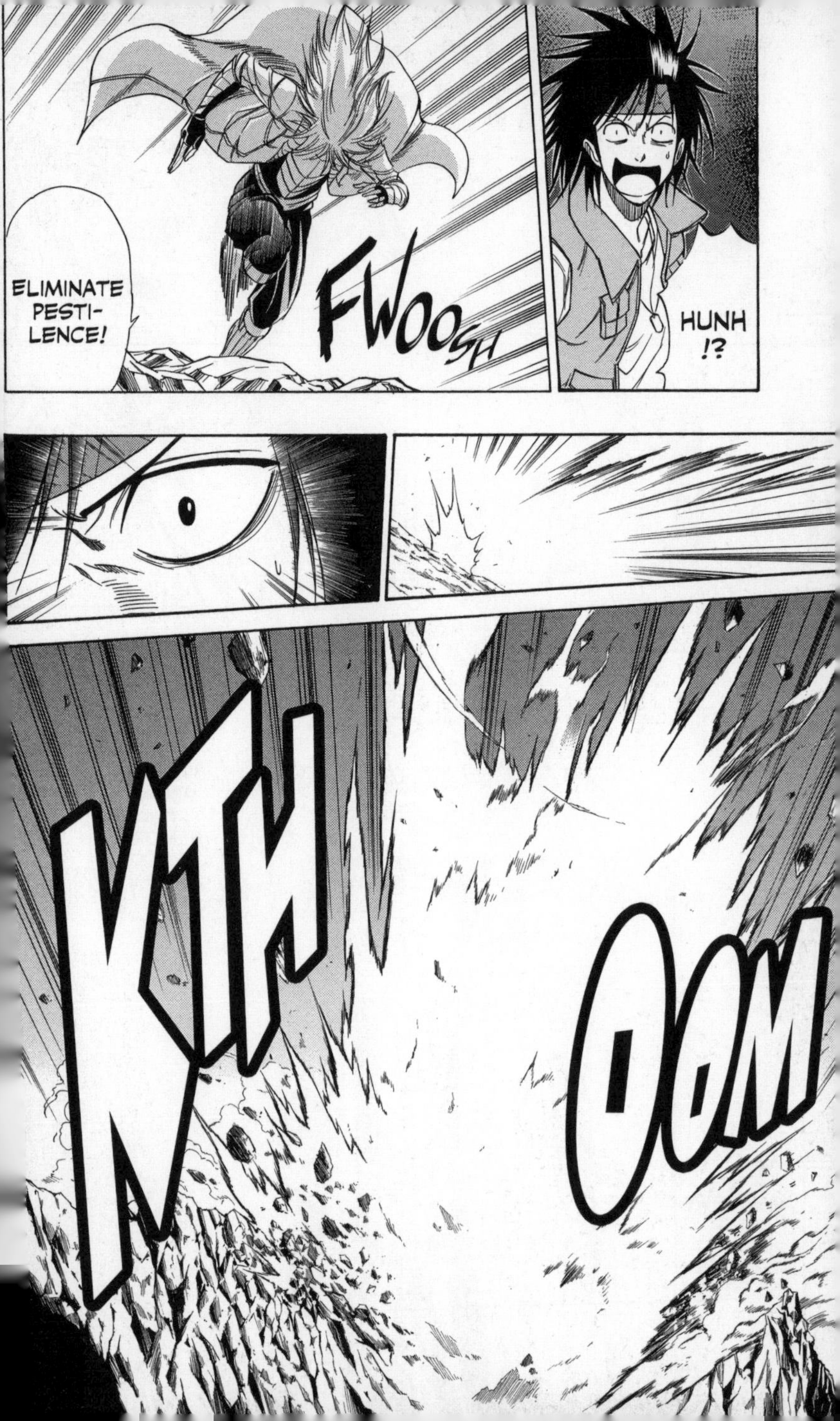
HUNH !?
ELIMINATE PESTI- LENCE!
FWOOSH
KTH
OOM

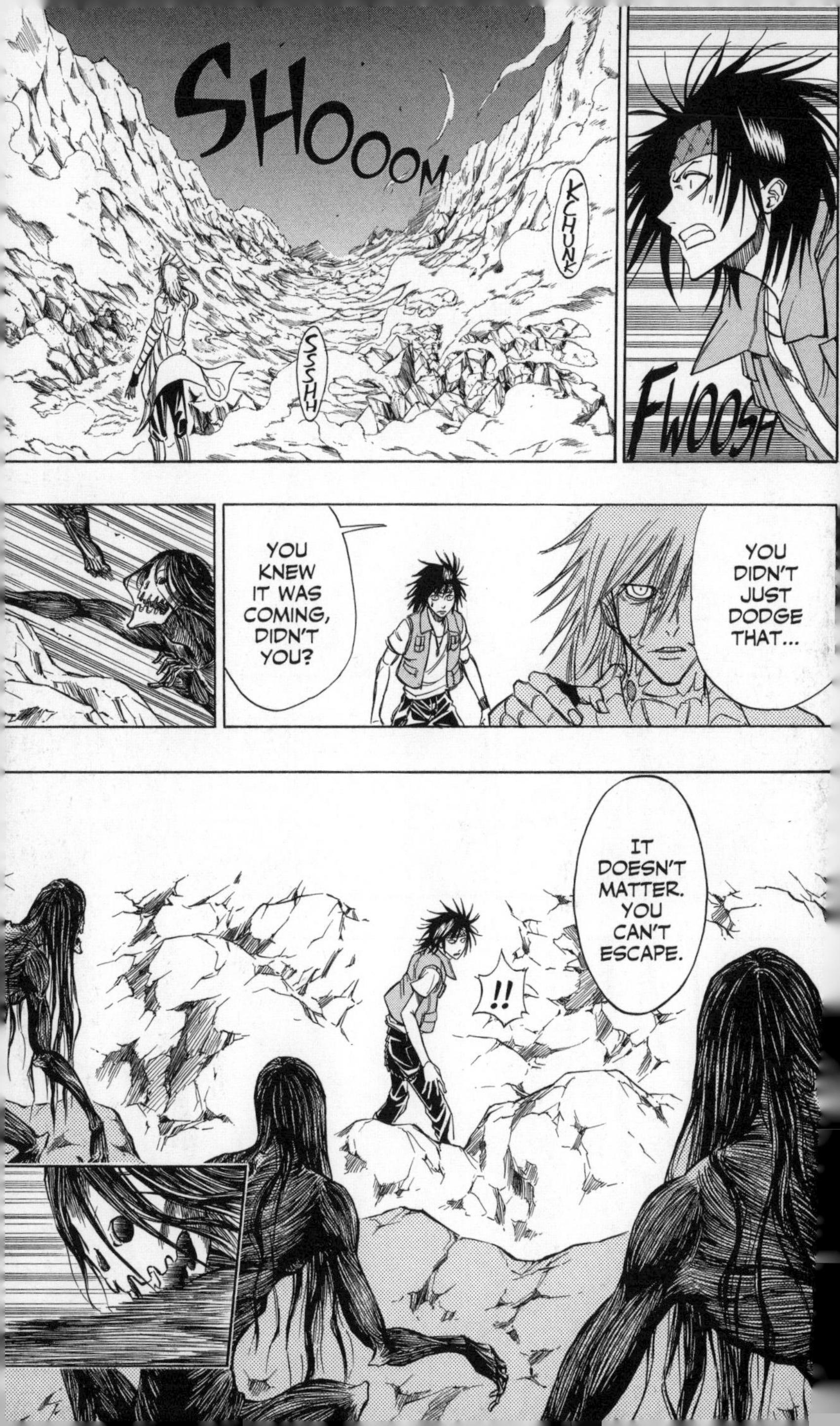
FWOOSH
SHOOOM
KCHUNK
SSSHH
YOU DIDN'T JUST DODGE THAT...
YOU KNEW IT WAS COMING, DIDN'T YOU?
IT DOESN'T MATTER. YOU CAN'T ESCAPE.
!!

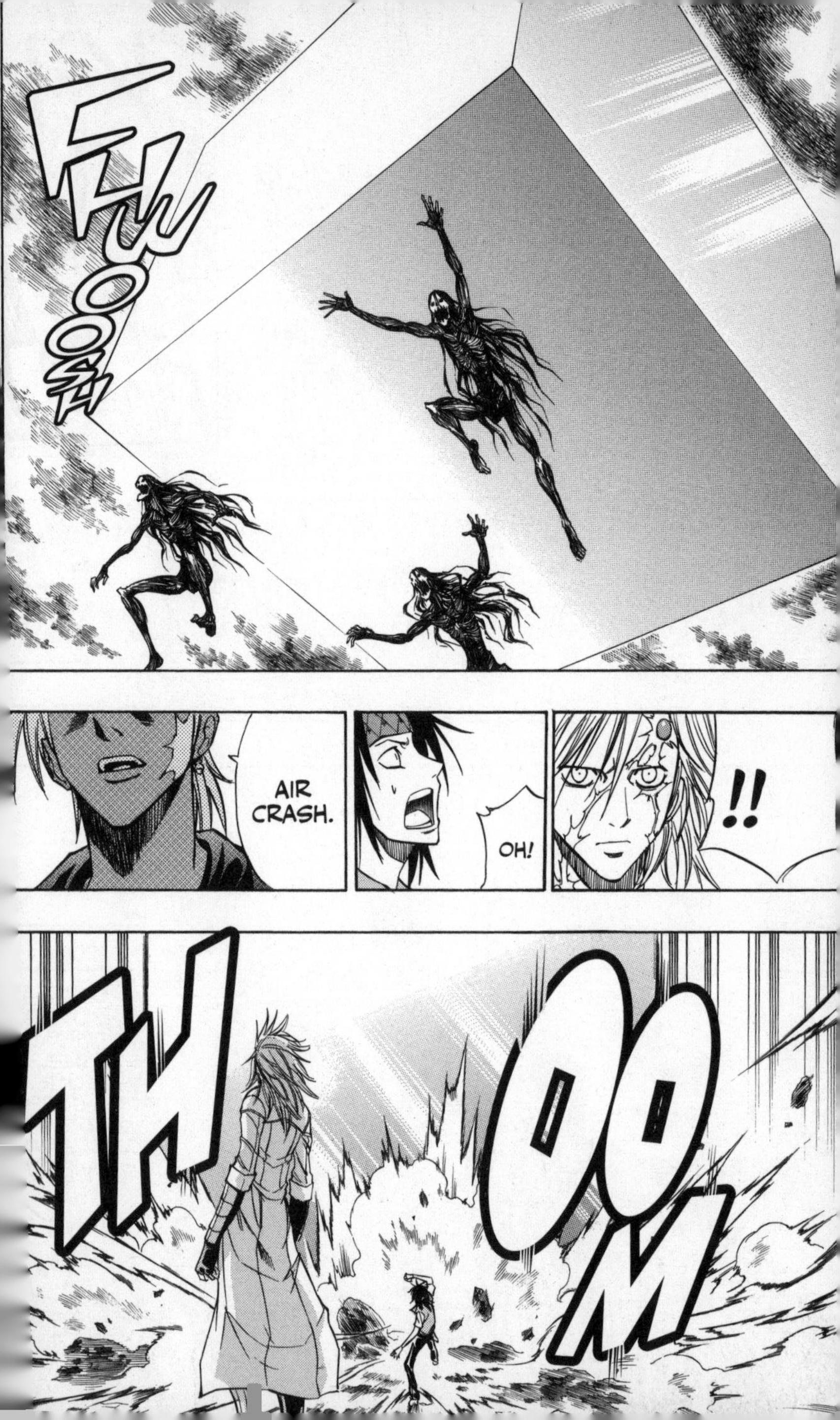
FWOOSH
!!
OH!
AIR CRASH.
THOOM

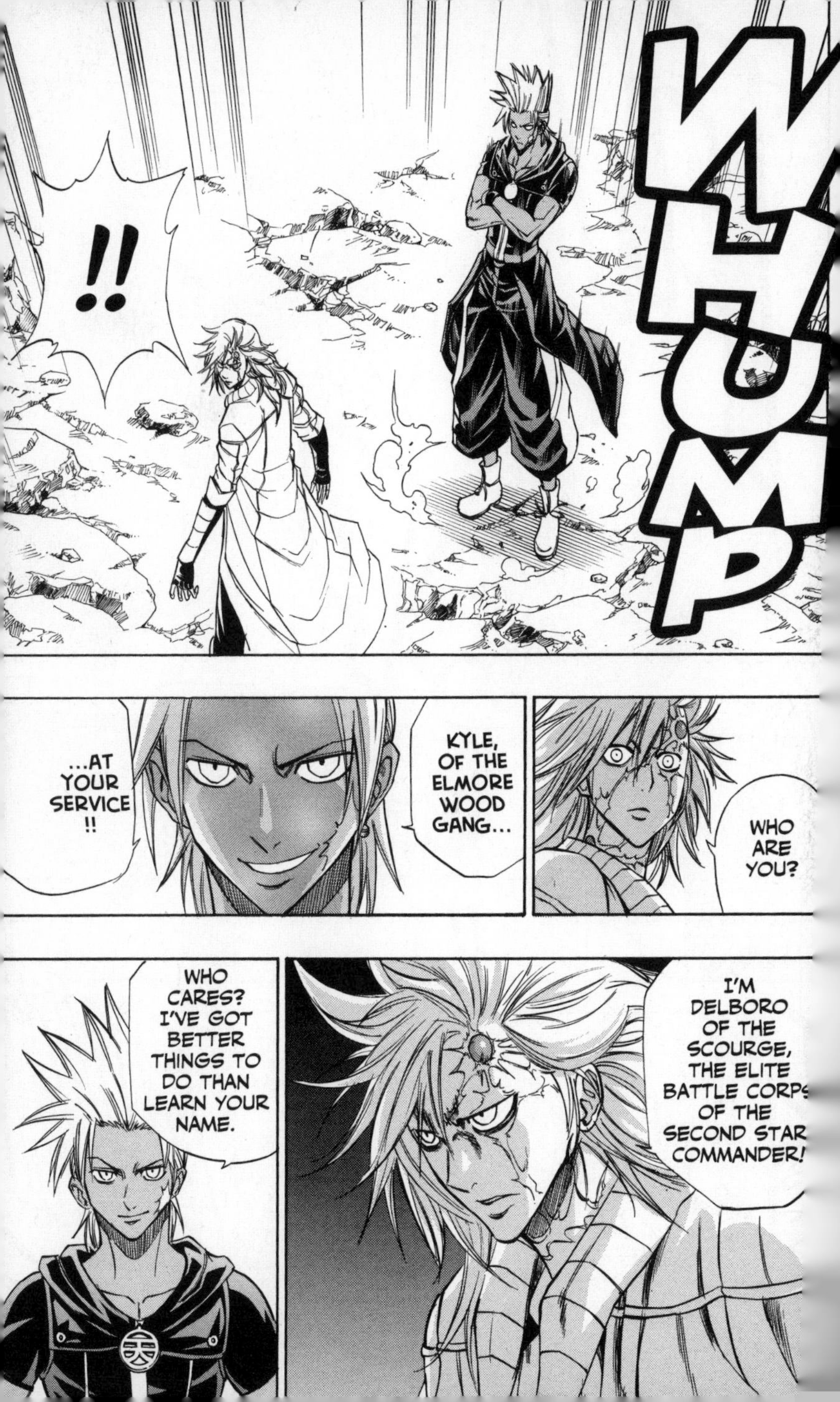
WHUMP
!!
WHO ARE YOU?
KYLE, OF THE ELMORE WOOD GANG...
...AT YOUR SERVICE !!
I'M DELBORO OF THE SCOURGE, THE ELITE BATTLE CORPS OF THE SECOND STAR COMMANDER!
WHO CARES? I'VE GOT BETTER THINGS TO DO THAN LEARN YOUR NAME.

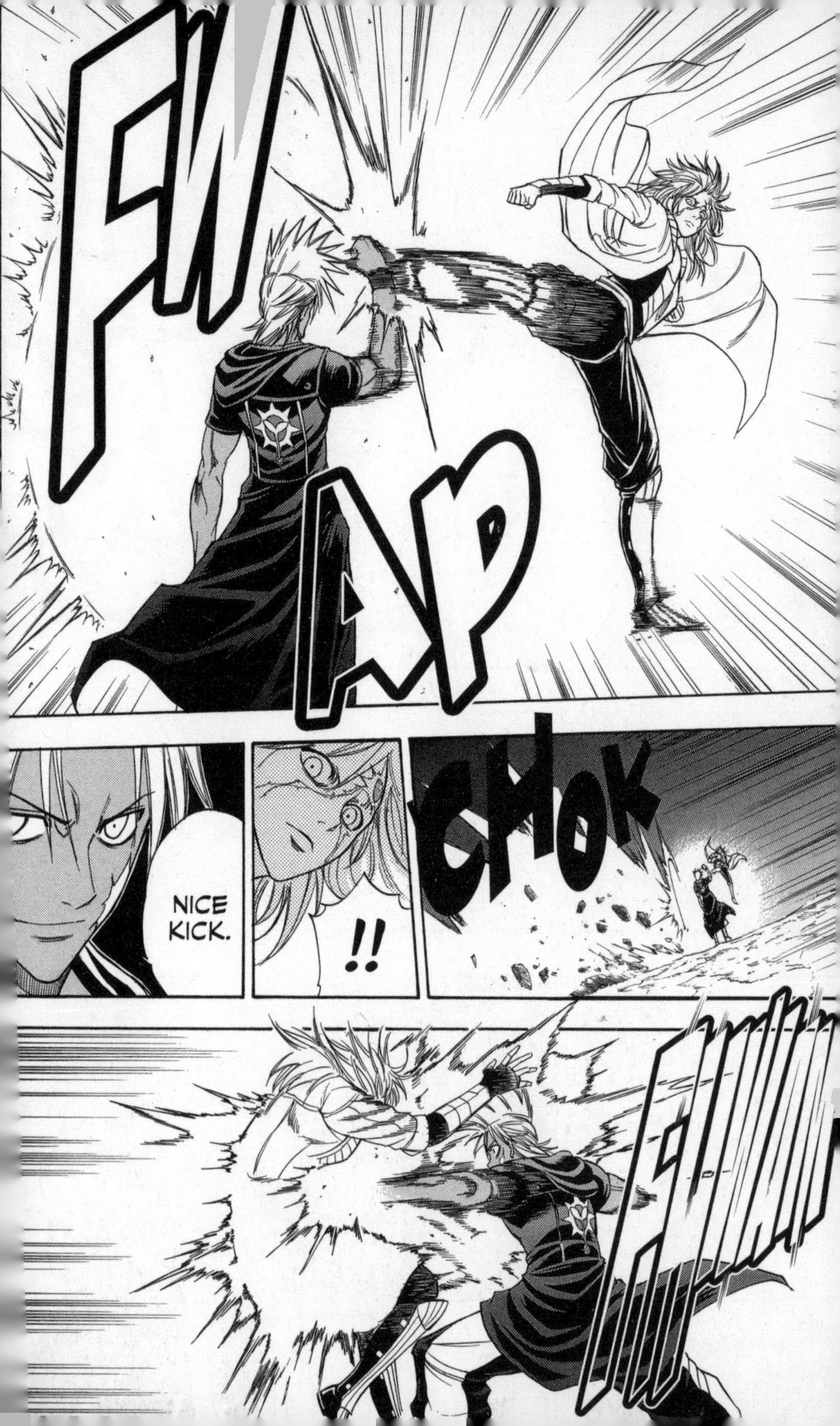
FW
AP
CHOK
!!
NICE KICK.

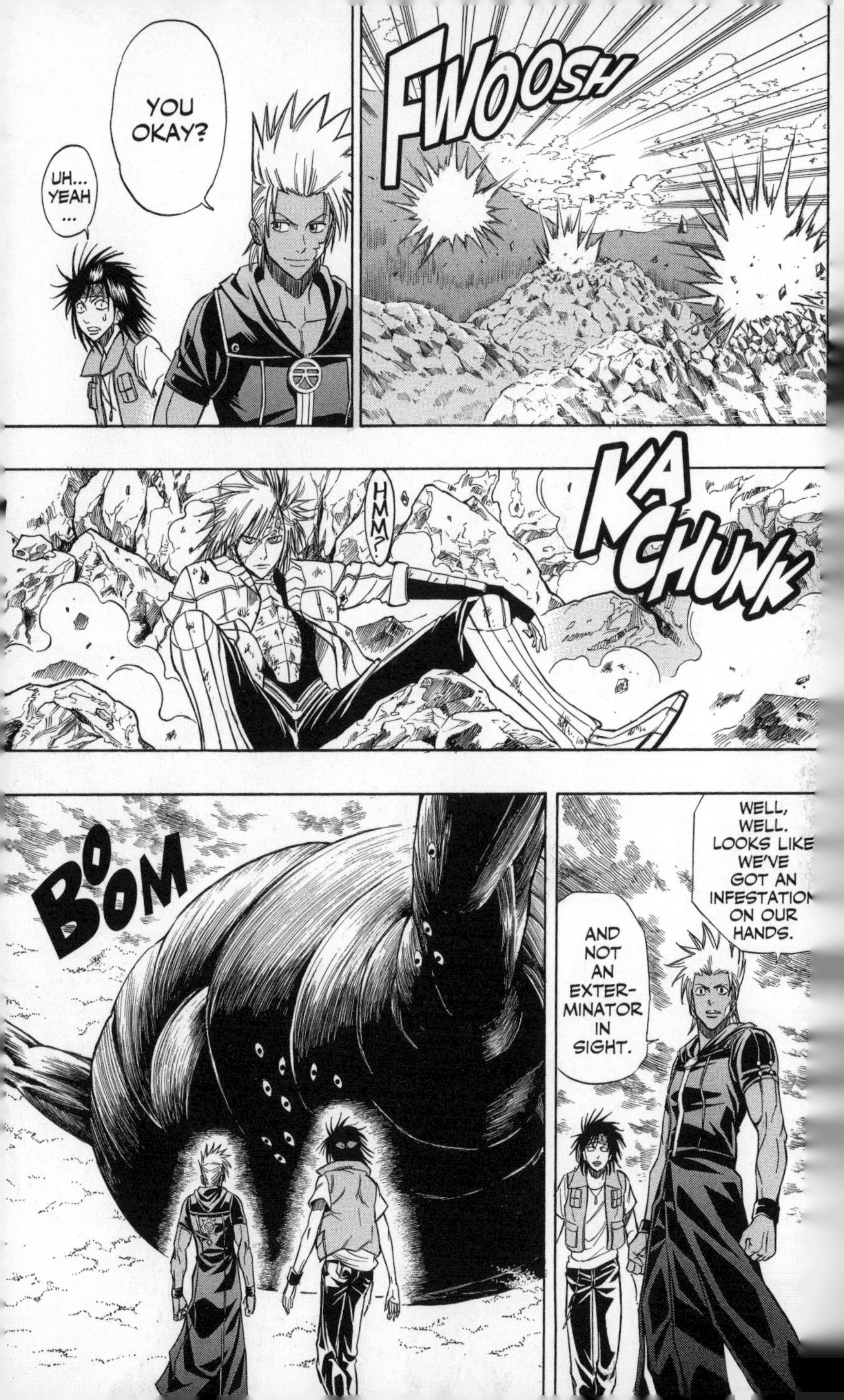
FWOOSH
YOU OKAY?
UH... YEAH ...
KA CHUNK
HMM?
WELL, WELL. LOOKS LIKE WE'VE GOT AN INFESTATION ON OUR HANDS.
AND NOT AN EXTER-MINATOR IN SIGHT.
BOOM

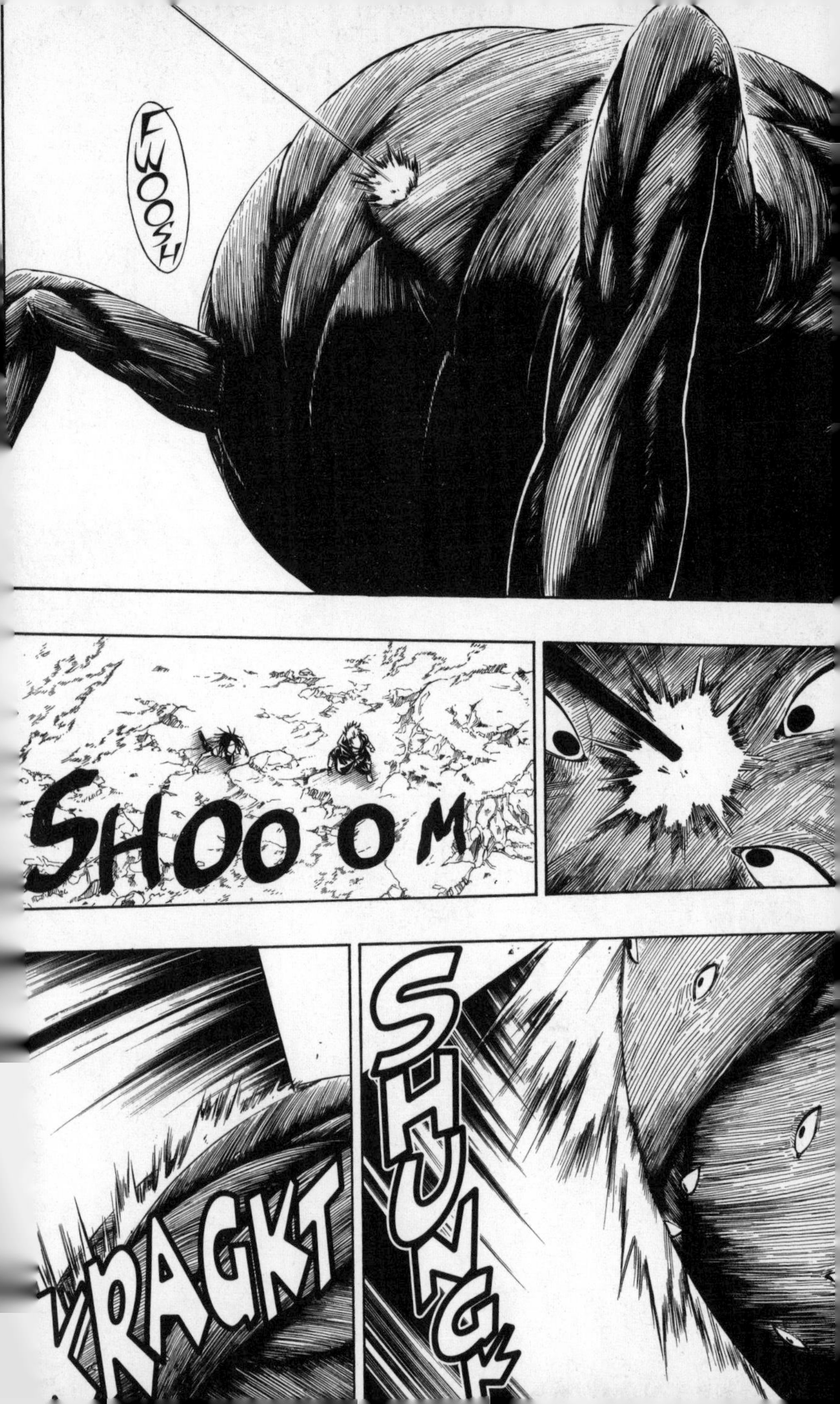
FWOOSH
SHOOOM
SHUNGK
RAGKT

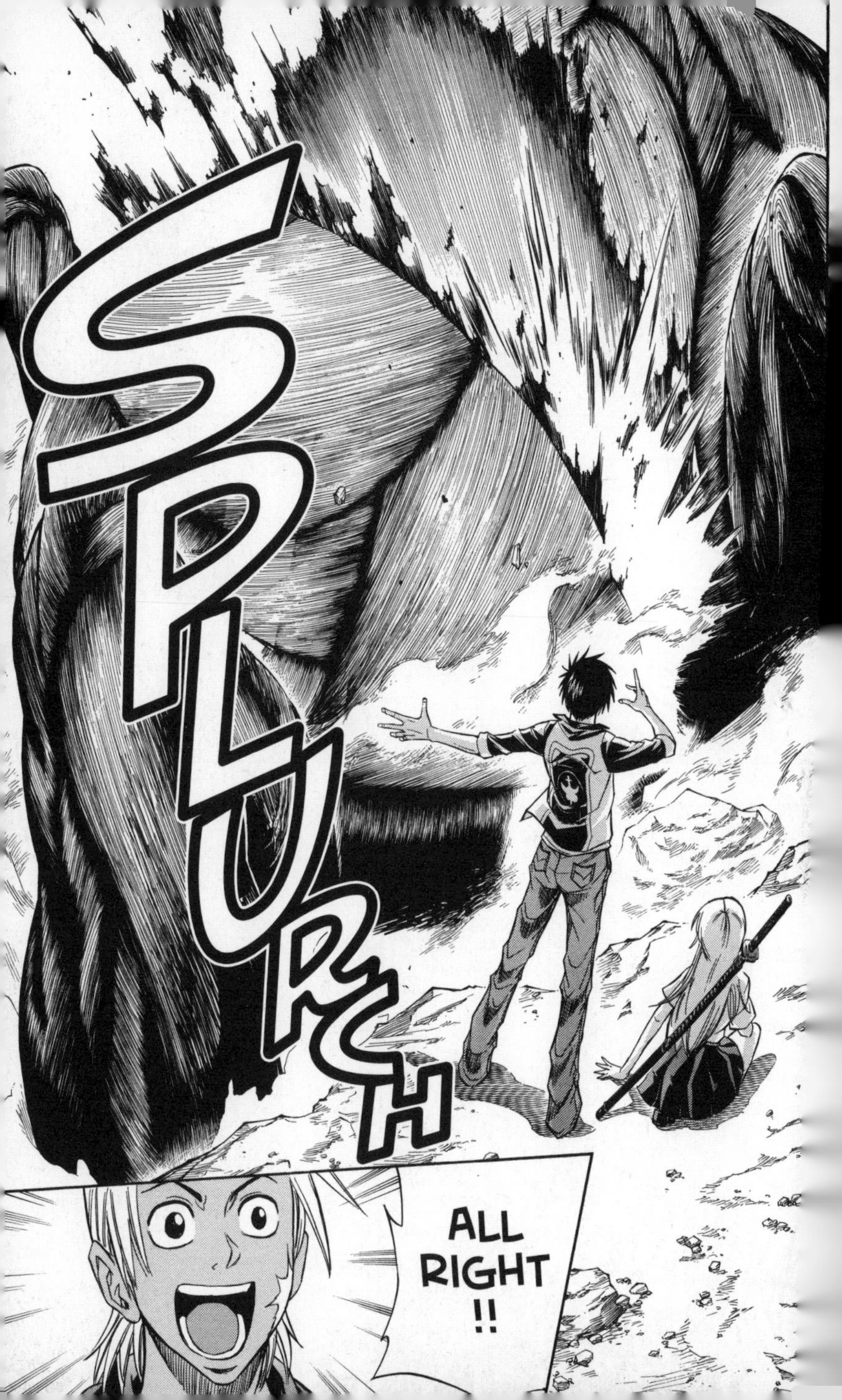
SPLURCH
ALL RIGHT !!

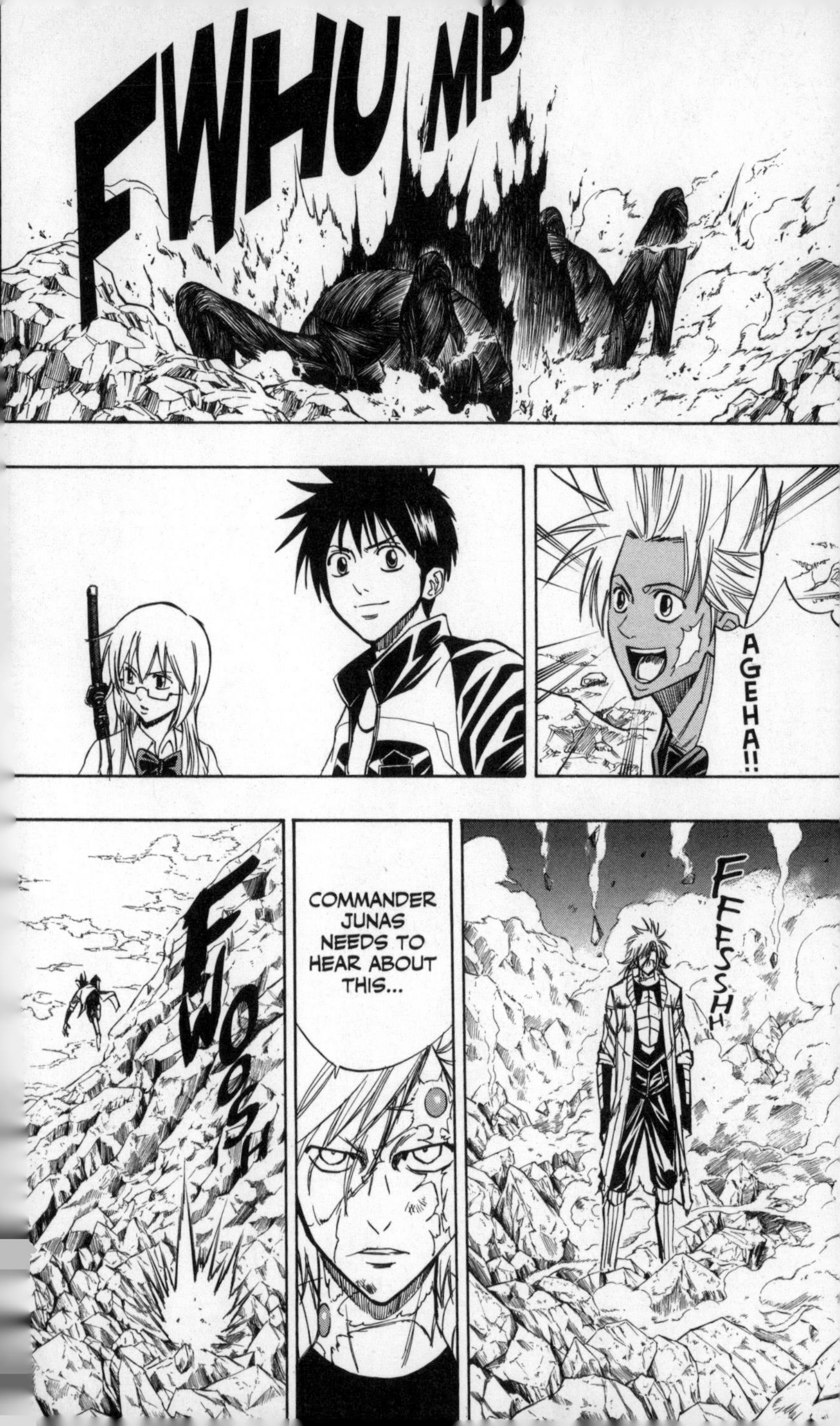
FWHUMP
AGEHA!!
FFFSSH
COMMANDER JUNAS NEEDS TO HEAR ABOUT THIS...
FWOOSH

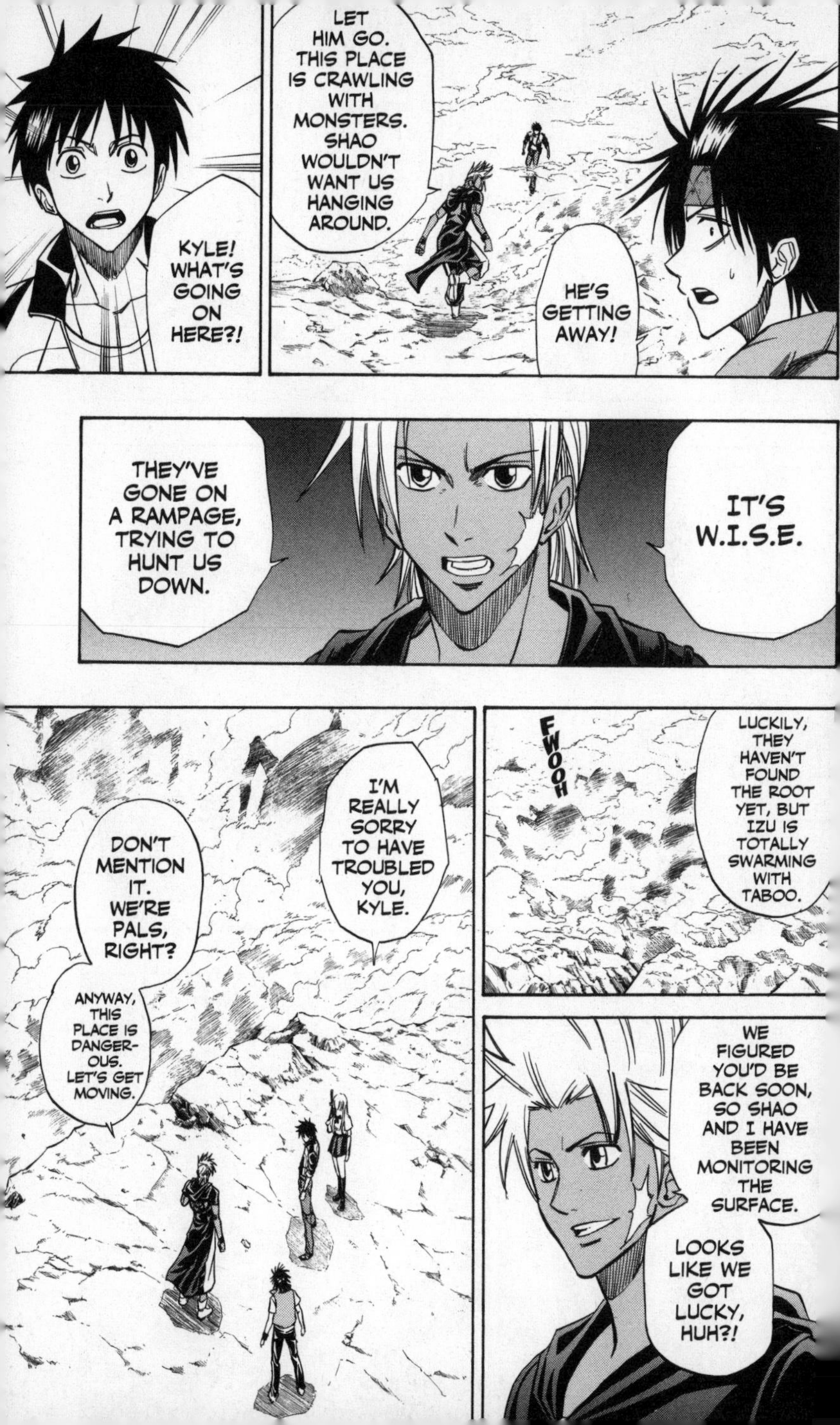
HE'S GETTING AWAY!
LET HIM GO. THIS PLACE IS CRAWLING WITH MONSTERS. SHAO WOULDN'T WANT US HANGING AROUND.
KYLE! WHAT'S GOING ON HERE?!
IT'S W.I.S.E.
THEY'VE GONE ON A RAMPAGE, TRYING TO HUNT US DOWN.
FWOOH
LUCKILY, THEY HAVEN'T FOUND THE ROOT YET, BUT IZU IS TOTALLY SWARMING WITH TABOO.
WE FIGURED YOU'D BE BACK SOON, SO SHAO AND I HAVE BEEN MONITORING THE SURFACE.
LOOKS LIKE WE GOT LUCKY, HUH?!
I'M REALLY SORRY TO HAVE TROUBLED YOU, KYLE.
DON'T MENTION IT. WE'RE PALS, RIGHT?
ANYWAY, THIS PLACE IS DANGER-OUS. LET'S GET MOVING.

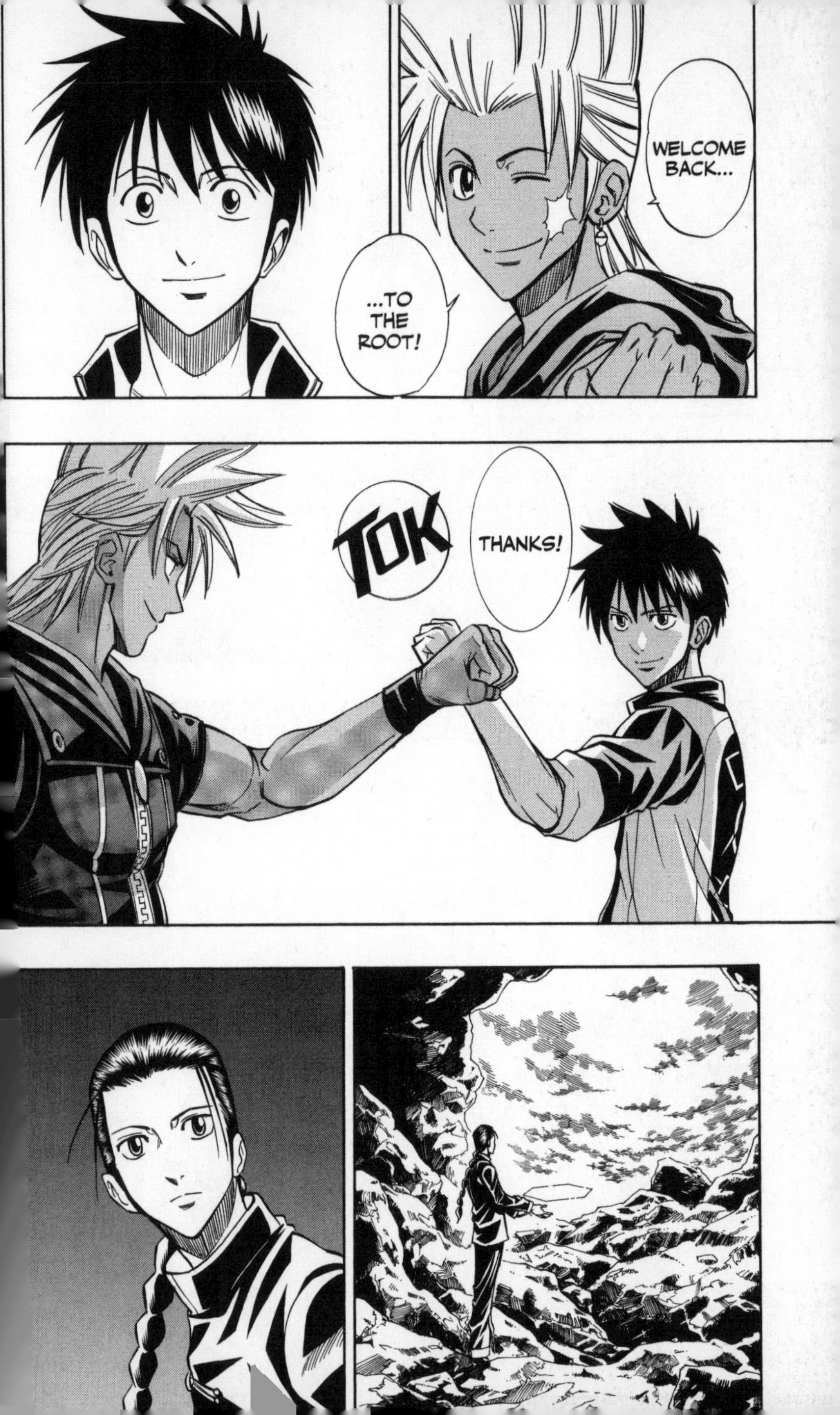
WELCOME BACK...
...TO THE ROOT!
THANKS!
TOK

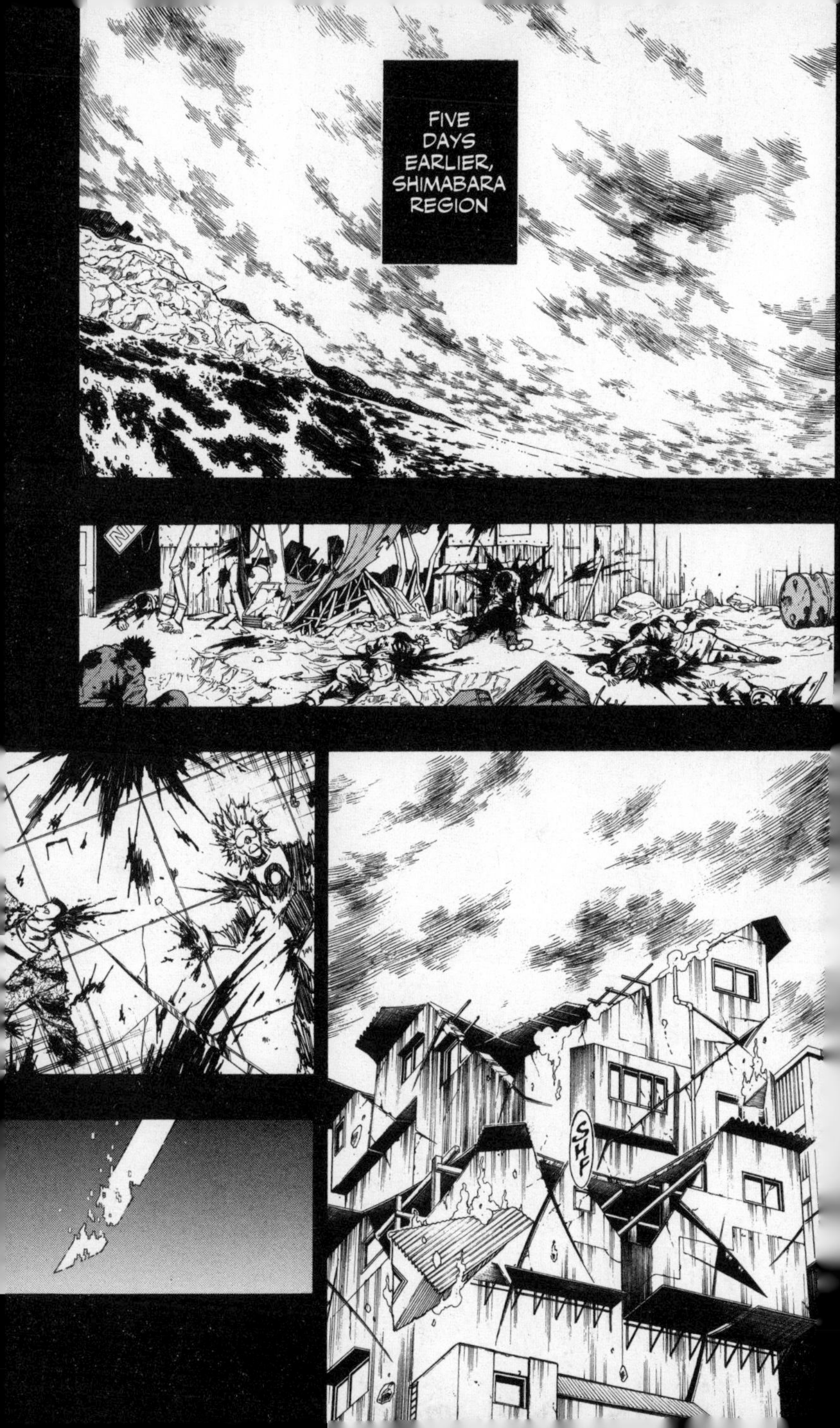
FIVE DAYS EARLIER, SHIMABARA REGION
SHF

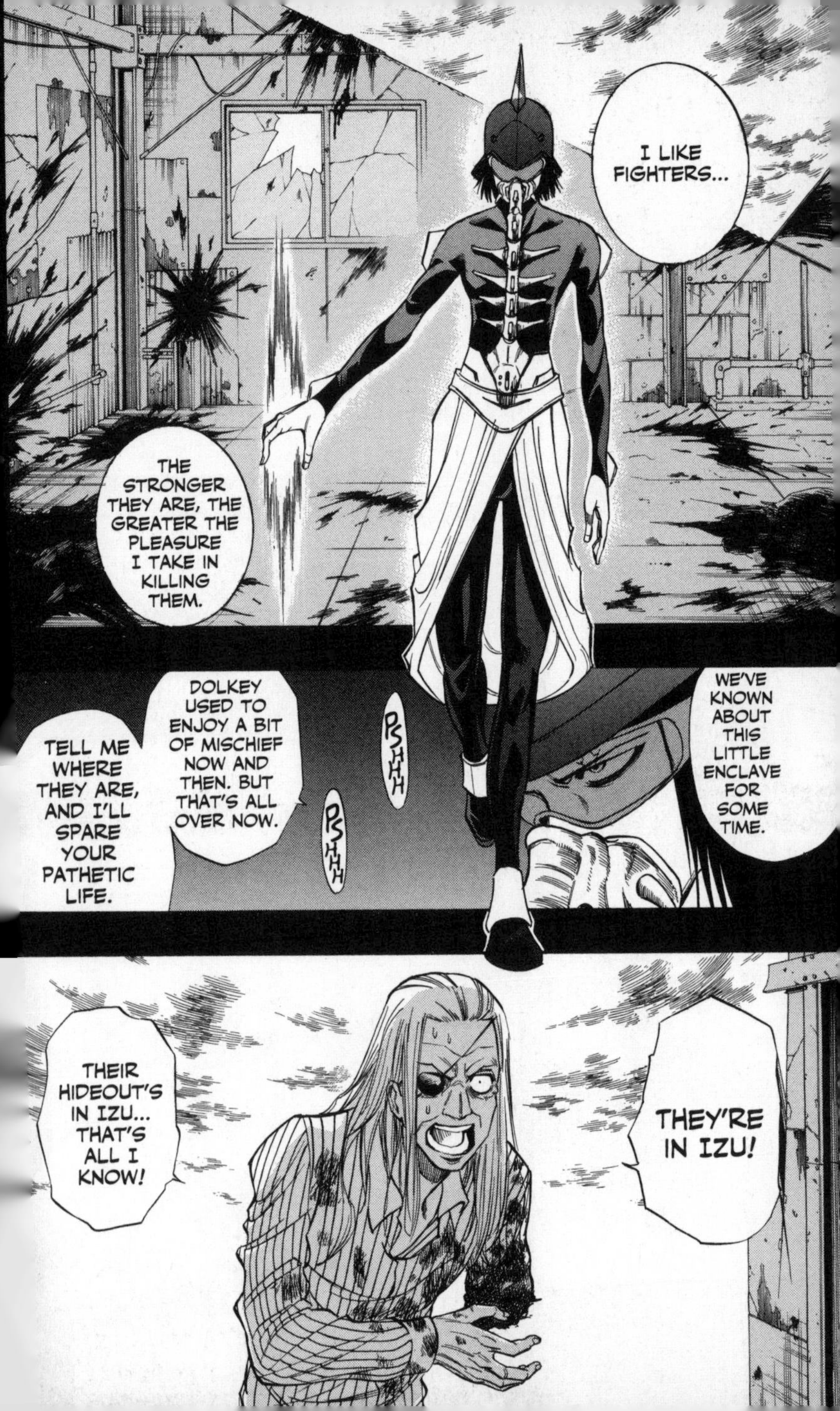
I LIKE FIGHTERS...
THE STRONGER THEY ARE, THE GREATER THE PLEASURE I TAKE IN KILLING THEM.
WE'VE KNOWN ABOUT THIS LITTLE ENCLAVE FOR SOME TIME.
PSHHH
PSHHH
DOLKEY USED TO ENJOY A BIT OF MISCHIEF NOW AND THEN. BUT THAT'S ALL OVER NOW.
TELL ME WHERE THEY ARE, AND I'LL SPARE YOUR PATHETIC LIFE.
THEY'RE IN IZU!
THEIR HIDEOUT'S IN IZU... THAT'S ALL I KNOW!

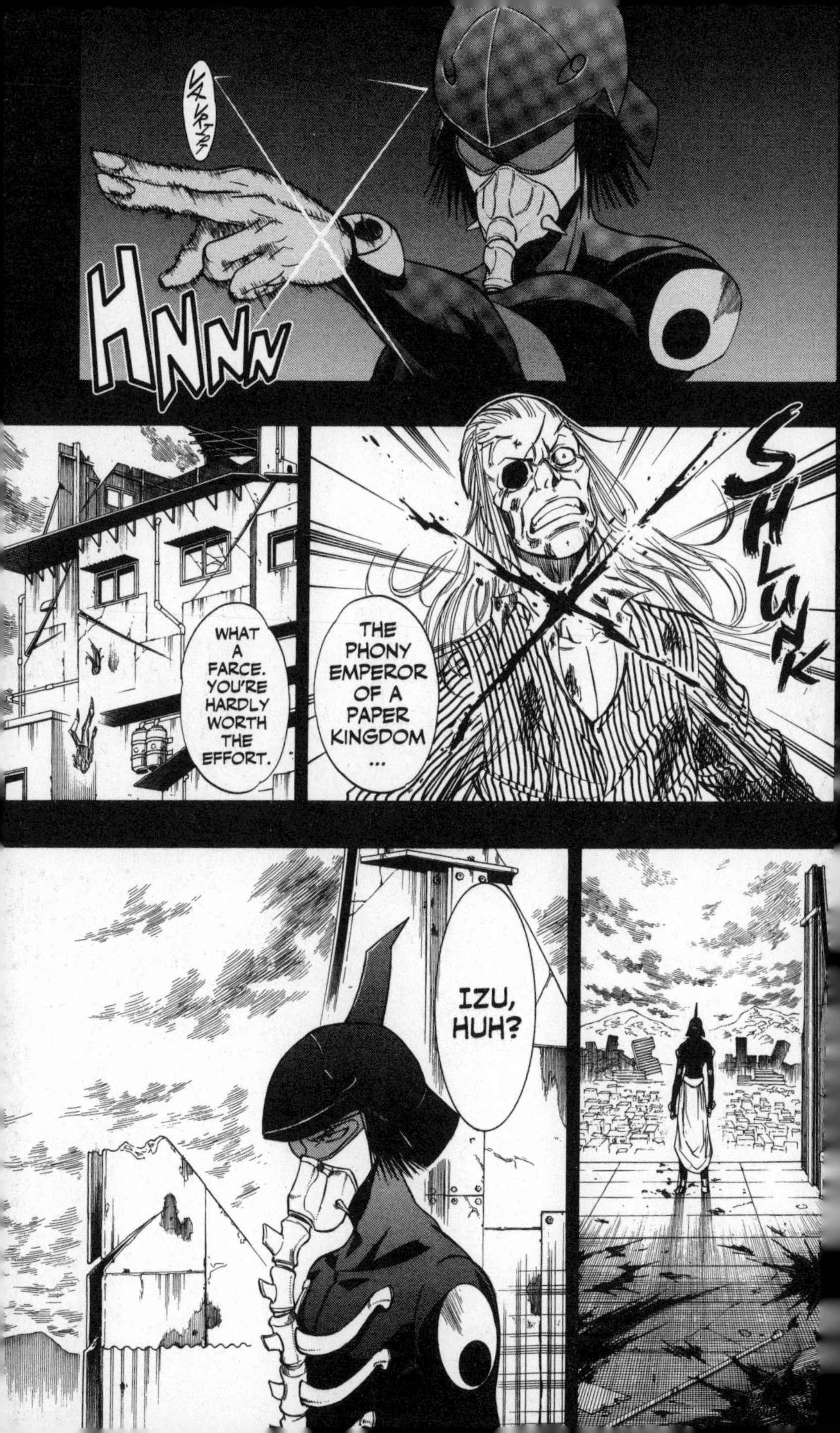
HNNN
SHLUNK
THE PHONY EMPEROR OF A PAPER KINGDOM...
WHAT A FARCE. YOU'RE HARDLY WORTH THE EFFORT.
IZU, HUH?

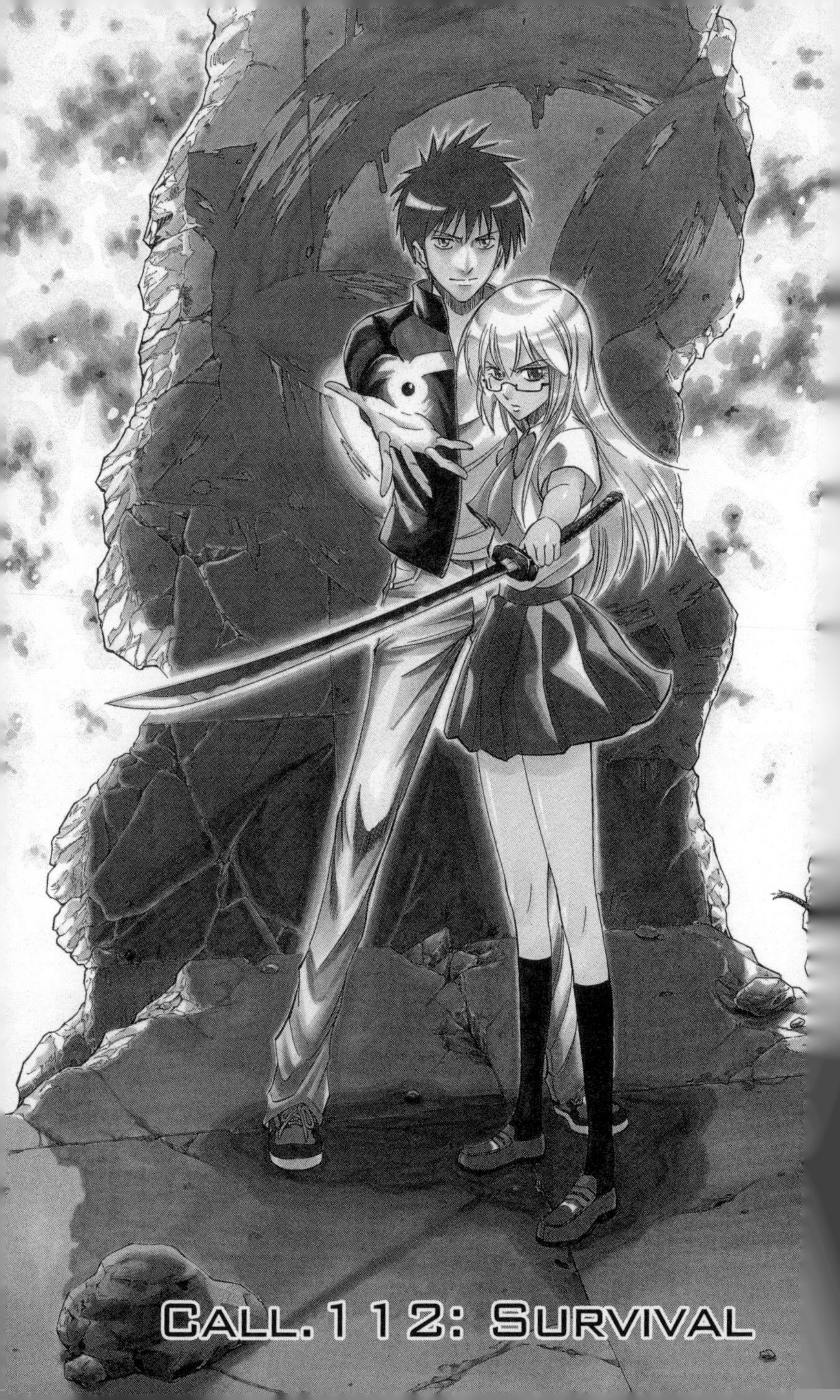
CALL. 112: SURVIVAL

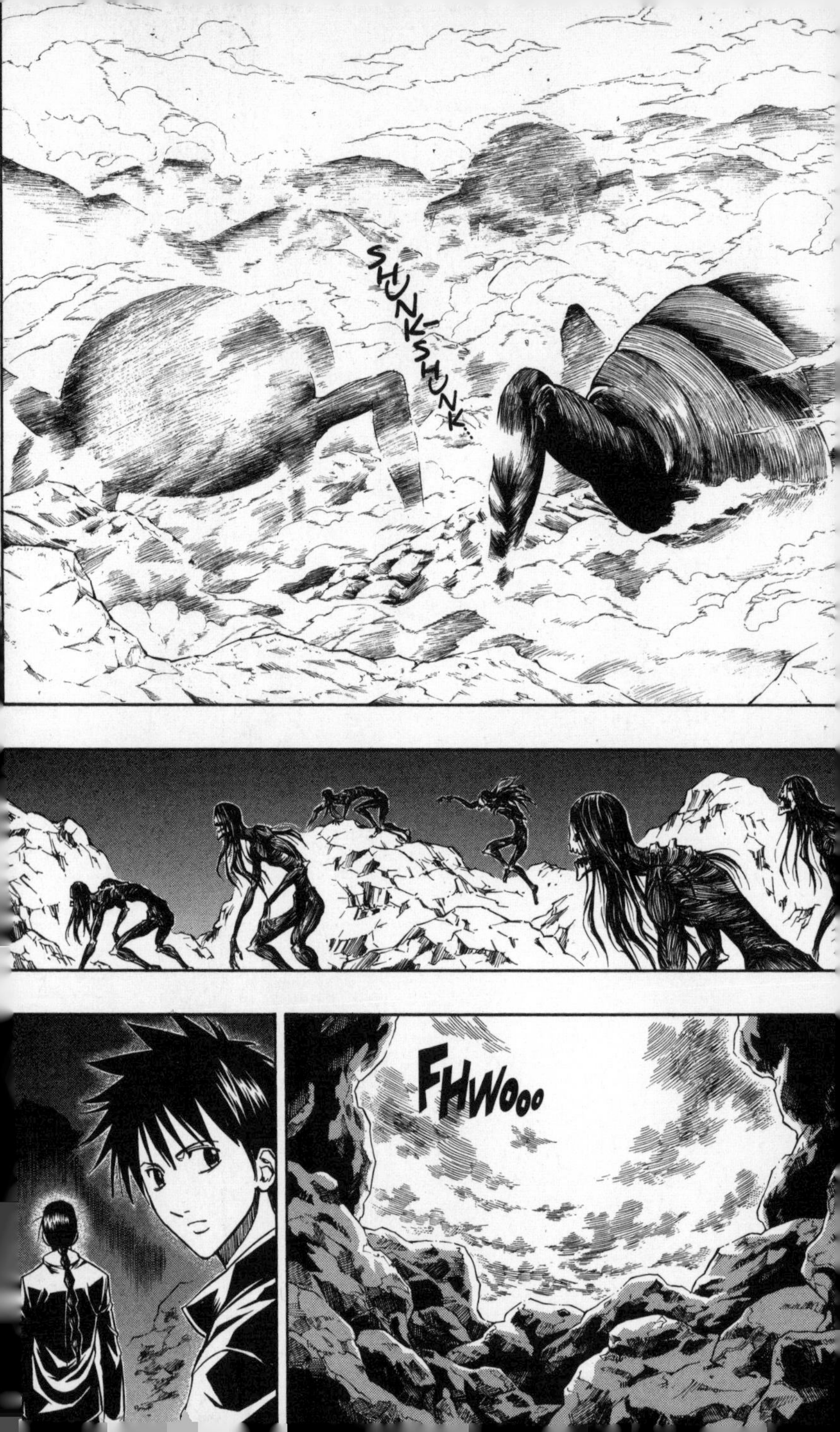
SHUNK SHUNK...
FHWOOO

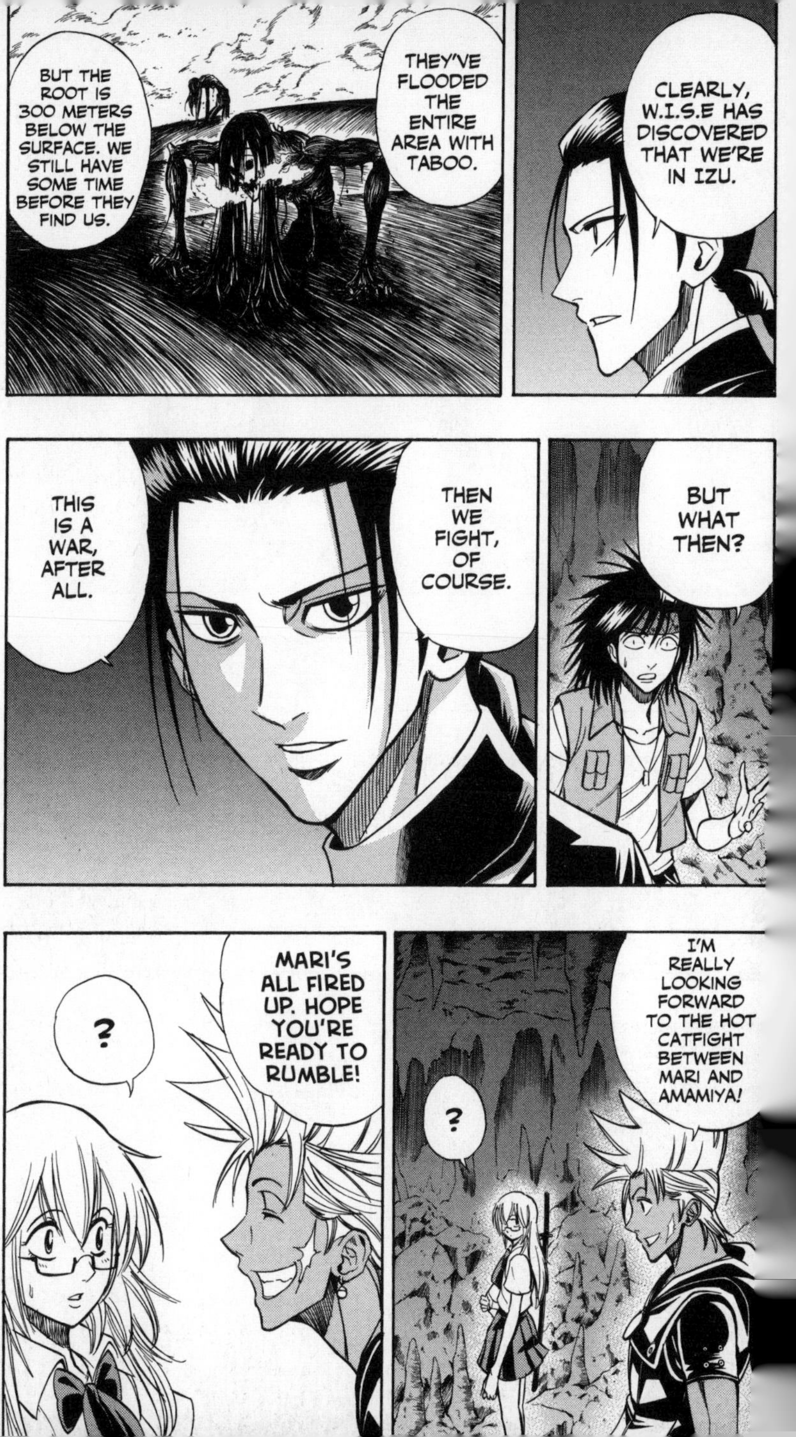
CLEARLY, W.I.S.E HAS DISCOVERED THAT WE'RE IN IZU.
THEY'VE FLOODED THE ENTIRE AREA WITH TABOO.
BUT THE ROOT IS 300 METERS BELOW THE SURFACE. WE STILL HAVE SOME TIME BEFORE THEY FIND US.
BUT WHAT THEN?
THEN WE FIGHT, OF COURSE.
THIS IS A WAR, AFTER ALL.
I'M REALLY LOOKING FORWARD TO THE HOT CATFIGHT BETWEEN MARI AND AMAMIYA!
?
MARI'S ALL FIRED UP. HOPE YOU'RE READY TO RUMBLE!
?

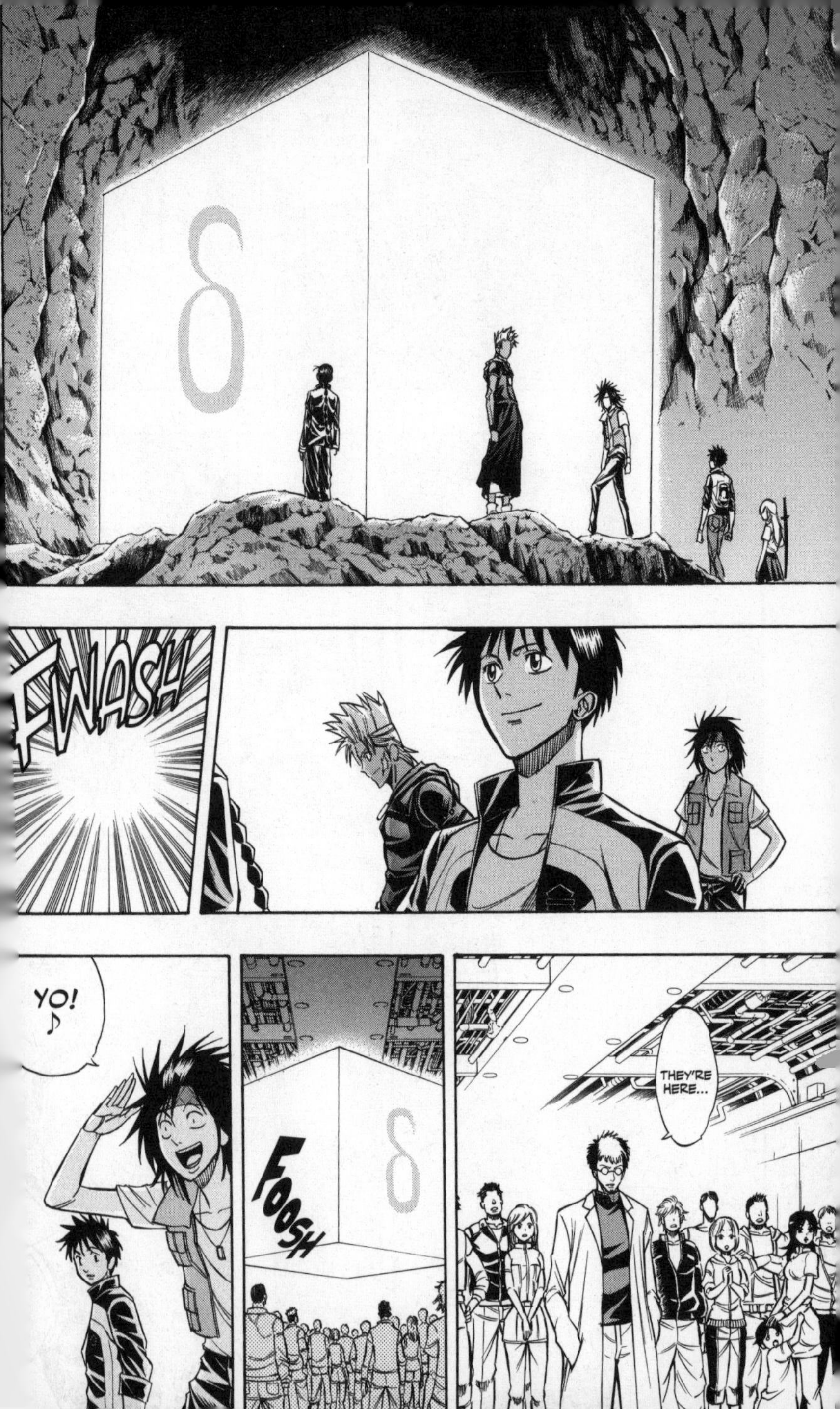
FWASH
THEY'RE HERE...
FOOSH
YO! ♪

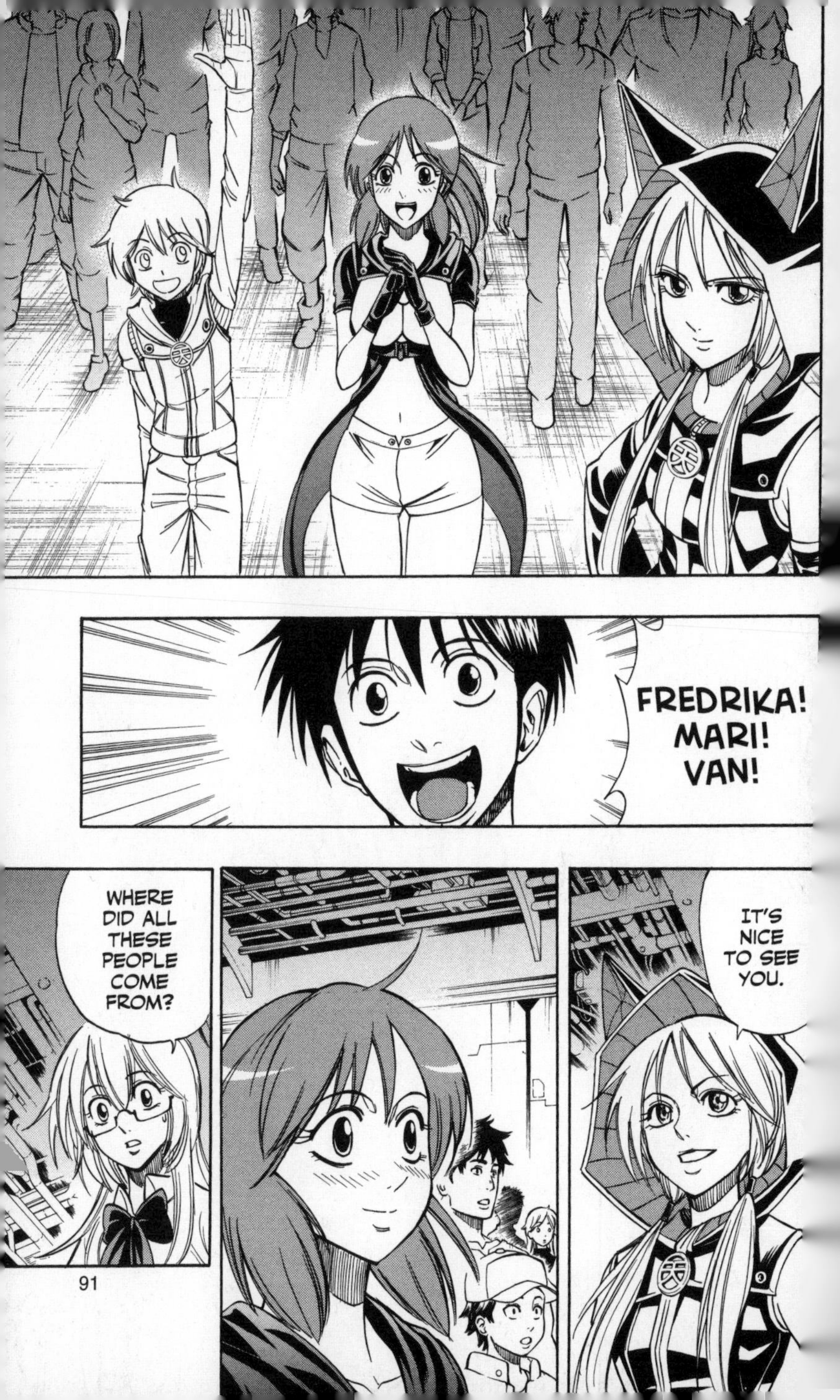
FREDRIKA! MARI! VAN!
IT'S NICE TO SEE YOU.
WHERE DID ALL THESE PEOPLE COME FROM?

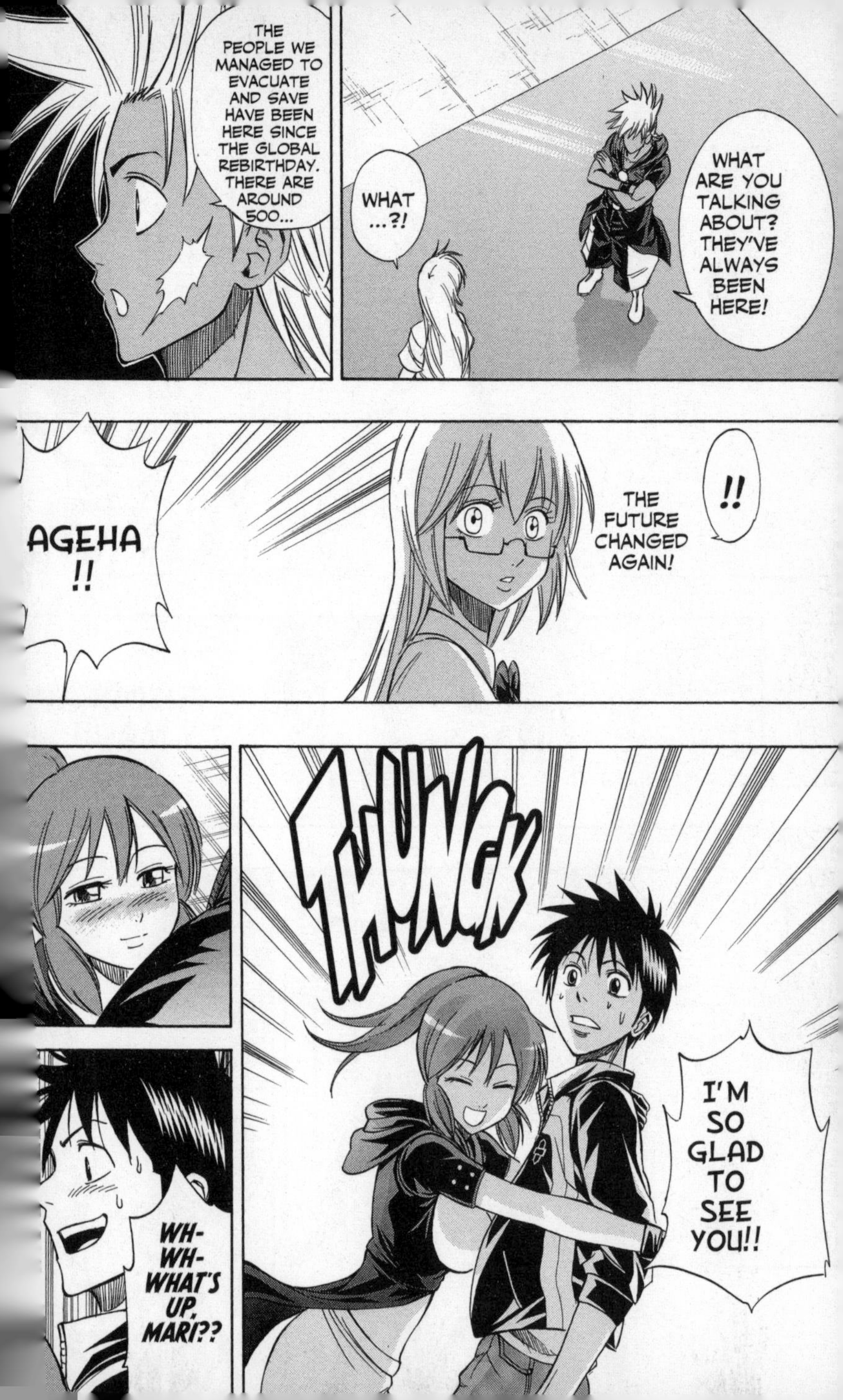
THE PEOPLE WE MANAGED TO EVACUATE AND SAVE HAVE BEEN HERE SINCE THE GLOBAL REBIRTHDAY. THERE ARE AROUND 500...
WHAT ...?!
WHAT ARE YOU TALKING ABOUT? THEY'VE ALWAYS BEEN HERE!
AGEHA !!
THE FUTURE CHANGED AGAIN!
!!
THUNCK
I'M SO GLAD TO SEE YOU!!
WH-WH-WHAT'S UP, MARI??

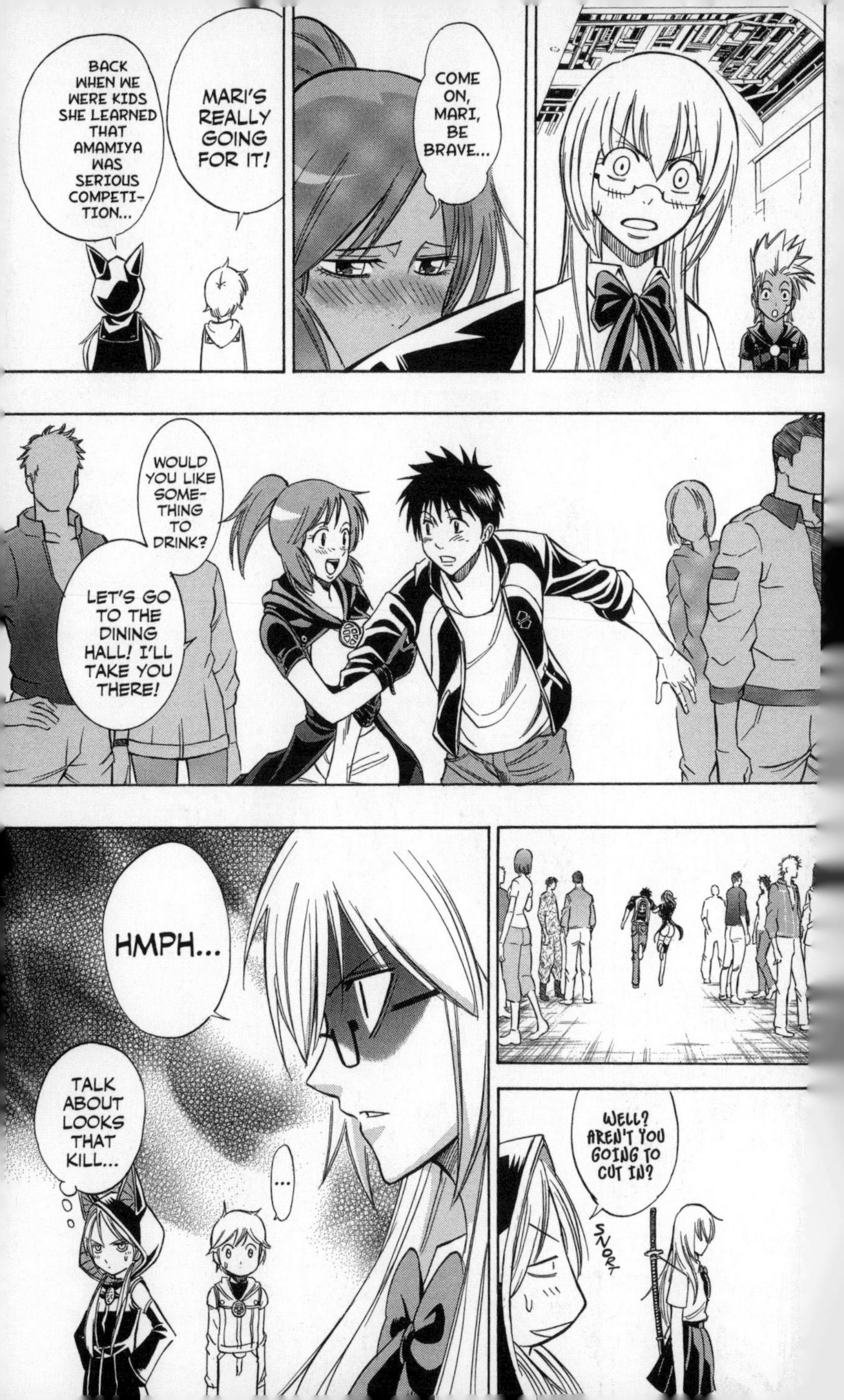
COME ON, MARI, BE BRAVE...
MARI'S REALLY GOING FOR IT!
BACK WHEN WE WERE KIDS SHE LEARNED THAT AMAMIYA WAS SERIOUS COMPETITION...
WOULD YOU LIKE SOMETHING TO DRINK?
LET'S GO TO THE DINING HALL! I'LL TAKE YOU THERE!
WELL? AREN'T YOU GOING TO CUT IN?
SNORT
HMPH...
...
TALK ABOUT LOOKS THAT KILL...

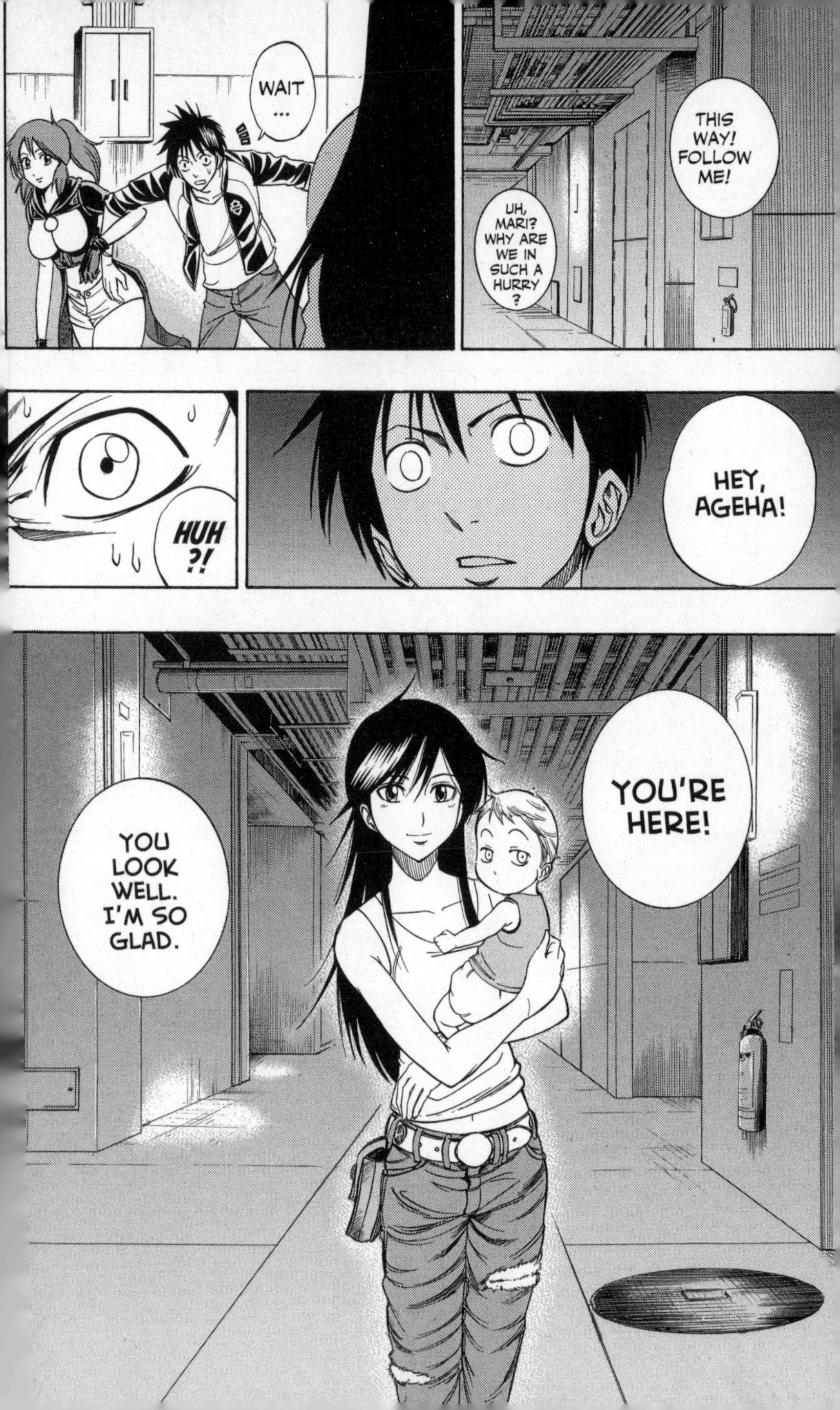
THIS WAY! FOLLOW ME!
UH, MARI? WHY ARE WE IN SUCH A HURRY?
WAIT ...
HEY, AGEHA!
HUH ?!
YOU'RE HERE!
YOU LOOK WELL. I'M SO GLAD.

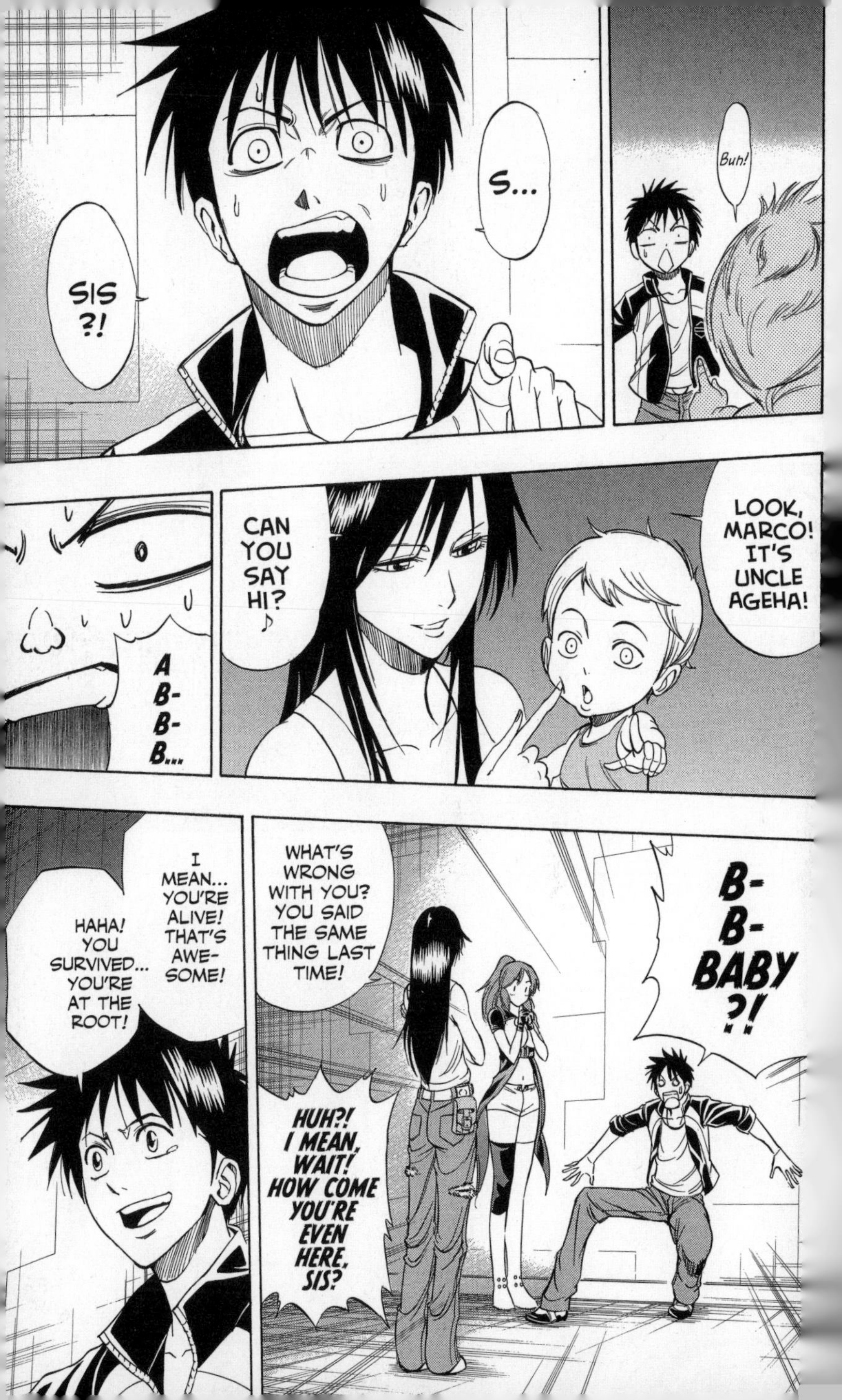
Bun!
S...
SIS ?!
LOOK, MARCO! IT'S UNCLE AGEHA!
CAN YOU SAY HI? ♪
ABB-B-B...
B-B-BABY?!
WHAT'S WRONG WITH YOU? YOU SAID THE SAME THING LAST TIME!
HUH?! I MEAN, WAIT! HOW COME YOU'RE EVEN HERE, SIS?
I MEAN... YOU'RE ALIVE! THAT'S AWESOME!
HAHA! YOU SURVIVED... YOU'RE AT THE ROOT!

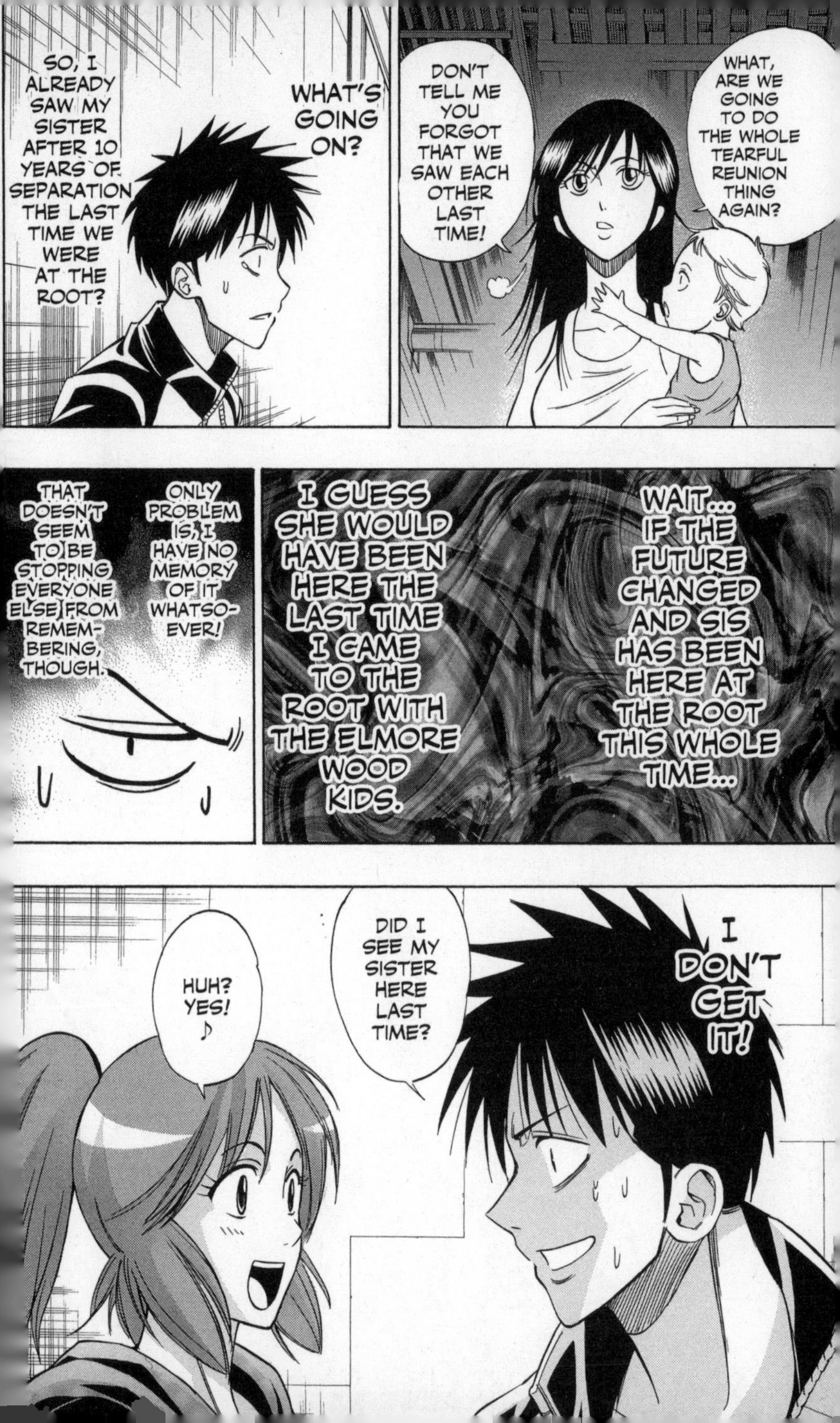
WHAT, ARE WE GOING TO DO THE WHOLE TEARFUL REUNION THING AGAIN?
DON'T TELL ME YOU FORGOT THAT WE SAW EACH OTHER LAST TIME!
WHAT'S GOING ON?
SO, I ALREADY SAW MY SISTER AFTER 10 YEARS OF SEPARATION THE LAST TIME WE WERE AT THE ROOT?
WAIT... IF THE FUTURE CHANGED AND SIS HAS BEEN HERE AT THE ROOT THIS WHOLE TIME...
I GUESS SHE WOULD HAVE BEEN HERE THE LAST TIME I CAME TO THE ROOT WITH THE ELMORE WOOD KIDS.
ONLY PROBLEM IS, I HAVE NO MEMORY OF IT WHATSO-EVER!
THAT DOESN'T SEEM TO BE STOPPING EVERYONE ELSE FROM REMEM-BERING, THOUGH.
I DON'T GET IT!
DID I SEE MY SISTER HERE LAST TIME?
HUH? YES! ♪

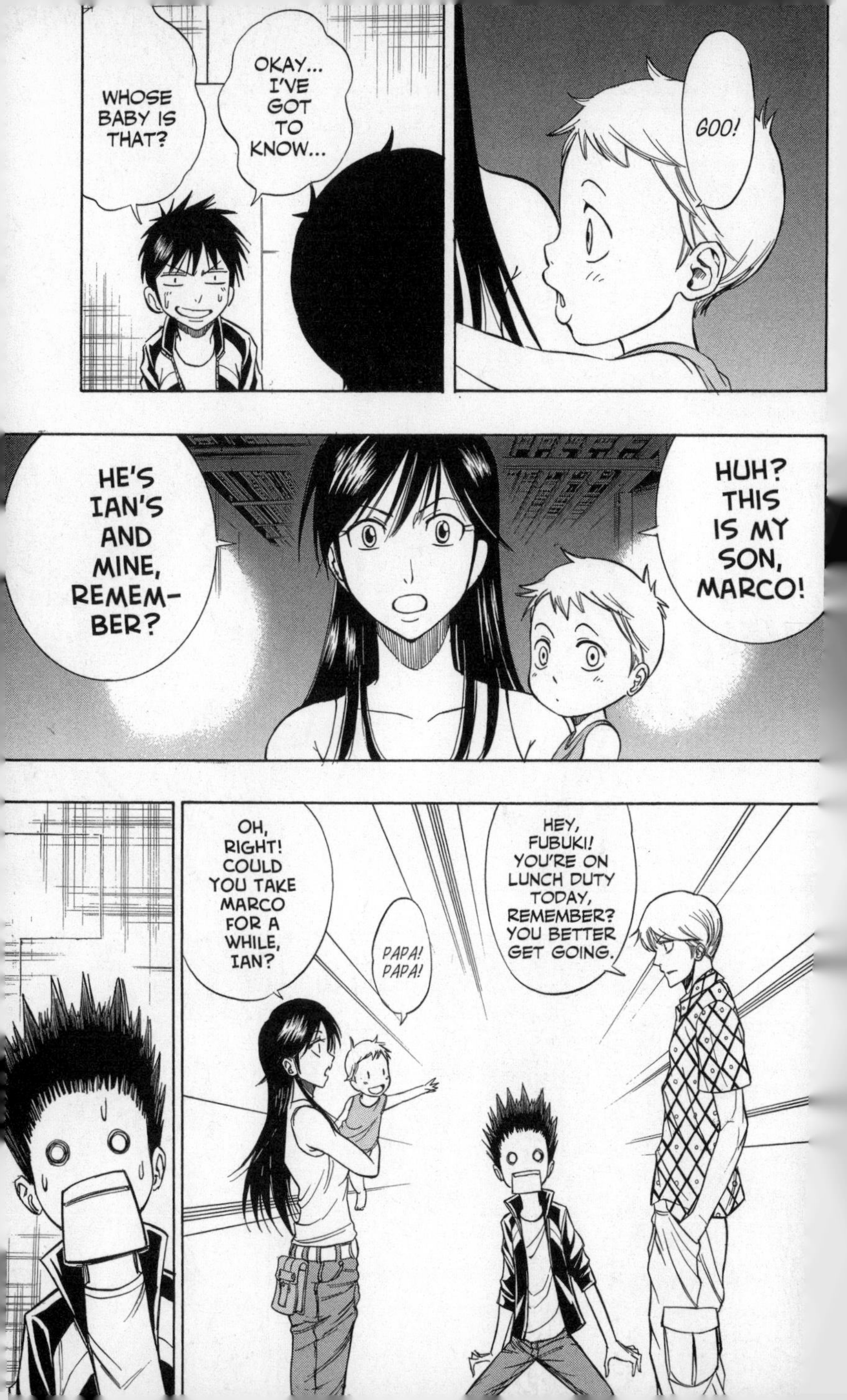
GOO!
OKAY... I'VE GOT TO KNOW...
WHOSE BABY IS THAT?
HUH? THIS IS MY SON, MARCO!
HE'S IAN'S AND MINE, REMEM-BER?
HEY, FUBUKI! YOU'RE ON LUNCH DUTY TODAY, REMEMBER? YOU BETTER GET GOING.
PAPA! PAPA!
OH, RIGHT! COULD YOU TAKE MARCO FOR A WHILE, IAN?

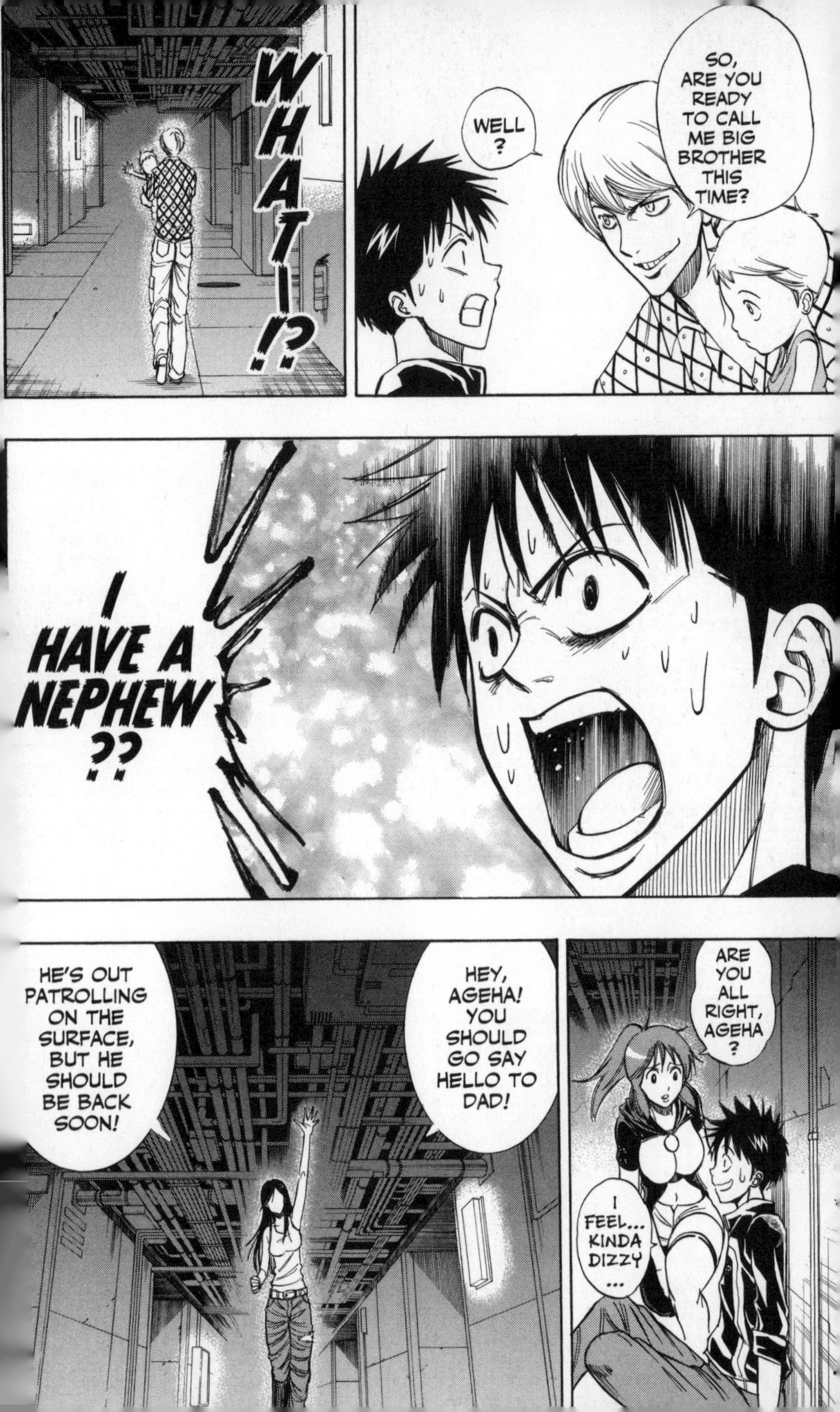
SO, ARE YOU READY TO CALL ME BIG BROTHER THIS TIME?
WELL?
WHAT!?
I HAVE A NEPHEW??
ARE YOU ALL RIGHT, AGEHA?
I FEEL... KINDA DIZZY...
HEY, AGEHA! YOU SHOULD GO SAY HELLO TO DAD!
HE'S OUT PATROLLING ON THE SURFACE, BUT HE SHOULD BE BACK SOON!

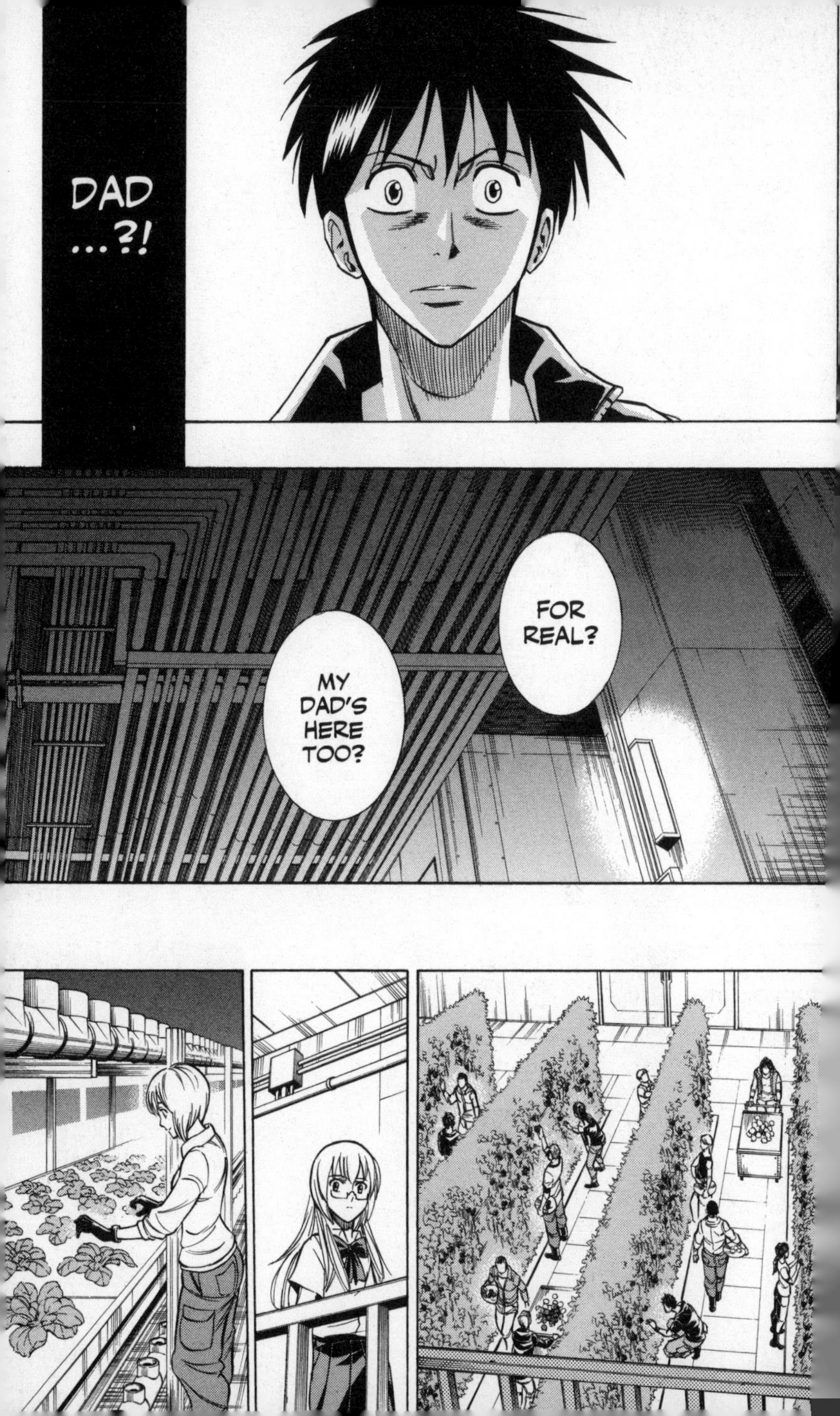
DAD ...?!
FOR REAL?
MY DAD'S HERE TOO?

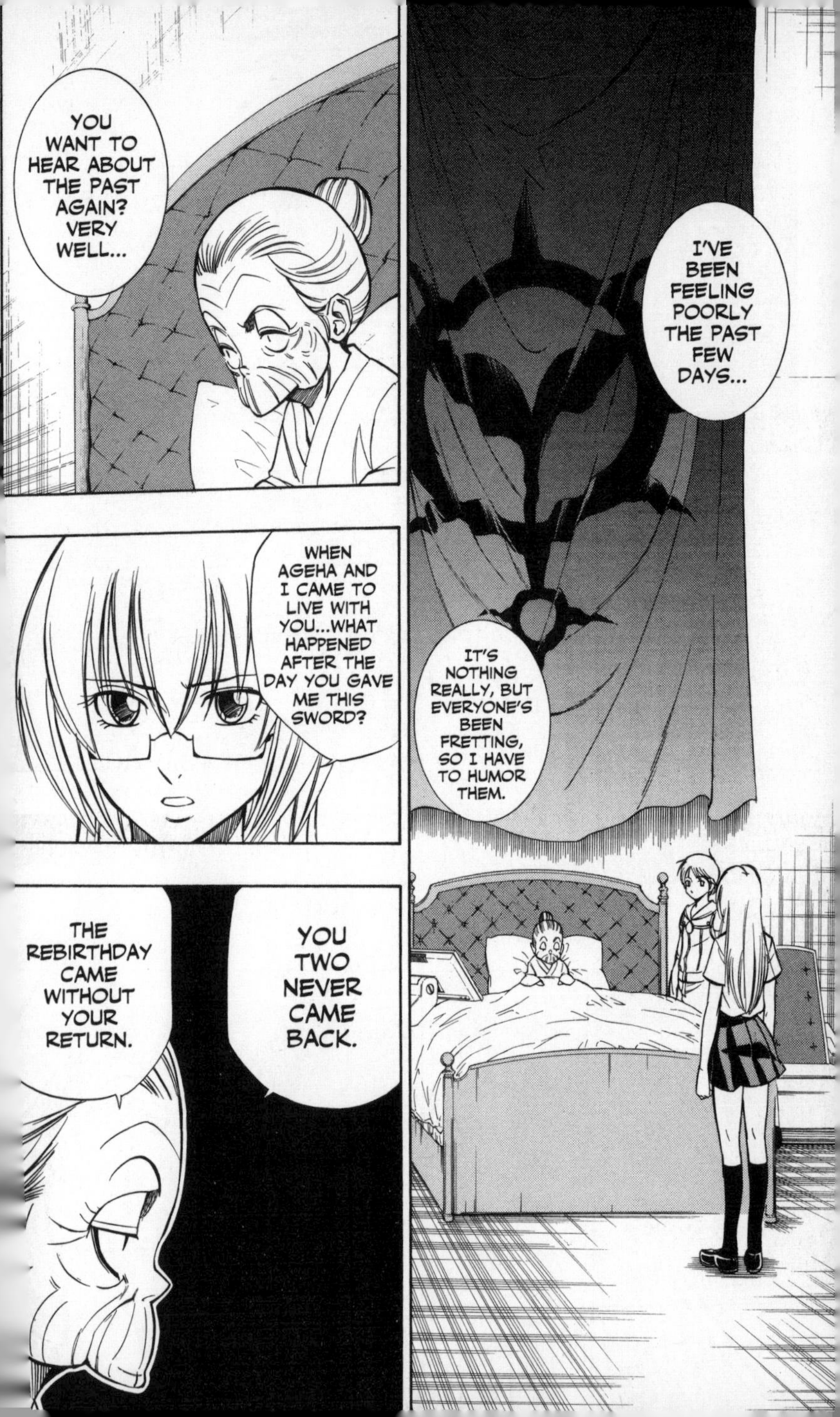
I'VE BEEN FEELING POORLY THE PAST FEW DAYS...
IT'S NOTHING REALLY, BUT EVERYONE'S BEEN FRETTING, SO I HAVE TO HUMOR THEM.
YOU WANT TO HEAR ABOUT THE PAST AGAIN? VERY WELL...
WHEN AGEHA AND I CAME TO LIVE WITH YOU...WHAT HAPPENED AFTER THE DAY YOU GAVE ME THIS SWORD?
YOU TWO NEVER CAME BACK.
THE REBIRTHDAY CAME WITHOUT YOUR RETURN.

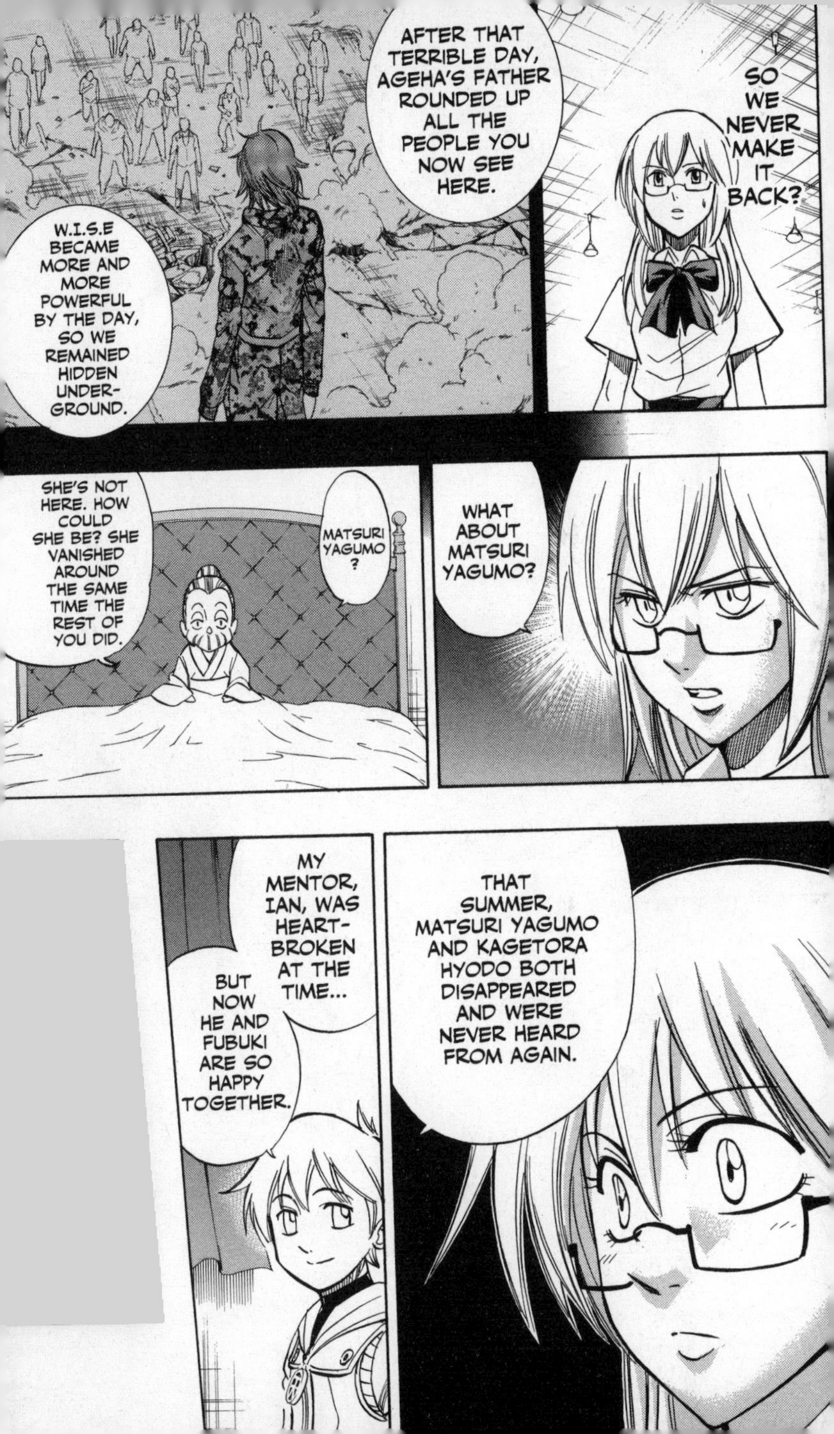
SO WE NEVER MAKE IT BACK?
AFTER THAT TERRIBLE DAY, AGEHA'S FATHER ROUNDED UP ALL THE PEOPLE YOU NOW SEE HERE.
W.I.S.E BECAME MORE AND MORE POWERFUL BY THE DAY, SO WE REMAINED HIDDEN UNDER-GROUND.
WHAT ABOUT MATSURI YAGUMO?
MATSURI YAGUMO?
SHE'S NOT HERE. HOW COULD SHE BE? SHE VANISHED AROUND THE SAME TIME THE REST OF YOU DID.
THAT SUMMER, MATSURI YAGUMO AND KAGETORA HYODO BOTH DISAPPEARED AND WERE NEVER HEARD FROM AGAIN.
MY MENTOR, IAN, WAS HEART-BROKEN AT THE TIME...
BUT NOW HE AND FUBUKI ARE SO HAPPY TOGETHER.

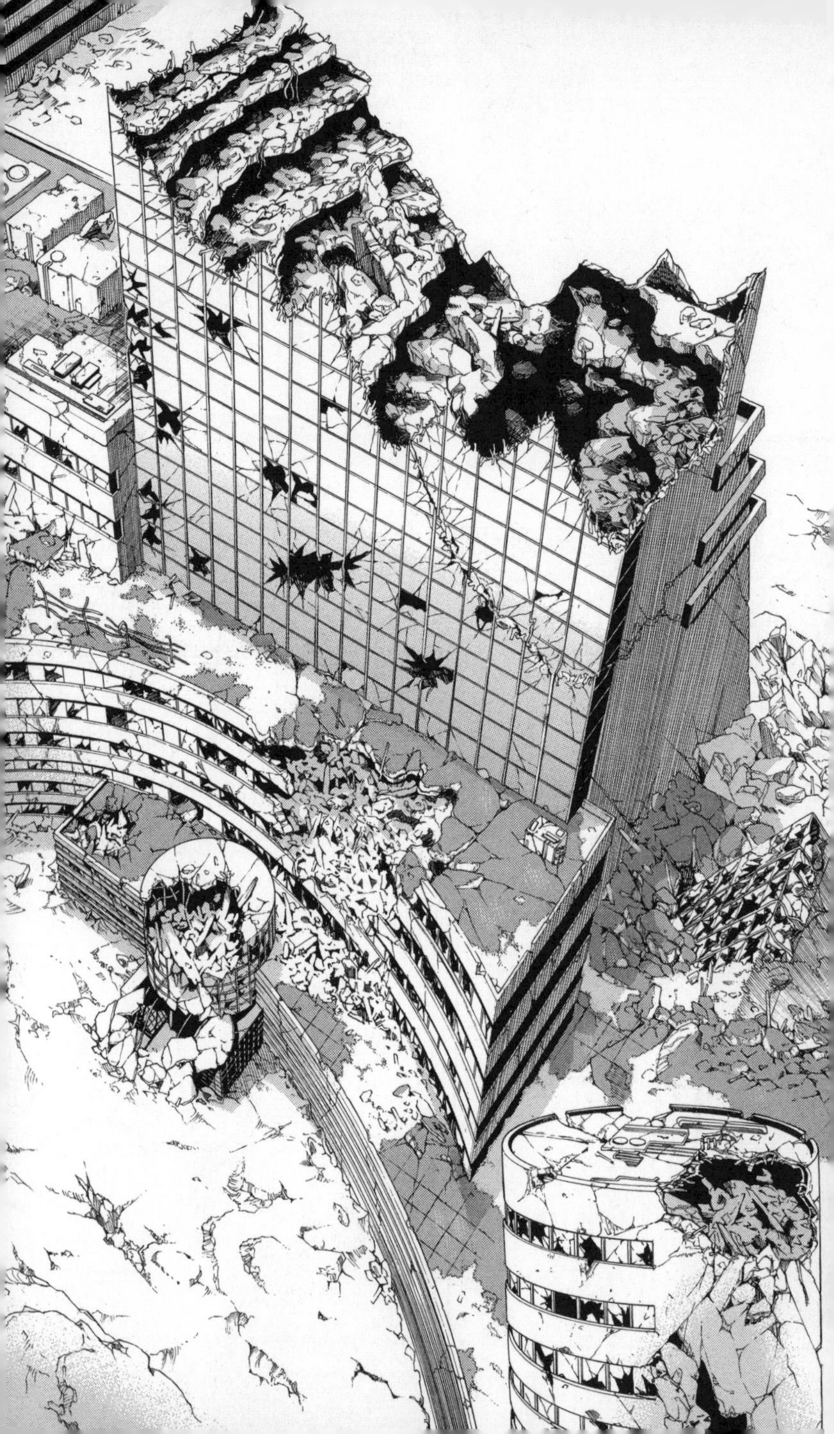

THEIR HIDEOUT MUST BE UNDERNEATH THIS BUILDING.

THE HEAVENLY TREE GENERAL HOSPITAL, FOUNDED BY ELMORE TENJUIN... IT TOOK A WHILE TO TRACK IT DOWN SINCE THERE AREN'T MANY RECORDS LEFT FROM THE OLD DAYS, ESPECIALLY OUT HERE IN THE BOONIES.

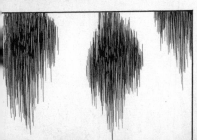

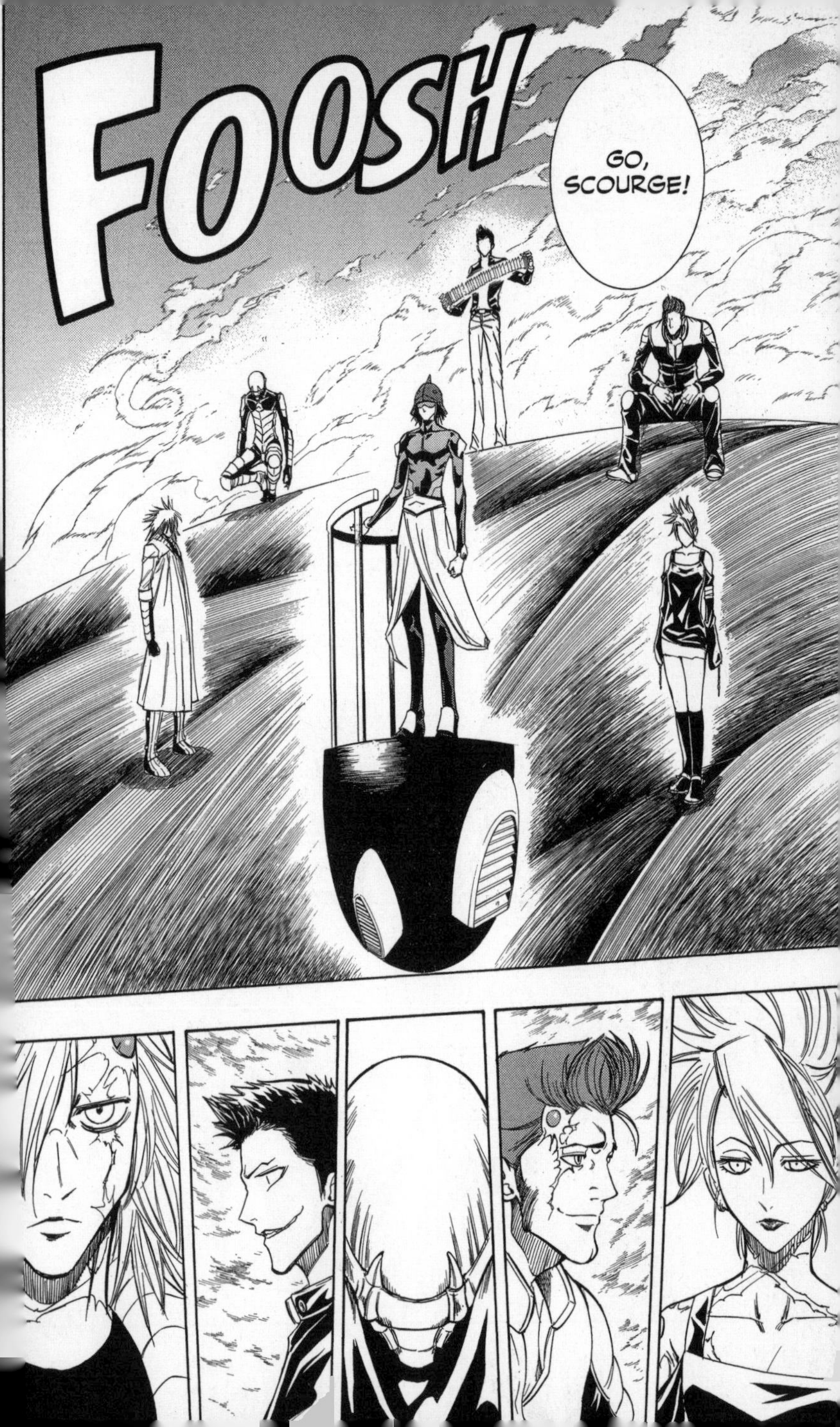
FOOSH
GO, SCOURGE!

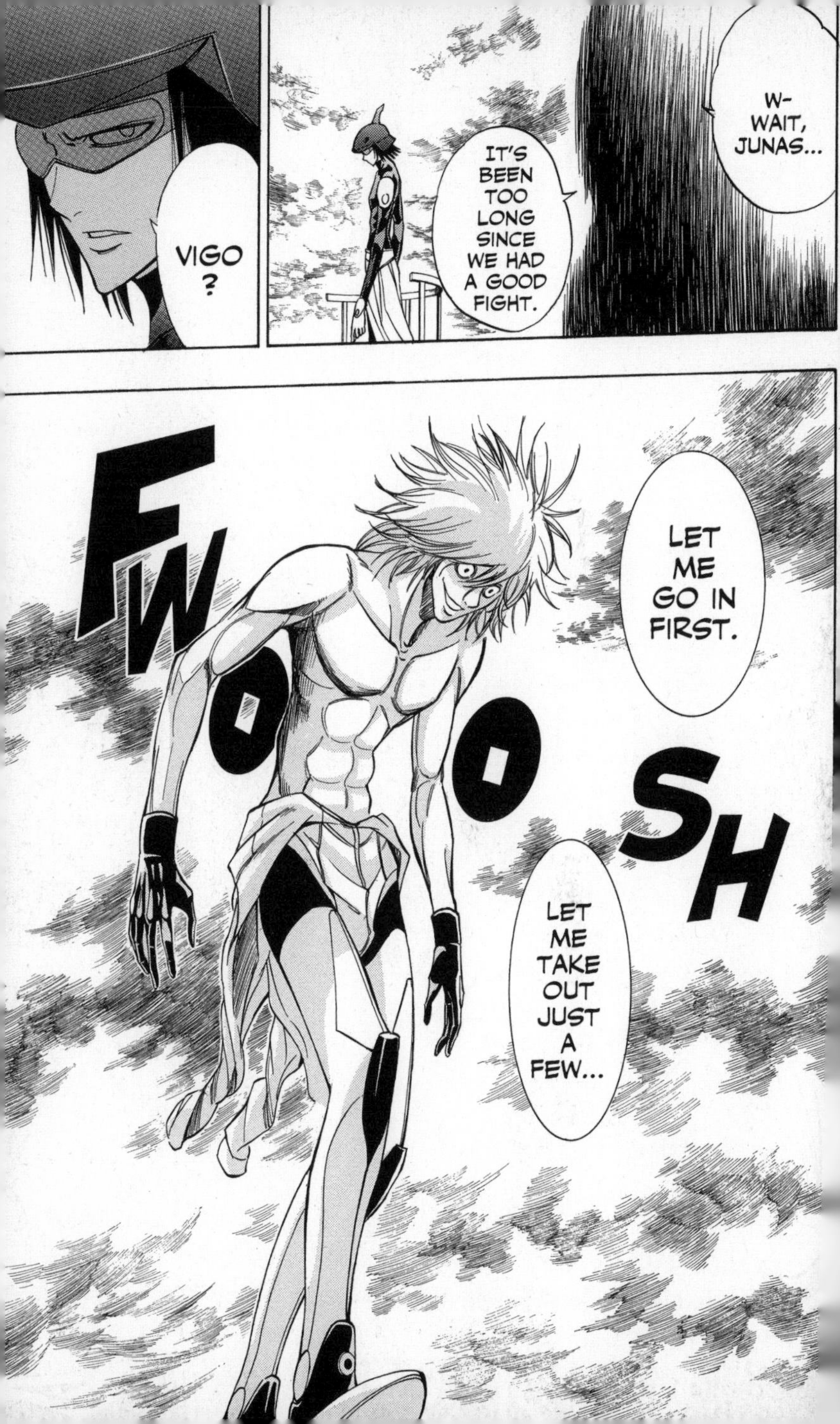
W- WAIT, JUNAS...
IT'S BEEN TOO LONG SINCE WE HAD A GOOD FIGHT.
VIGO?
LET ME GO IN FIRST.
FWOOOSH
LET ME TAKE OUT JUST A FEW...

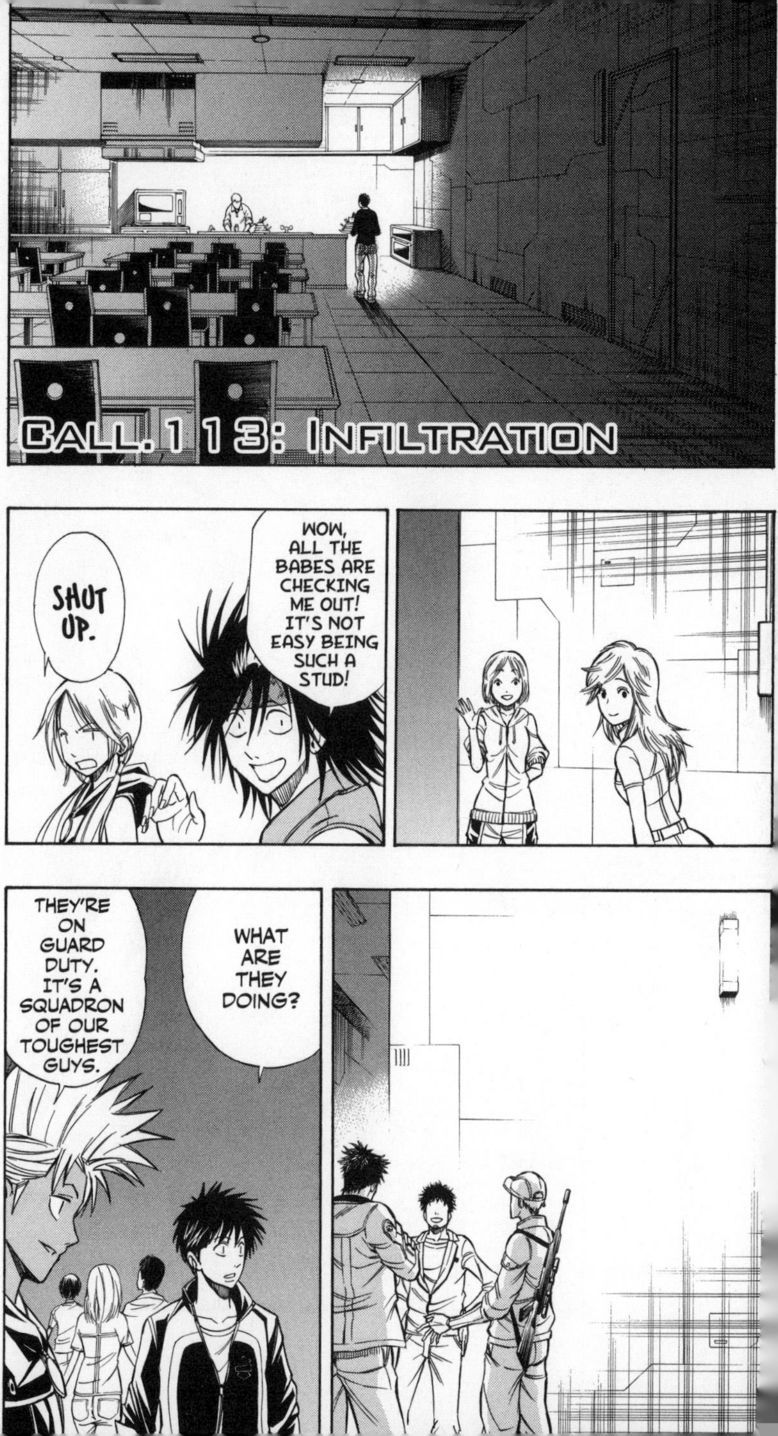
CALL.113: INFILTRATION
WOW, ALL THE BABES ARE CHECKING ME OUT! IT'S NOT EASY BEING SUCH A STUD!
SHUT UP.
WHAT ARE THEY DOING?
THEY'RE ON GUARD DUTY. IT'S A SQUADRON OF OUR TOUGHEST GUYS.

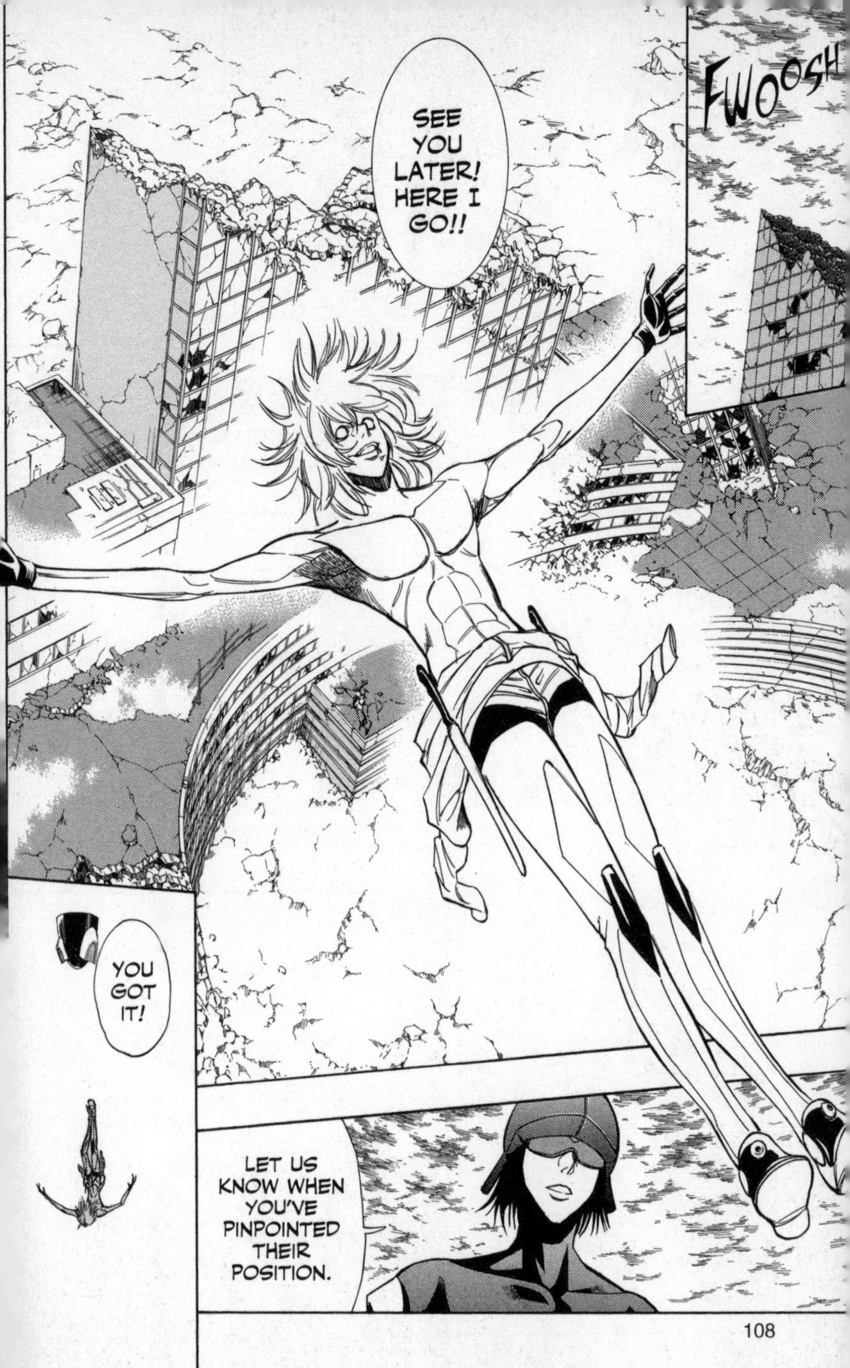
FWOOSH
SEE YOU LATER! HERE I GO!!
LET US KNOW WHEN YOU'VE PINPOINTED THEIR POSITION.
YOU GOT IT!

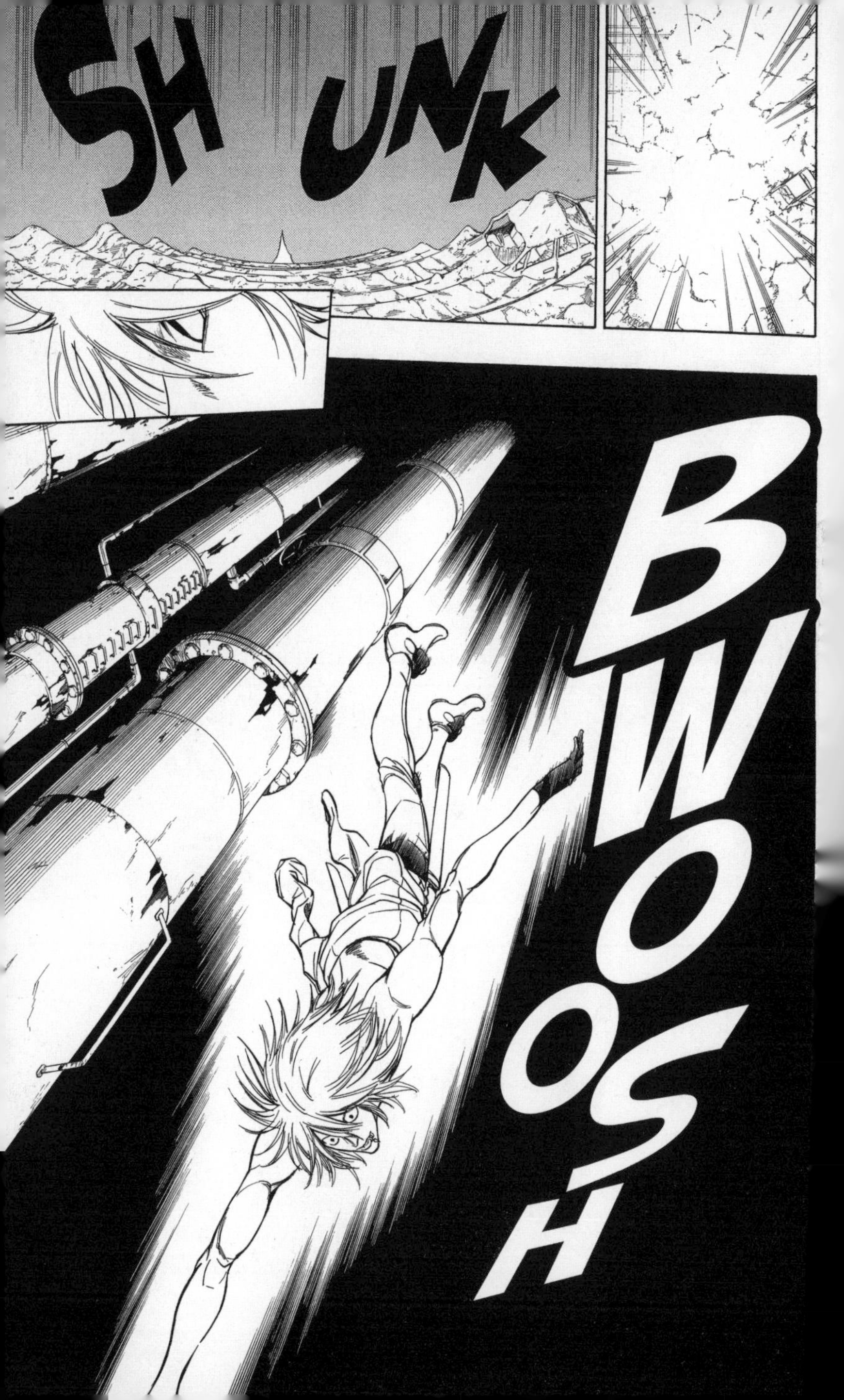
SHUNK
BWOOSH

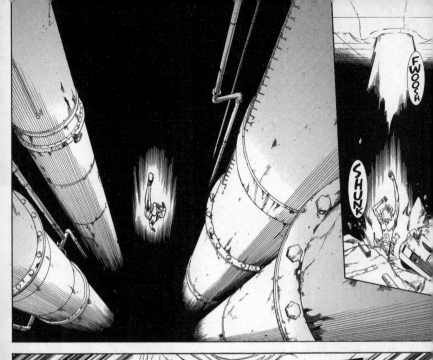

DEEP, DEEP DOWN UNDER-GROUND... THERE'S SOME-THING HUGE UP AHEAD!

FWOOSH

THIS IS IT!

TUNK

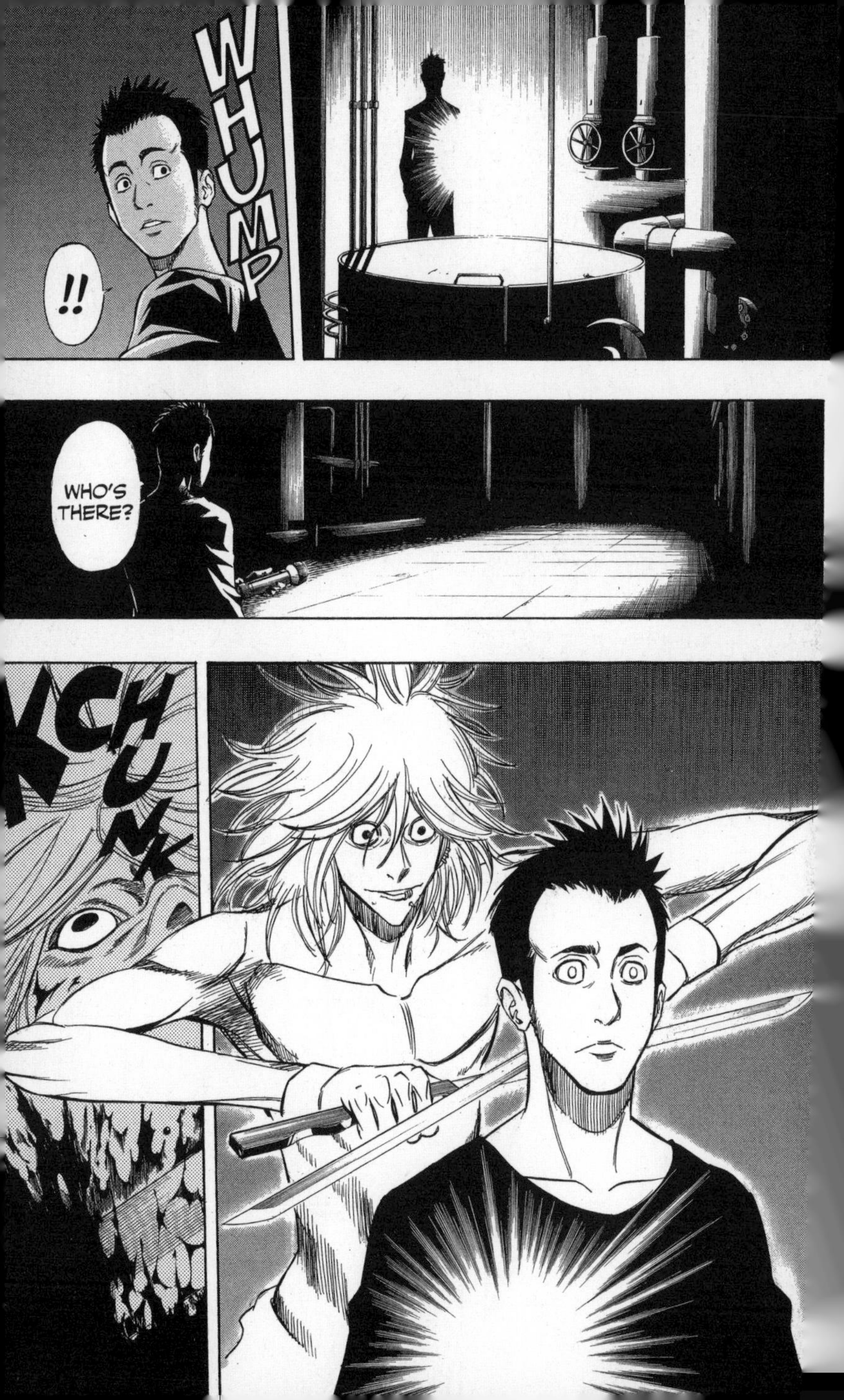
WHUMP
!!
WHO'S THERE?
KCHUNK

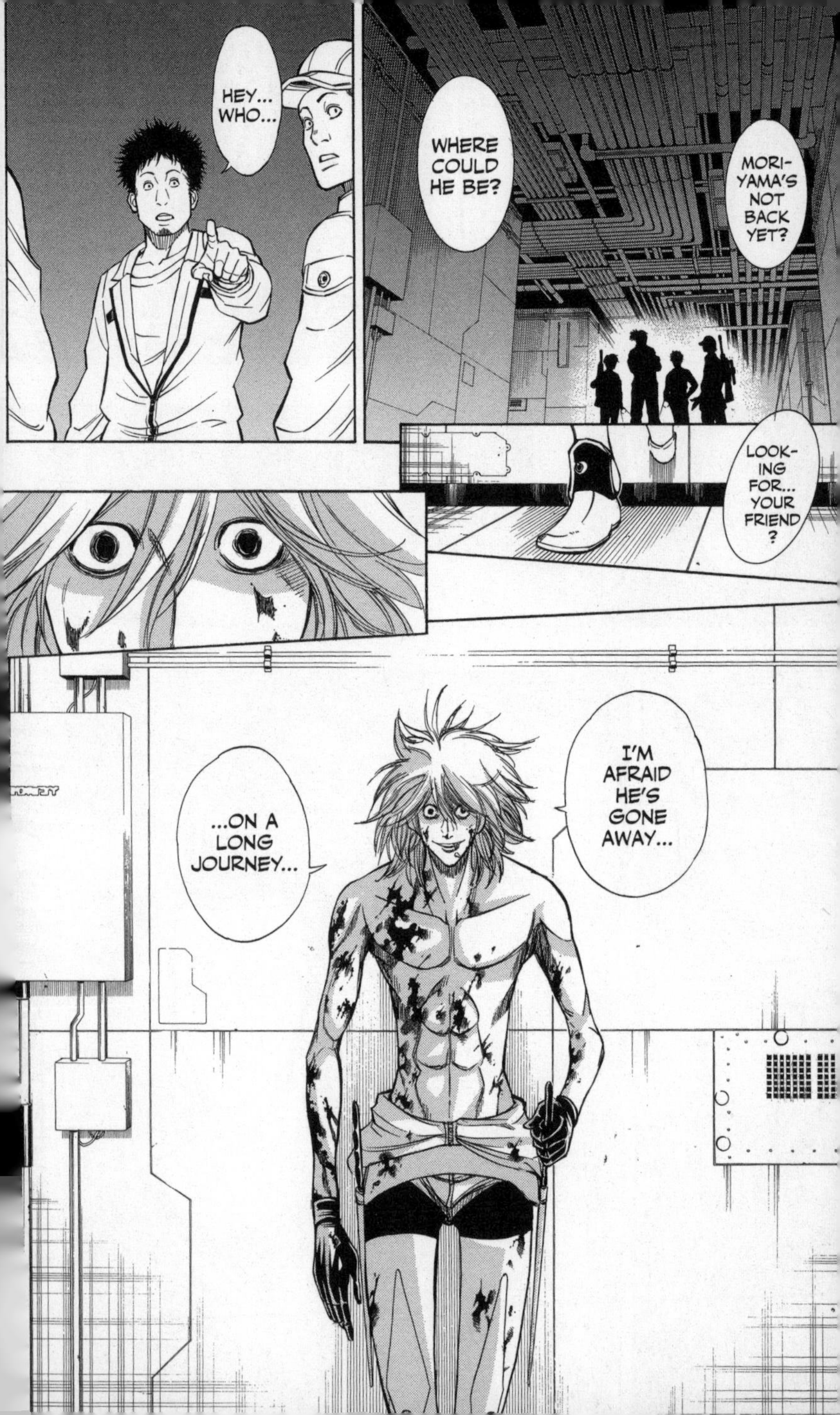
MORI-YAMA'S NOT BACK YET?
WHERE COULD HE BE?
HEY... WHO...
LOOK-ING FOR... YOUR FRIEND?
I'M AFRAID HE'S GONE AWAY...
...ON A LONG JOURNEY...

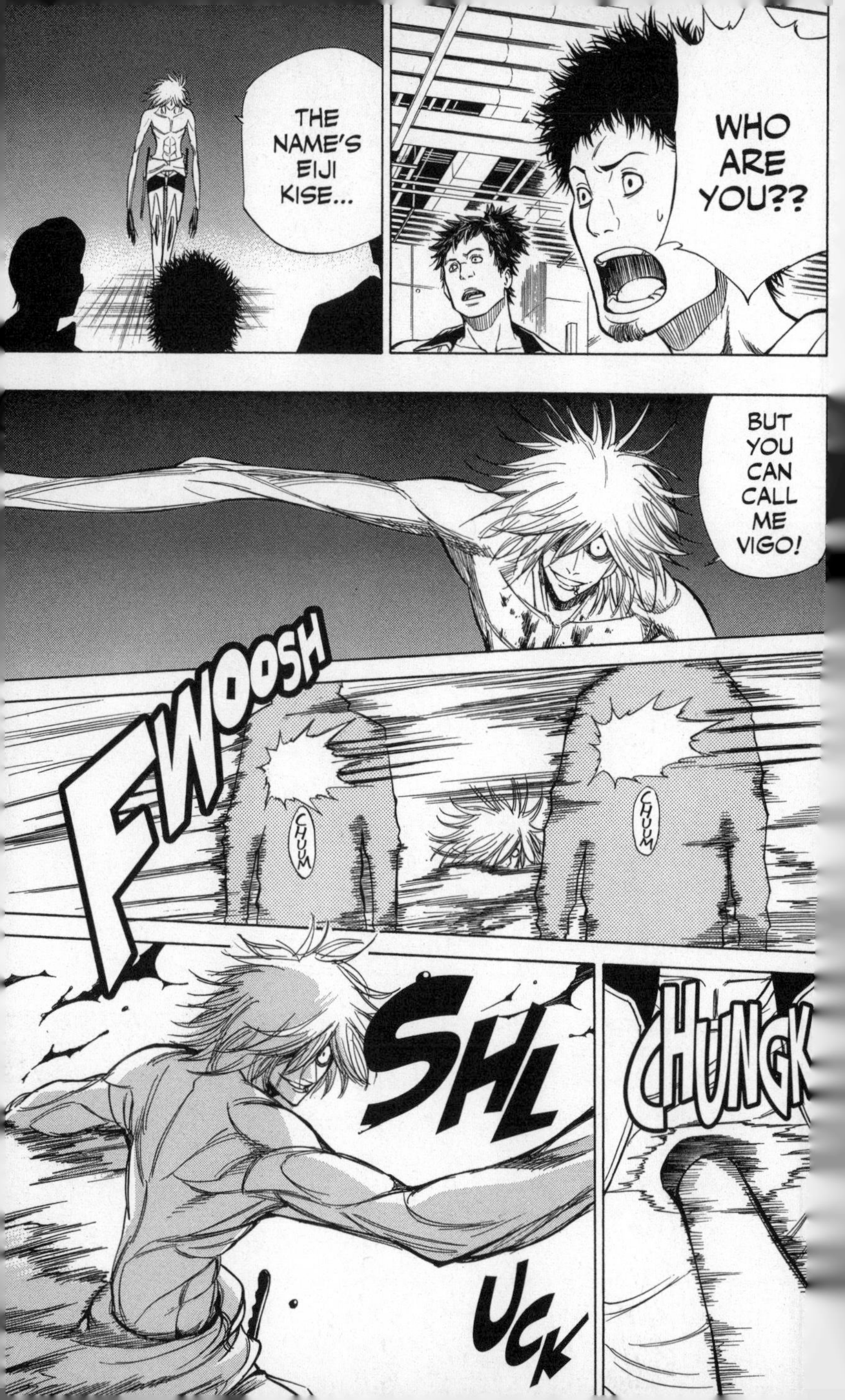
WHO ARE YOU??
THE NAME'S EIJI KISE...
BUT YOU CAN CALL ME VIGO!
FWOOSH
CHUUM
CHUUM
CHUNGK
SHL
UCK

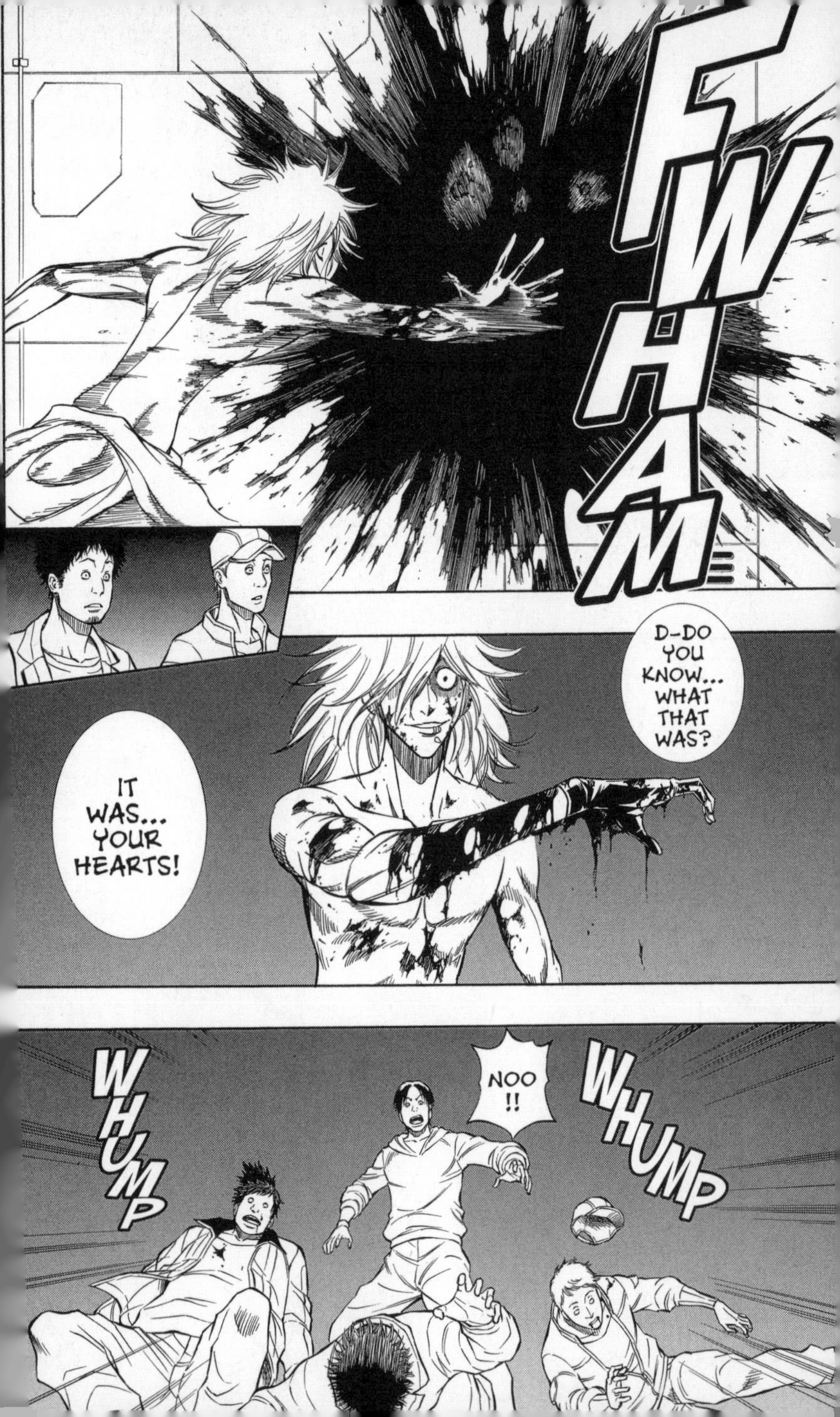
FWHAM
D-DO YOU KNOW... WHAT THAT WAS?
IT WAS... YOUR HEARTS!
WHUMP
NOO !!
WHUMP

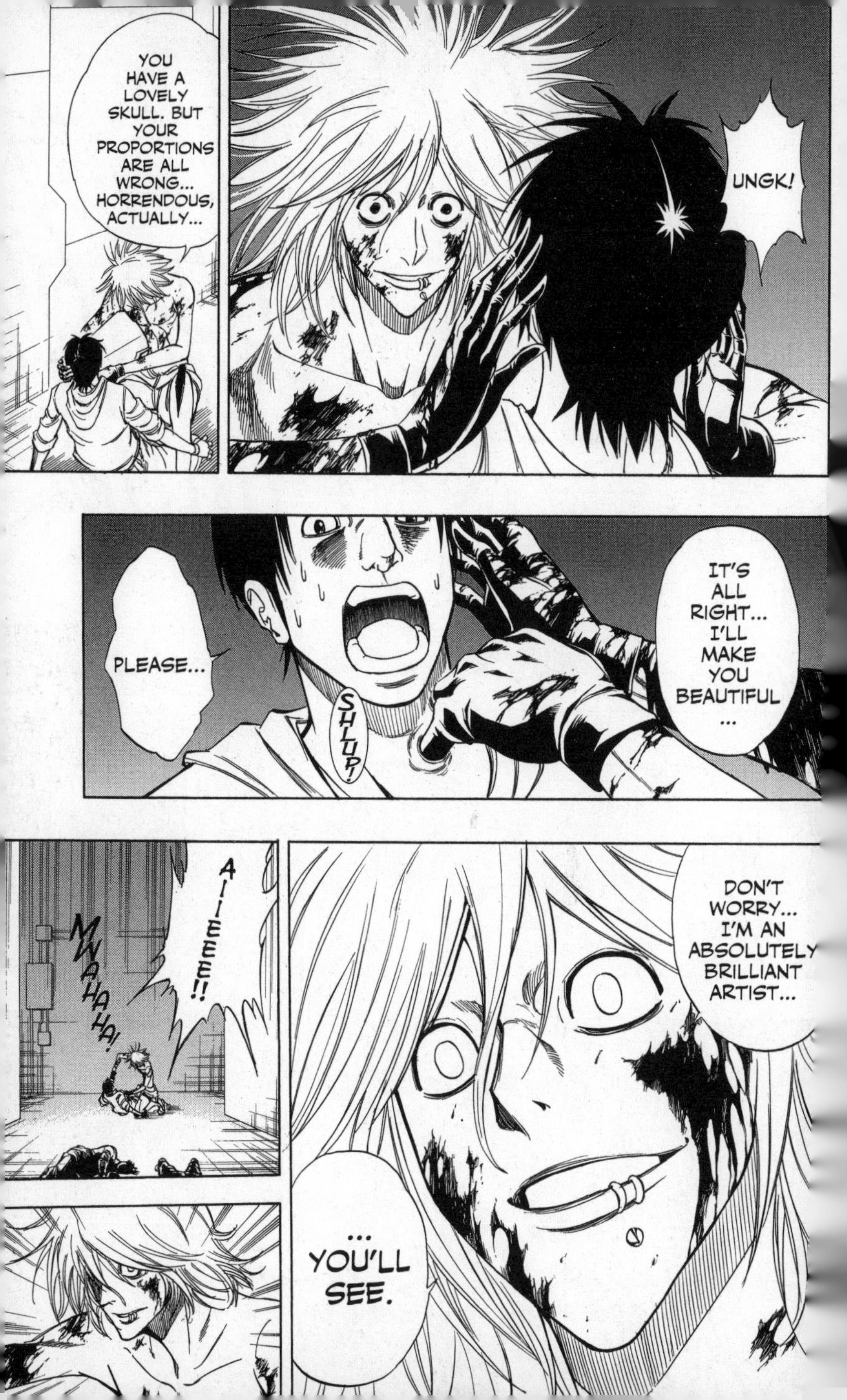
UNGK!
YOU HAVE A LOVELY SKULL. BUT YOUR PROPORTIONS ARE ALL WRONG... HORRENDOUS, ACTUALLY...
IT'S ALL RIGHT... I'LL MAKE YOU BEAUTIFUL ...
SHLUP!
PLEASE...
DON'T WORRY... I'M AN ABSOLUTELY BRILLIANT ARTIST...
... YOU'LL SEE.
AIIEEEE!!
MWAHAHAHA!

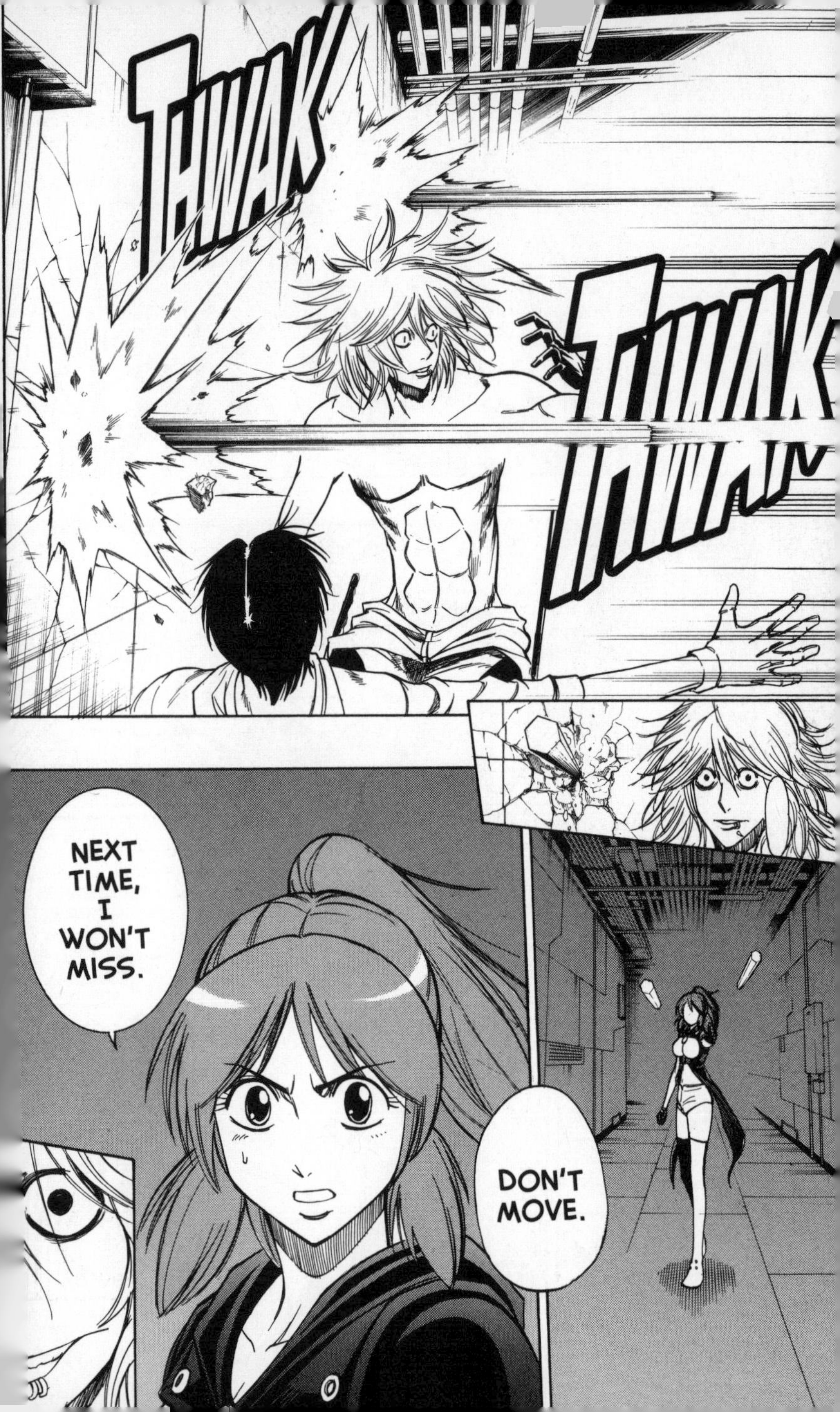
THWAK
THWAK
DON'T MOVE.
NEXT TIME, I WON'T MISS.

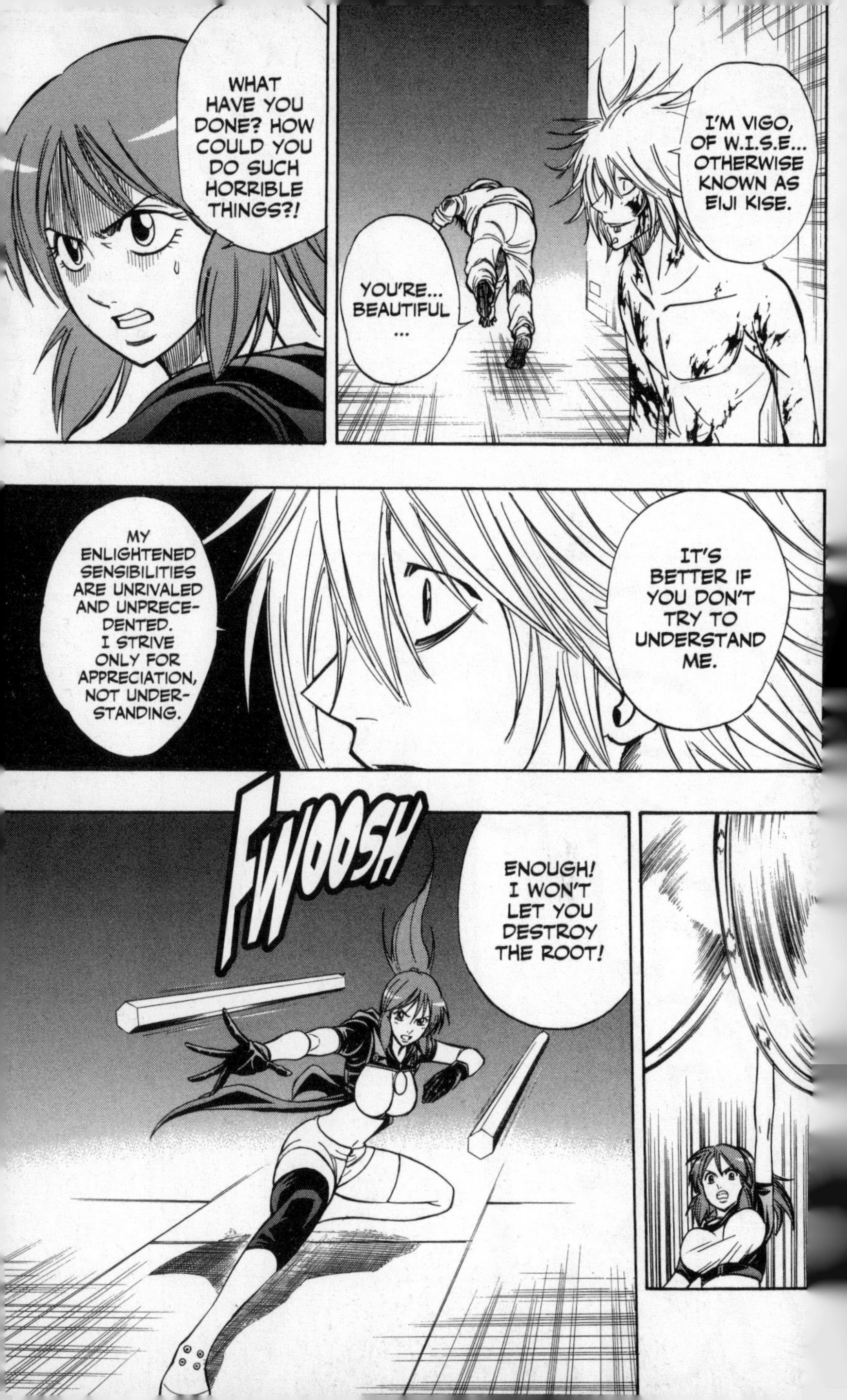
I'M VIGO, OF W.I.S.E... OTHERWISE KNOWN AS EIJI KISE.
YOU'RE... BEAUTIFUL ...
WHAT HAVE YOU DONE? HOW COULD YOU DO SUCH HORRIBLE THINGS?!
IT'S BETTER IF YOU DON'T TRY TO UNDERSTAND ME.
MY ENLIGHTENED SENSIBILITIES ARE UNRIVALED AND UNPRECE-DENTED. I STRIVE ONLY FOR APPRECIATION, NOT UNDER-STANDING.
ENOUGH! I WON'T LET YOU DESTROY THE ROOT!
FWOOSH

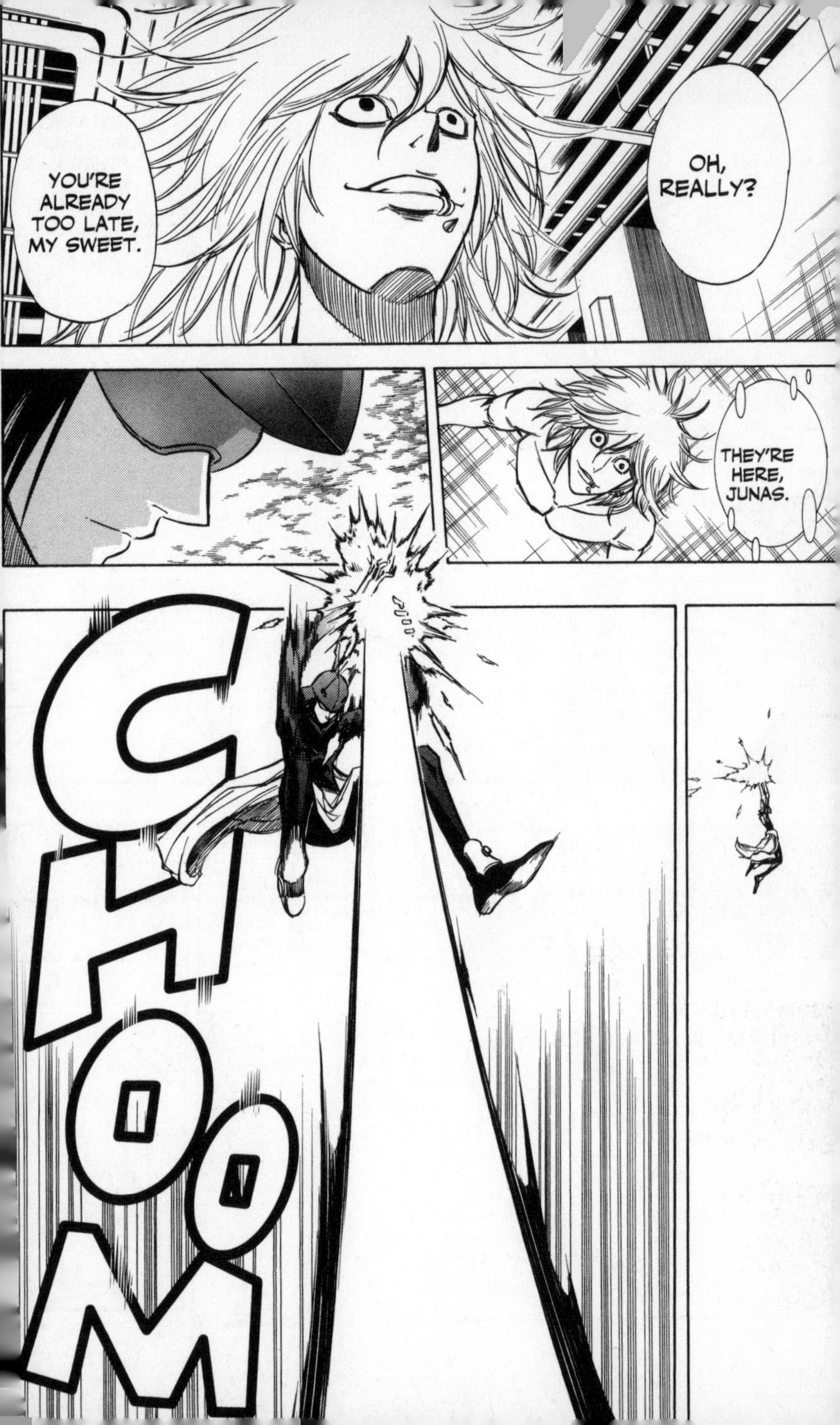
OH, REALLY?
YOU'RE ALREADY TOO LATE, MY SWEET.
THEY'RE HERE, JUNAS.
CHOOOM

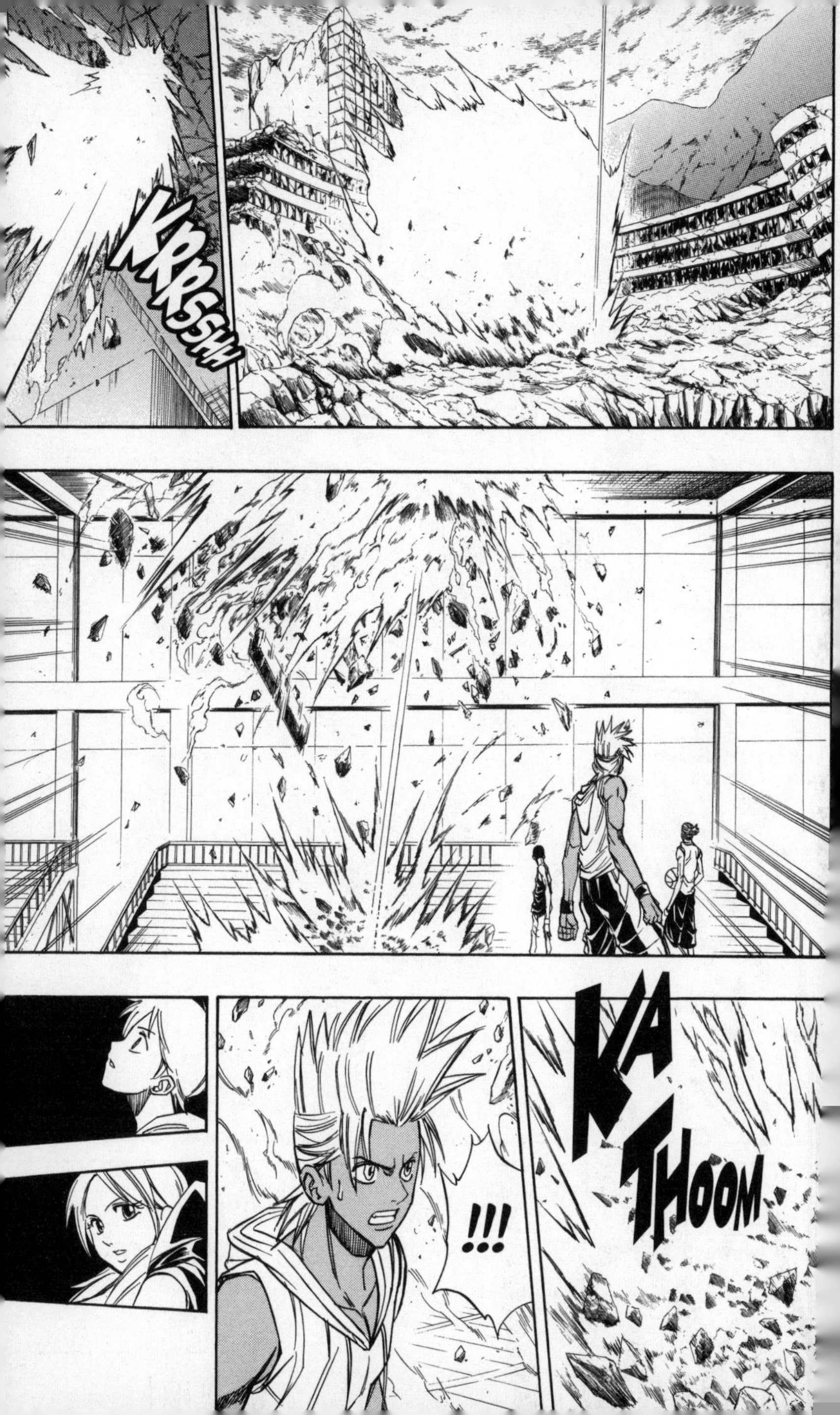
KRRSSHH
KA THOOM
!!!

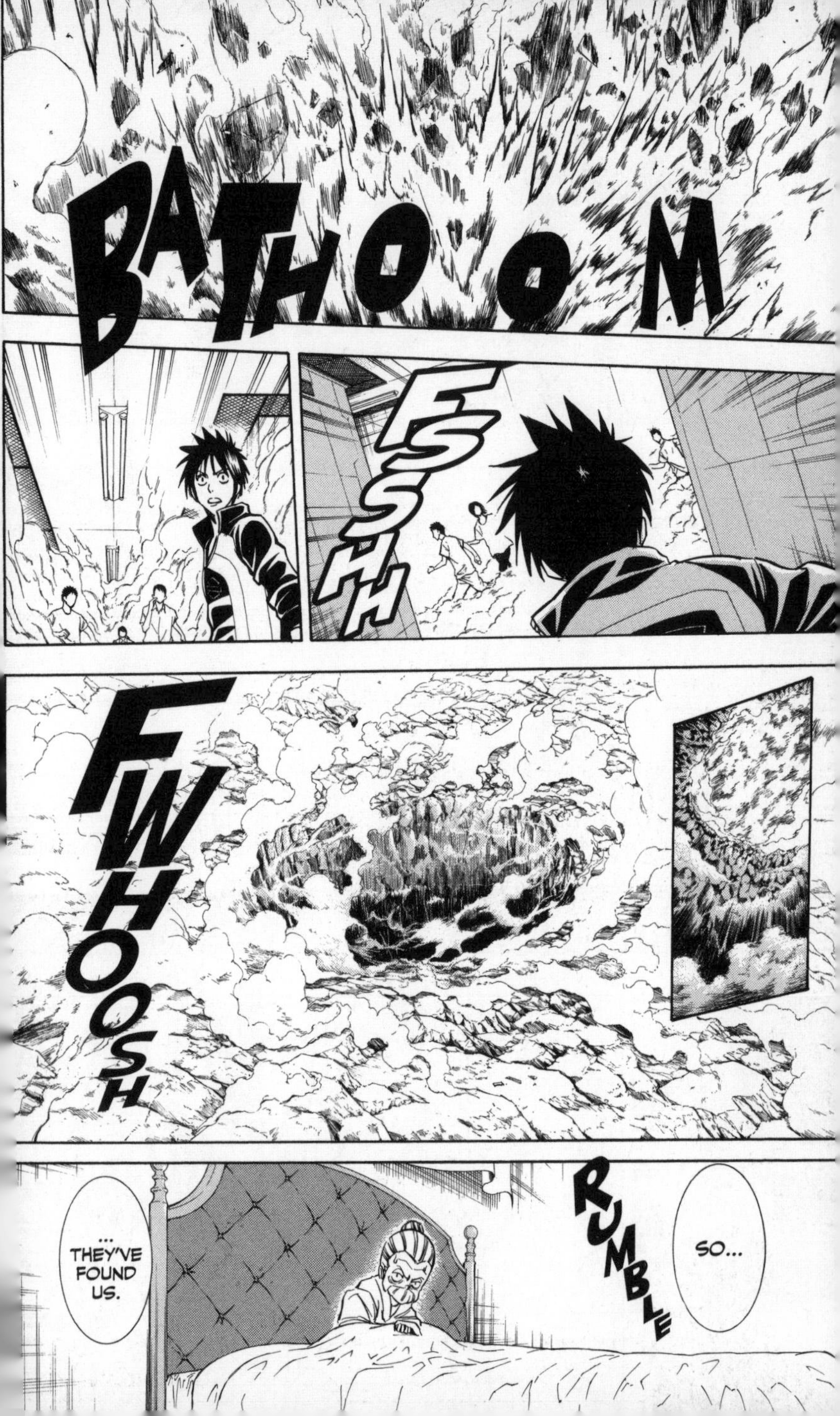
BATHOOM
FSSHH
FWHOOSH
SO...
RUMBLE
... THEY'VE FOUND US.

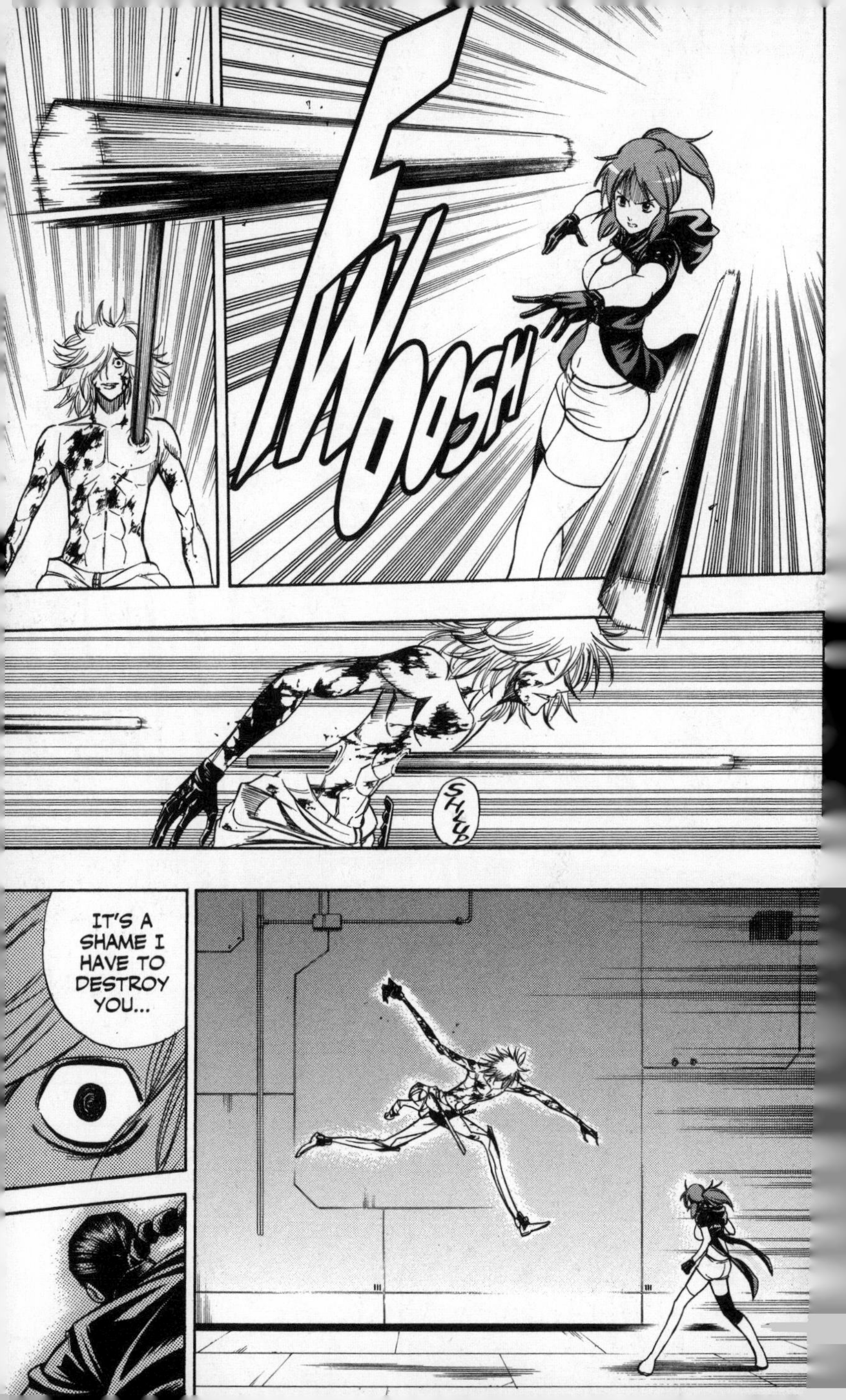
WHOOSH
SHLUP
IT'S A SHAME I HAVE TO DESTROY YOU...

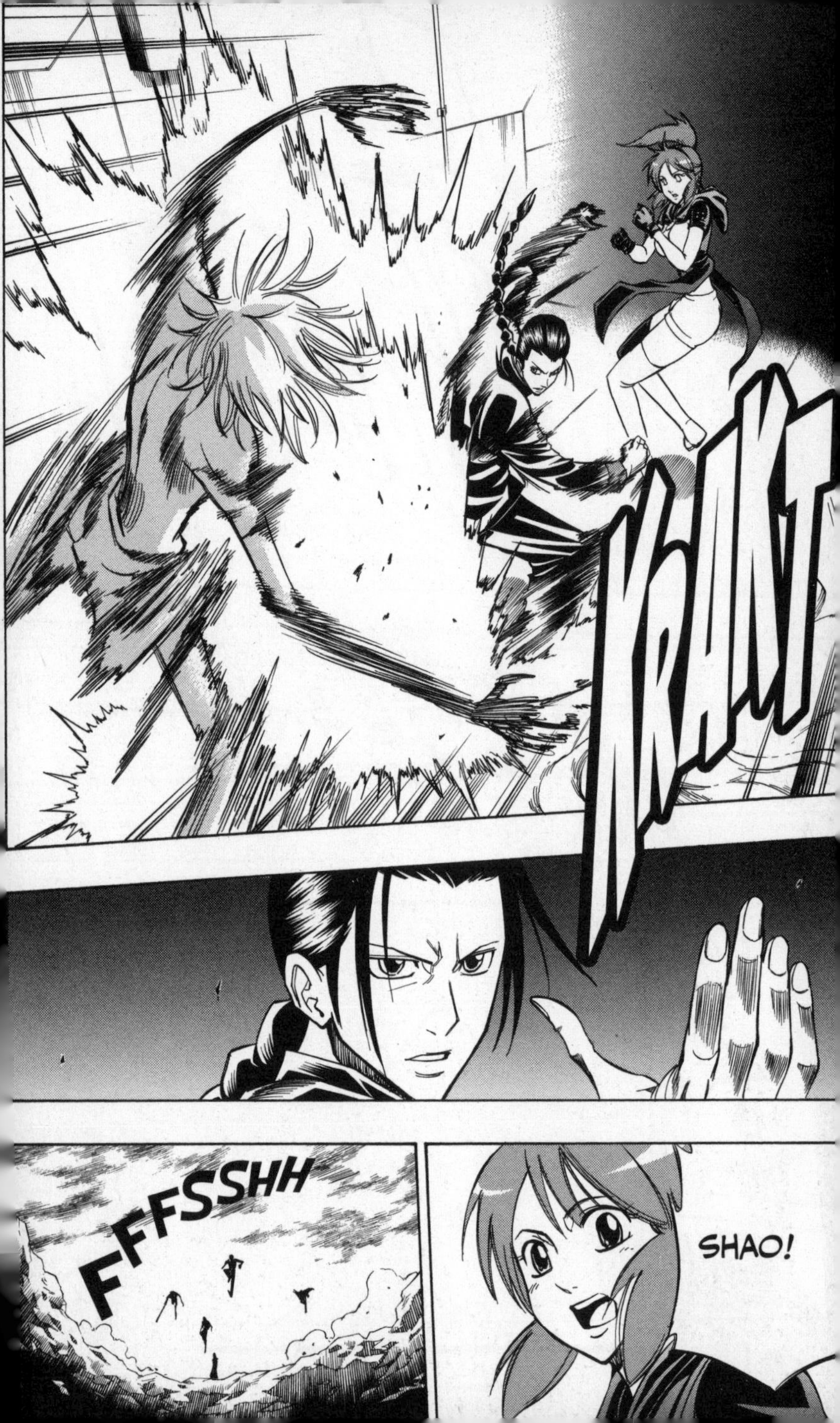
KRAKT
SHAO!
FFFSSHH

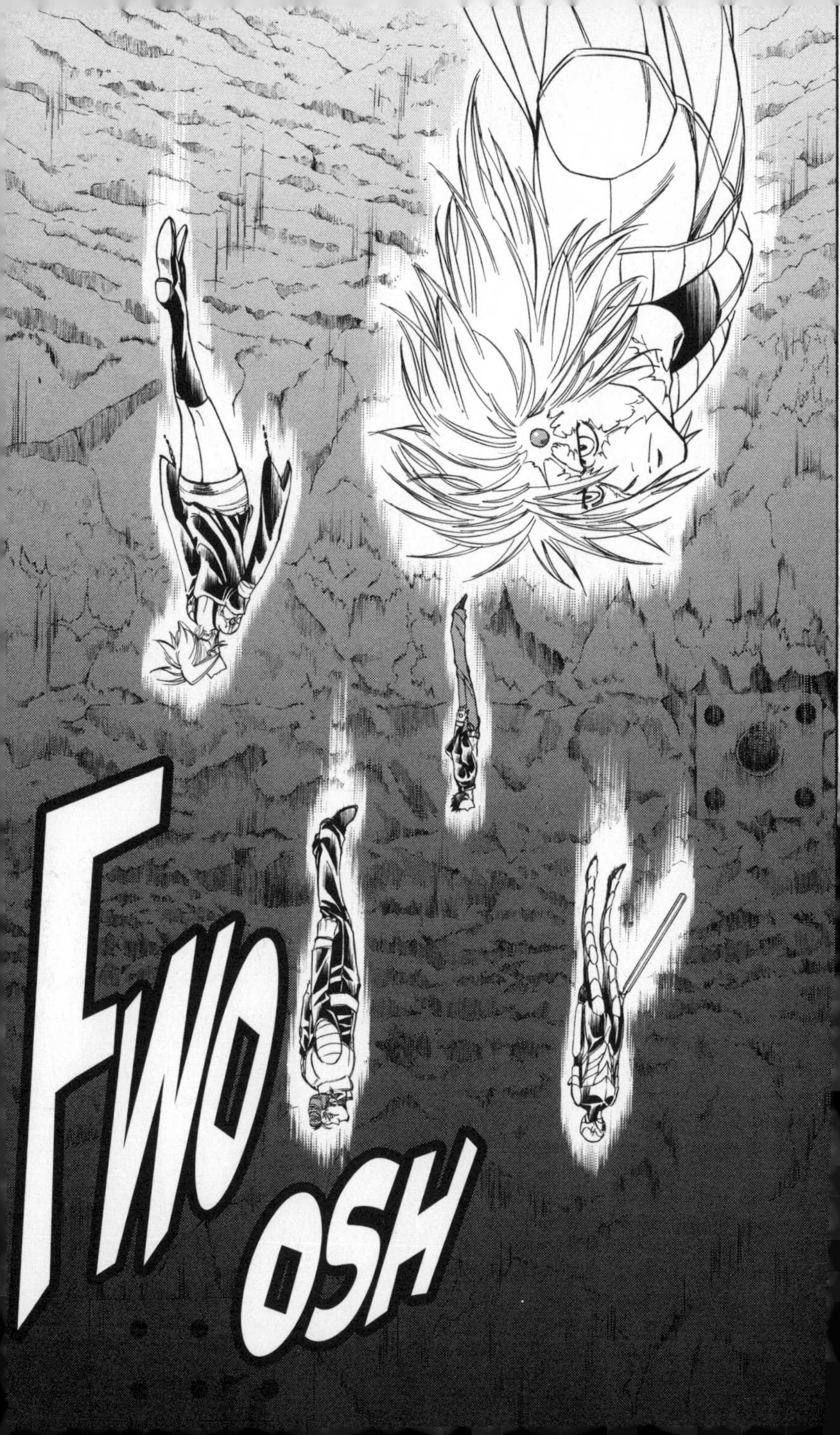
FWOOSH

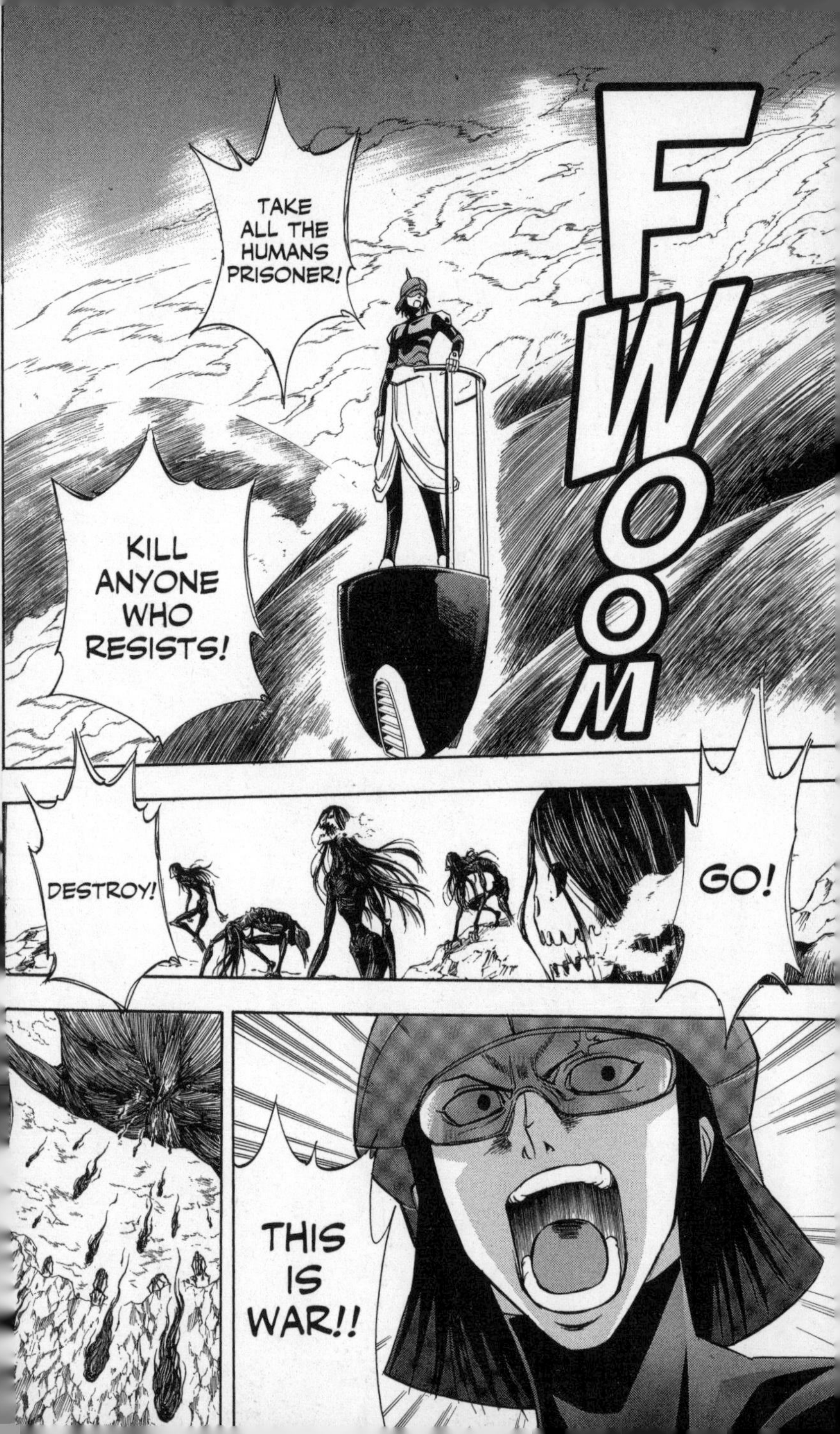
FWOOM
TAKE ALL THE HUMANS PRISONER!
KILL ANYONE WHO RESISTS!
GO!
DESTROY!
THIS IS WAR!!

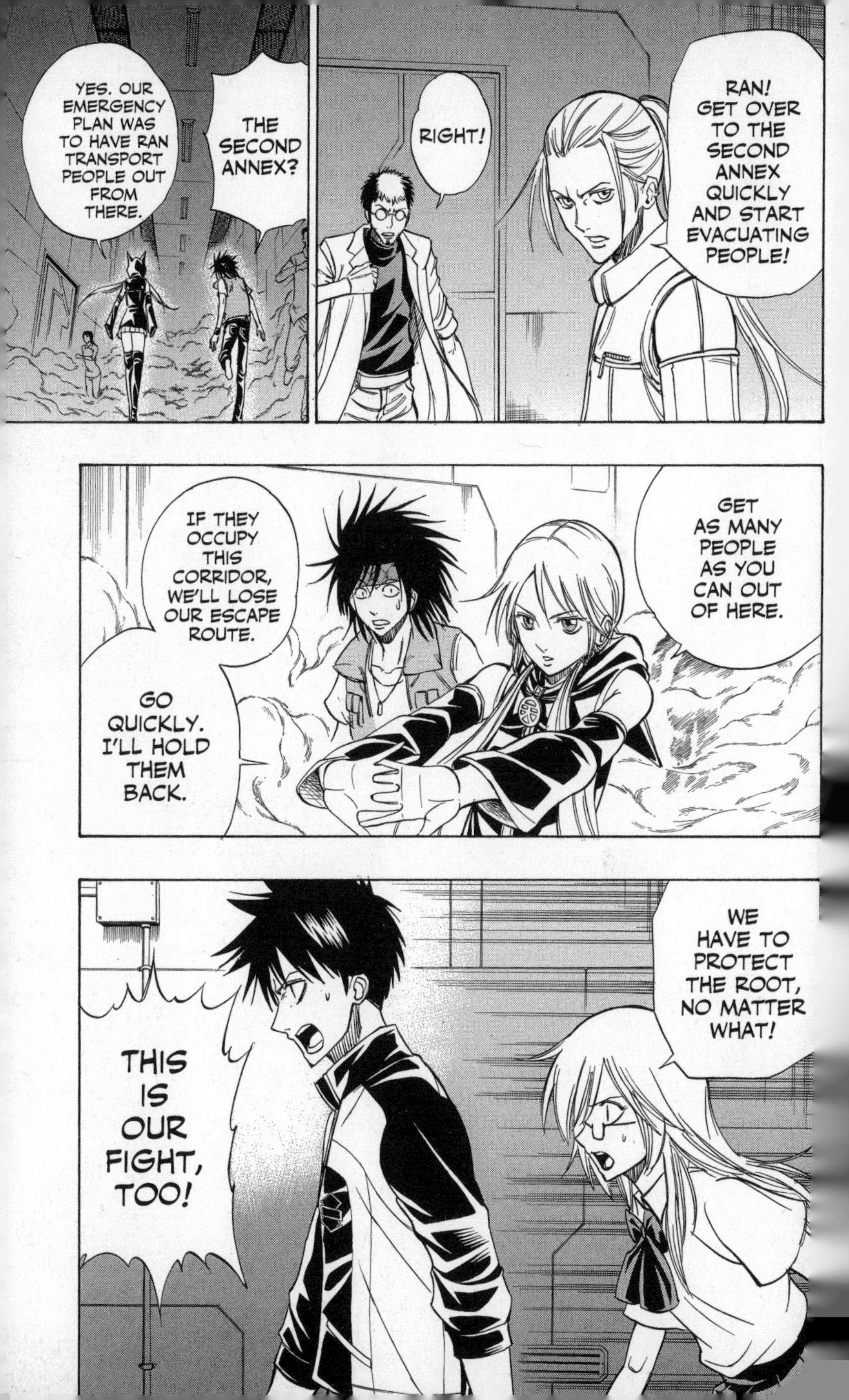
RAN! GET OVER TO THE SECOND ANNEX QUICKLY AND START EVACUATING PEOPLE!
RIGHT!
THE SECOND ANNEX?
YES. OUR EMERGENCY PLAN WAS TO HAVE RAN TRANSPORT PEOPLE OUT FROM THERE.
GET AS MANY PEOPLE AS YOU CAN OUT OF HERE.
IF THEY OCCUPY THIS CORRIDOR, WE'LL LOSE OUR ESCAPE ROUTE.
GO QUICKLY. I'LL HOLD THEM BACK.
WE HAVE TO PROTECT THE ROOT, NO MATTER WHAT!
THIS IS OUR FIGHT, TOO!

Mutters and mumblings

LATELY, MY G-PENS HAVE BEEN
ACTING UP. I BUY THEM BY THE
BOX, SO I STILL HAVE A LOT
LEFT, BUT NONE OF THEM ARE
WORKING SMOOTHLY...WISH I
COULD FIGURE OUT A SOLUTION.

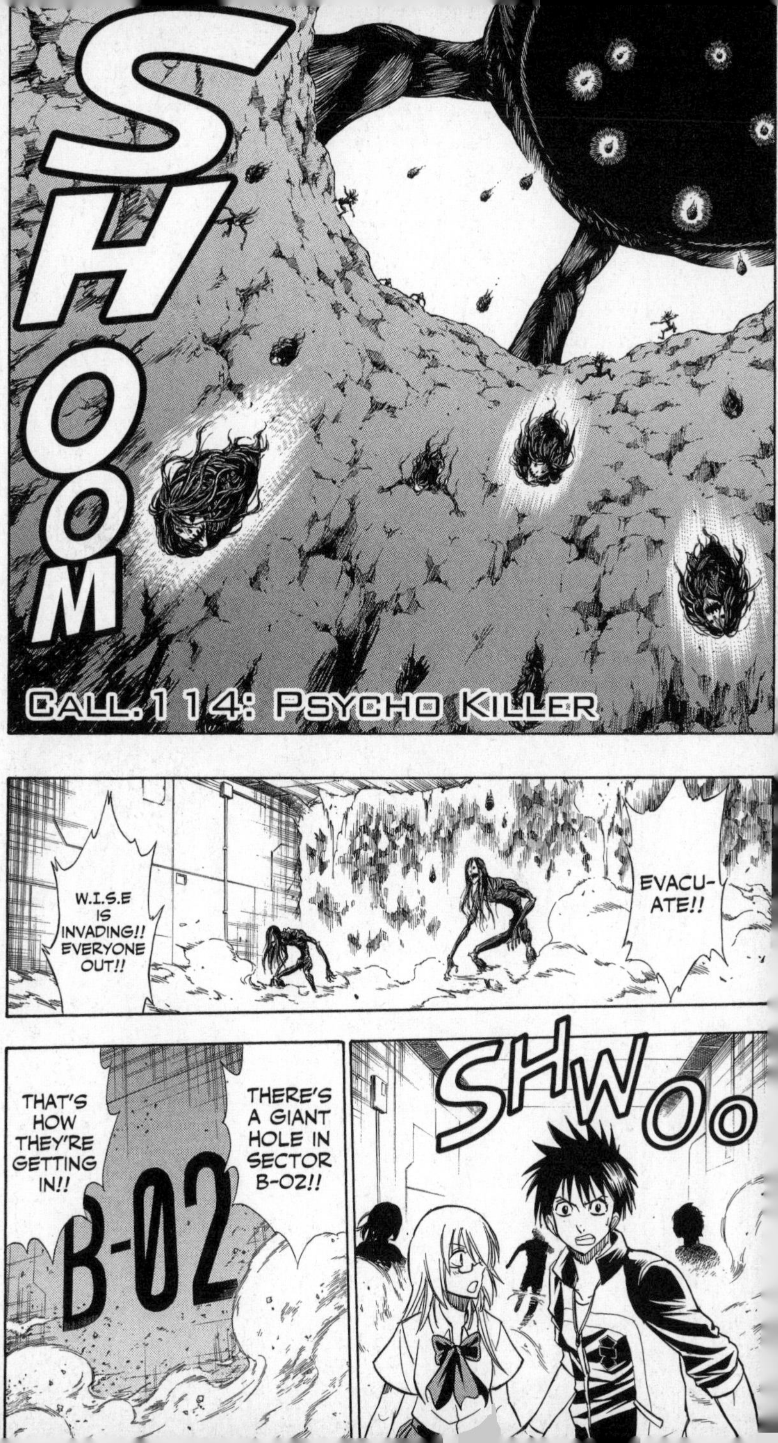
SHOOOM
Call.114: Psycho Killer
EVACUATE!!
W.I.S.E IS INVADING!! EVERYONE OUT!!
SHWOO
THERE'S A GIANT HOLE IN SECTOR B-02!!
THAT'S HOW THEY'RE GETTING IN!!
B-02

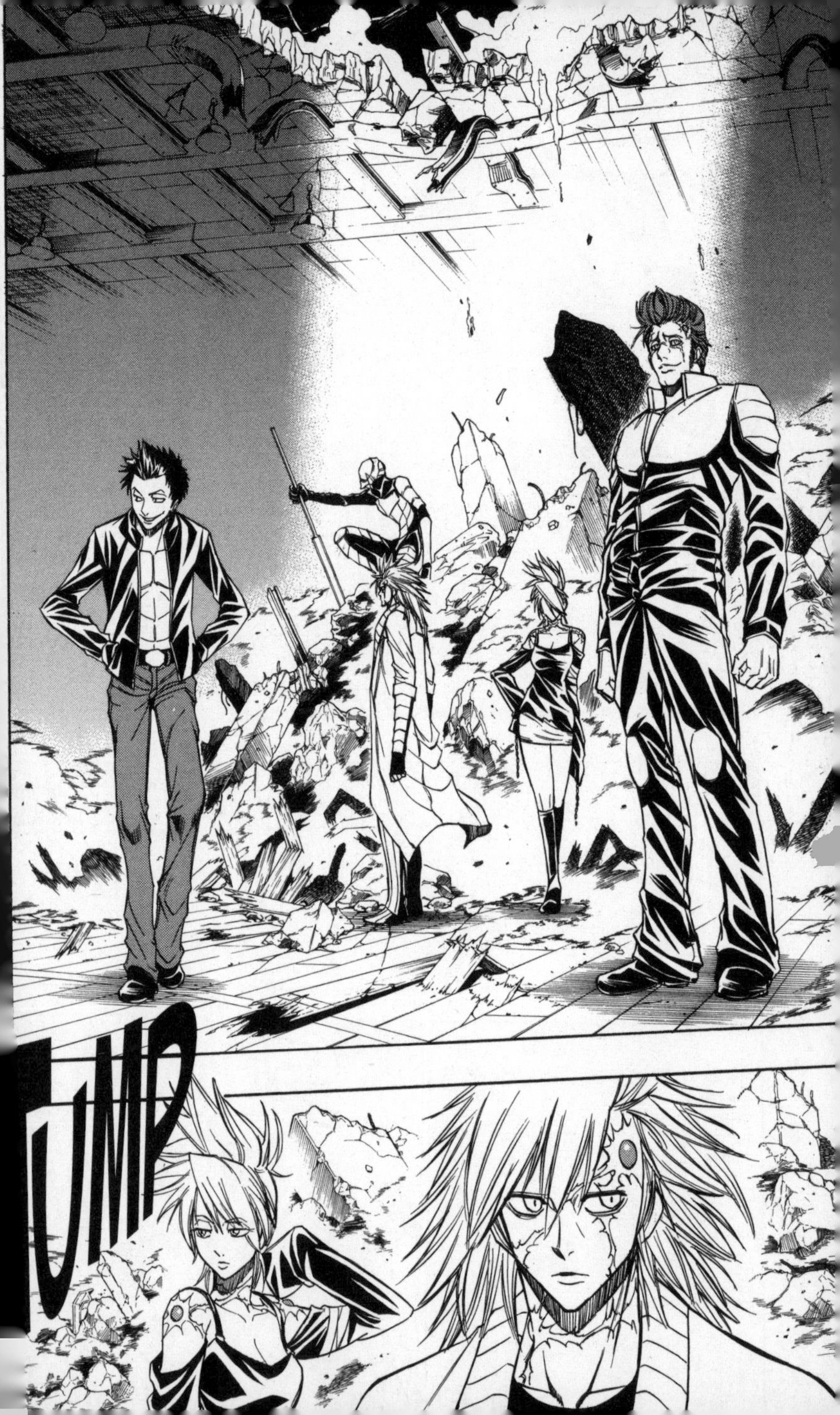

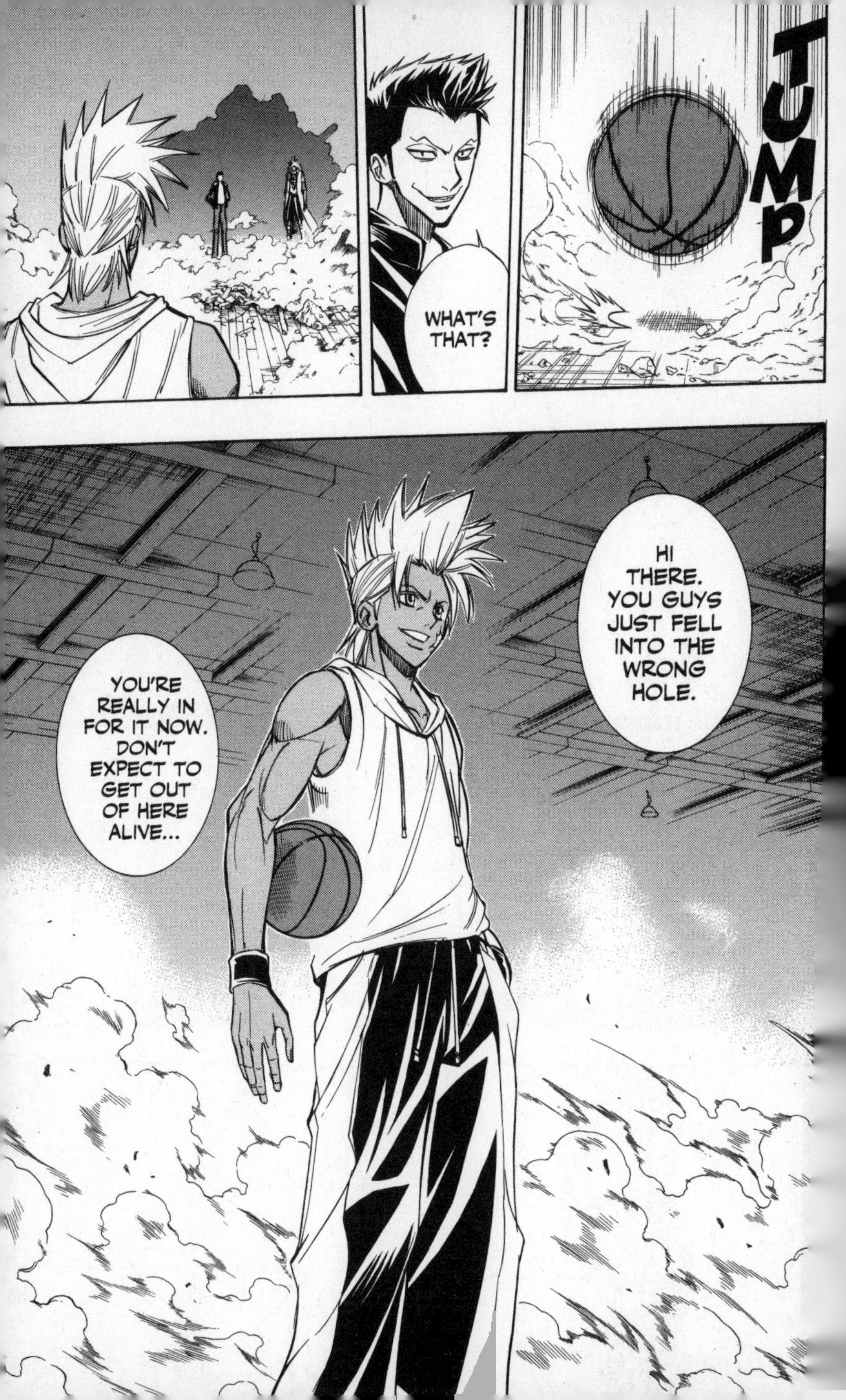
TUMP
WHAT'S THAT?
HI THERE. YOU GUYS JUST FELL INTO THE WRONG HOLE.
YOU'RE REALLY IN FOR IT NOW. DON'T EXPECT TO GET OUT OF HERE ALIVE...

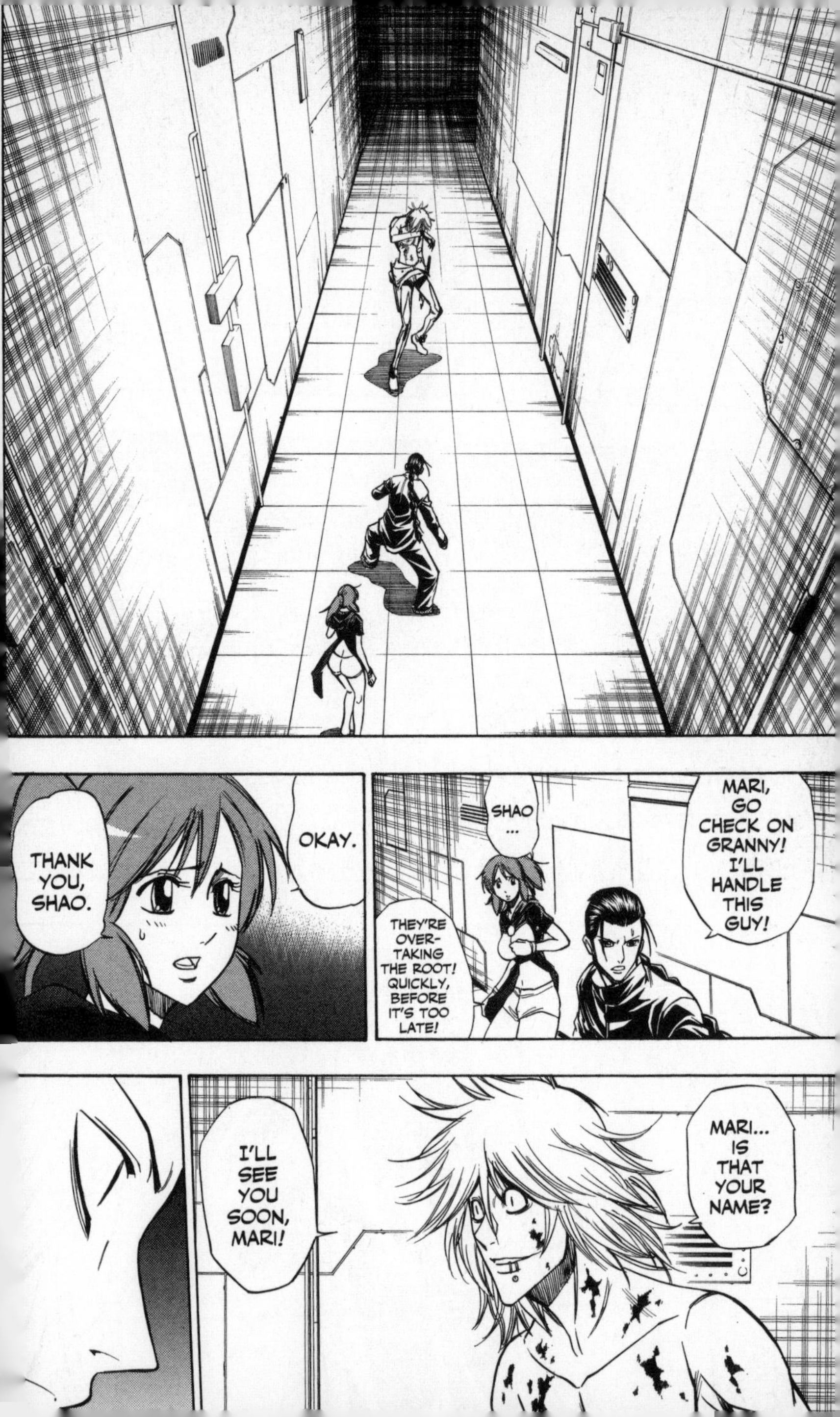
MARI, GO CHECK ON GRANNY! I'LL HANDLE THIS GUY!
SHAO ...
THEY'RE OVER-TAKING THE ROOT! QUICKLY, BEFORE IT'S TOO LATE!
OKAY.
THANK YOU, SHAO.
MARI... IS THAT YOUR NAME?
I'LL SEE YOU SOON, MARI!

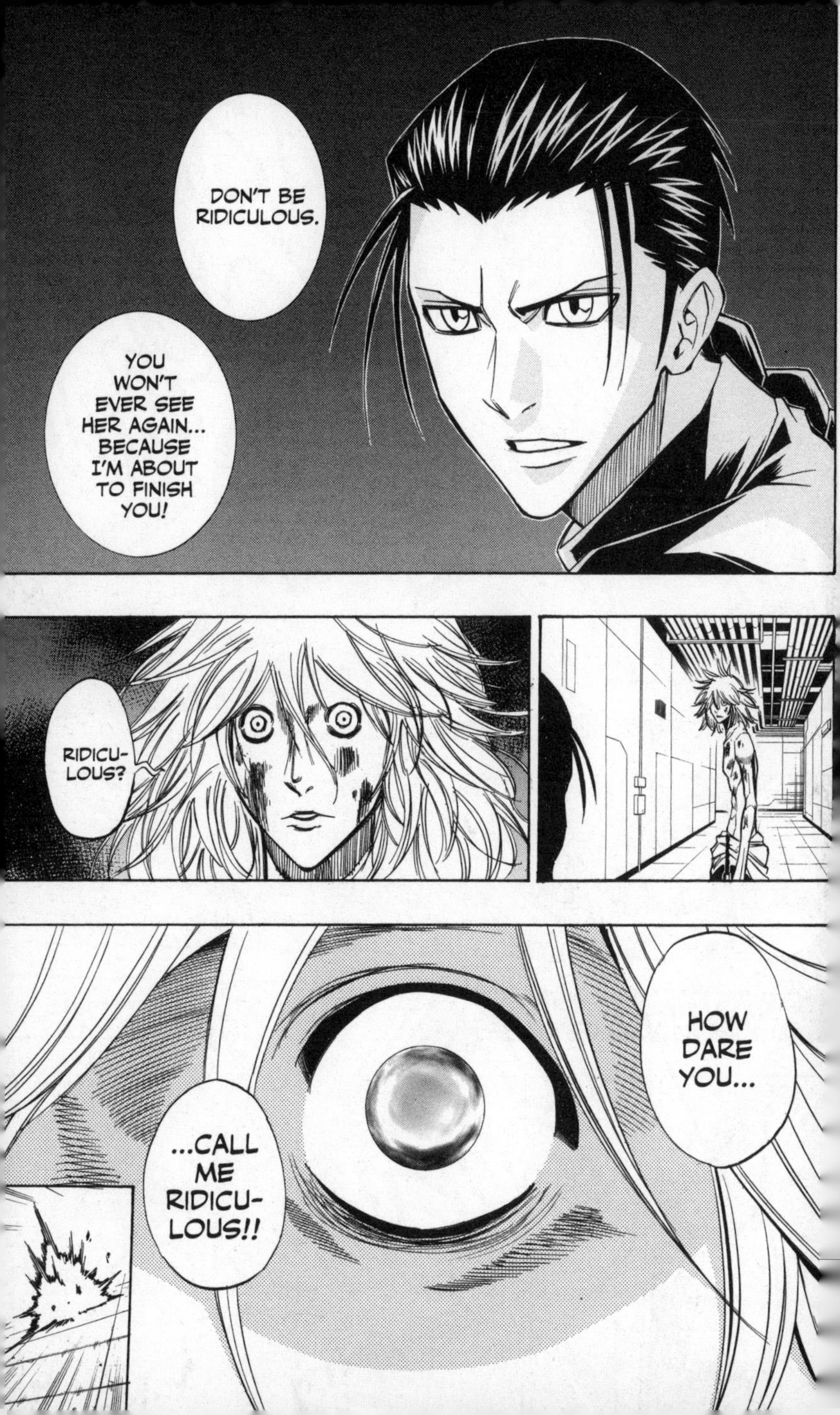
DON'T BE RIDICULOUS.
YOU WON'T EVER SEE HER AGAIN... BECAUSE I'M ABOUT TO FINISH YOU!
RIDICU-LOUS?
HOW DARE YOU...
...CALL ME RIDICU-LOUS!!

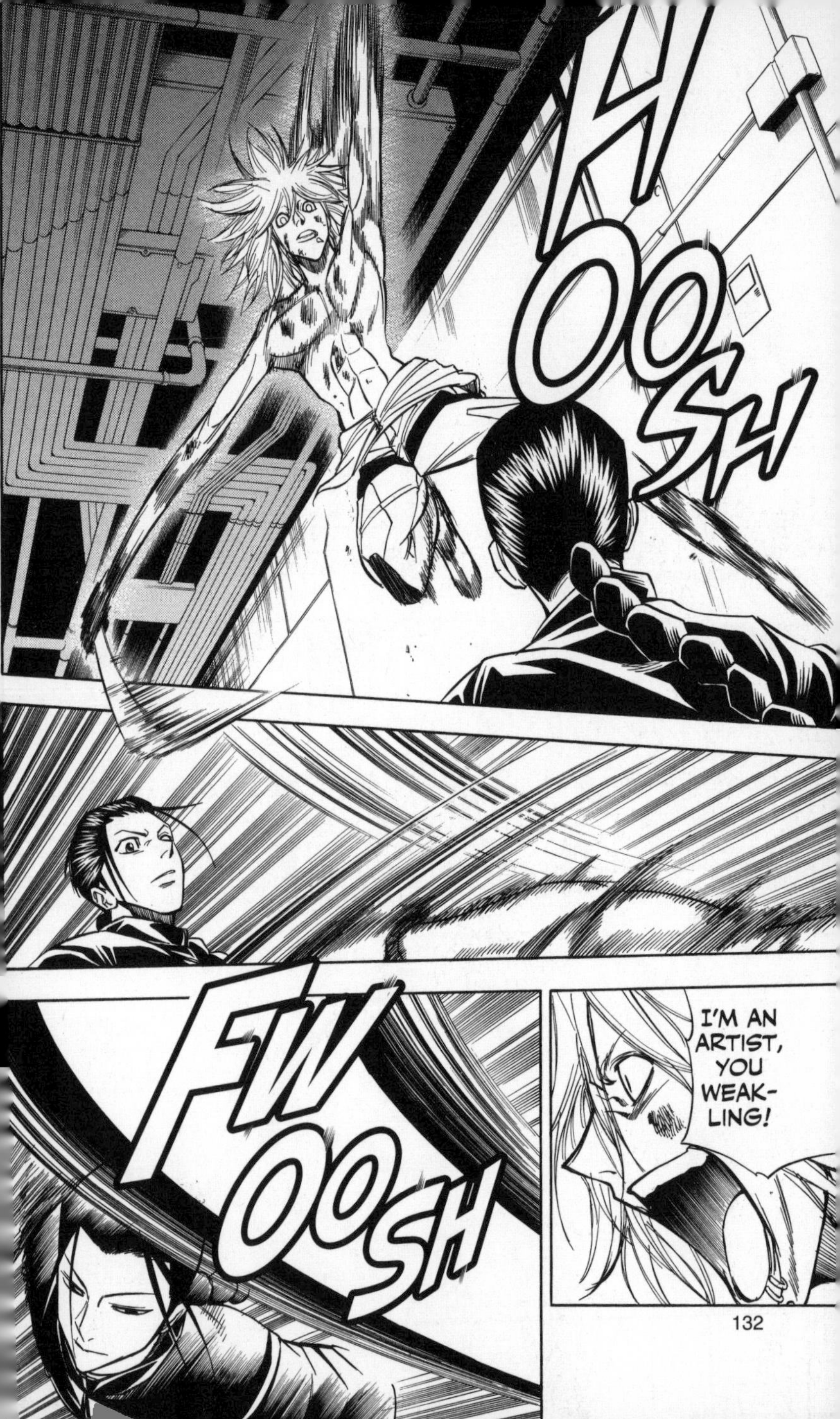
HOOSH
I'M AN ARTIST, YOU WEAK-LING!
FWOOSH

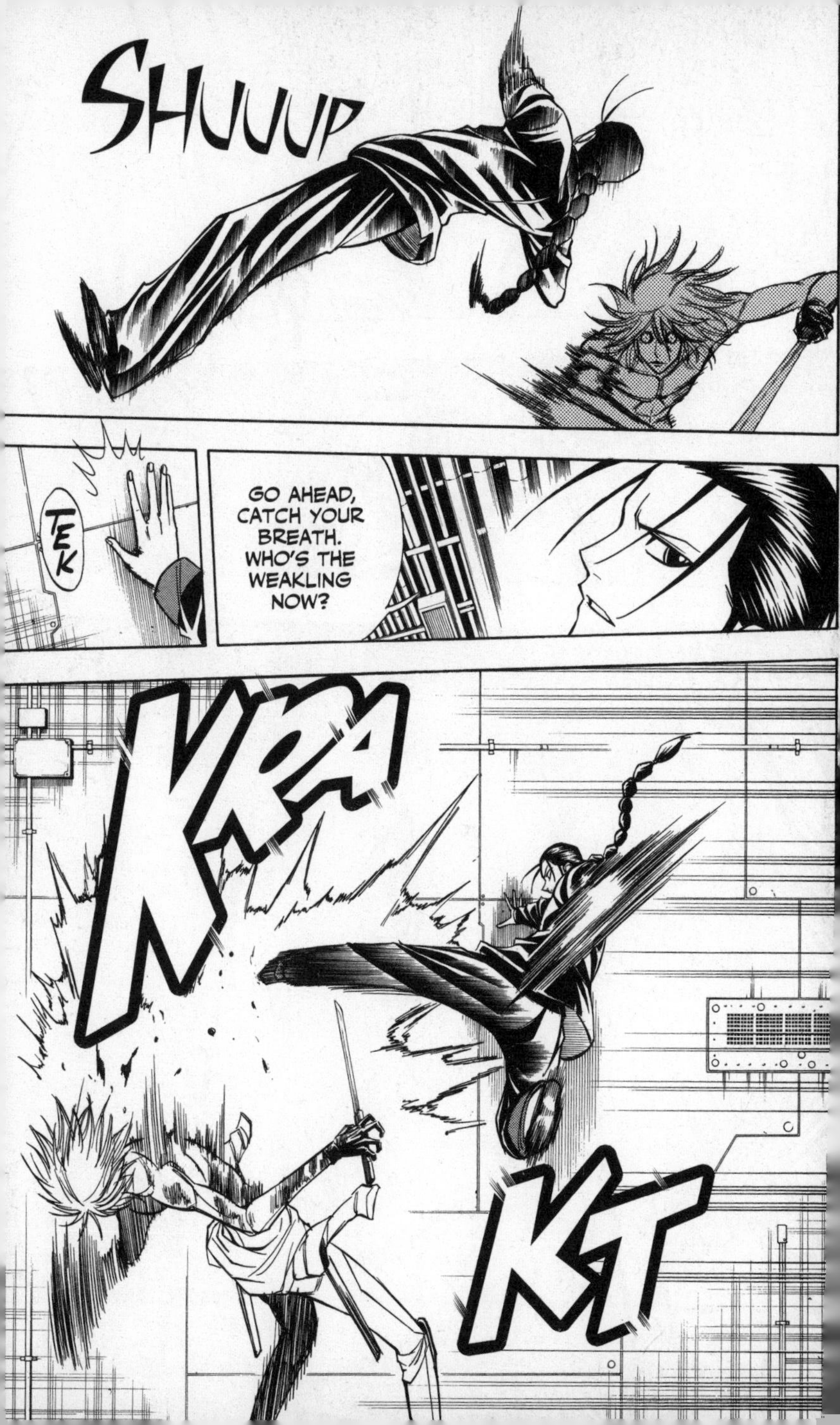
SHUUUP
GO AHEAD, CATCH YOUR BREATH. WHO'S THE WEAKLING NOW?
TEK
KPA
KT

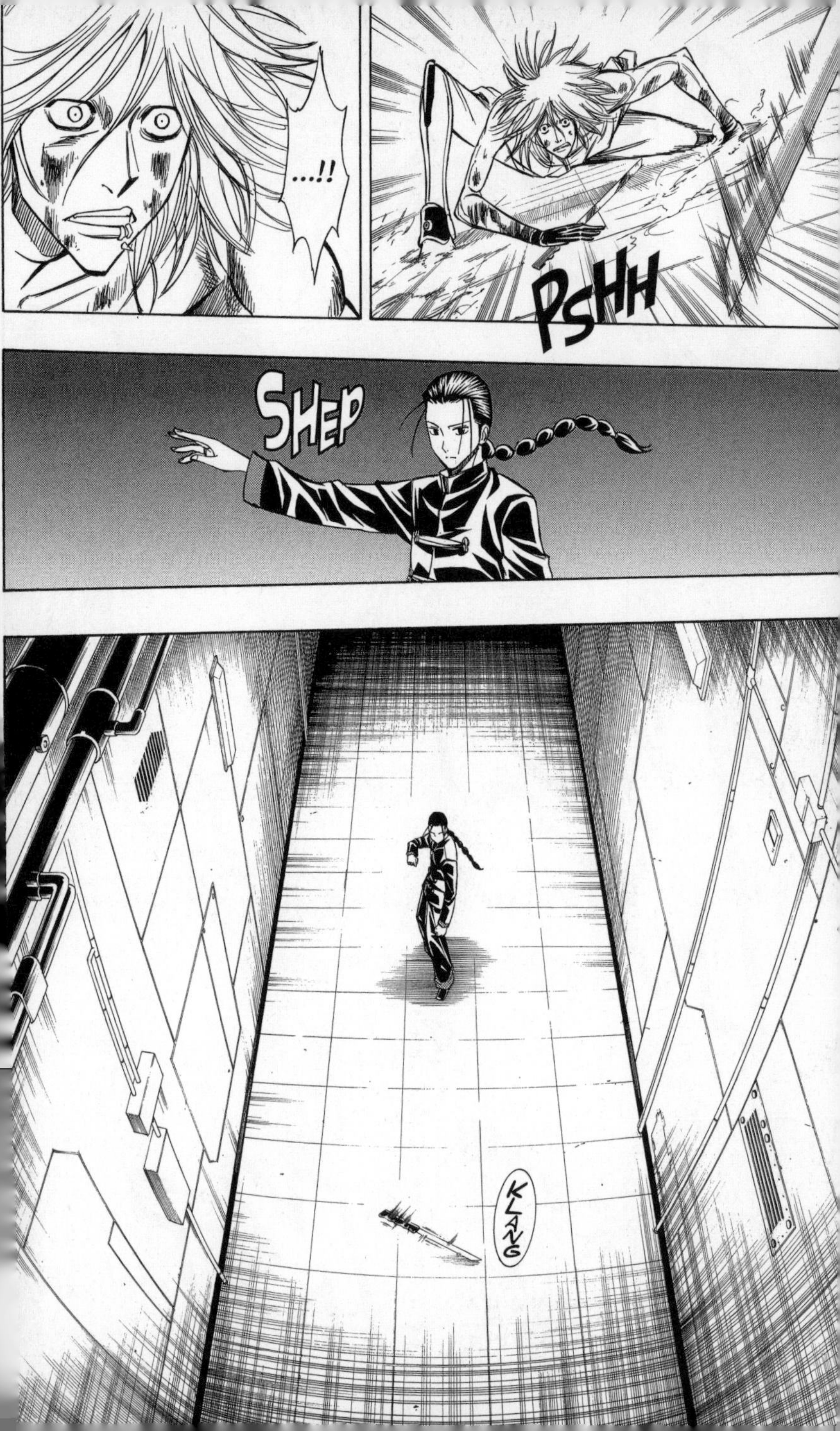
PSHH
...!!
SHEP
KLANG

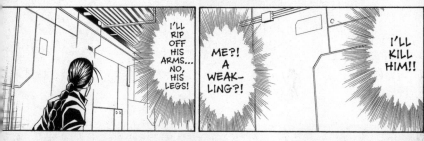

I'LL RIP OFF HIS ARMS... NO, HIS LEGS!

ME?! A WEAKLING?!

I'LL KILL HIM!!

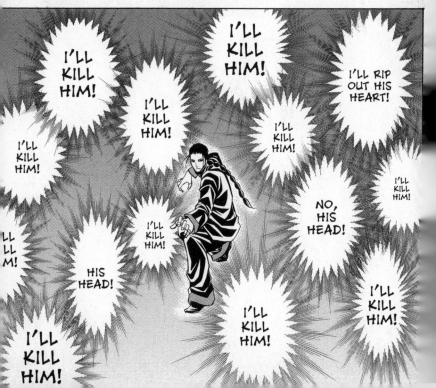

I'LL KILL HIM!

I'LL KILL HIM!

I'LL KILL HIM!

I'LL RIP OUT HIS HEART!

I'LL KILL HIM!

I'LL KILL HIM!

I'LL KILL HIM!

I'LL KILL HIM!

NO, HIS HEAD!

LL LL M!

I'LL KILL HIM!

HIS HEAD!

I'LL KILL HIM!

I'LL KILL HIM!

I'LL KILL HIM!

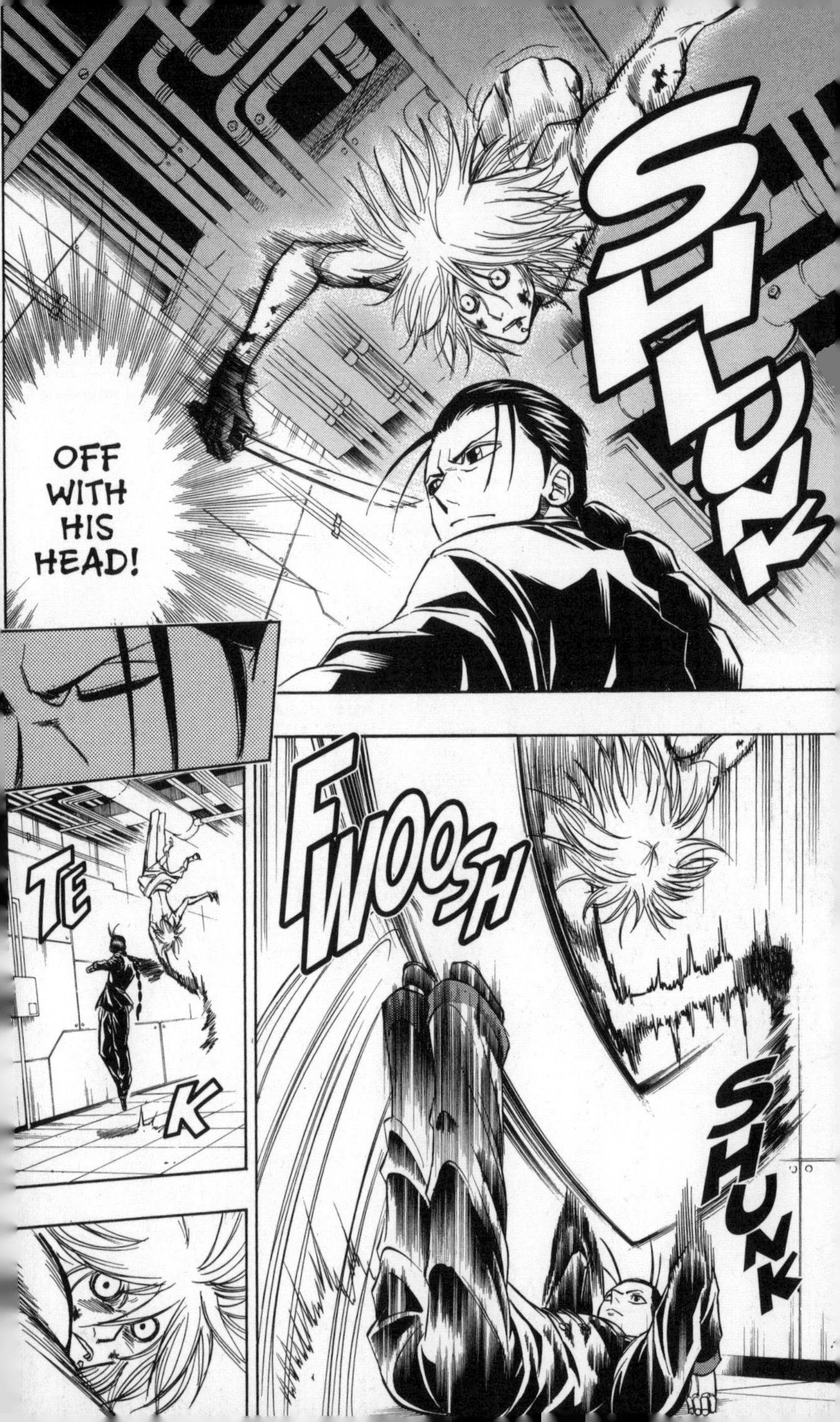
SHLUNK
OFF WITH HIS HEAD!
FWOOSH
SHUNK
TE
K

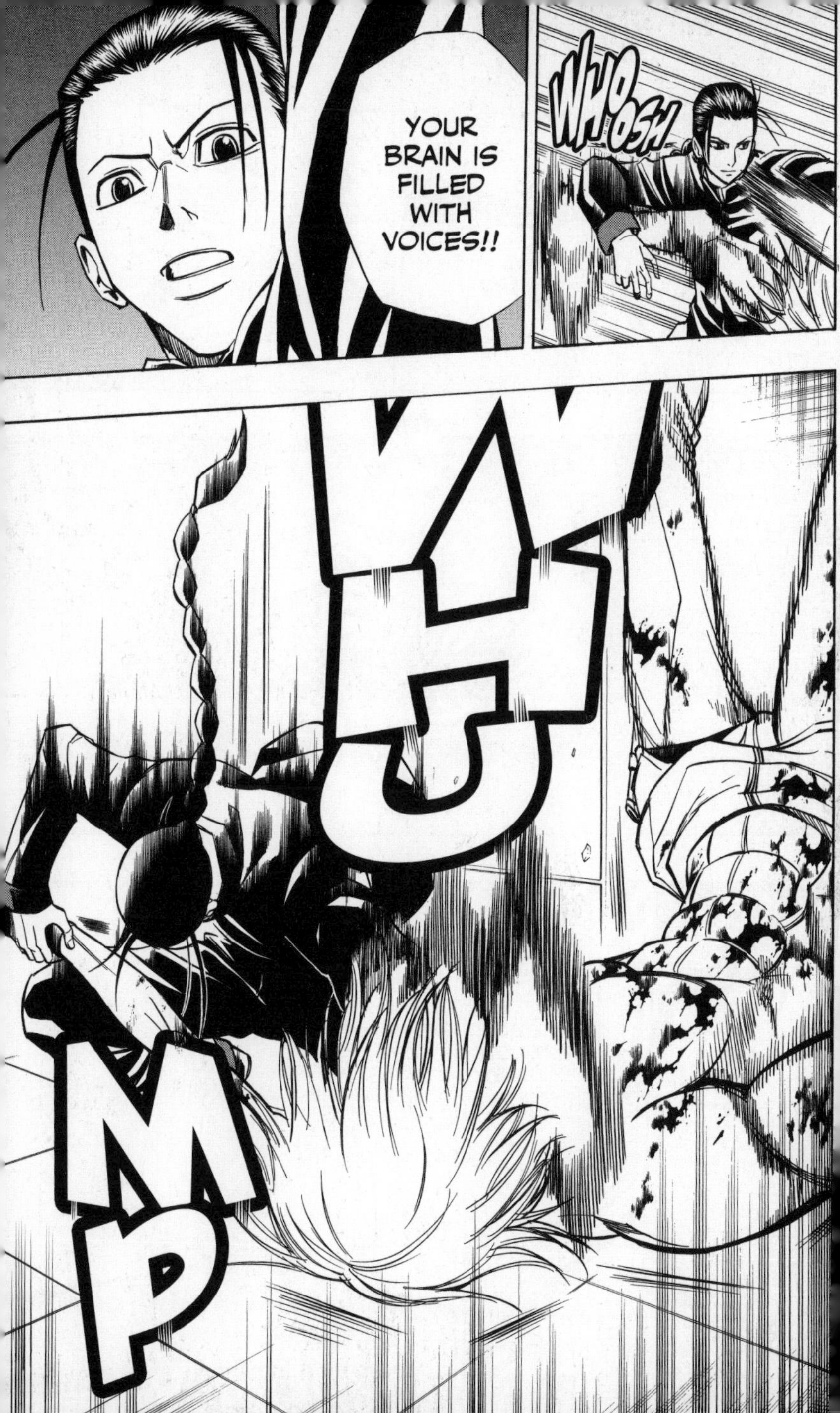
WHOOSH
YOUR BRAIN IS FILLED WITH VOICES!!
WHUMP

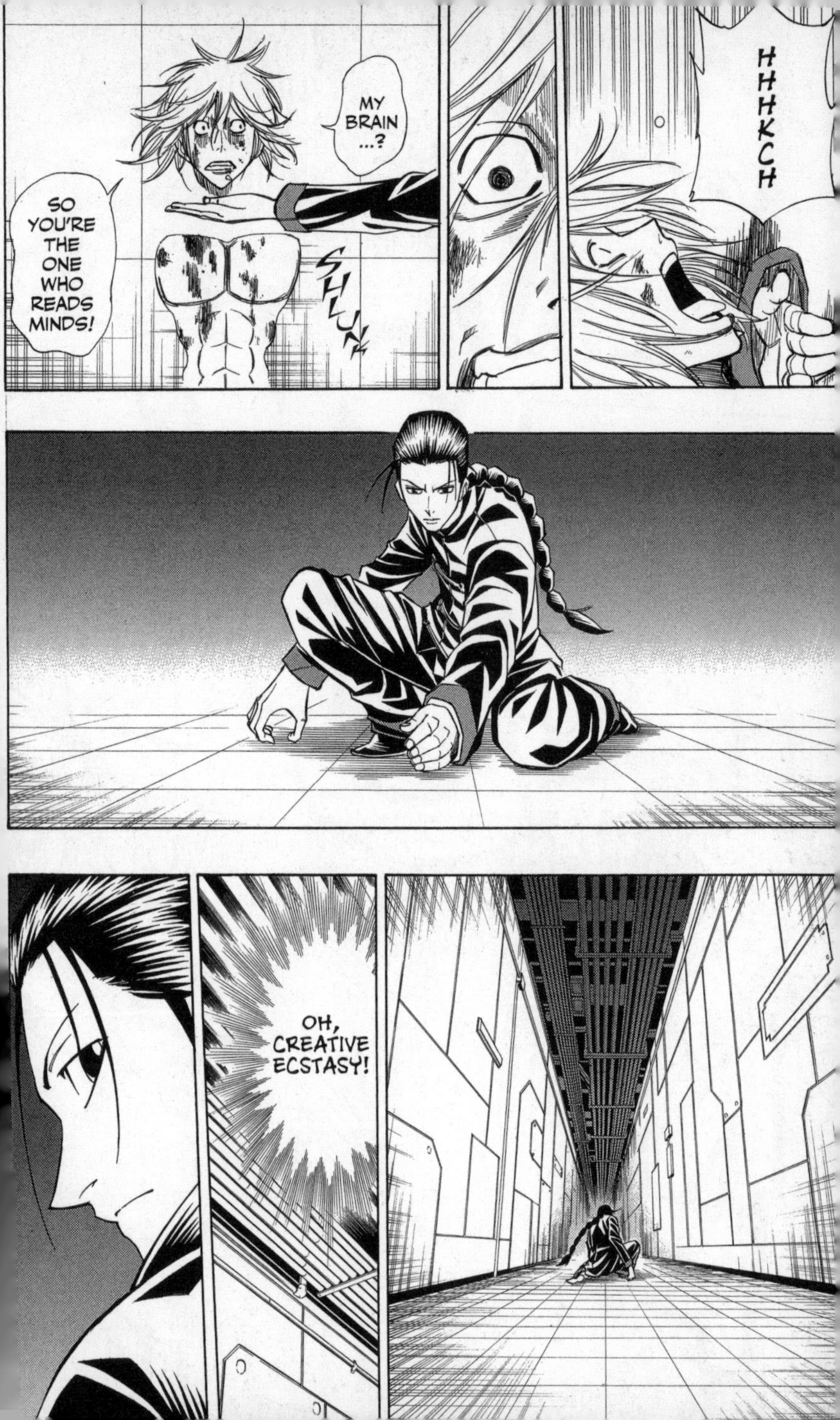
HHHKCH
MY BRAIN ...?
SO YOU'RE THE ONE WHO READS MINDS!
SHLUNK
OH, CREATIVE ECSTASY!

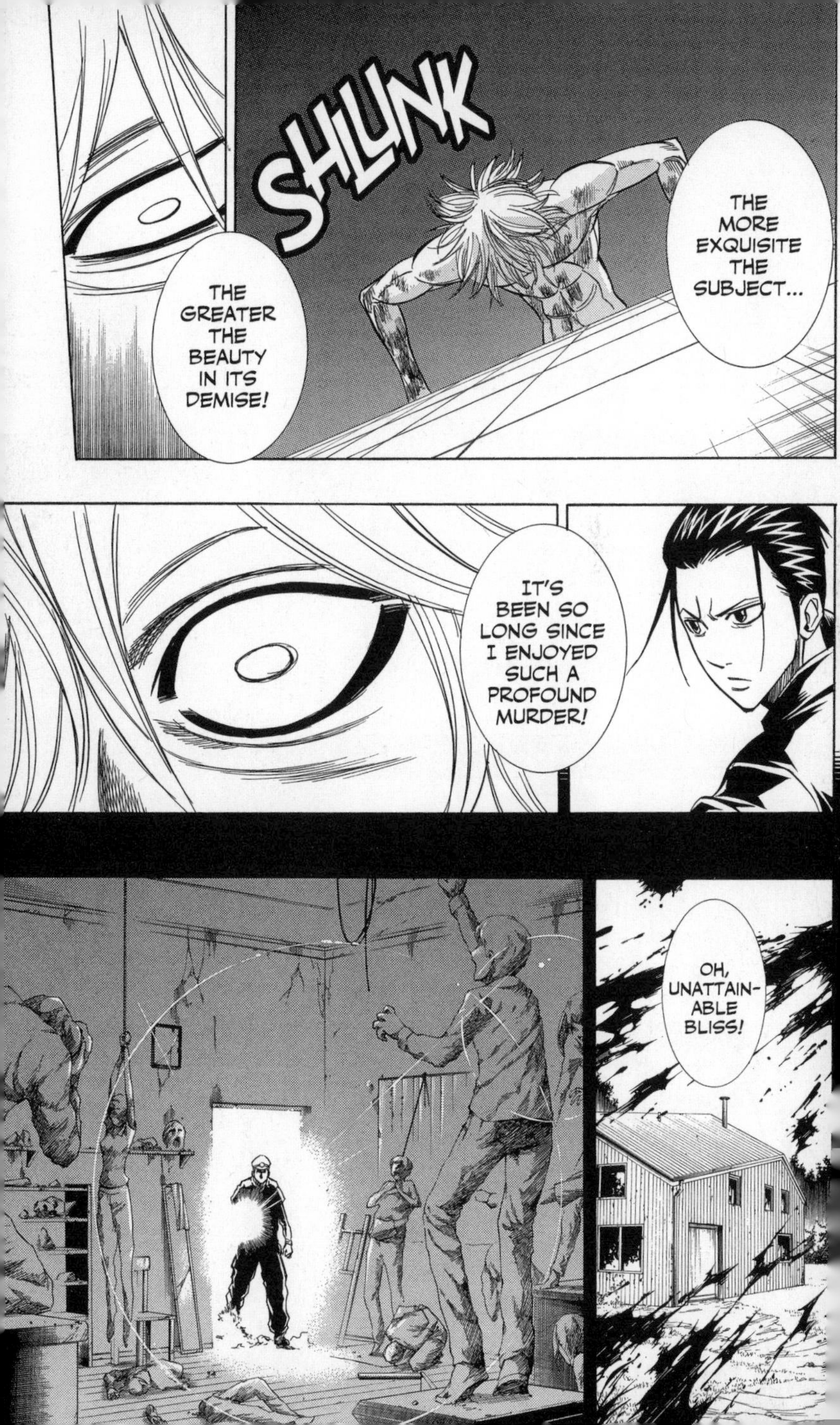
SHLUNK
THE MORE EXQUISITE THE SUBJECT...
THE GREATER THE BEAUTY IN ITS DEMISE!
IT'S BEEN SO LONG SINCE I ENJOYED SUCH A PROFOUND MURDER!
OH, UNATTAIN-ABLE BLISS!

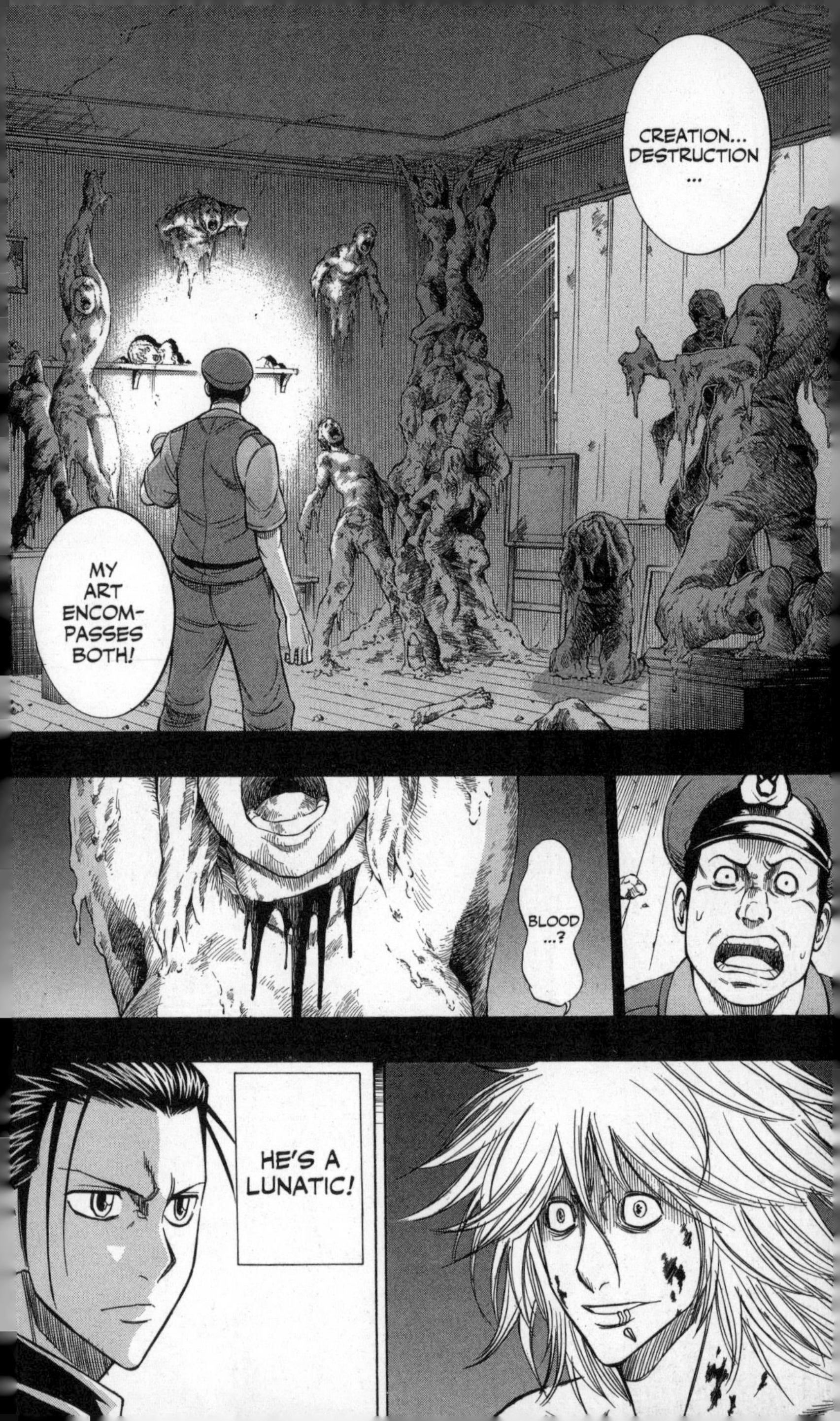
CREATION... DESTRUCTION ...
MY ART ENCOM-PASSES BOTH!
BLOOD ...?
HE'S A LUNATIC!

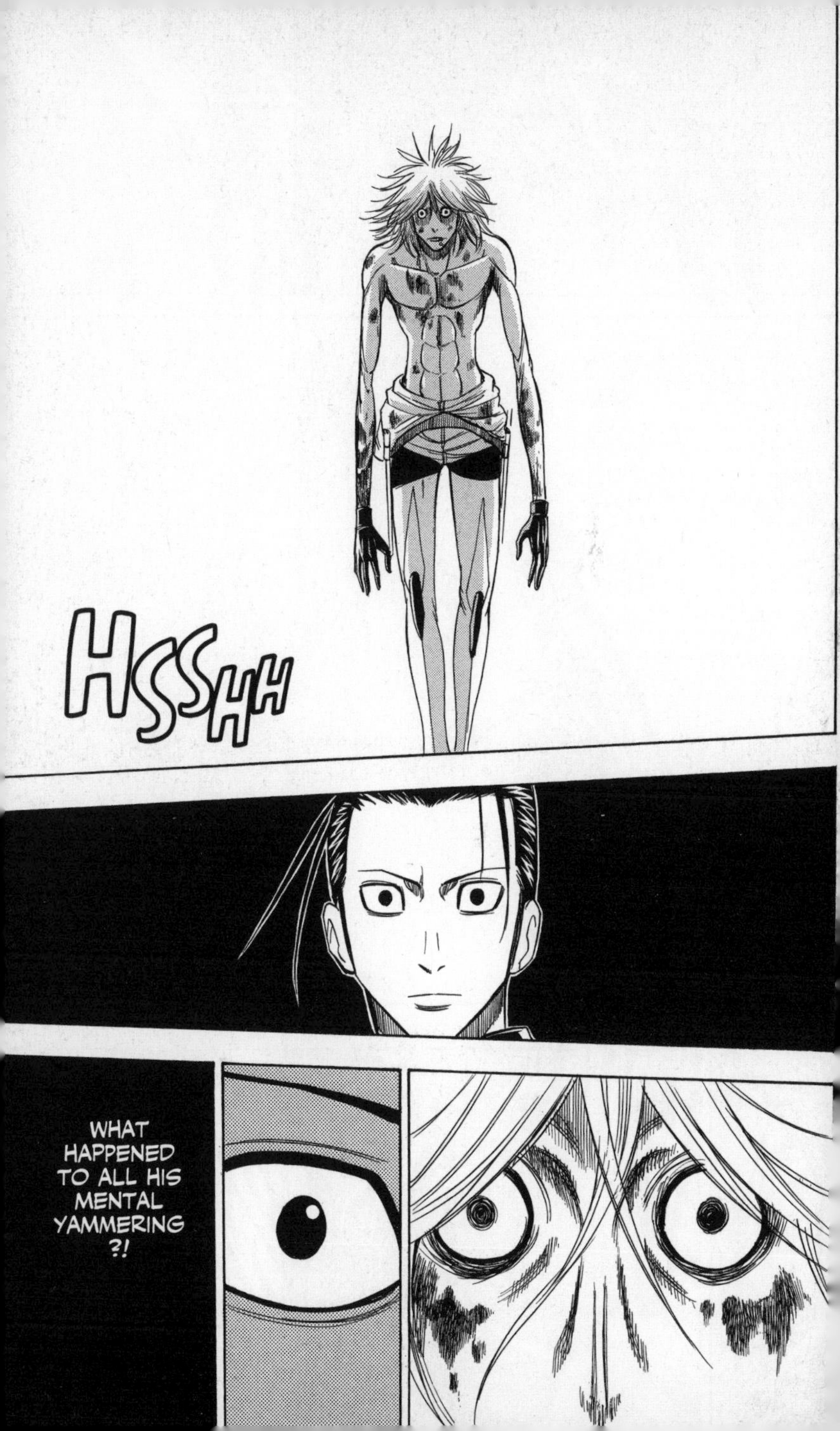
HSSHH
WHAT HAPPENED TO ALL HIS MENTAL YAMMERING ?!

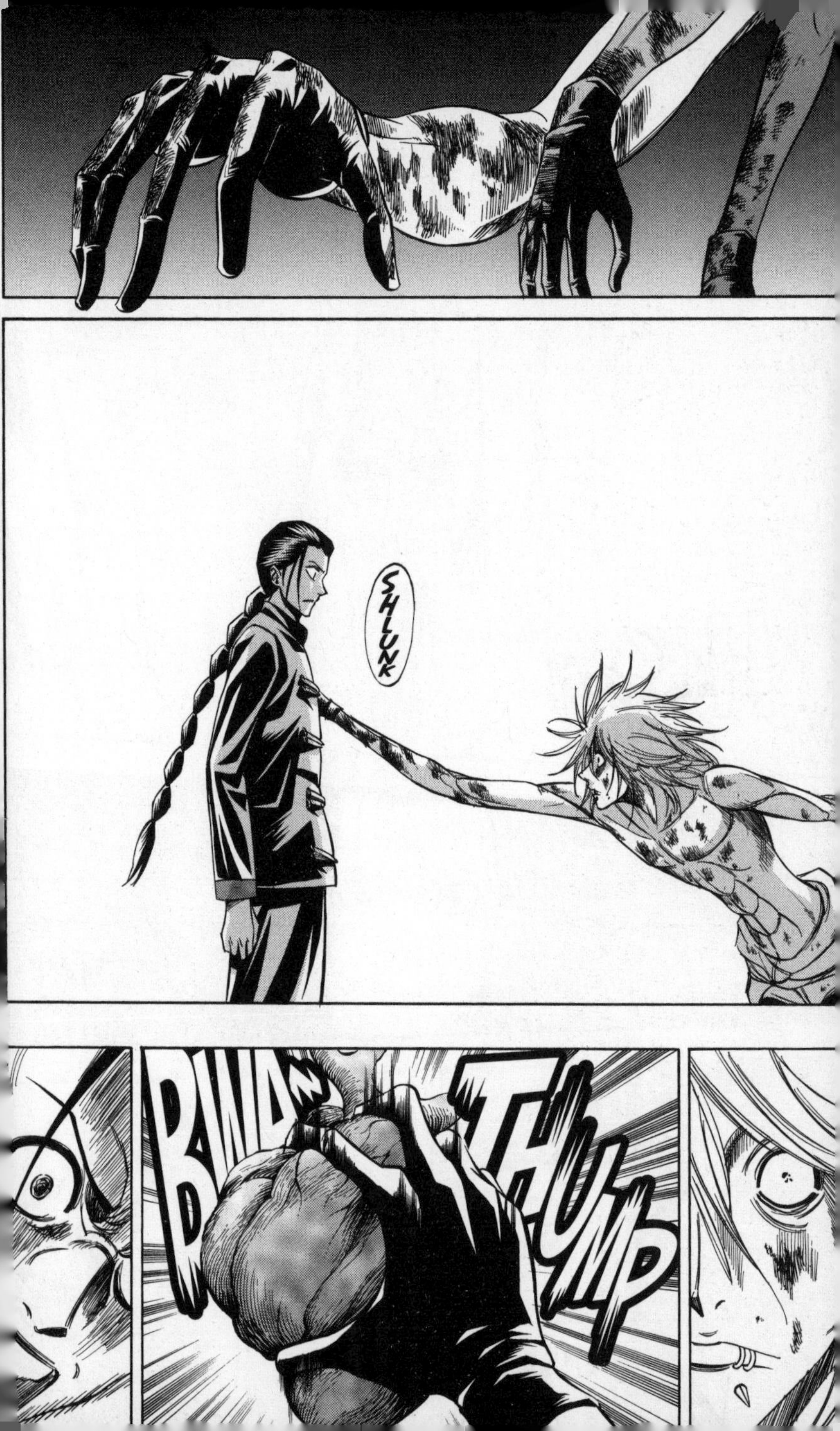
SHLUNK
BA-THUMP

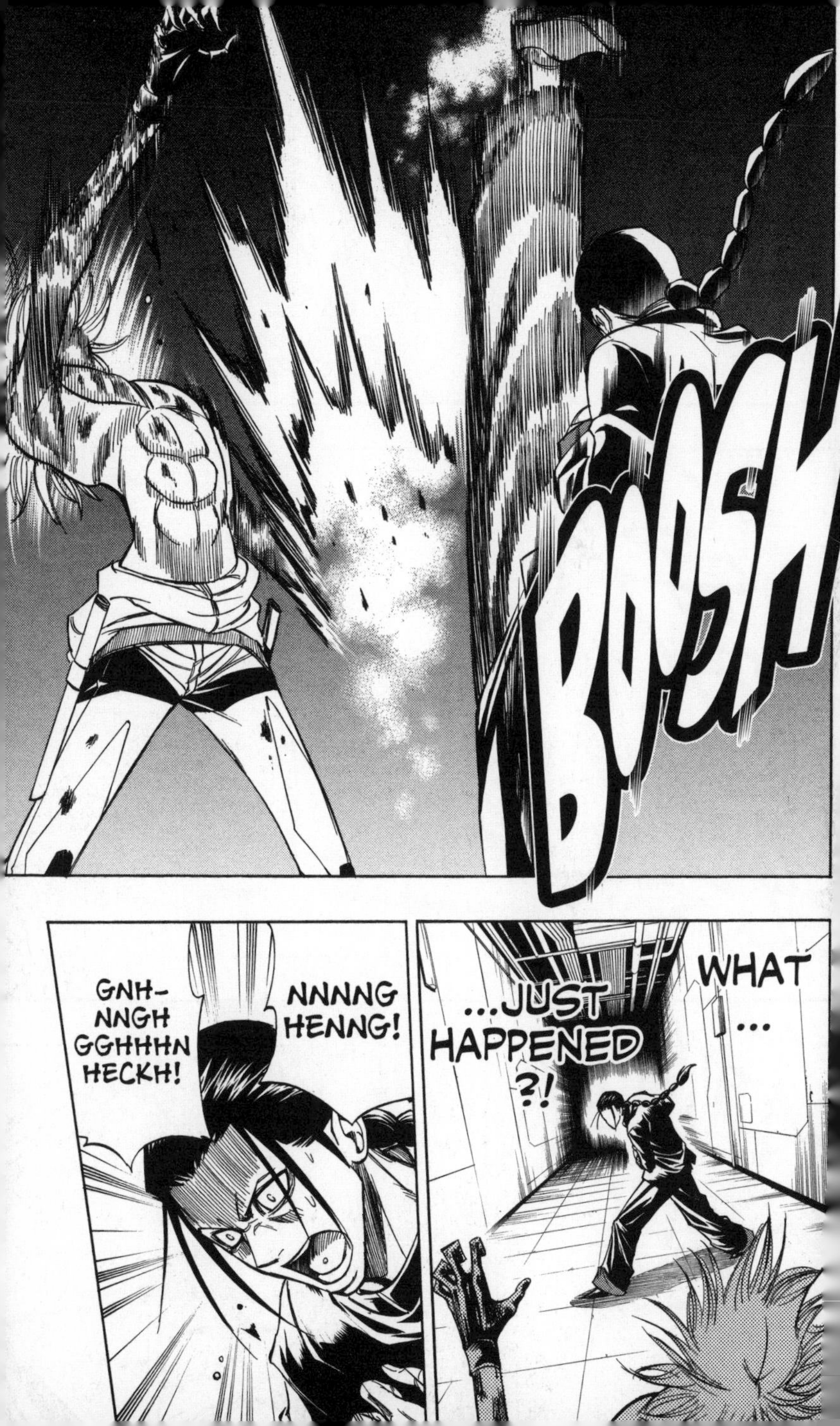
BOOSH
WHAT ...
...JUST HAPPENED ?!
NNNNG HENNG!
GNH-NNGH GGHHHN HECKH!

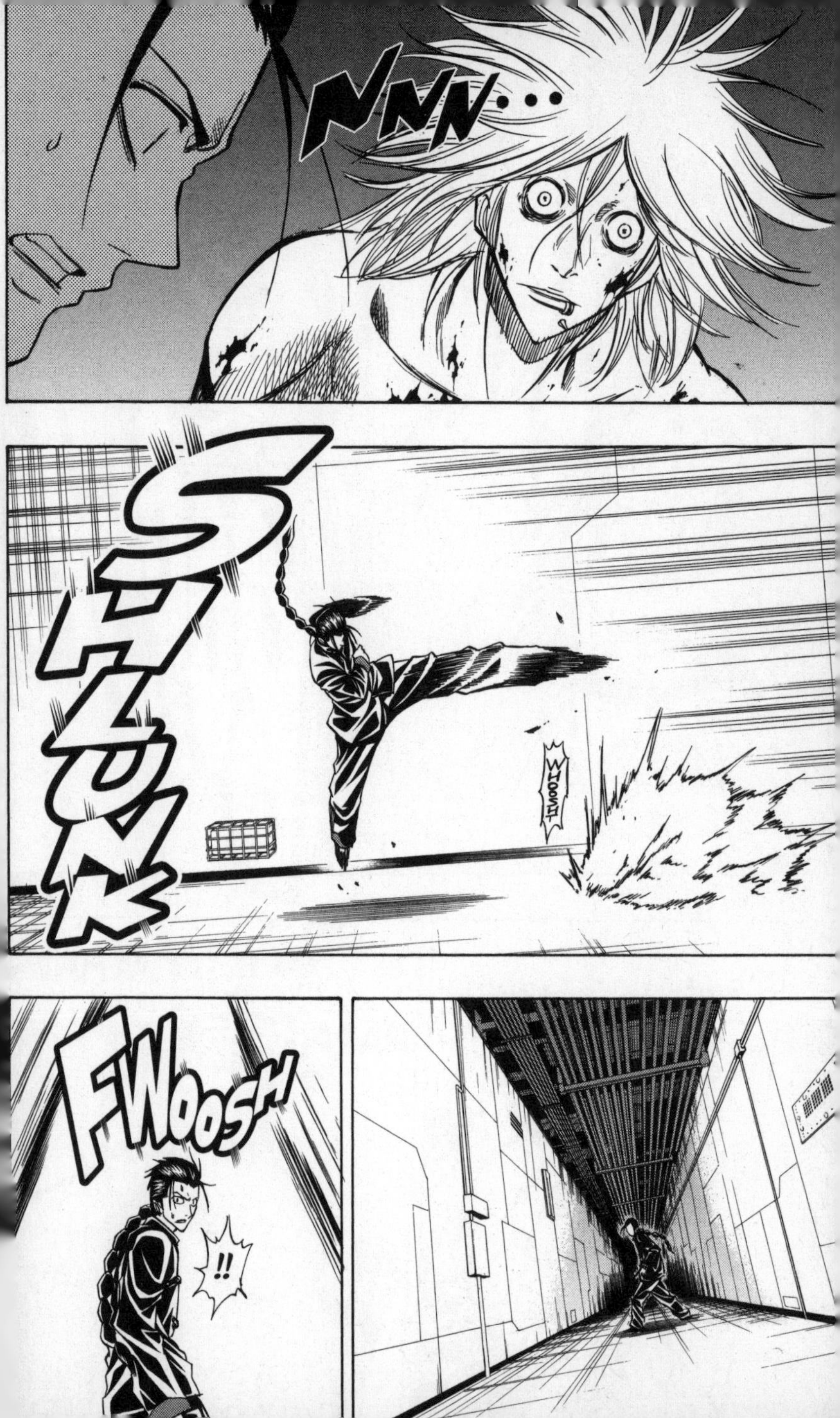
NNN...
SHUNK
WHOOSH
FWOOSH
!!

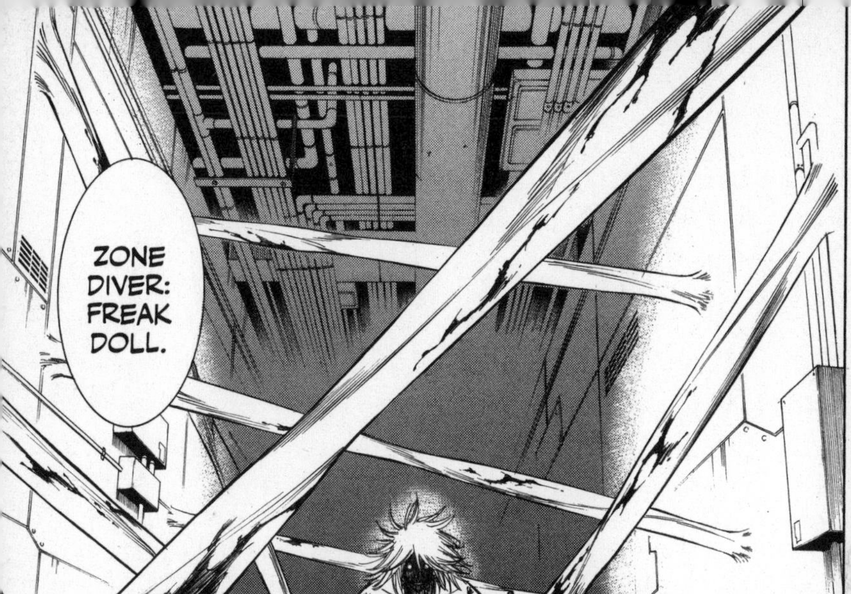
ZONE DIVER: FREAK DOLL.

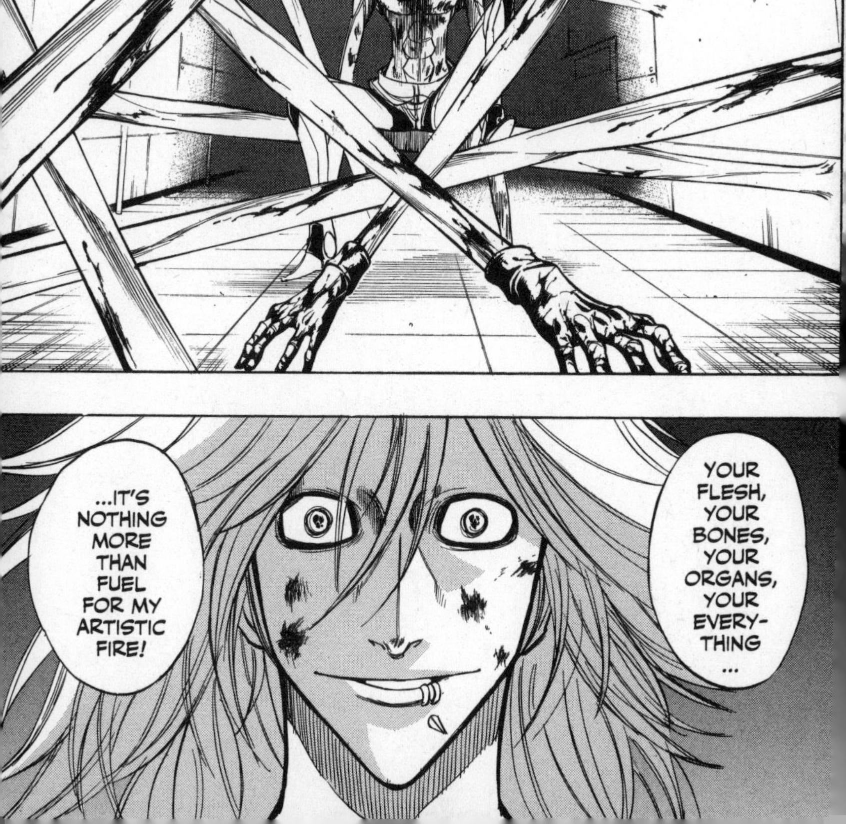
YOUR FLESH, YOUR BONES, YOUR ORGANS, YOUR EVERY-THING ...
...IT'S NOTHING MORE THAN FUEL FOR MY ARTISTIC FIRE!

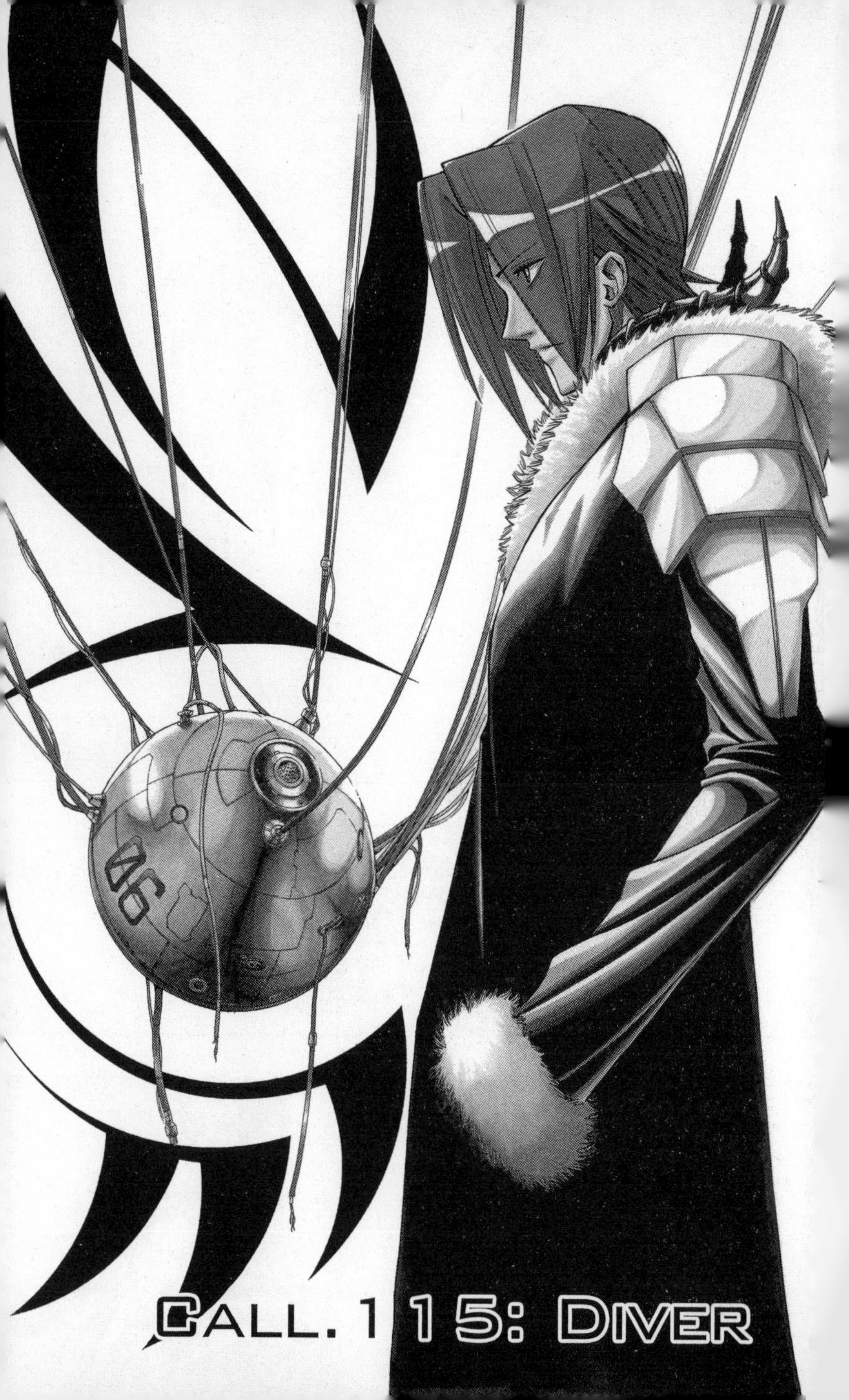

CALL. 115: DIVER

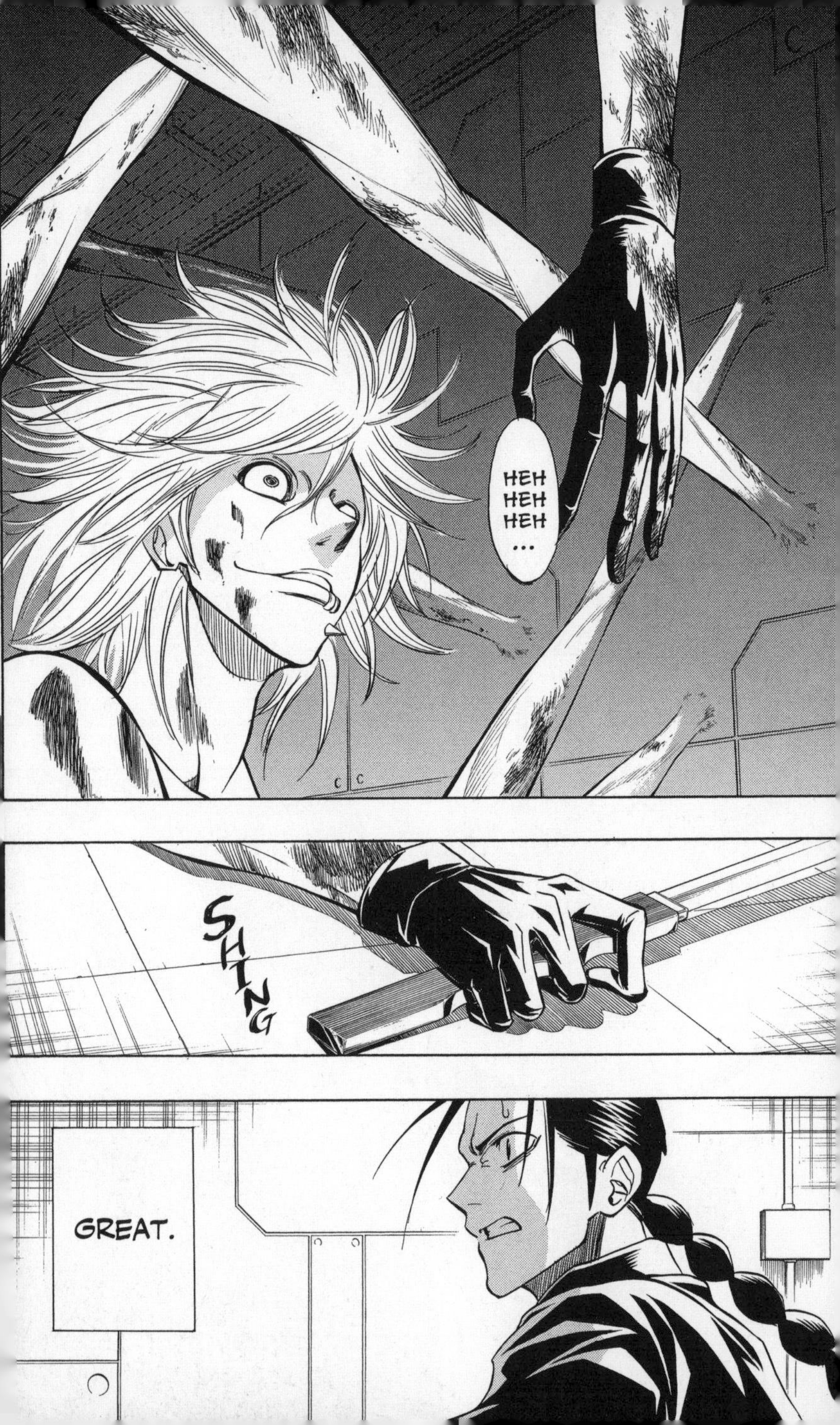
HEH HEH HEH ...
SHING
GREAT.

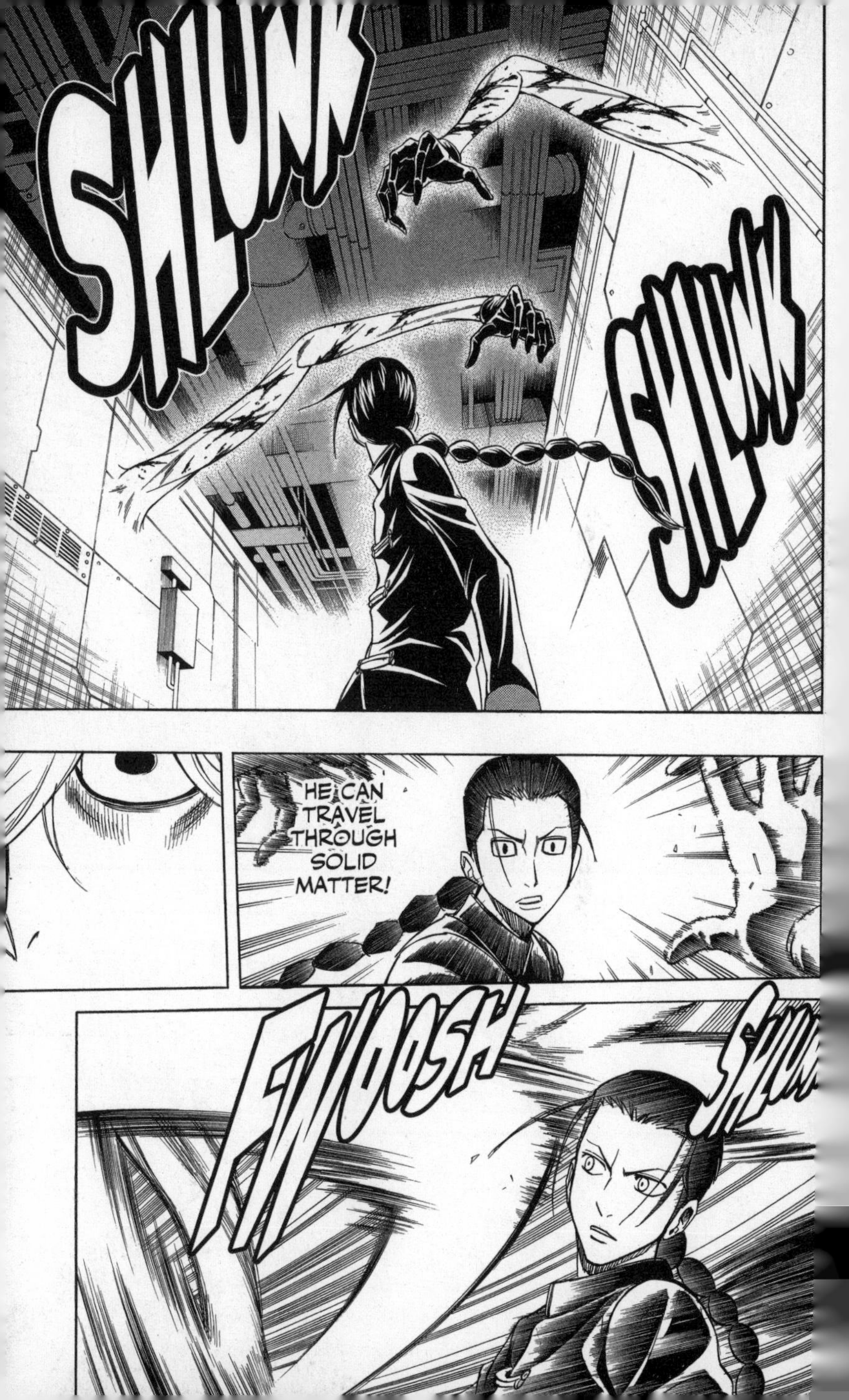
SHLUNK
SHLUNK
HE CAN TRAVEL THROUGH SOLID MATTER!
FWOOSH

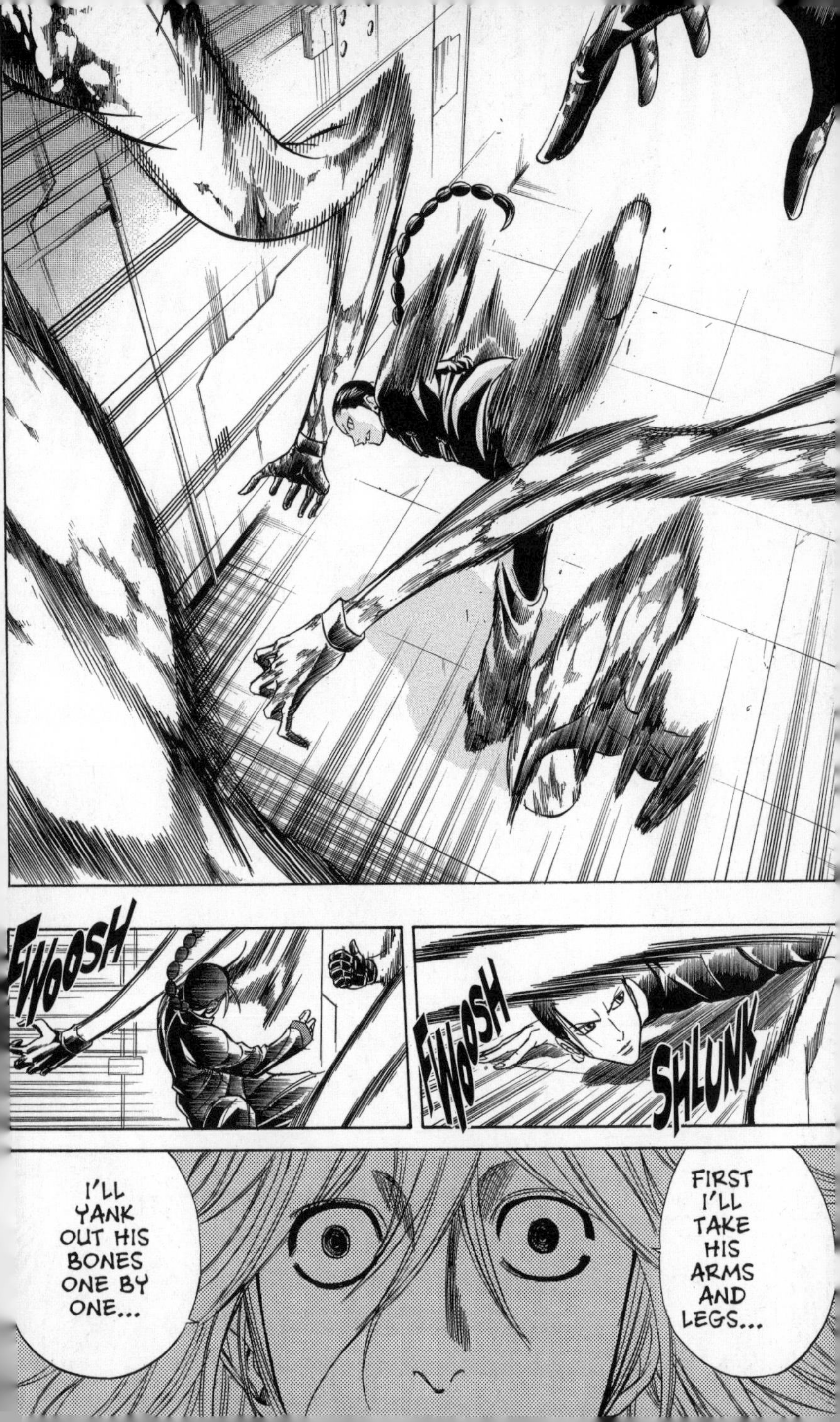
FWOOSH
SHLUNK
FWOOSH
FIRST I'LL TAKE HIS ARMS AND LEGS...
I'LL YANK OUT HIS BONES ONE BY ONE...

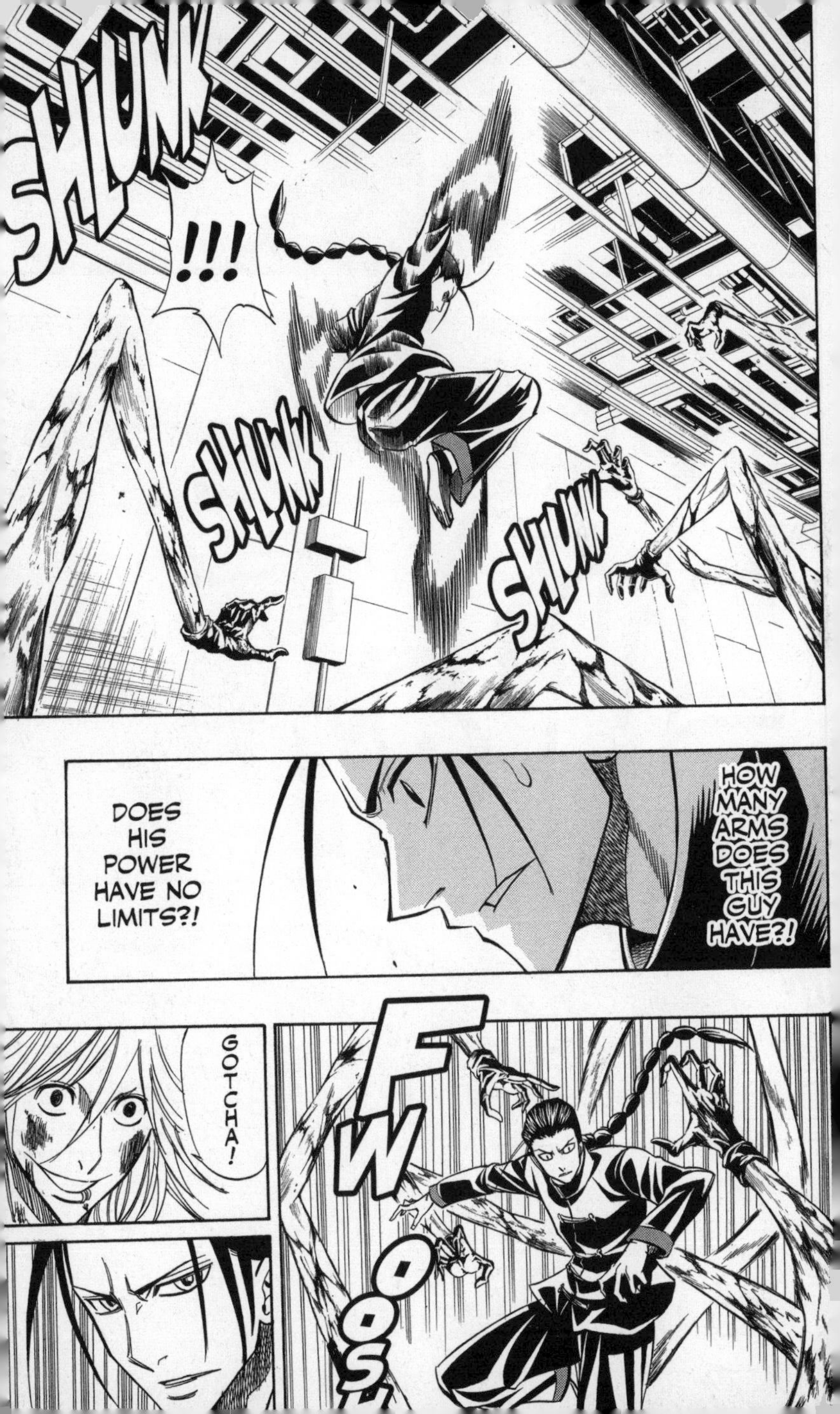
SHLUNK
!!!
SHLUNK
SHLUNK
HOW MANY ARMS DOES THIS GUY HAVE?!
DOES HIS POWER HAVE NO LIMITS?!
FWOOOSH
GOTCHA!

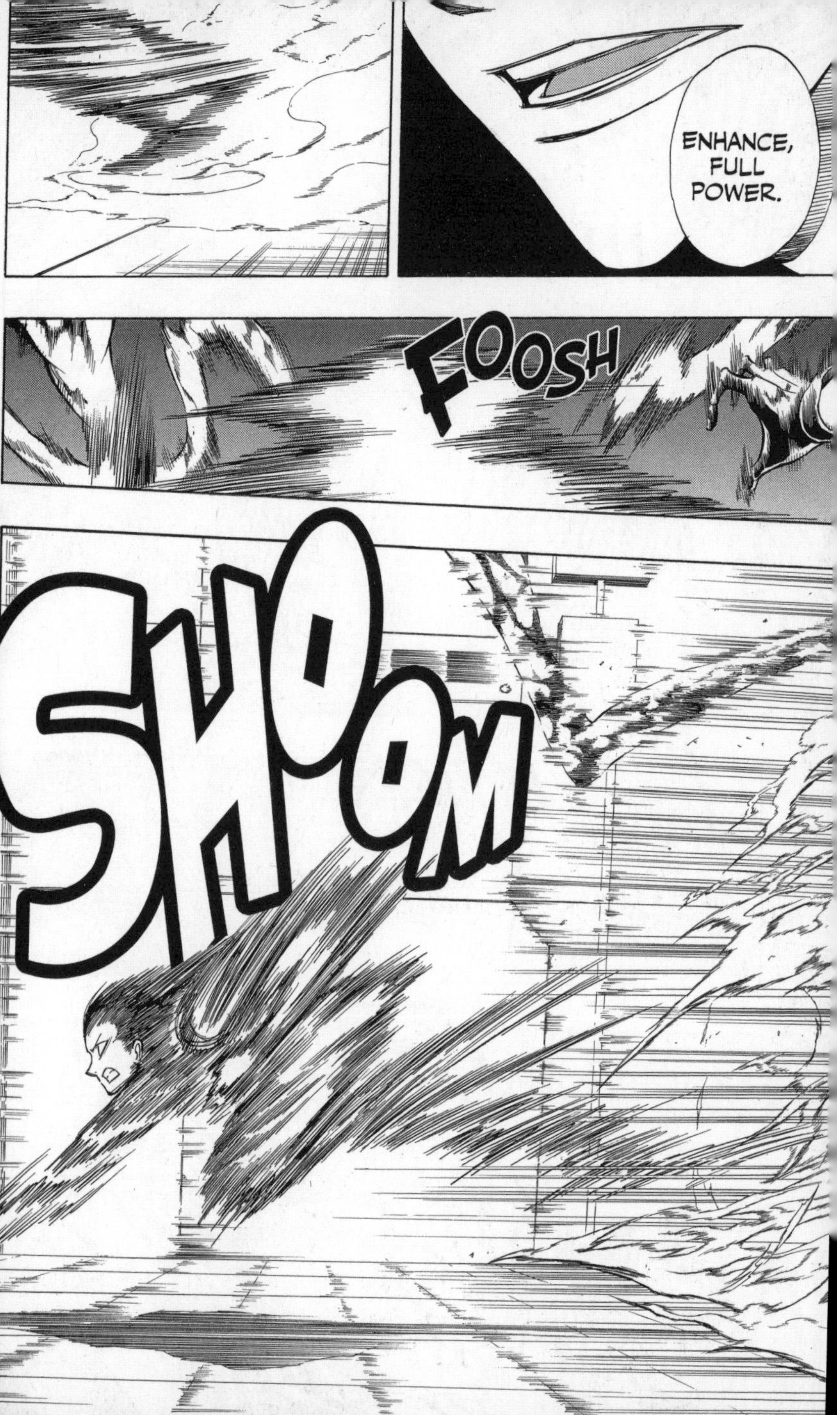
ENHANCE, FULL POWER.
FOOSH
SHOOM

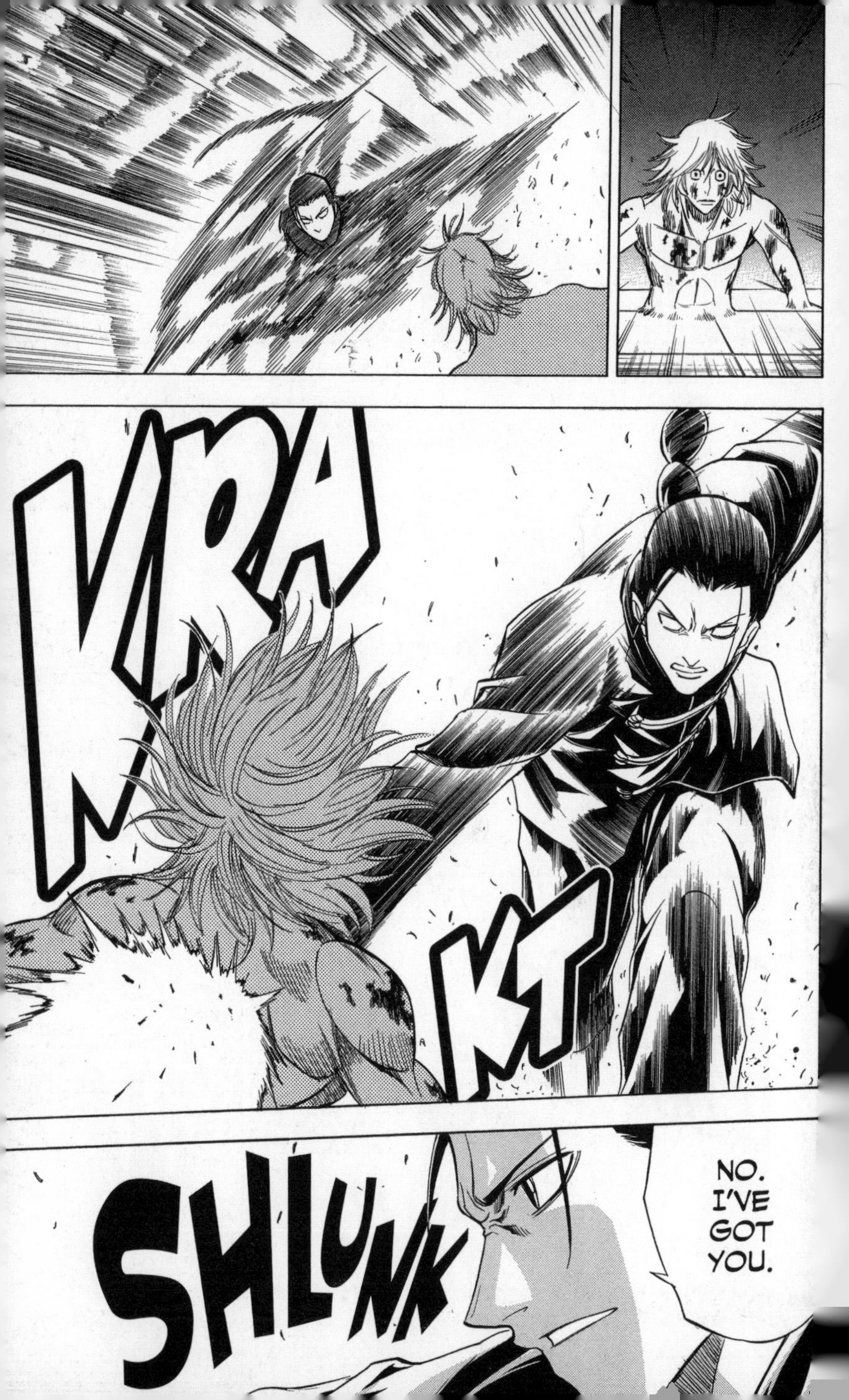
KRA
KT
NO. I'VE GOT YOU.
SHLUNK

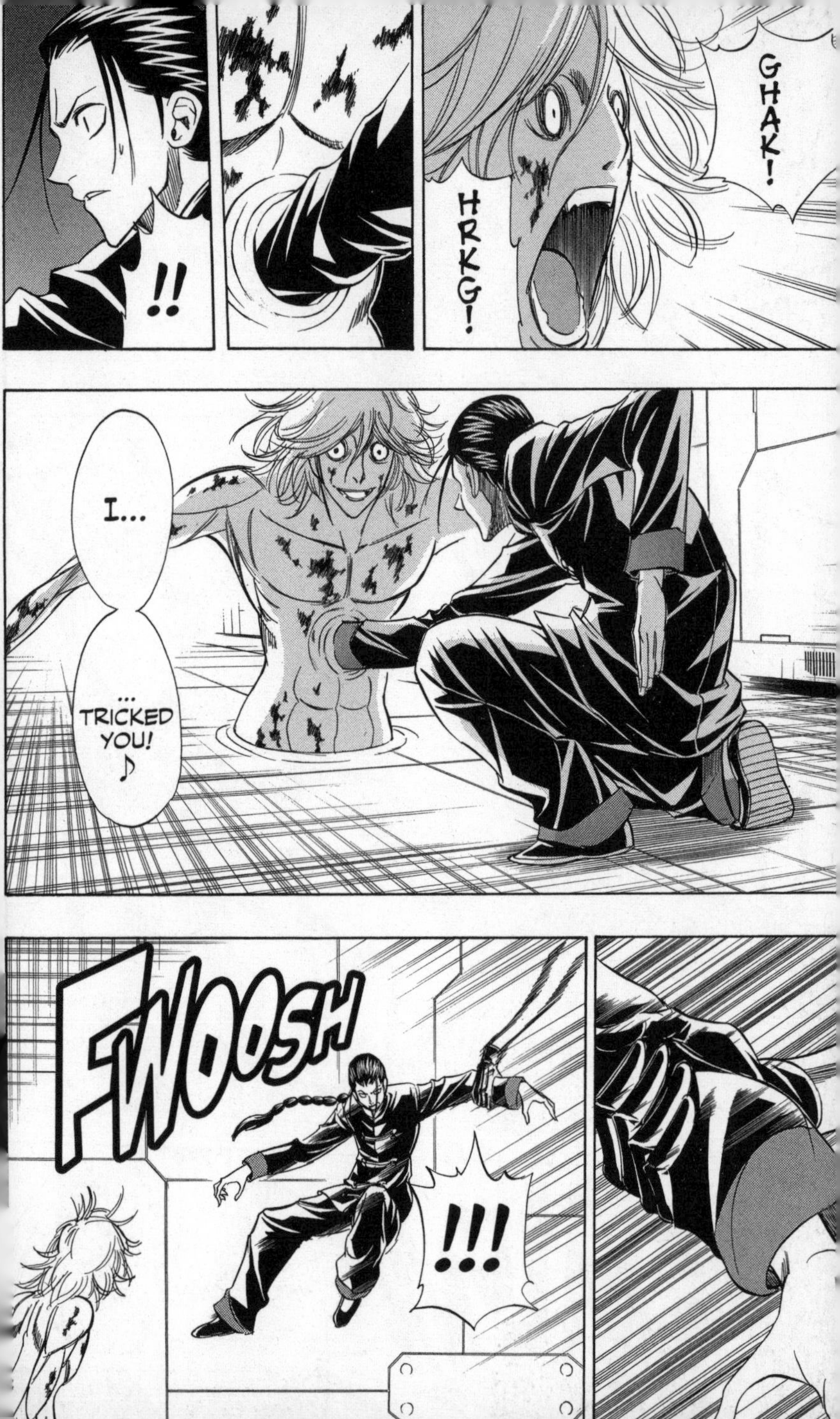
GHAK!
HRKG!
!!
I...
...TRICKED YOU! ♪
FWOOSH
!!!

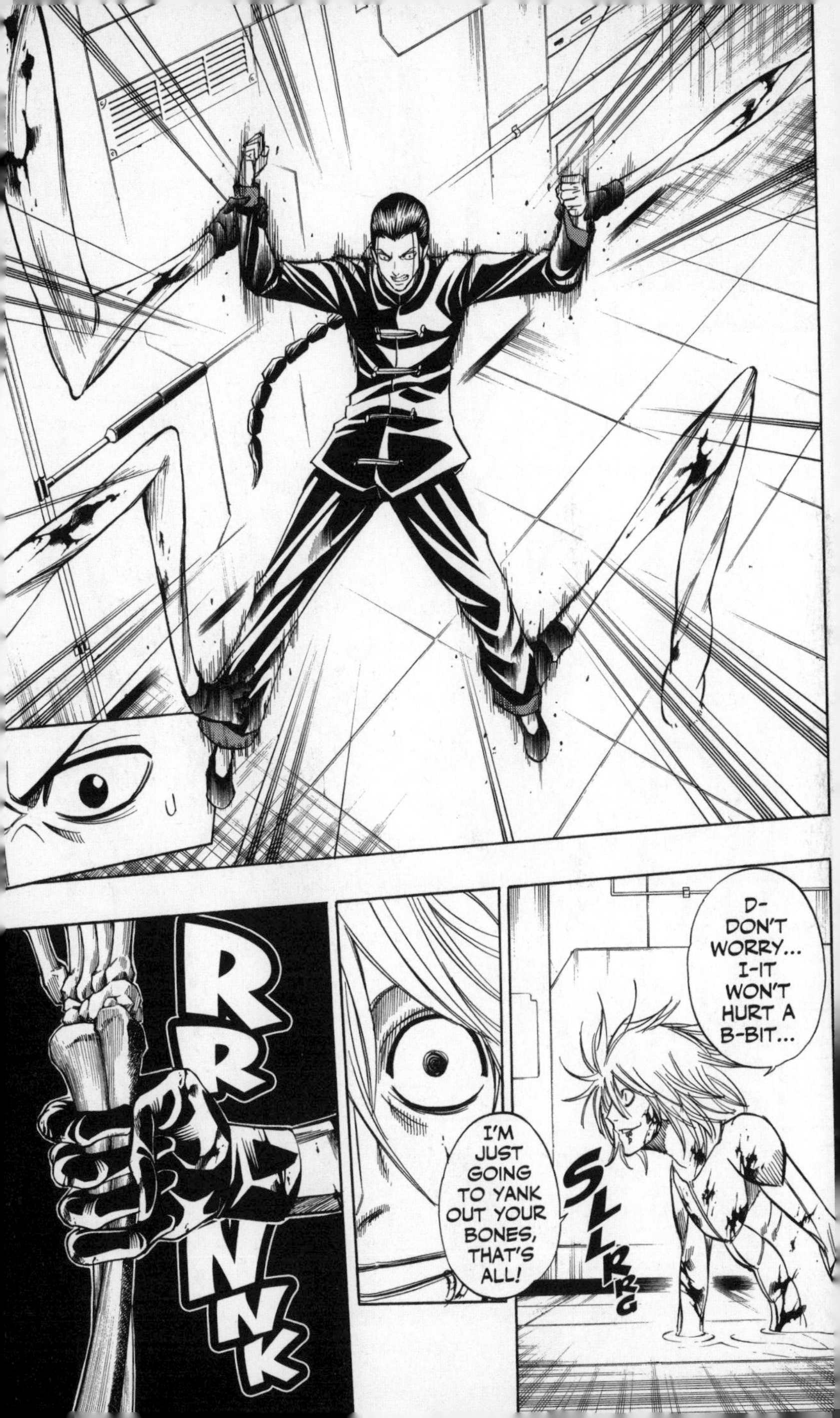
D-DON'T WORRY... I-IT WON'T HURT A B-BIT...
I'M JUST GOING TO YANK OUT YOUR BONES, THAT'S ALL!
SLLRRG
RRNNK

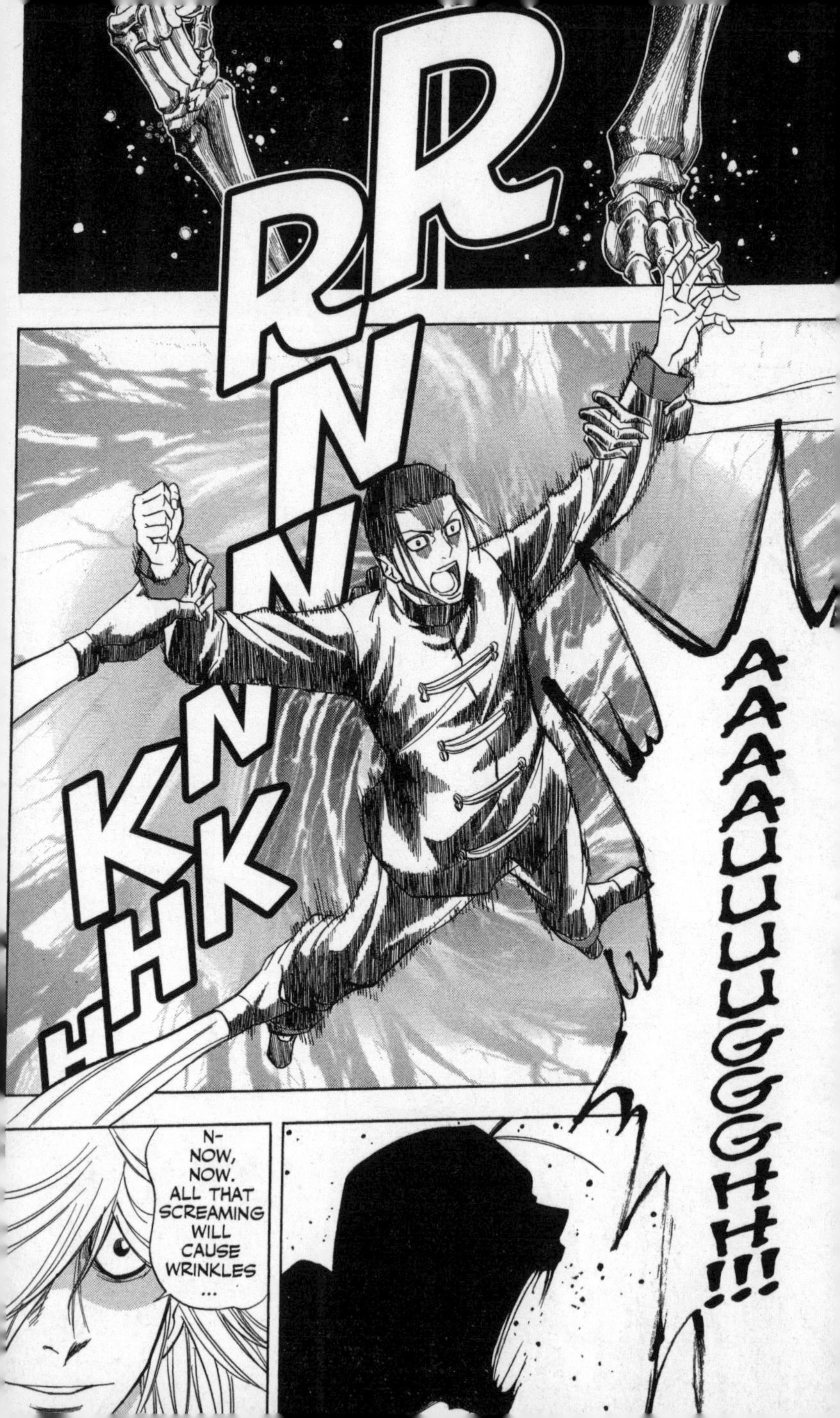
RRNNN
KNHHK
AAAAUUUUGGGGHHH!!!
N-NOW, NOW. ALL THAT SCREAMING WILL CAUSE WRINKLES...

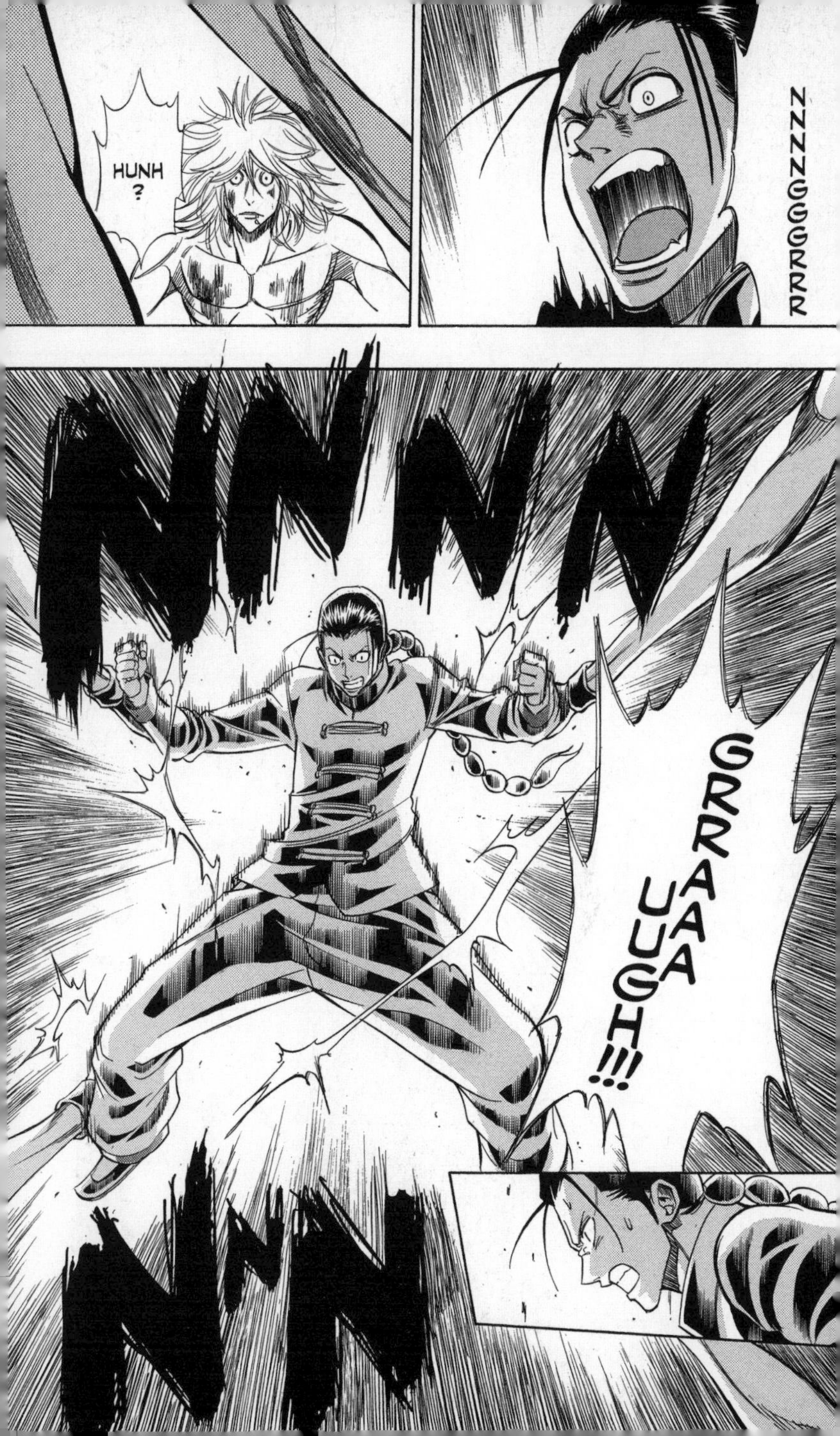
NNNNGGGRRR
HUNH ?
NNNN
GRRAAAUUGH!!!
NNN

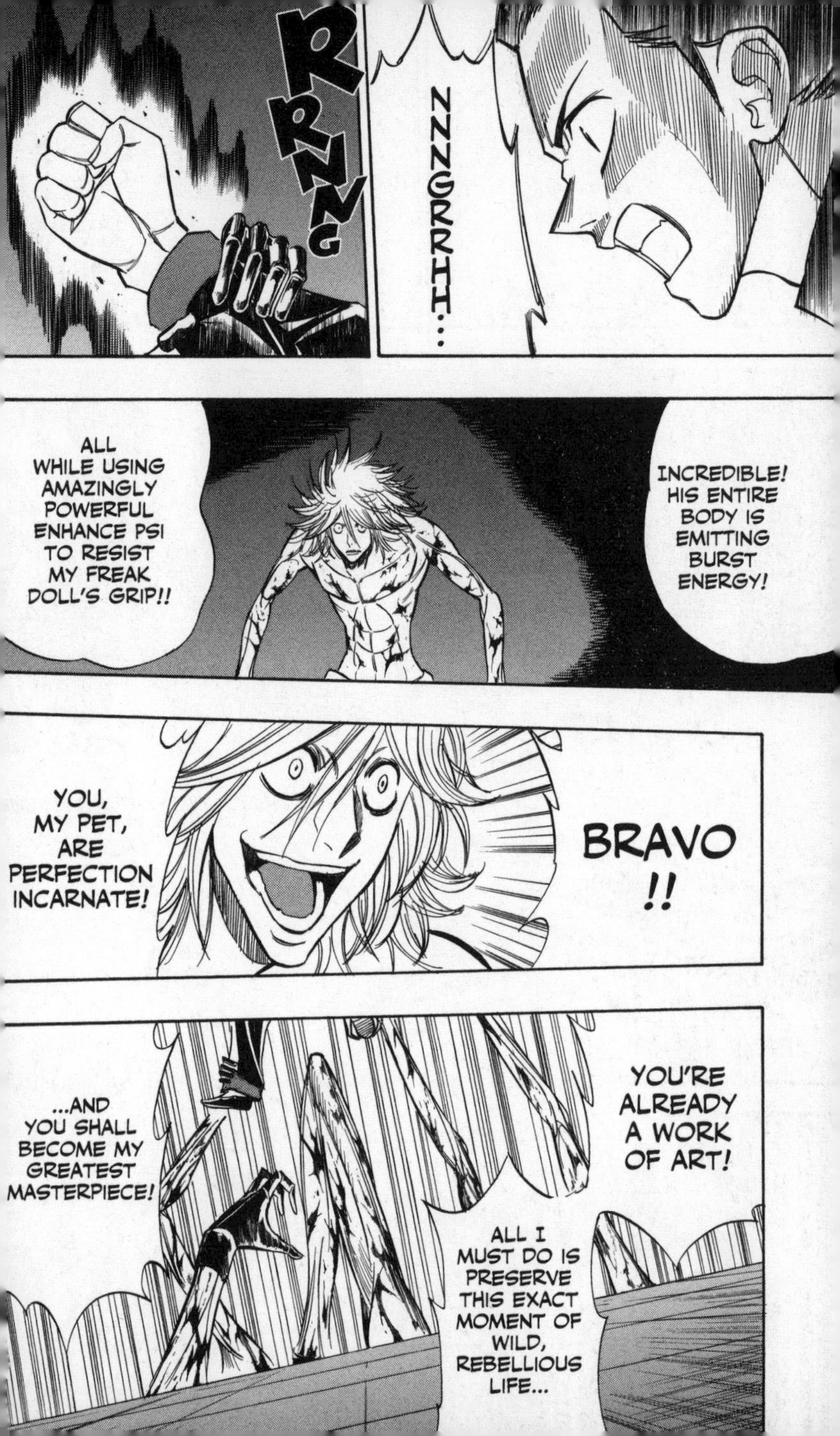
NNNGRRHH...
RRNNG
INCREDIBLE! HIS ENTIRE BODY IS EMITTING BURST ENERGY!
ALL WHILE USING AMAZINGLY POWERFUL ENHANCE PSI TO RESIST MY FREAK DOLL'S GRIP!!
BRAVO !!
YOU, MY PET, ARE PERFECTION INCARNATE!
YOU'RE ALREADY A WORK OF ART!
ALL I MUST DO IS PRESERVE THIS EXACT MOMENT OF WILD, REBELLIOUS LIFE...
...AND YOU SHALL BECOME MY GREATEST MASTERPIECE!

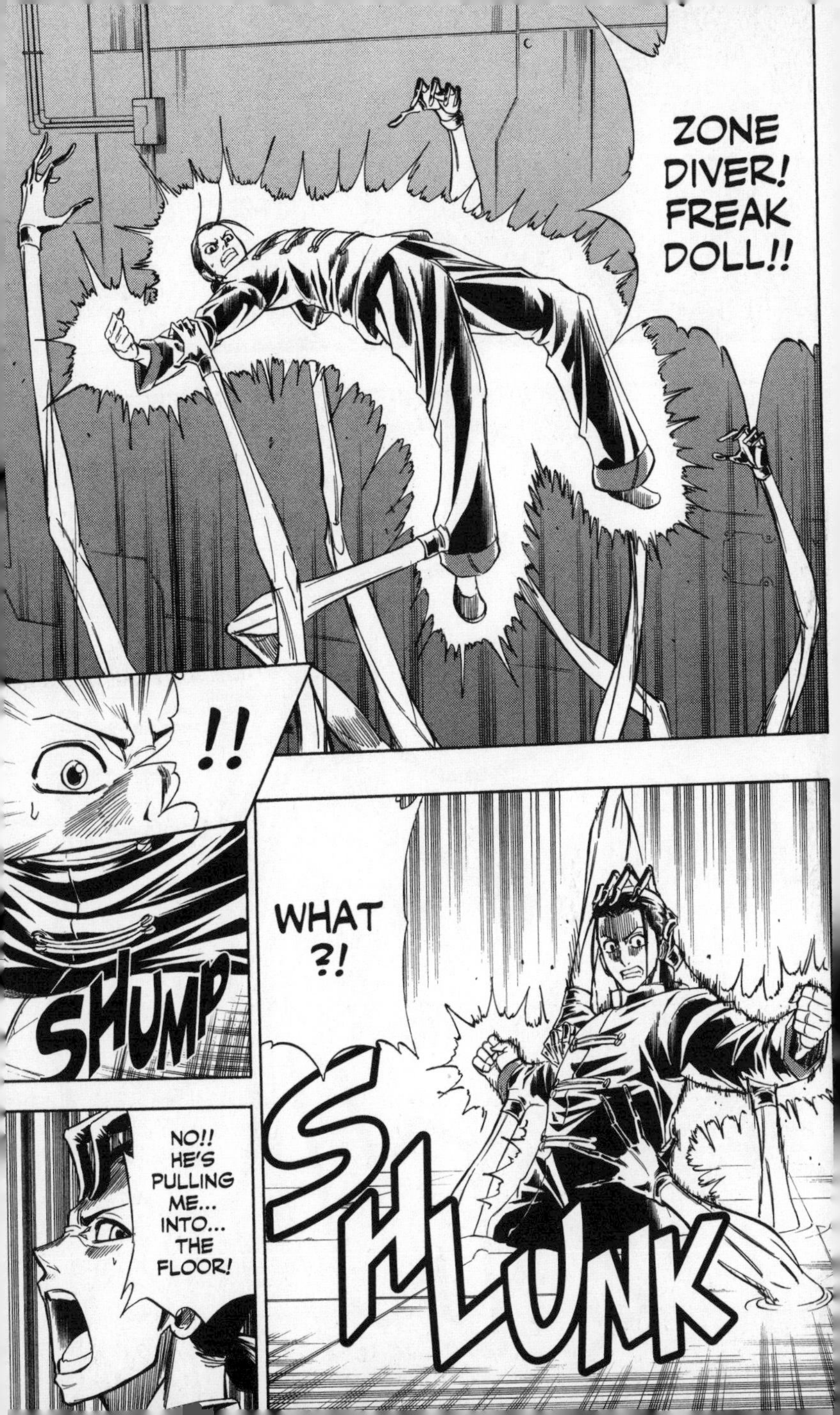
ZONE DIVER! FREAK DOLL!!
!!
WHAT ?!
SHUMP
SHLUNK
NO!! HE'S PULLING ME... INTO... THE FLOOR!

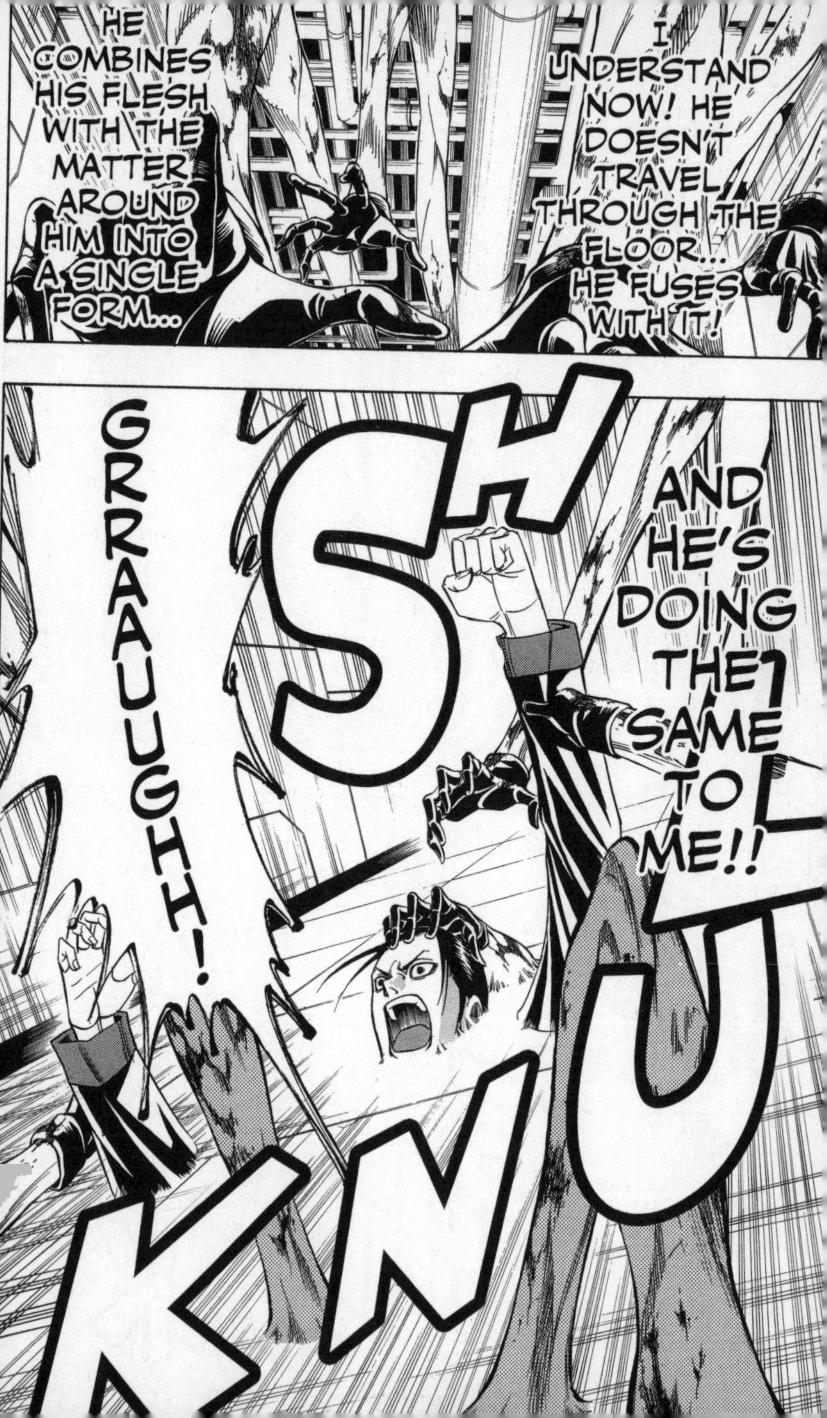
I UNDERSTAND NOW! HE DOESN'T TRAVEL THROUGH THE FLOOR... HE FUSES WITH IT!
HE COMBINES HIS FLESH WITH THE MATTER AROUND HIM INTO A SINGLE FORM...
AND HE'S DOING THE SAME TO ME!!
SHLUNK
GRRAAUUGHH!

SHLUNK
MY MASTER-PIECE WILL BE COMPLETE IN 45 SECONDS!
WHEN THE CONCRETE HAS FULLY BLENDED WITH YOUR BONES...
I'LL PULL YOU OUT AND DISENGAGE MY PSI. THEN YOU'LL BE FINISHED!
TUNK
YOU'LL BE PERFECT...
KSHUNCK
?!

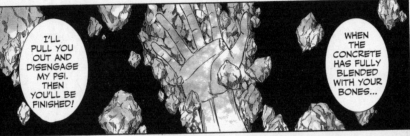

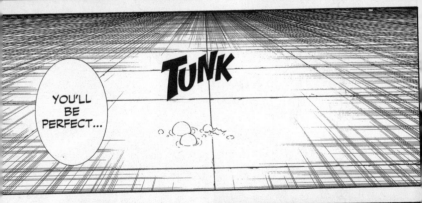

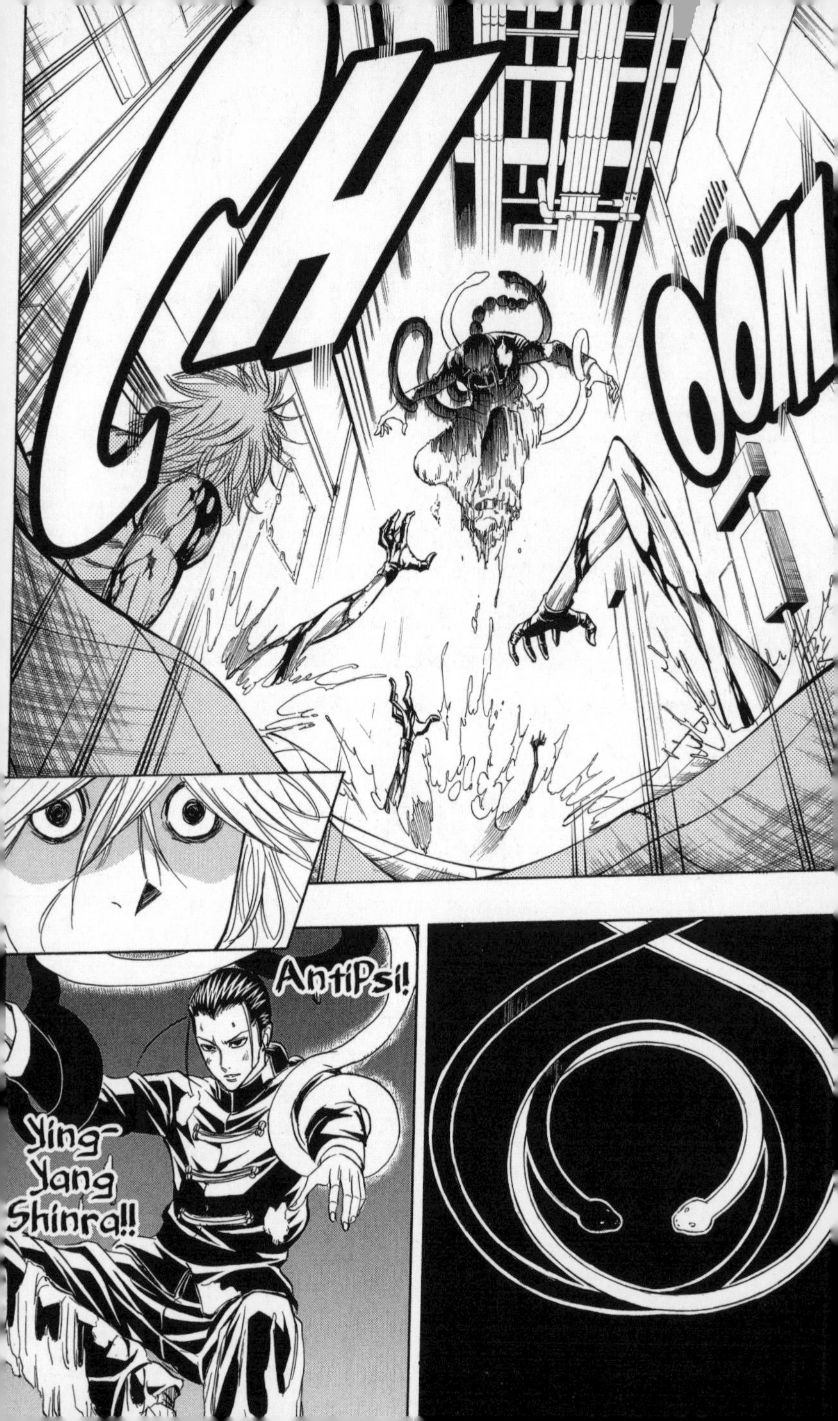
CH
OOM
AntiPsi!
Ying-Yang Shinra!!

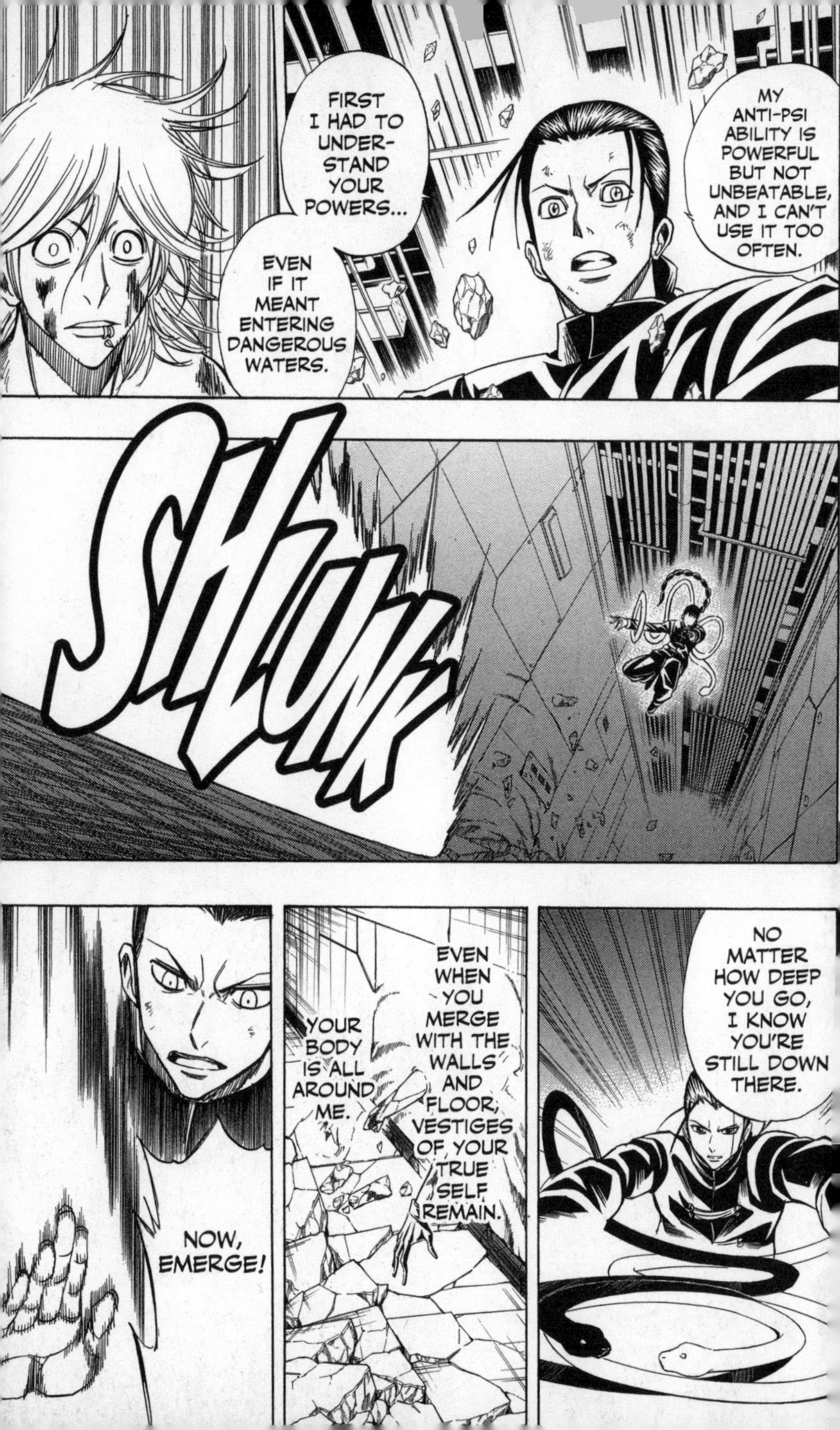
MY ANTI-PSI ABILITY IS POWERFUL BUT NOT UNBEATABLE, AND I CAN'T USE IT TOO OFTEN.
FIRST I HAD TO UNDER-STAND YOUR POWERS...
EVEN IF IT MEANT ENTERING DANGEROUS WATERS.
SHLUNK
NO MATTER HOW DEEP YOU GO, I KNOW YOU'RE STILL DOWN THERE.
EVEN WHEN YOU MERGE WITH THE WALLS AND FLOOR, VESTIGES OF YOUR TRUE SELF REMAIN.
YOUR BODY IS ALL AROUND ME.
NOW, EMERGE!

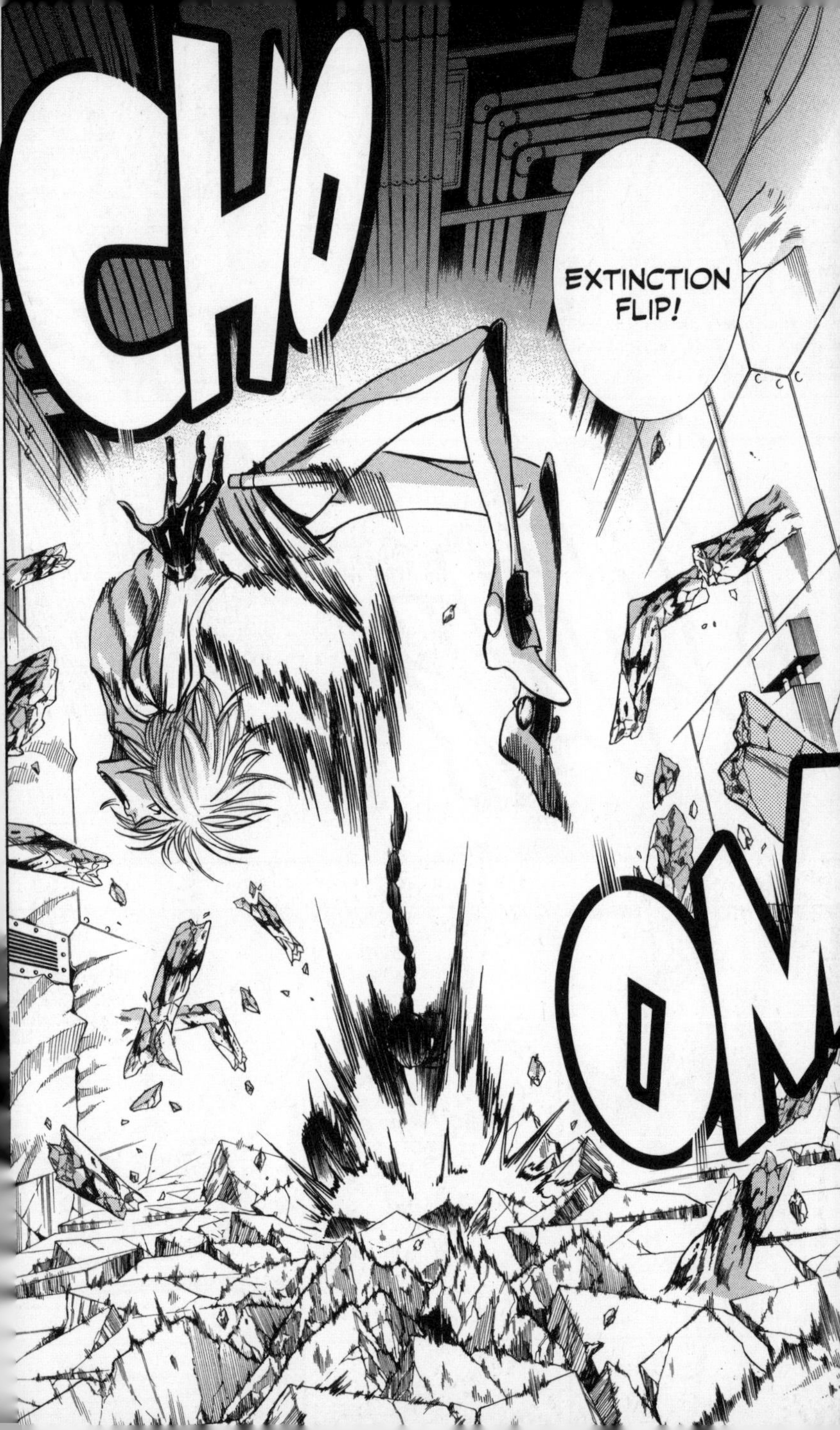
EXTINCTION FLIP!
CHO
OM

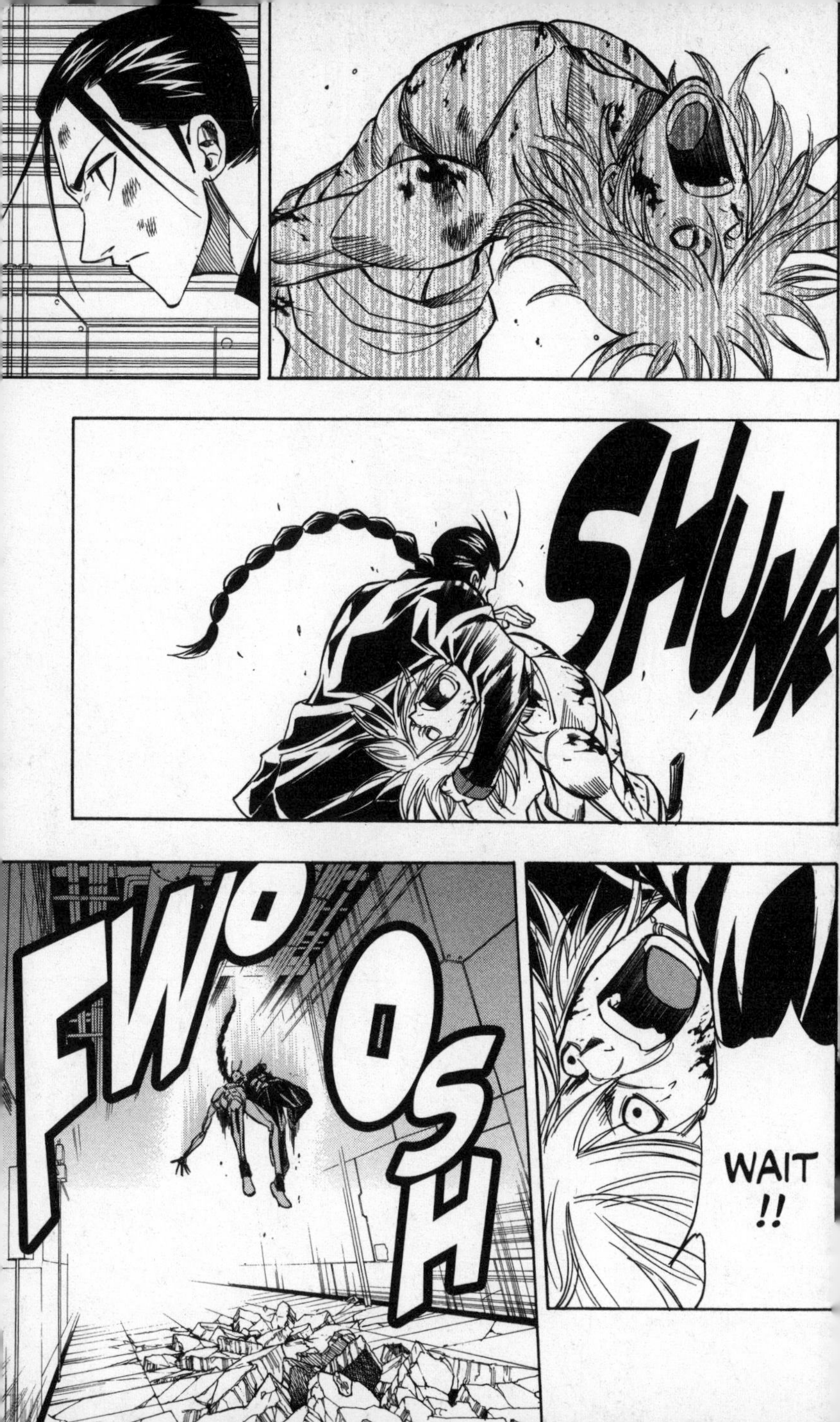
SHUNK
WAIT !!
FWOOSH

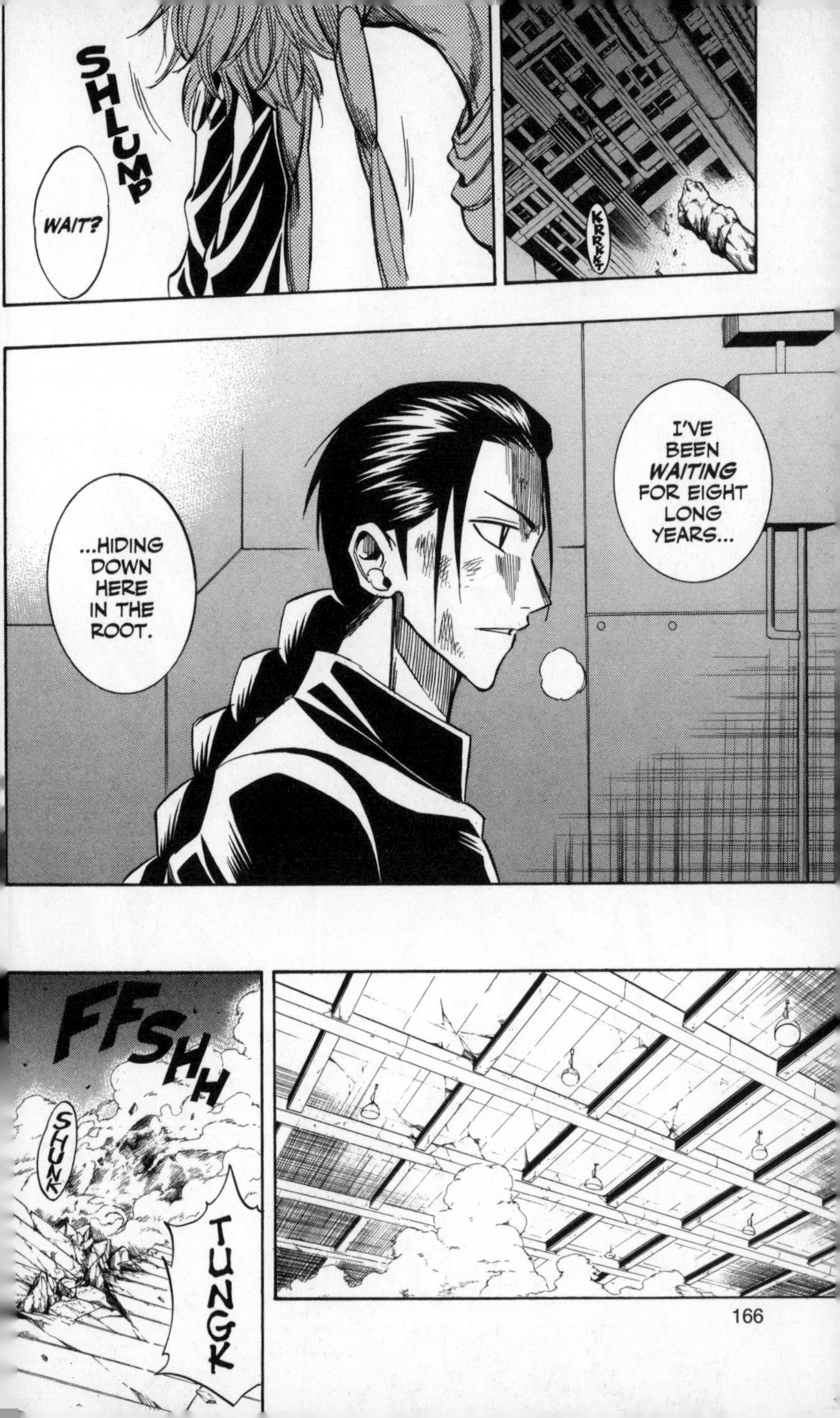
KRRKT
SHLUMP
WAIT?
I'VE BEEN *WAITING* FOR EIGHT LONG YEARS...
...HIDING DOWN HERE IN THE ROOT.
FFSHH
SHUNK
TUNGK

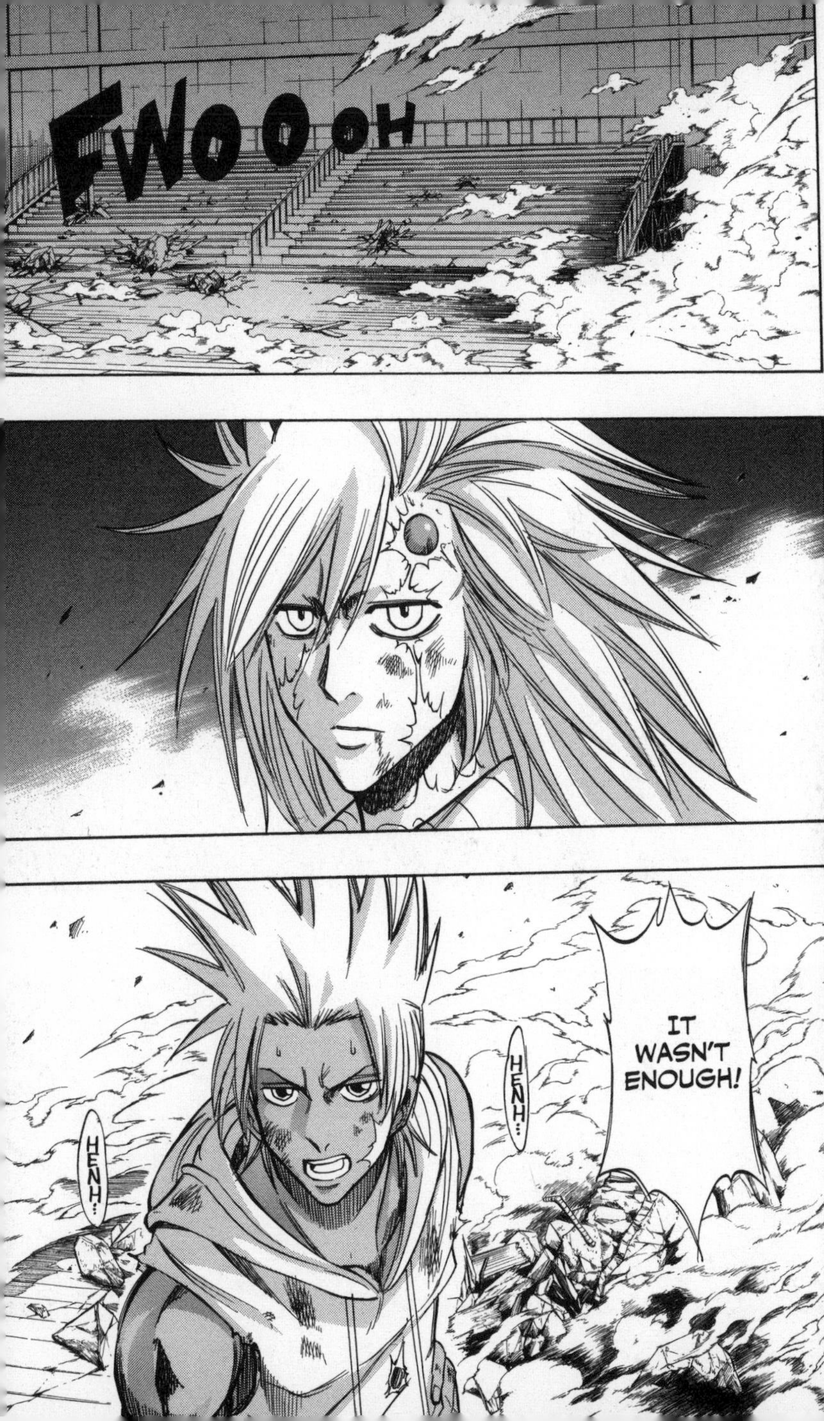
FWOOOH
IT WASN'T ENOUGH!
HENH...
HENH...

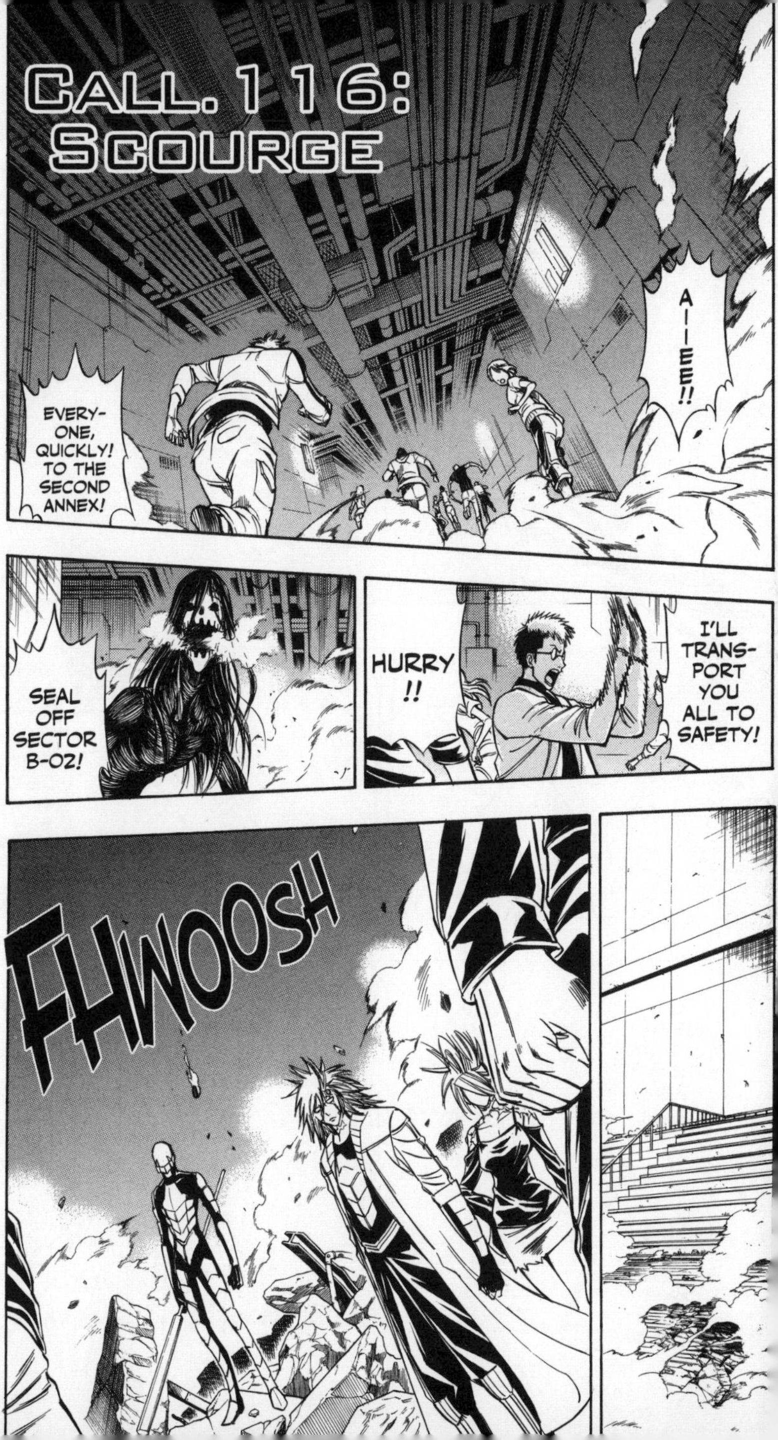
CALL. 116:
SCOURGE
AIIEE!!
EVERY-ONE, QUICKLY! TO THE SECOND ANNEX!
I'LL TRANS-PORT YOU ALL TO SAFETY!
HURRY!!
SEAL OFF SECTOR B-02!
FHWOOSH

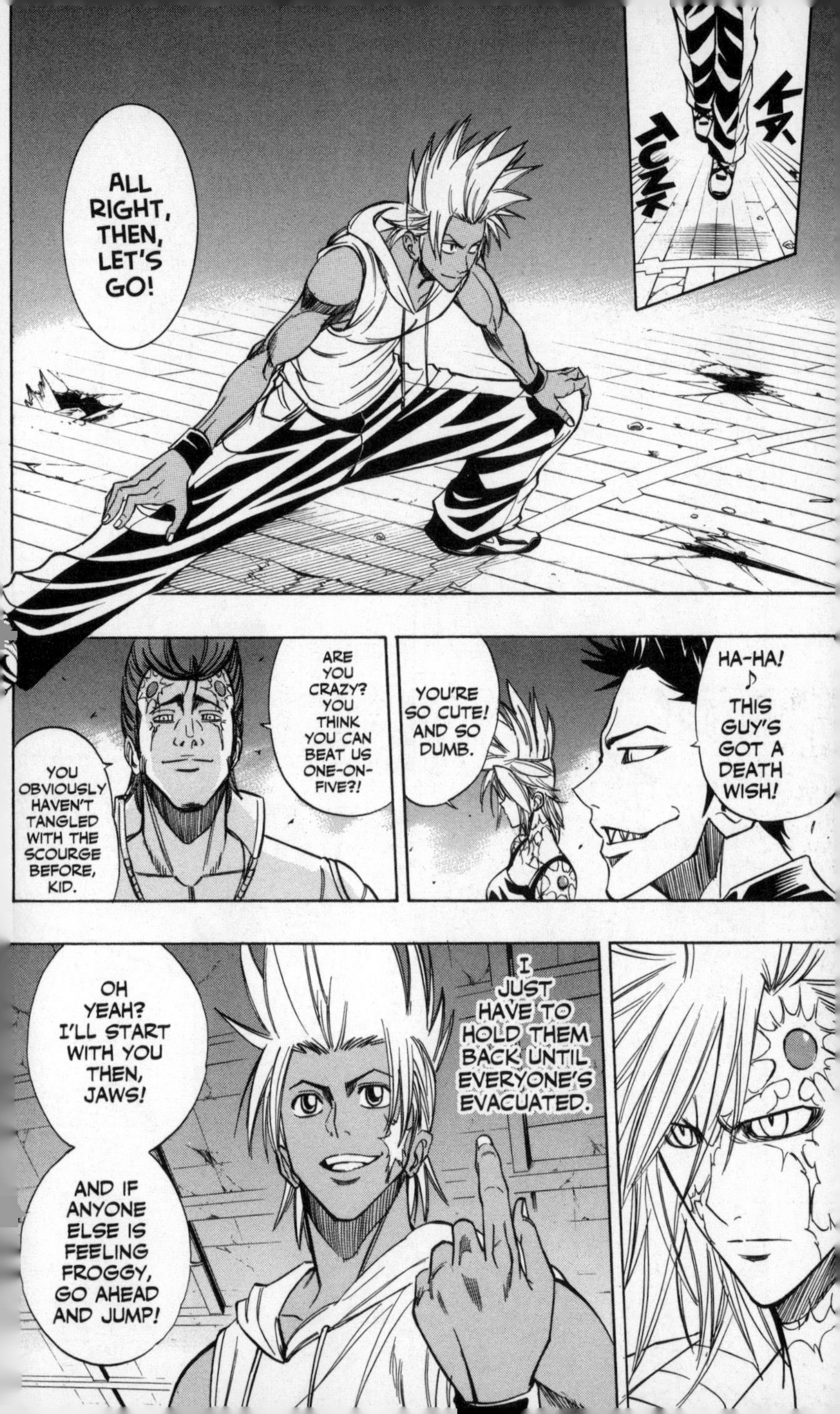
KA-TUNK
ALL RIGHT, THEN, LET'S GO!
HA-HA! ♪ THIS GUY'S GOT A DEATH WISH!
YOU'RE SO CUTE! AND SO DUMB.
ARE YOU CRAZY? YOU THINK YOU CAN BEAT US ONE-ON-FIVE?!
YOU OBVIOUSLY HAVEN'T TANGLED WITH THE SCOURGE BEFORE, KID.
I JUST HAVE TO HOLD THEM BACK UNTIL EVERYONE'S EVACUATED.
OH YEAH? I'LL START WITH YOU THEN, JAWS!
AND IF ANYONE ELSE IS FEELING FROGGY, GO AHEAD AND JUMP!

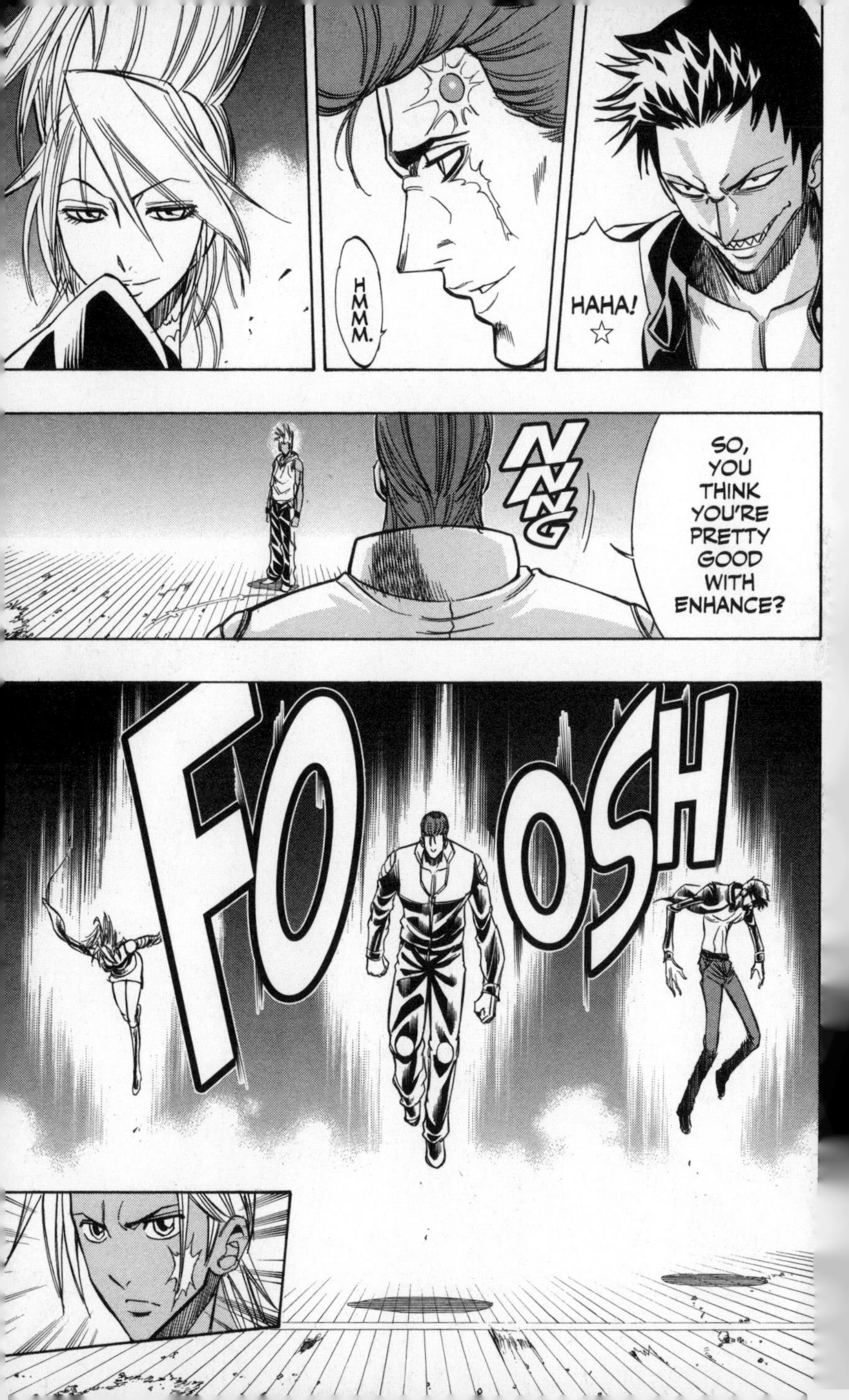
HAHA! ☆
HMMM.
SO, YOU THINK YOU'RE PRETTY GOOD WITH ENHANCE?
NNNG
FOOSH

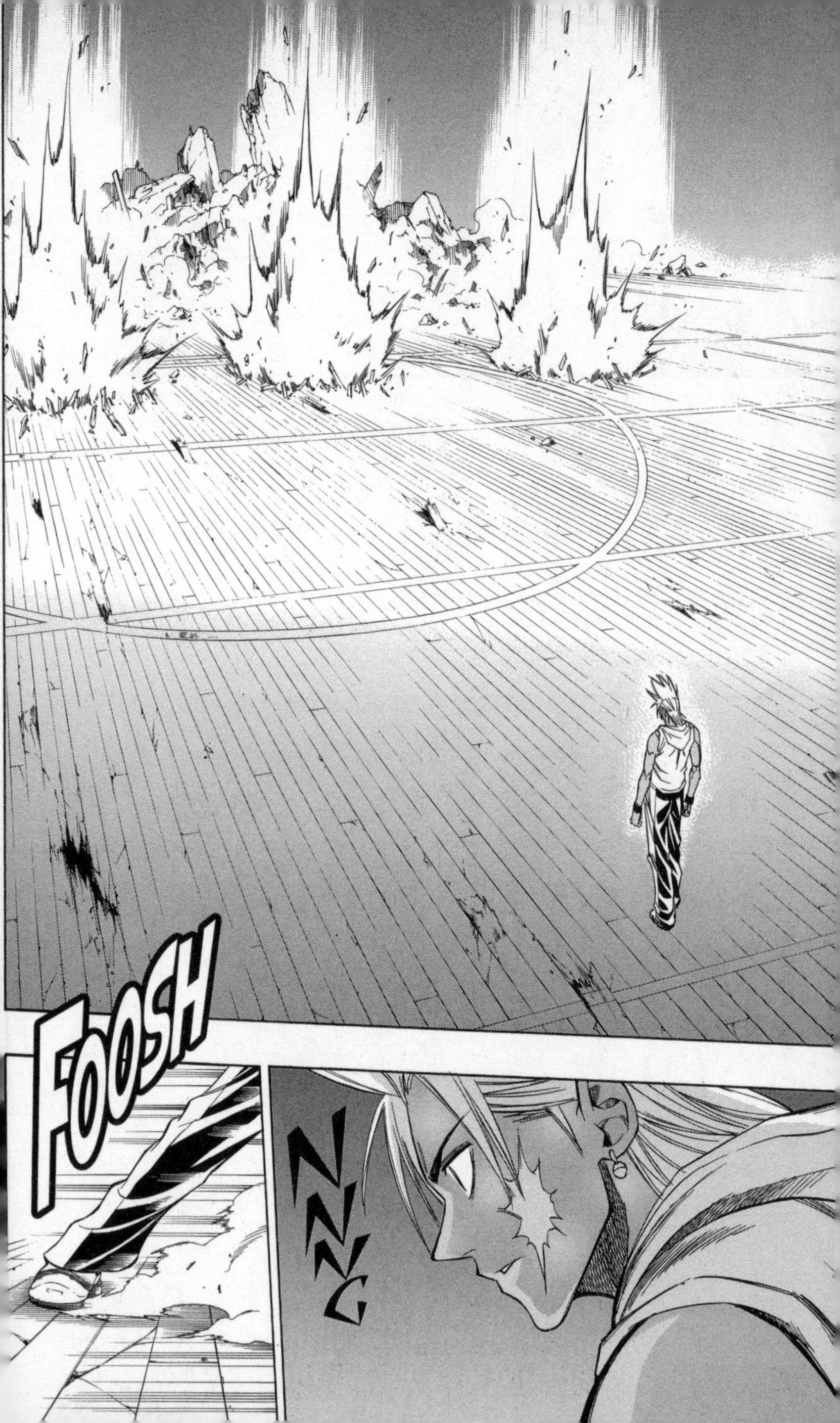
NNNG
FOOSH

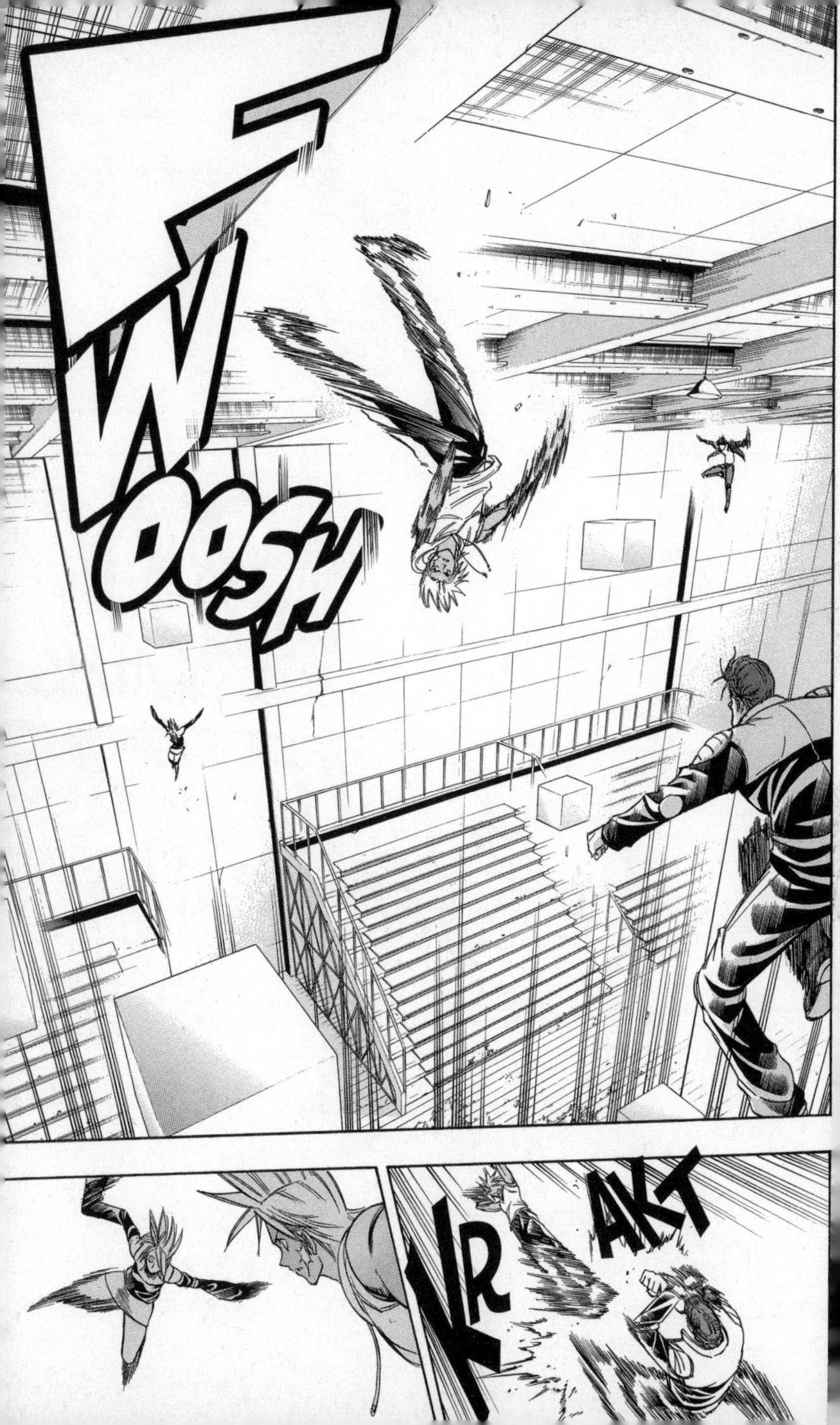
WOOSH
KRAKT

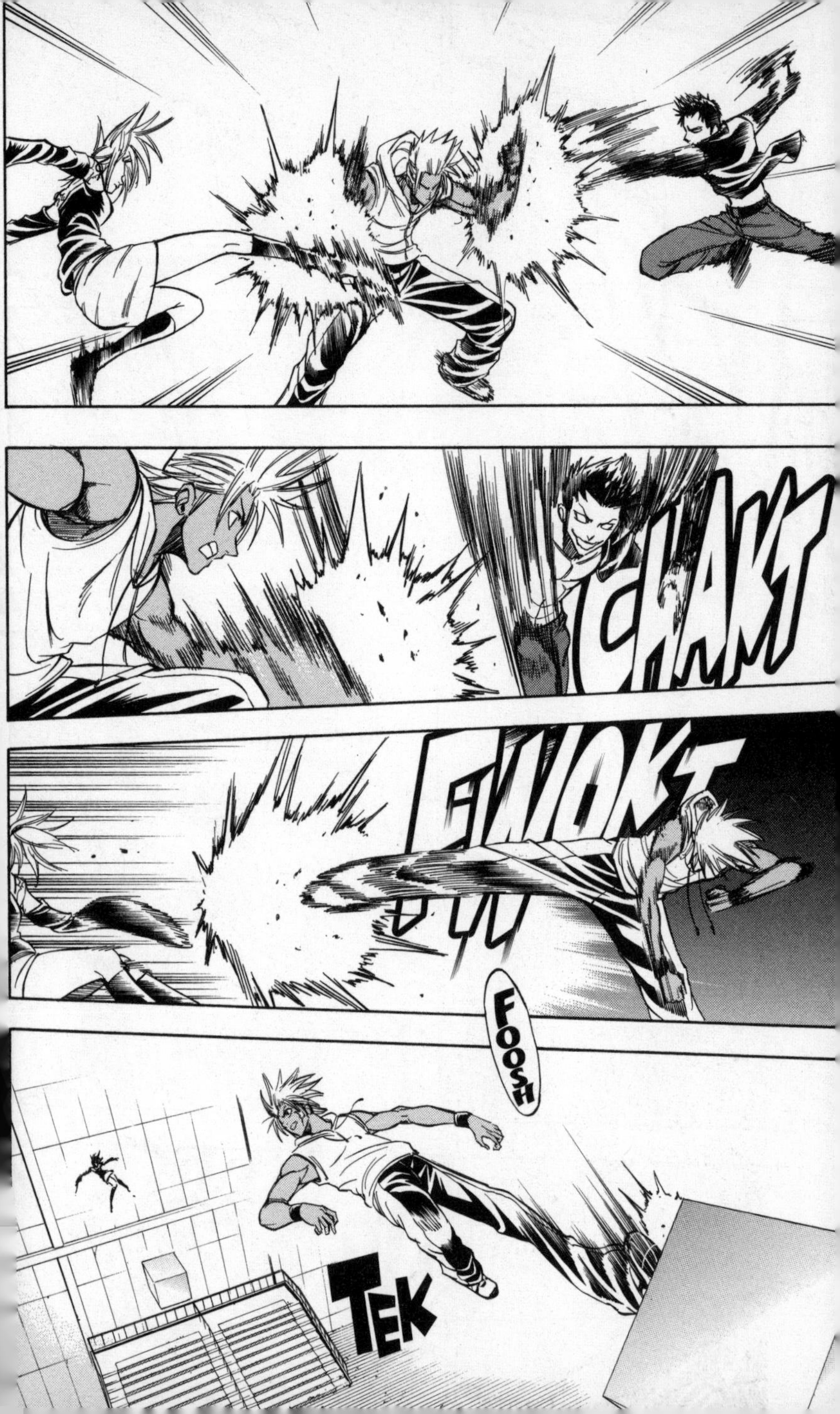
CHAK
FWOK
FOOSH
TEK

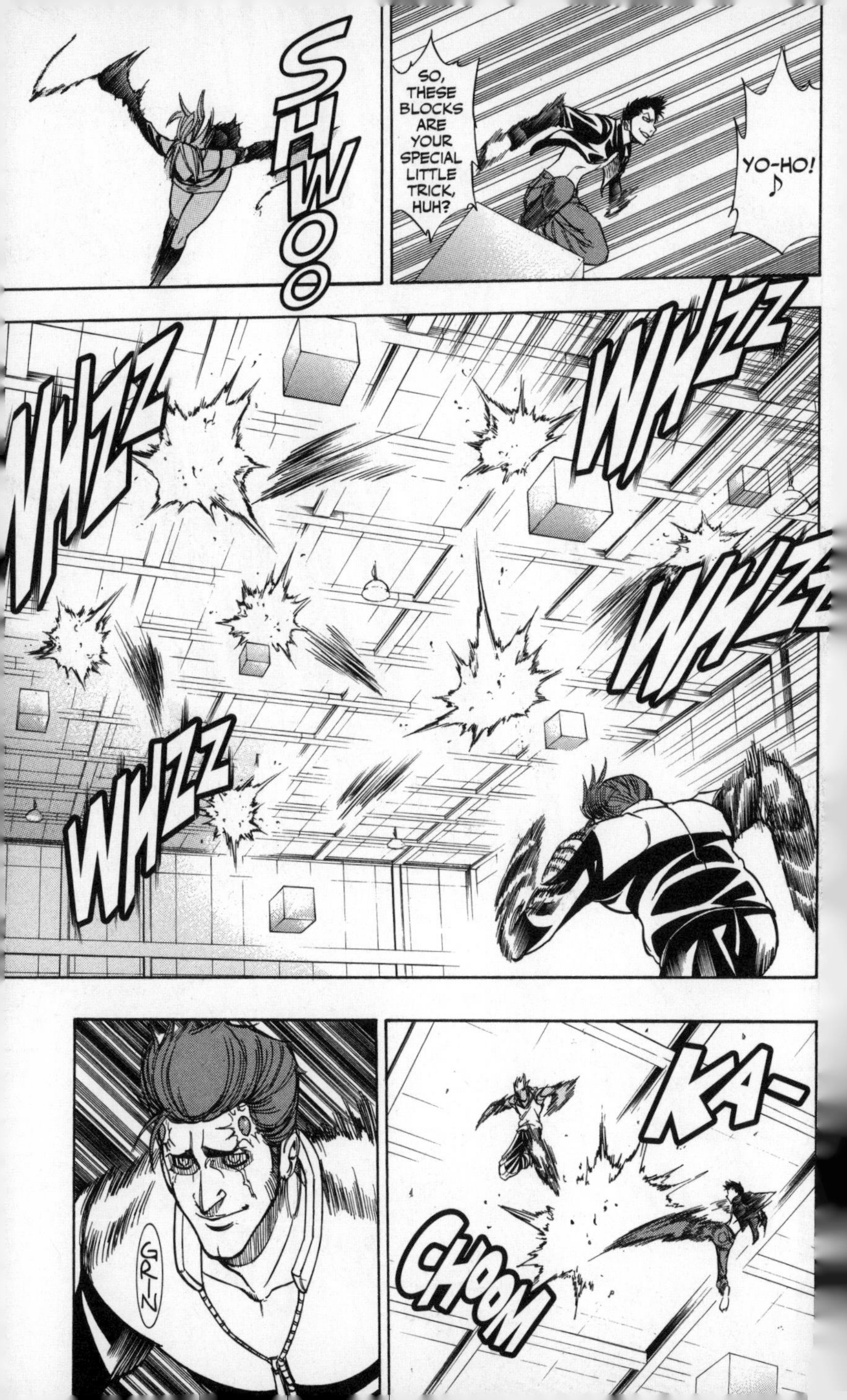
SO, THESE BLOCKS ARE YOUR SPECIAL LITTLE TRICK, HUH?
YO-HO! ♪
SHWOOO
WHIZZ
WHIZZ
WHIZZ
WHIZZ
KA-
CHOOM
GRIN

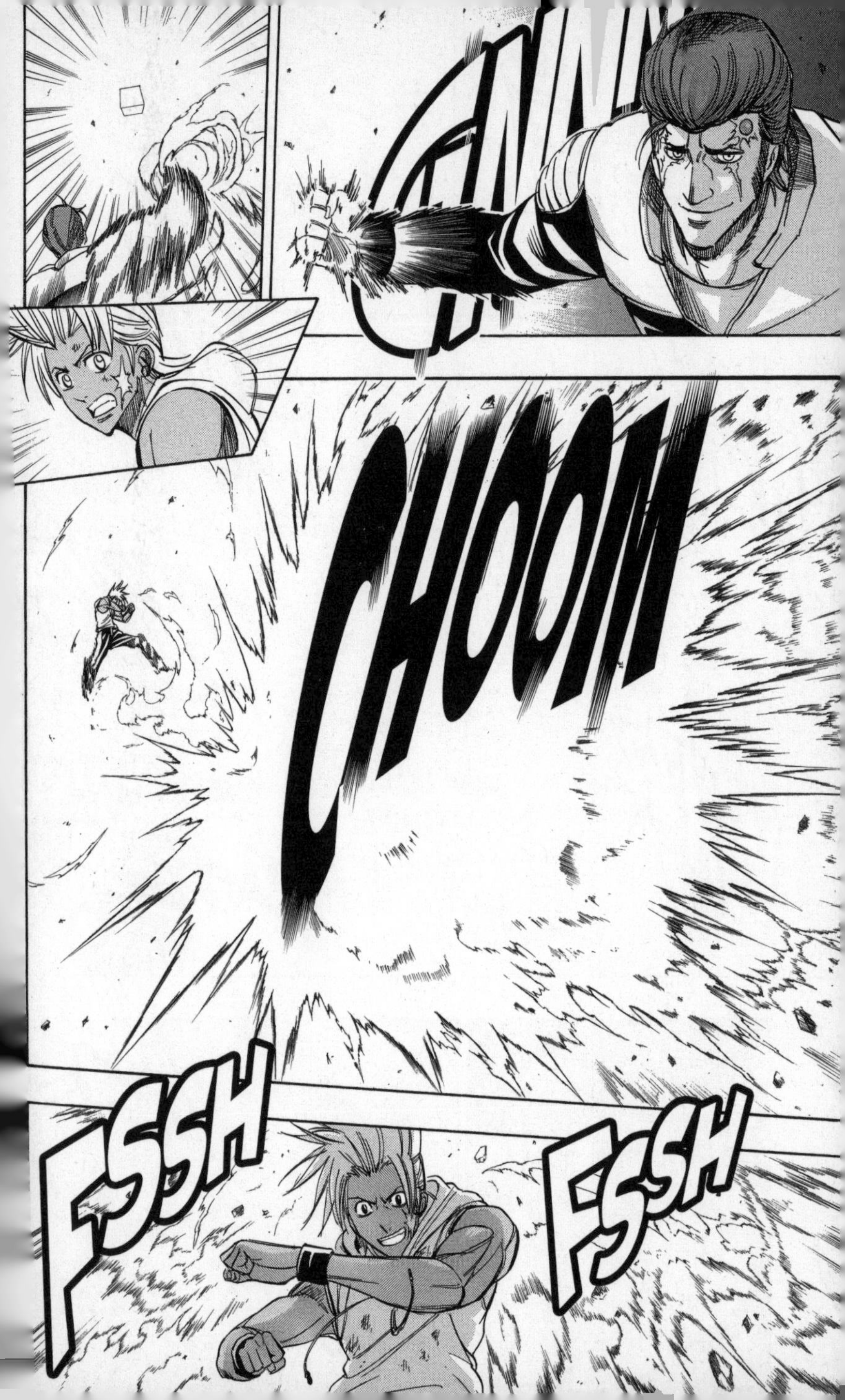
CHOOM
FSSH
FSSH

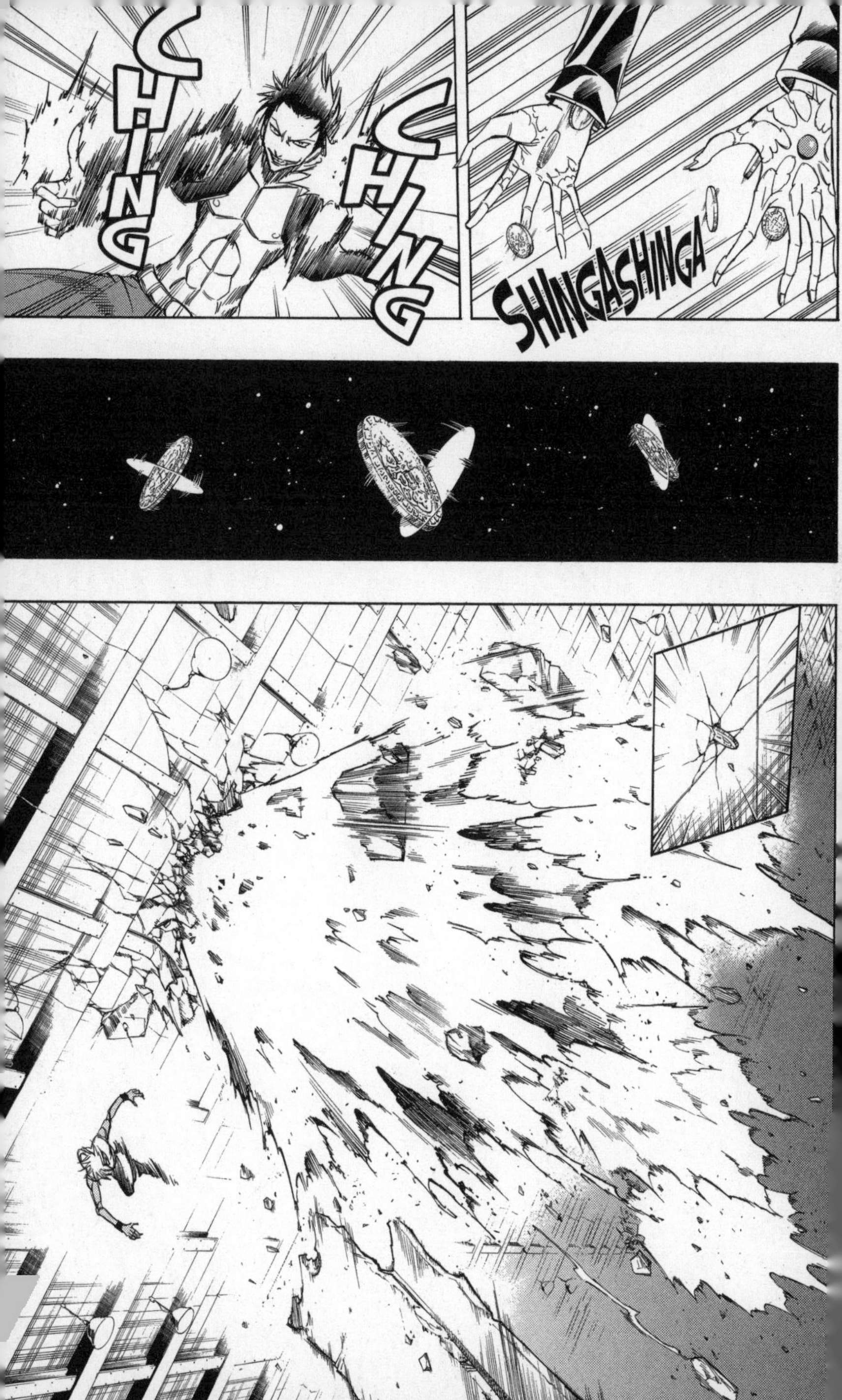
SHINGASHINGA
CHING
CHING

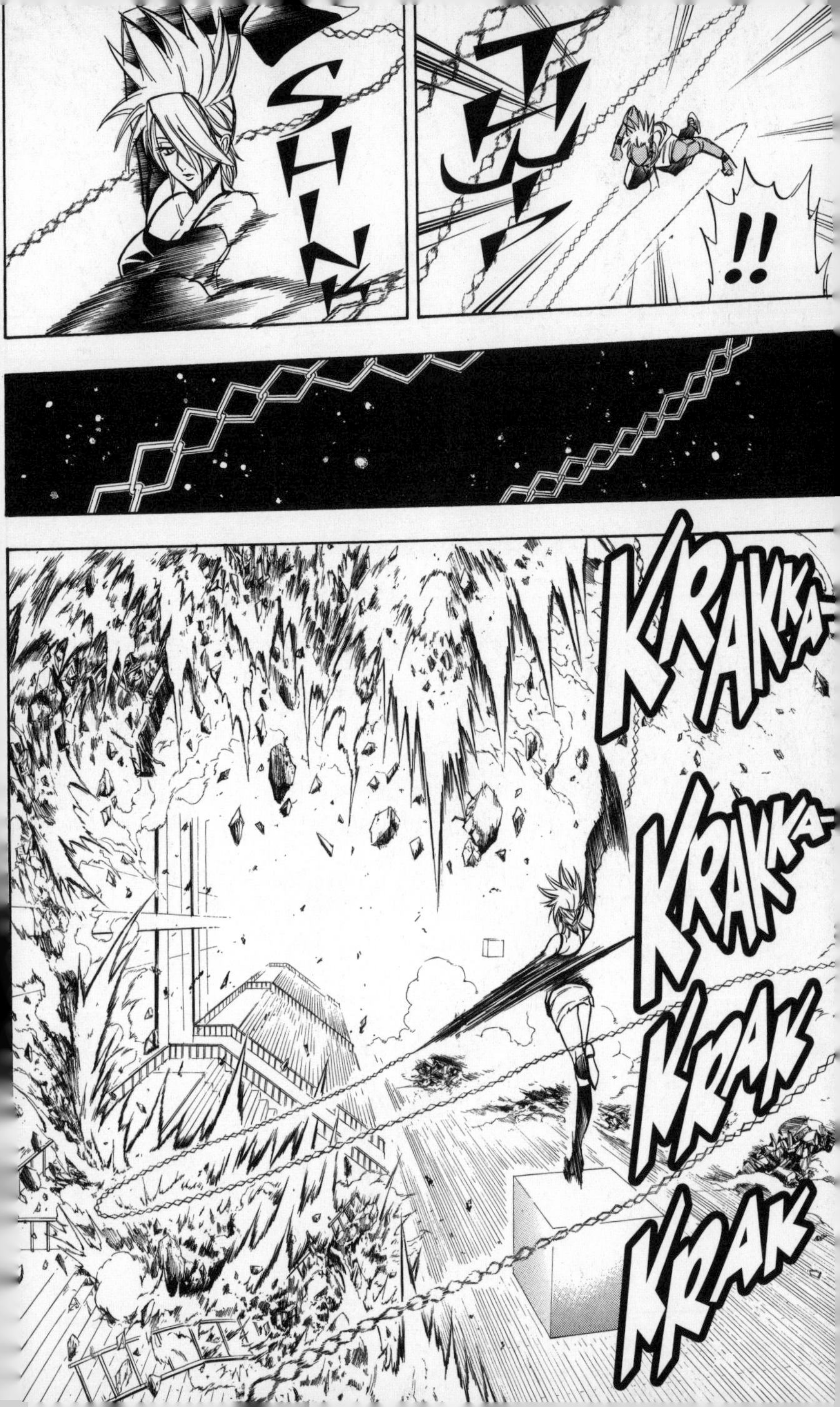
!!
SHINK
KRAKKA-
KRAKKA-
KRAK
KRAK

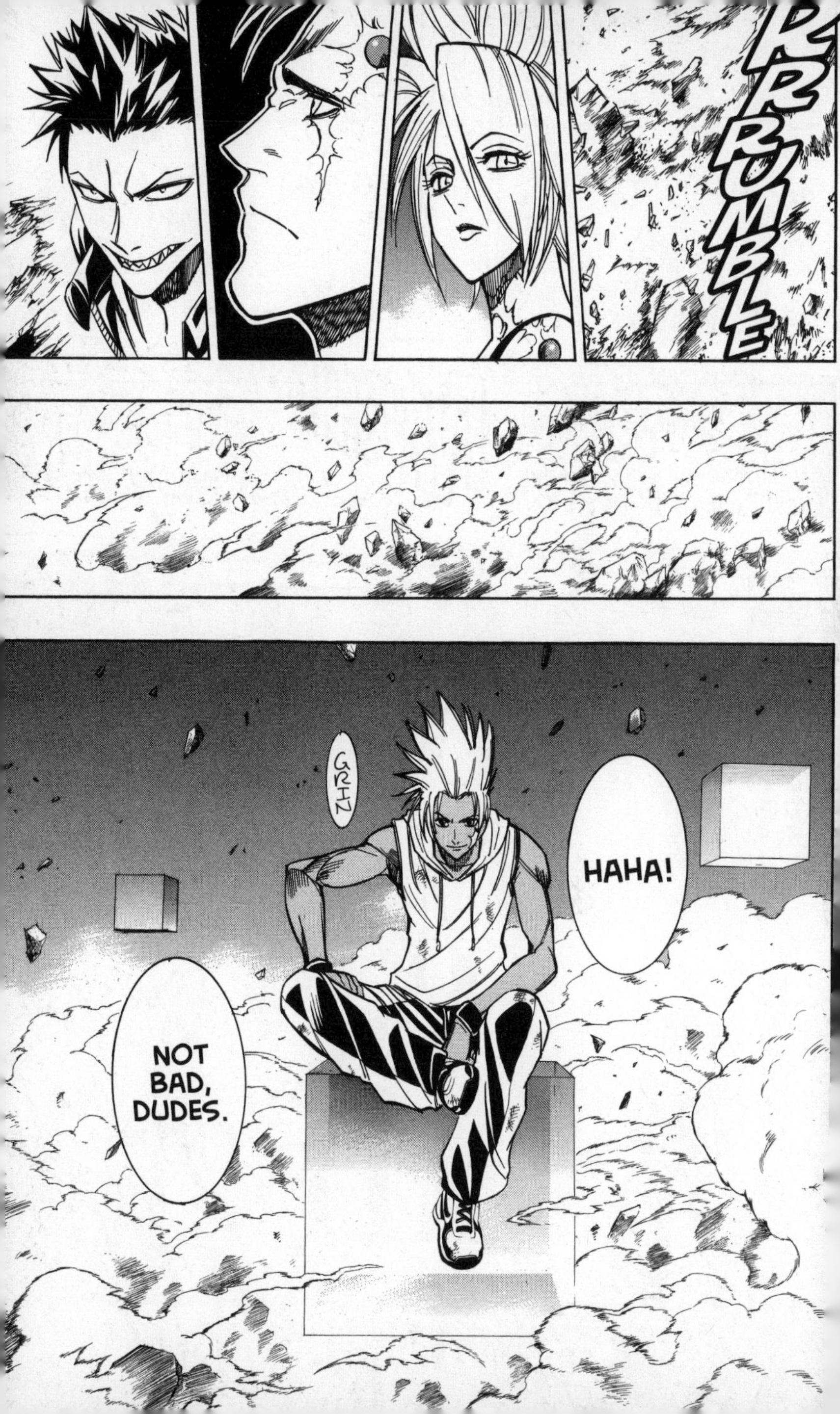
DRRUMBLE
HAHA!
GRIN
NOT BAD, DUDES.

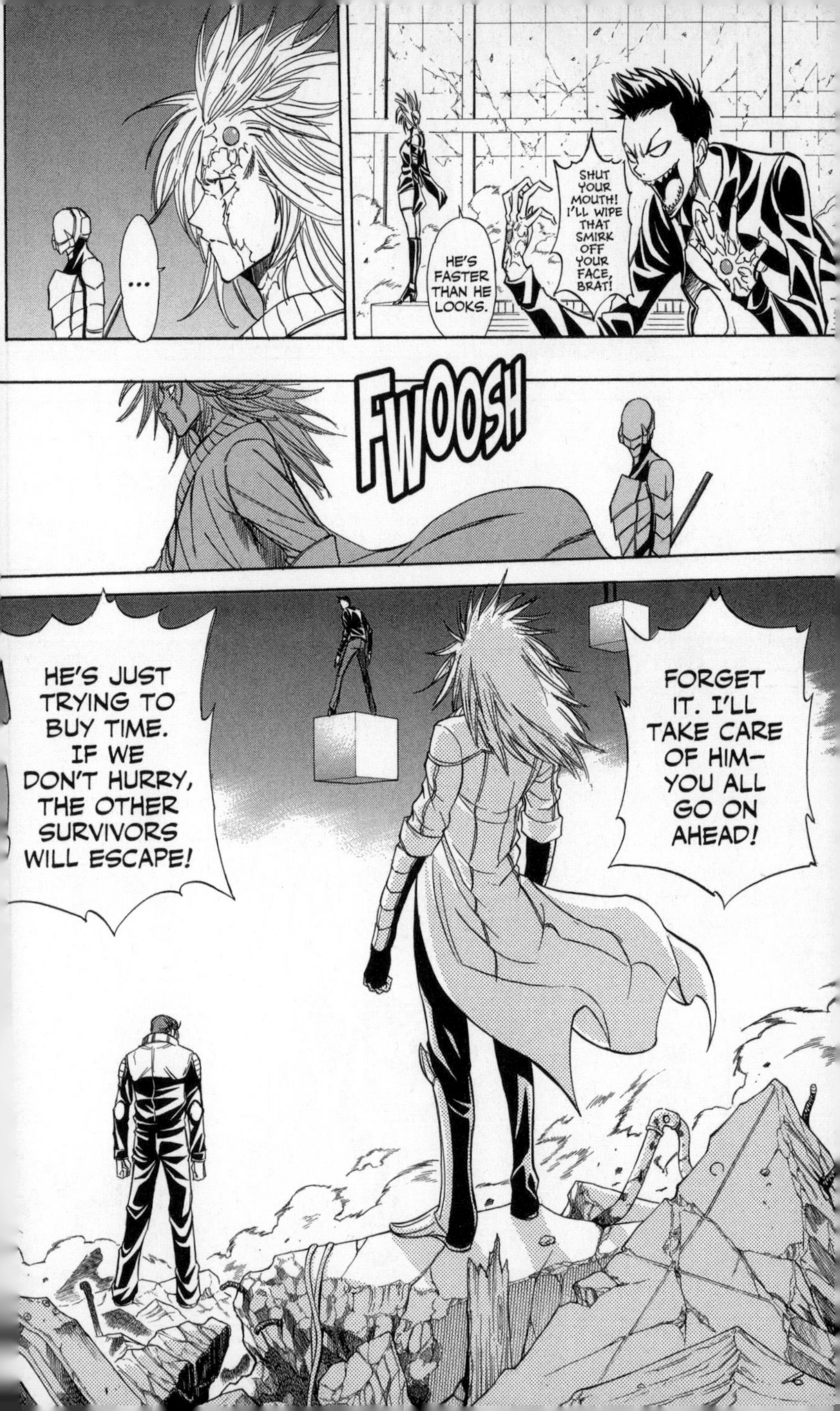
SHUT YOUR MOUTH! I'LL WIPE THAT SMIRK OFF YOUR FACE, BRAT!
HE'S FASTER THAN HE LOOKS.
...
FWOOSH
FORGET IT. I'LL TAKE CARE OF HIM— YOU ALL GO ON AHEAD!
HE'S JUST TRYING TO BUY TIME. IF WE DON'T HURRY, THE OTHER SURVIVORS WILL ESCAPE!

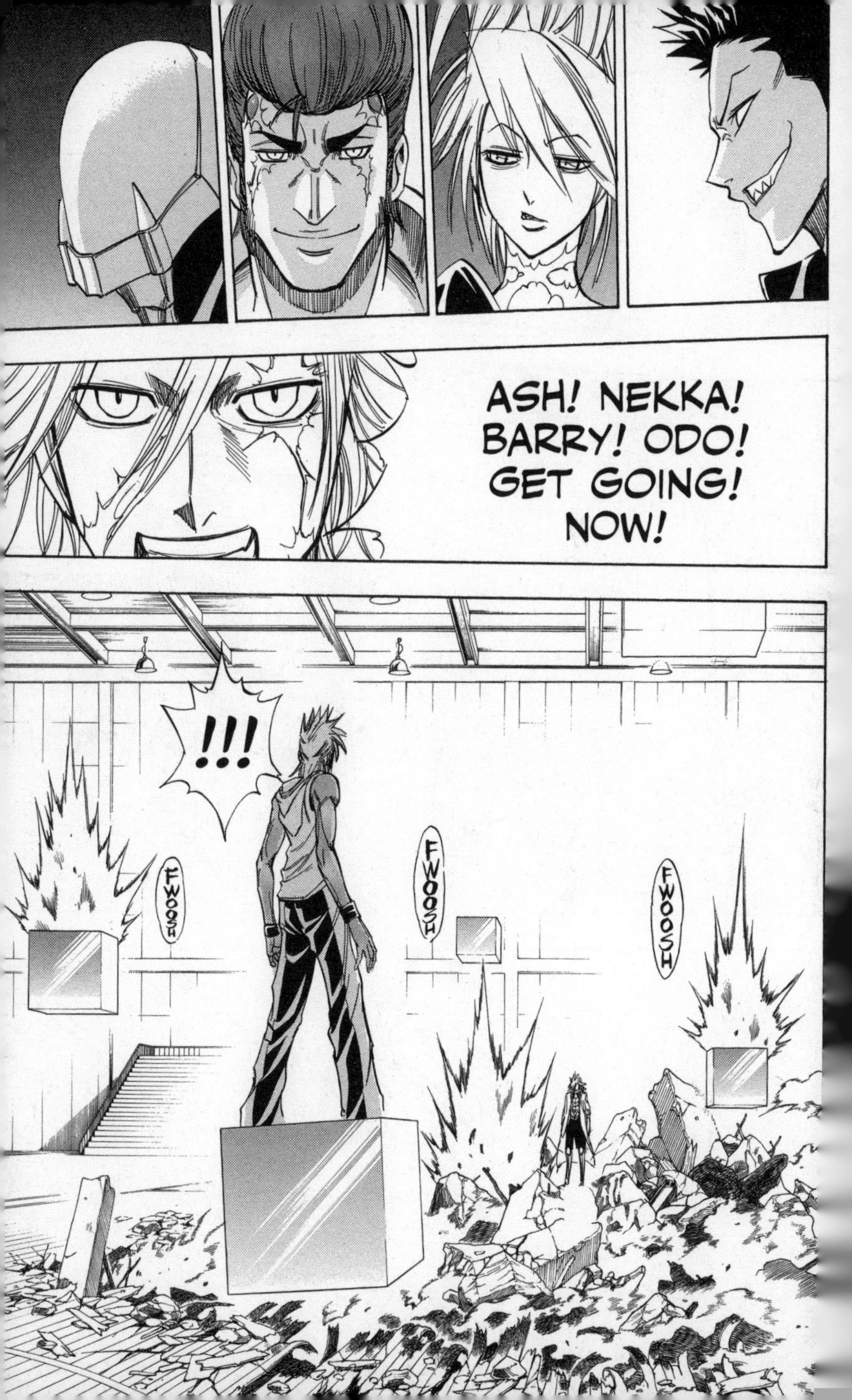
ASH! NEKKA! BARRY! ODO! GET GOING! NOW!
!!!
FWOOSH
FWOOSH
FWOOSH

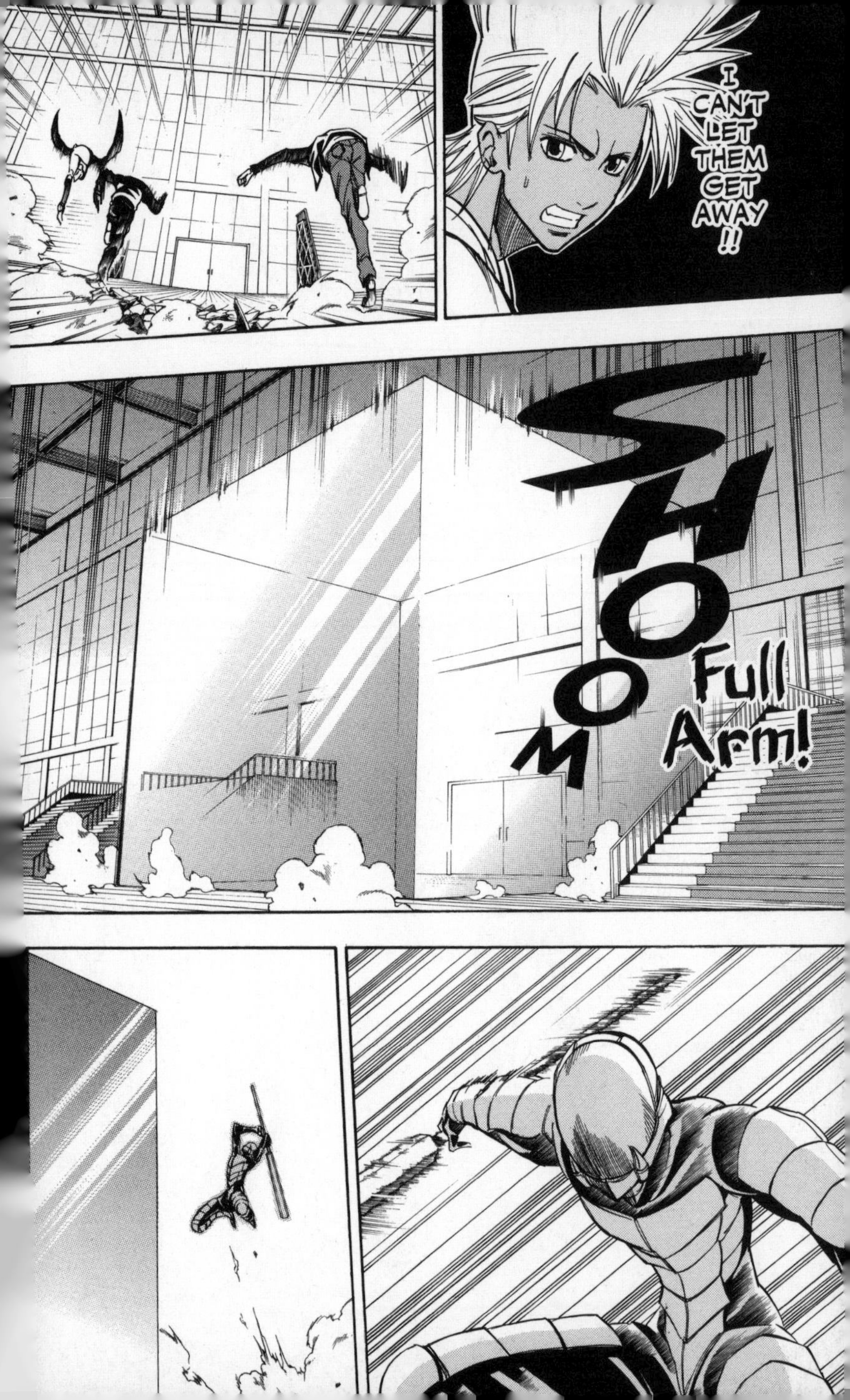
I CAN'T LET THEM GET AWAY!!
SHOOOM
Full Arm!

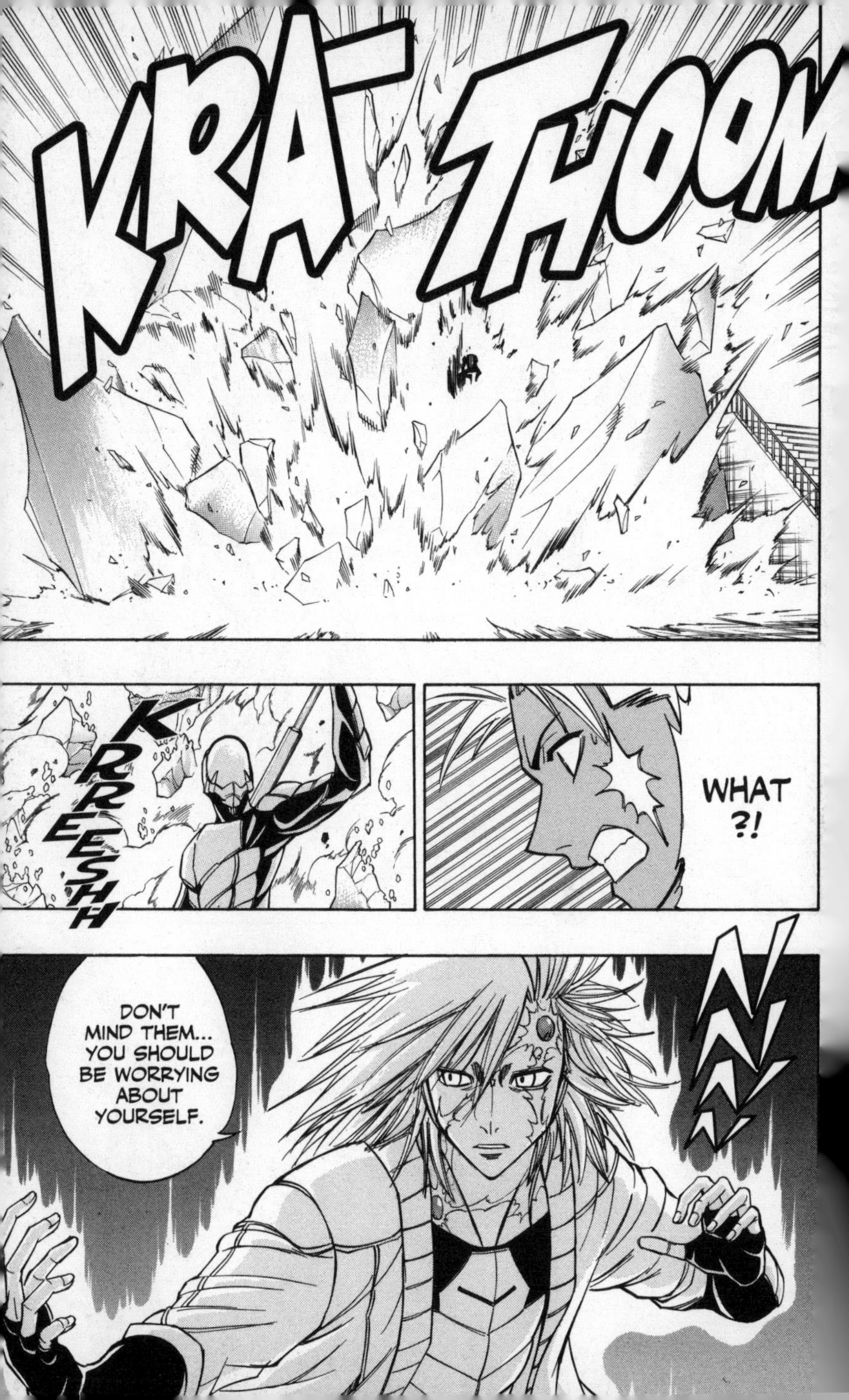
KRA-THOOM
WHAT ?!
KRREESHH
DON'T MIND THEM... YOU SHOULD BE WORRYING ABOUT YOURSELF.

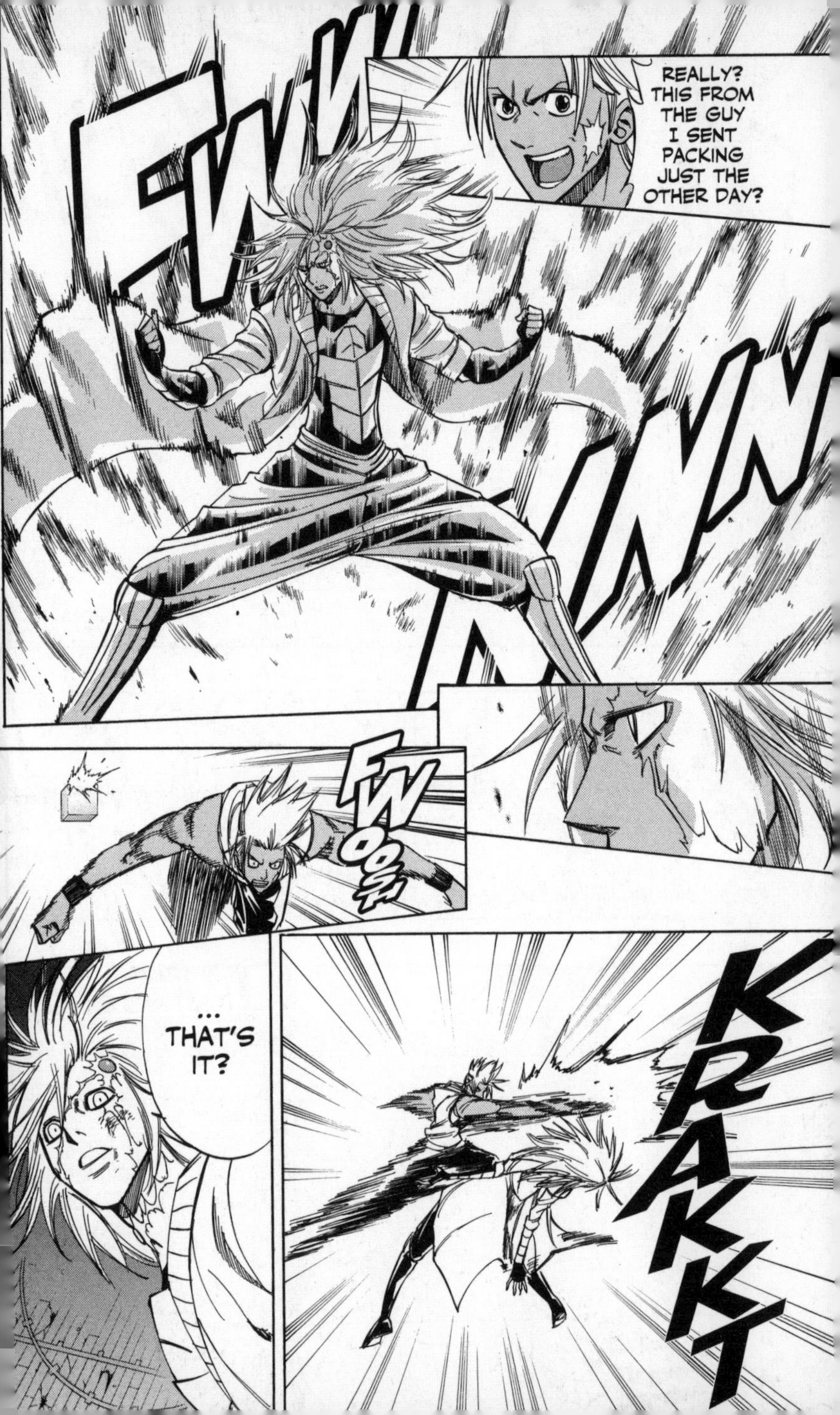
REALLY? THIS FROM THE GUY I SENT PACKING JUST THE OTHER DAY?
FWOOSH
KRAKT
... THAT'S IT?

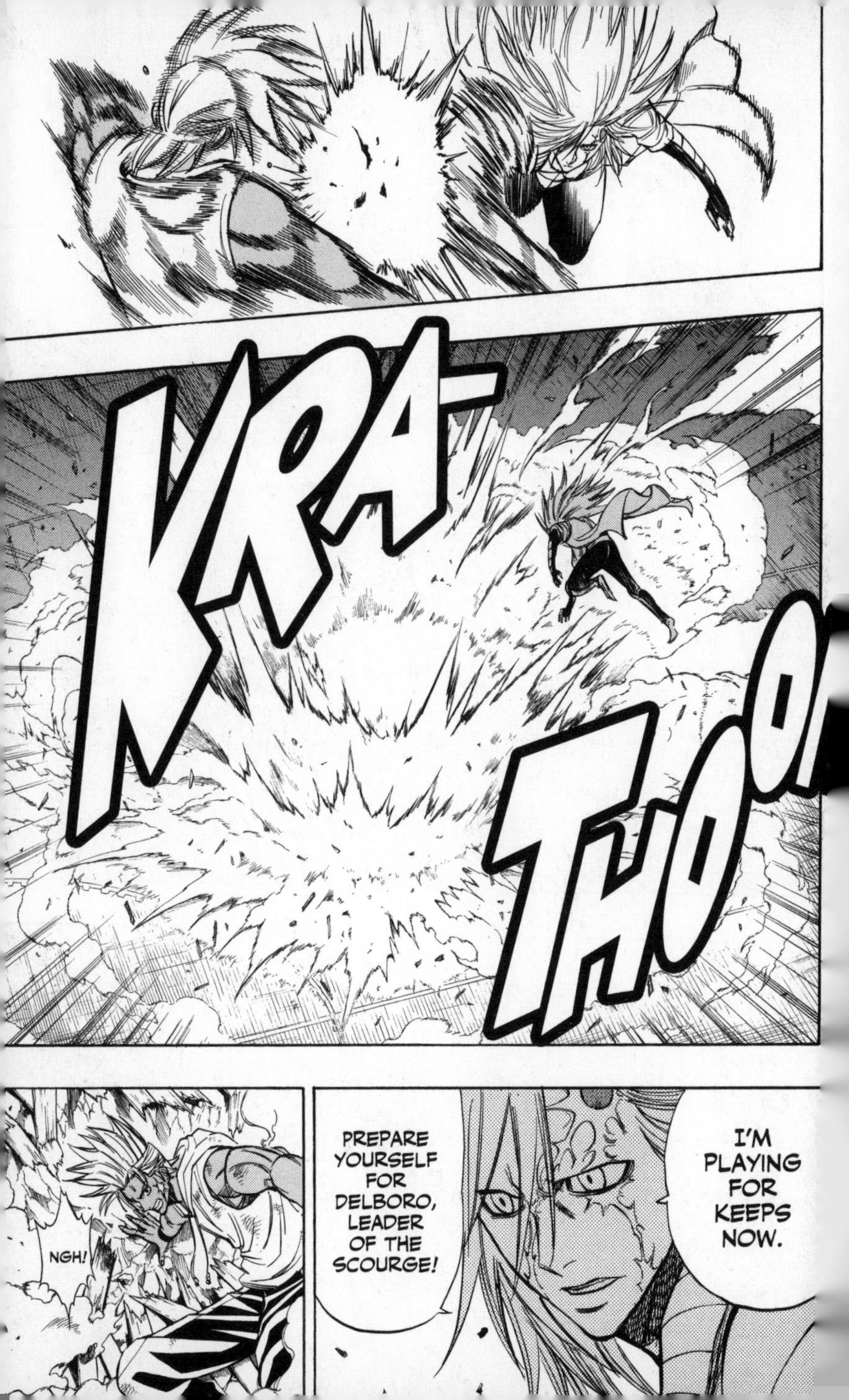
KRA-
THOO
I'M PLAYING FOR KEEPS NOW.
PREPARE YOURSELF FOR DELBORO, LEADER OF THE SCOURGE!
NGH!

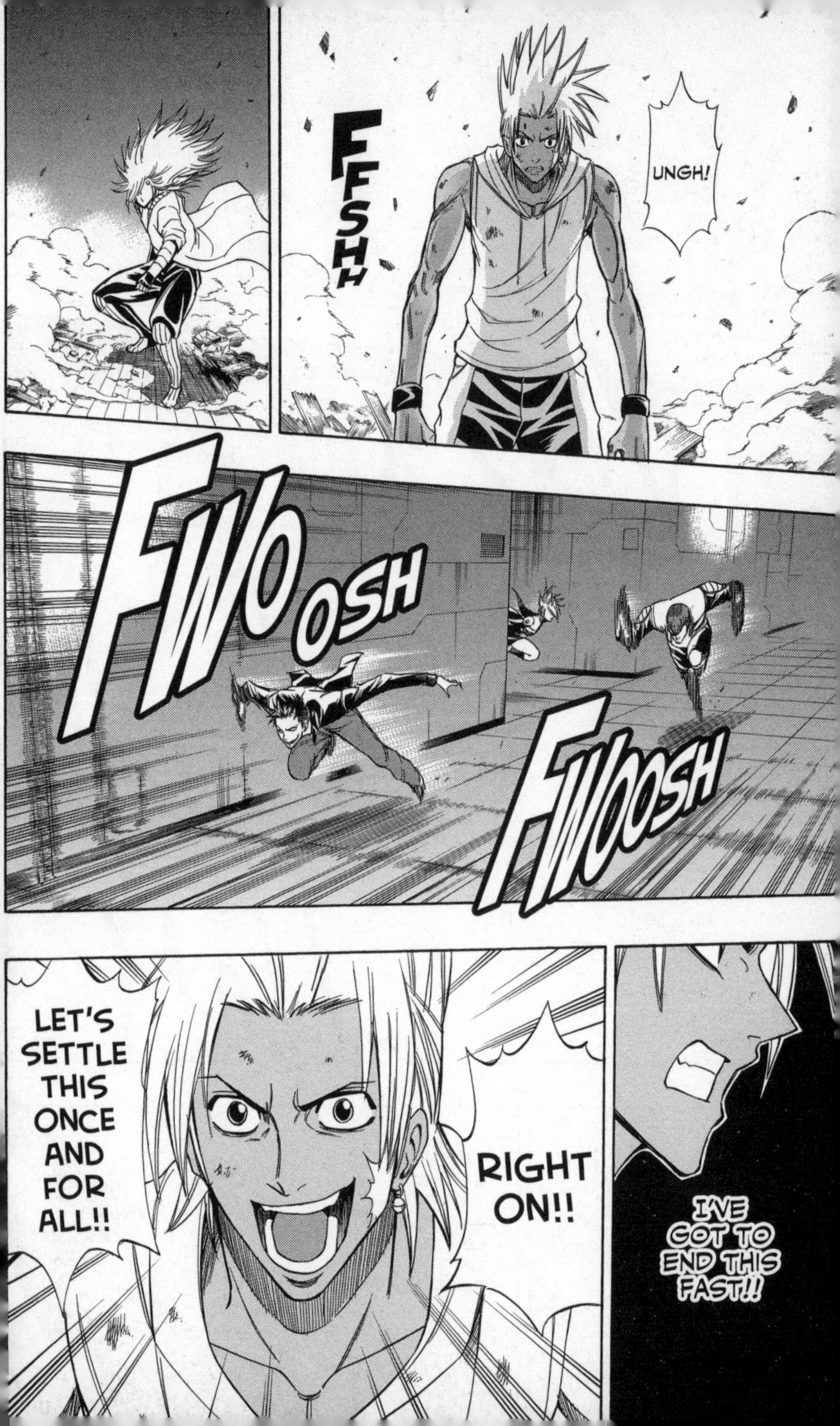
FFSHHH
UNGH!
FWOOSH
FWOOSH
I'VE GOT TO END THIS FAST!!
RIGHT ON!!
LET'S SETTLE THIS ONCE AND FOR ALL!!

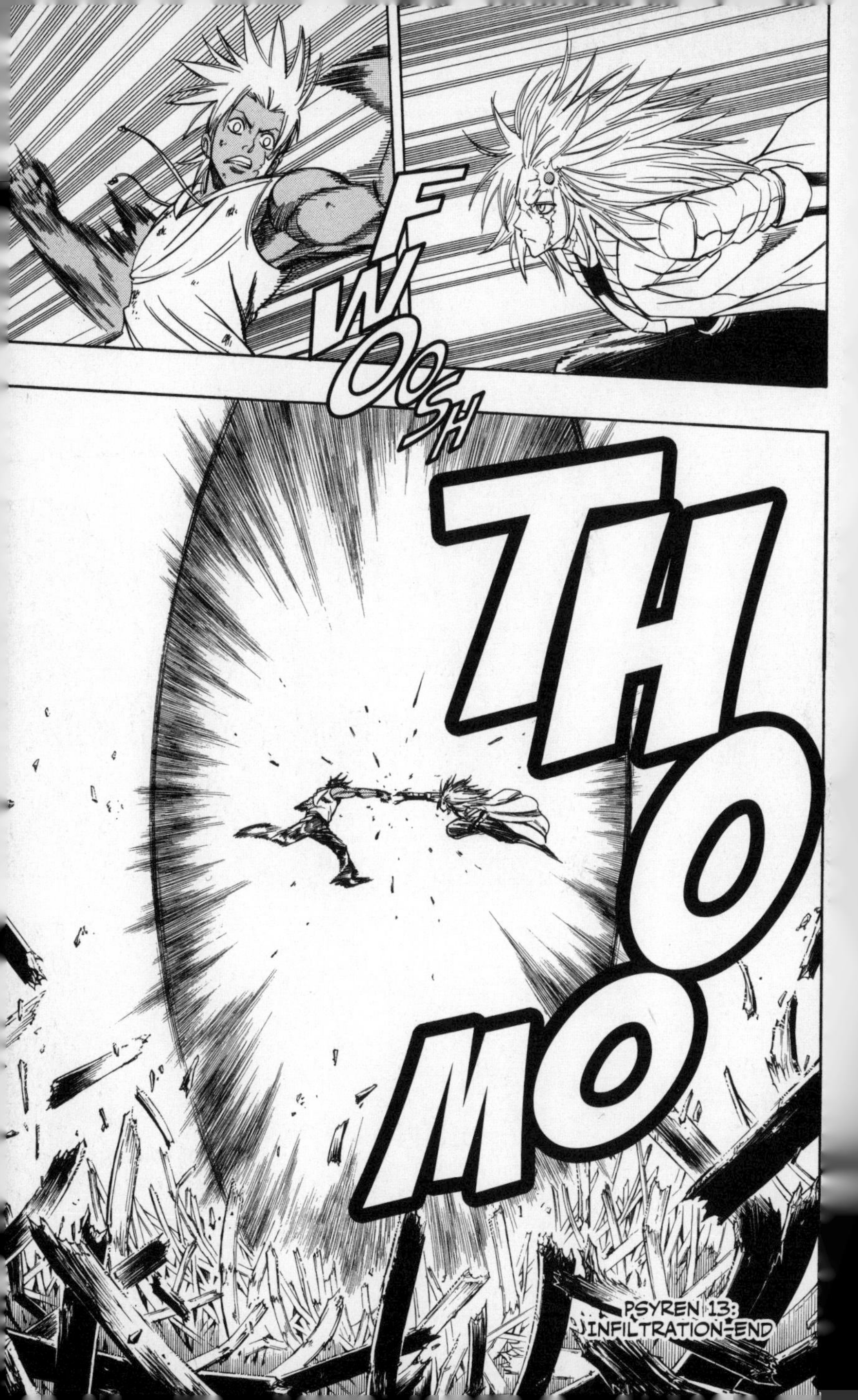
FWOOSH
THOOM
PSYREN 13: INFILTRATION-END

PSYREN

Afterword 13

THANK YOU FOR BUYING
VOLUME 13!!

THIS VOLUME'S ALL ABOUT THE
BATTLE WHEN ENEMIES INVADE
THE ROOT.

IT'S BEEN ABOUT TWO MONTHS
SINCE I FINISHED WORK ON VOLUME
12, BUT I HAVEN'T HAD A SINGLE DAY
OFF SINCE THEN AND I'VE BARELY
SET FOOT OUTSIDE...SO I DON'T
REALLY HAVE ANYTHING TO TELL
YOU ABOUT! (*SOB*)

MY LIFE HAS BASICALLY BEEN
TOTALLY UNCHANGED SINCE THE
LAST VOLUME...BOO-HOO!
I'D BETTER GET OUT AND DO
SOMETHING BEFORE VOLUME 14...

TOSHIAKI IWASHIRO, AUGUST 2010

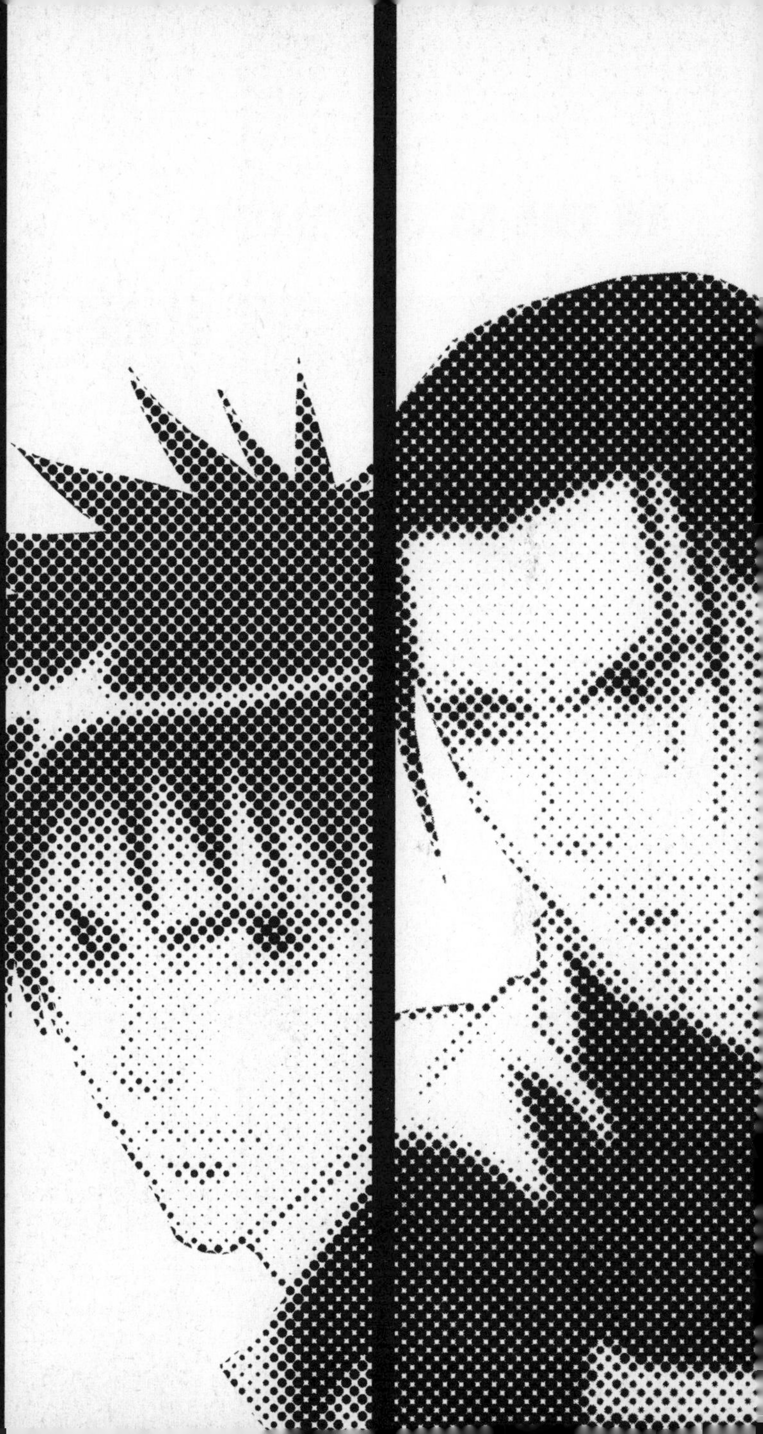

IN THE NEXT VOLUME...

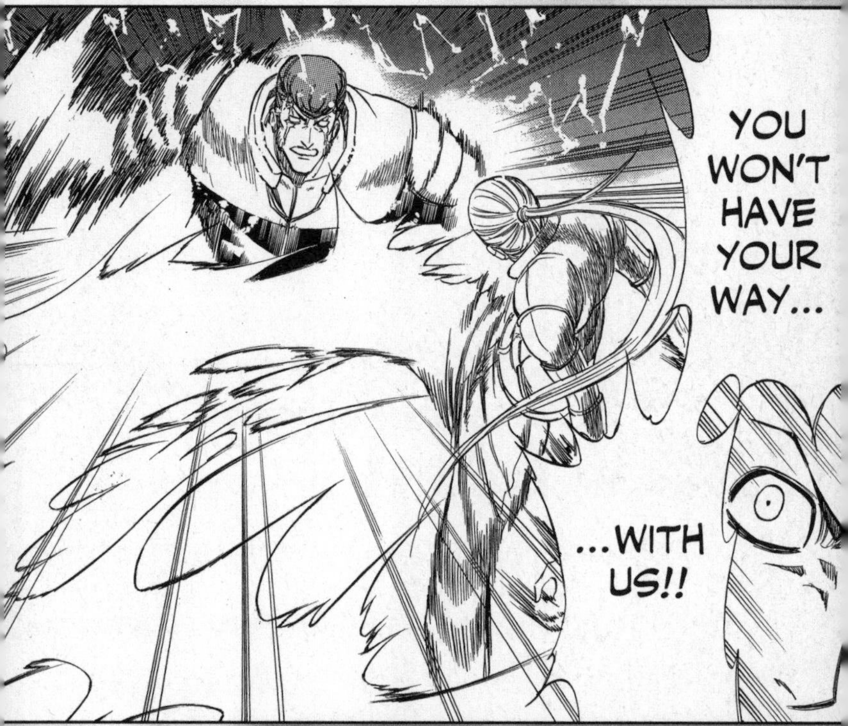
YOU WON'T HAVE YOUR WAY...
...WITH US!!

NOVA

W.I.S.E's elite battle force, nicknamed the "Scourge," is attacking the Root! After a fierce battle, Ageha, his fellow Psionists and the Elmore Wood Gang succeed in driving them away. But when Star Commander Junas shows up, Ageha finds himself driven into a corner...

Available JANUARY 2014!

You're Reading in the Wrong Direction!!

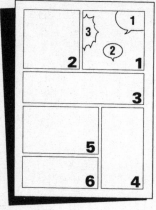

Whoops! Guess what? You're starting at the wrong end of the comic!

...It's true! In keeping with the original Japanese format, **Psyren** is meant to be read from right to left, starting in the upper-right corner.

Unlike English, which is read from left to right, Japanese is read from right to left, meaning that action, sound effects and word-balloon order are completely reversed—something which can make readers unfamiliar with Japanese feel pretty backwards themselves. For this reason, manga or Japanese comics published in the U.S. in English have sometimes been published "flopped"—that is, printed in exact reverse order, as though seen from the other side of a mirror.

By flopping pages, U.S. publishers can avoid confusing readers, but the compromise is not without its downside. For one thing, a character in a flopped manga series who once wore in the original Japanese version a T-shirt emblazoned with "M A Y" (as in "the merry month of") now wears one which reads "Y A M"! Additionally, many manga creators in Japan are themselves unhappy with the process, as some feel the mirror-imaging of their art changes their original intentions.

We are proud to bring you Toshiaki Iwashiro's **Psyren** in the original unflopped format. For now, though, turn to the other side of the book and let the fun begin...!

—Editor